Praise for Franchising For Dummies, 2nd Edition

"It is increasingly important that prospective investors know how to properly investigate franchising before taking the big step. *Franchising For Dummies,* 2nd Edition, is a crucial guide for anyone who is seriously considering the path to small-business ownership. Michael and Dave's long experience and expertise in franchising makes them exceptional guides."

Matthew Shay
President, International Franchise Association

"Dave Thomas, the legendary founder of Wendy's, and Michael Seid, one of the nation's leading franchise consultants, have written the ultimate franchise primer. Whether you are planning to become a franchisee or looking to start your own franchise system, don't go into franchising without it."

Lawrence "Doc" Cohen, CFE
Franchisee; Great American Cookies, Pretzel Time, and Coffee Beanery
Chairman, International Franchise Association

"I have had the privilege of knowing Michael Seid for many, many years, and there is no human being on the planet with more knowledge about franchising than Michael. I have read his publications over and over again — and each time I learn something new that helps me grow my business. Anyone who makes his or her living in the franchising world is doing himself or herself a gross injustice by not making the time or effort to read this book."

Sidney Feltenstein, CFE
Chairman, Sagittarius Brands
Captain D's Seafood and Del Taco
Past Chairman, International Franchise Association

"*Franchising For Dummies,* 2nd Edition, is the most important book prospective franchisees and those interested in becoming franchisors should read. We routinely turn to Michael Seid & Associates to perform critical assignments for our clients —

including such industry leaders as Pizza Hut, 7-Eleven, Arby's, and The Miss Universe Organization — and in this book you get what you need to know straight from the nation's leading consulting expert."

David Kaufmann
Senior Partner
Kaufmann, Feiner, Yamin, Gildin & Robbins LLP
New York

"At every Wing Zone Discovery Day, our prospective franchisees receive two disclosure documents. The first is the Uniform Franchise Offering Circular, as prescribed by law and the second is *Franchising For Dummies,* 2nd Edition. There is no easier way to translate legalese into layman's English than placing these two documents side by side."

Stan Friedman, CFE
Executive Vice President, Wing Zone

"Michael brings insight and a wealth of practical experience to *Franchising For Dummies,* 2nd Edition. I have worked for many years with Michael, and his expertise has made him the leading consultant in franchising and invariably our clients' first choice as an advisor."

Arthur L. Pressman
Co-Chair, Franchise and Distribution Practice Team
Nixon Peabody LLP, Boston, MA

"I have had the privilege of working with Michael Seid for many years in support of franchising at the International Franchise Association. Michael Seid and Dave Thomas have penned a must-read for anyone interested in creating a successful franchise system or becoming a franchisee. Franchisees and franchisors alike owe a debt of gratitude to Michael and Dave for this fine work."

James H. "Jim" Amos Jr., CFE
Chairman Emeritus, MBE/UPS
Chairman of SONA MED Spa
Past Chairman, International Franchise Association

Franchising FOR DUMMIES®
2ND EDITION

by Michael Seid and Dave Thomas

WILEY

Wiley Publishing, Inc.

Franchising For Dummies®, 2nd Edition

Published by
Wiley Publishing, Inc.
111 River St.
Hoboken, NJ 07030-5774
www.wiley.com

Copyright © 2010 by Wiley Publishing, Inc., Indianapolis, Indiana

Published simultaneously in Canada

For general information on our other products and services, please contact our Customer Care Department within the U.S. at 877-762-2974, outside the U.S. at 317-572-3993, or fax 317-572-4002.

For technical support, please visit www.wiley.com/techsupport.

Wiley also publishes its books in a variety of electronic formats. Some content that appears in print may not be available in electronic books.

Library of Congress Control Number: 2006927771

ISBN: 978-0-470-04581-7

Manufactured in the United States of America

10 9 8

WILEY

About the Authors

Michael H. Seid, Founder and Managing Director, Michael H. Seid & Associates: Michael Seid (West Hartford, CT) is founder and Managing Director of Michael H. Seid & Associates (MSA), the nation's leading consulting firm specializing in franchising and other methods of distribution. At the age of 6, Michael began to work in his family's business, Ruth and Dave's in Brooklyn, New York, and he traces his success as a businessperson to the lessons taught to him by his parents. From working with his parents, his brother (Mark), and his sister (Carol), he learned the lifelong meaning of quality, consistency, entrepreneurship, ethics, fair play, and respect for the customer.

During his 25+ years in franchising, Michael has been a Senior Operations and Financial Executive or Consultant for companies within the franchise, retail, hospitality, restaurant, and service industries. He has also been a franchisee. Michael is the past Chairman of the International Franchise Association (IFA) Supplier Forum, a former member of the IFA's Executive Committee, and the first supplier ever directly elected to the IFA's Board of Directors. Michael is a Certified Franchise Executive (CFE) and a very non-practicing Certified Public Accountant (CPA).

MSA's clients are diverse, and Michael routinely works with large multinational Fortune 10 companies as well as small emerging businesses. MSA assists emerging franchisors in the design and development of their franchise systems and established franchisors and other companies in the development of their tactical planning for domestic and international expansion and support. MSA also provides headquarters and field support systems, manuals and training programs, marketing and expansion strategies, franchise relations, crisis management, expert witnesses, litigation support, and the strategic restructuring of established franchise systems. Michael has been the backup servicer for several of the nation's largest transactions related to royalty securitization for franchisors.

Michael is a noted author of numerous articles on franchising, an oft-quoted expert in the field, and a frequent lecturer on the subject of franchising. Michael is married to his wife of 30 years, Susan, and has two children, Rachel and Andrew. For more information on the services offered by MSA, including speaking or consulting services, call 860-523-4257. Michael's e-mail address is mseid@msaworldwide.com, and MSA's Web site is www.msaworldwide.com.

Dave Thomas, Late Founder of Wendy's International: Dave Thomas began his lifelong career in the restaurant industry at the age of 12, working the counter at the Regas Restaurant in Knoxville, Tennessee. There, he fell in love with the restaurant business and learned that he could be anything he wanted to be if he worked hard and had a burning desire to succeed. Dave passed away in 2002.

Dave was a franchisee of Kentucky Fried Chicken (KFC) until 1968, when at the age of 35 the restaurants were sold back to KFC and Dave became a millionaire. In 1969, Dave opened the first Wendy's Old Fashioned Hamburgers restaurant in downtown Columbus, Ohio. By 1973, Dave began franchising Wendy's, and today, more than 6,700 Wendy's restaurants dot the globe.

In 1989, Dave agreed to appear in a few Wendy's commercials. He appeared in more than 800 commercials during the campaign's 13-year run and, admittedly, rarely said his lines correctly in one take. He was one of the nation's most recognizable television spokesmen. If dropping out of high school was Dave's biggest mistake, it led to one of his greatest accomplishments. In 1993, 45 years after leaving school, Dave earned his GED certificate and received his high school diploma from Coconut Creek High School in Fort Lauderdale. He was voted Most Likely to Succeed by the graduating class and attended the prom with his wife, Lorraine, where they were named Prom King and Queen.

Dave always believed in giving back to the community. He was a long-time supporter of a variety of children's charities, but the cause closest to his heart was adoption. As an adopted child, Dave knew the importance of a permanent home and family. Dave spoke before Congress and participated in several adoption celebrations at the White House. In 1992, Dave established the Dave Thomas Foundation for Adoption, donating speakers' fees and profits from sales of his books to adoption causes. He accomplished a great deal, but he considered his family — Lorraine, 5 children, and 15 grandchildren — his greatest accomplishment. For more information about Dave Thomas and Wendy's, visit the Web site at www.wendys.com.

Dedication

When Dave Thomas passed away in 2002, he left behind several important legacies: his family, his adoption foundation, and Wendy's Old Fashioned Hamburgers, the company he founded and nurtured into the world-class franchise organization it is today.

Dave was the patriarch of the Wendy's family, and we are committed to continuing Dave's vision and upholding his standards for quality, service, and cleanliness. The values Dave used to build the company are deeply rooted in our culture. Simply said, Dave's values are Wendy's values, and we are dedicated to maintaining these values in all we do.

—Lorraine Thomas and the Thomas Family, in memory of Dave

This book is dedicated to my parents — Ruth and David Seid. It is from them that I began my business education at the age of 6 and from where I learned the lessons of hard work, integrity, and compassion. Their wisdom has been part of every aspect of my life, and I am forever in their debt for their continued guidance, support, and love.

This book is also dedicated to my wife, Susan, and our children, Rachel and Andrew. They are what make life perfect. Rachel and Andrew, you are my inspiration, and you have exceeded every expectation we as parents have had for you. It is through you that I know that God has blessed me beyond imagination.

To my three cousins — Alan and Debbie Klein, franchisees for Maaco, and Gloria Halpern, the mother of a franchise player. I miss you every day since the accident and know that you rest with the angels.

To the franchisors and franchisees who drive this innovative engine of small-business growth and from whom I have learned my craft — I wish you continued prosperity. And finally, to the members and leadership of the International Franchise Association (IFA). It is largely because of the IFA that franchising has become the preeminent method for people to achieve their goal of economic independence in an environment that is safe and well respected worldwide.

—Michael Seid

Editor's note: Michael Seid will donate all the proceeds from the sale of this book to the Dave Thomas Foundation for Adoption, which generates awareness for the thousands of children waiting for a permanent home and loving family of their own.

Author's Acknowledgments

From Michael Seid: I realized as we wrote this book why Dave was an immensely important person in the field of franchising and, even more so, as a human being. I am forever in his debt for teaching me, after more than 25 years in franchising, why great franchise systems operate the way they do and how to be a better franchise executive. I am also forever in his debt for sharing his personal beliefs on what is important — the immense satisfaction of caring about other people. He was truly a great gentleman and someone to emulate. I am privileged to have had the opportunity to collaborate with him on the first edition of *Franchising For Dummies,* having had Wendy's as one of our clients, and, even more so, to have called Dave my friend and mentor. He is missed each and every day.

Other folks were also instrumental to *Franchising For Dummies,* 2nd Edition. Certainly, my family for putting up with the long hours, the interruptions in our lives, and the lack of attention I gave them as we crunched through the book. I am inspired daily by my talented partner, Kay Marie Ainsley. Her wisdom on the totality of the subject of franchising, and her ability to both teach clients on how to be great franchisors and inspire them to reach their potential, are unique skills and gifts. I would not be a good businessman if I did not thank MSA's clients for putting up with me during the process of writing this book. Their encouragement, their willingness to adjust their schedules at the last minute to accommodate my schedule, and — most important for any business — their commitment to always paying their bills on time, made the job easier.

Several other important people contributed in large and small ways to the success of this book: Marisa Faunce and David Koch (Wiley Rein & Fielding — Washington, D.C.); Joyce Mazero (Haynes & Boone — Dallas, Texas); Rupert Barkoff (Kilpatrick Stockton LLC — Atlanta, Georgia); Andrew Selden (Briggs & Morgan — Minneapolis, Minnesota); Michael Garner (Dady & Garner — Minneapolis, Minnesota); Lane Fisher (Fisher Zucker — Philadelphia, Pennsylvania); Jim McKenna (McKenna & Associates — Boston, Massachusetts); Lee Plave, Brett Lowell, Stuart Hirschman, and Mark Kirsch (DLA Piper — Washington, D.C., and Chicago, Illinois); and David Kaufmann (Kaufmann, Feiner — New York, New York). These friends and experts contributed to *Franchising For Dummies* and also reviewed parts of the manuscript, making suggestions for changes and improvements. I am grateful for their support, their talents, and the time they generously provided to me. They each have made *Franchising For Dummies,* 2nd Edition, a better tool for you to use in making your franchise decision.

Publisher's Acknowledgments

We're proud of this book; please send us your comments at http://dummies.custhelp.com. For other comments, please contact our Customer Care Department within the U.S. at 877-762-2974, outside the U.S. at 317-572-3993, or fax 317-572-4002.

Some of the people who helped bring this book to market include the following:

Acquisitions, Editorial, and Media Development

Project Editor: Kristin DeMint

(Previous Edition: Jeanne Criswell)

Acquisitions Editor: Stacy Kennedy

Copy Editors: Elizabeth Kuball, Darren Meiss, Kelly Ewing

(Previous Edition: Susan Diane Smith, Donna Frederick, Tina Sims)

Assistant Editor: Erin Calligan Mooney

Senior Editorial Assistant: David Lutton

Technical Editor: Charles Cowgill

Media Development Producer: Jenny Swisher

Senior Editorial Manager: Jennifer Ehrlich

Editorial Supervisor and Reprint Editor: Carmen Krikorian

Editorial Assistants: Rachelle Amick, Jennette ElNaggar

Cover Photo: © Britt Erlanson/Getty

Cartoons: Rich Tennant, www.the5thwave.com

Composition Services

Project Coordinator: Bill Ramsey

Layout and Graphics: Carl Byers, Timothy C. Detrick

Proofreaders: Evelyn Wellborn

Indexer: Rebecca Salerno

Special Help
Elizabeth Kuball, Sarah Westfall

Publishing and Editorial for Consumer Dummies

Diane Graves Steele, Vice President and Publisher, Consumer Dummies

Kristin Ferguson-Wagstaffe, Product Development Director, Consumer Dummies

Ensley Eikenburg, Associate Publisher, Travel

Kelly Regan, Editorial Director, Travel

Publishing for Technology Dummies

Andy Cummings, Vice President and Publisher, Dummies Technology/General User

Composition Services

Debbie Stailey, Director of Composition Services

Contents at a Glance

Table of Contents

Introduction

M any people think they understand a thing or two about franchising because they shop in franchised locations nearly every day. But what they probably don't know is that, over the years, myths have developed about franchising, its rate of success, and its ease of entry, as well as about how franchise systems should be managed and grown. As such, we, your authors, are here to dispel those myths — we have been fortunate to work for many successful years in franchising and are grateful to have often been called the world's leading experts in the field of franchise management and development.

You likely know the late Dave Thomas, who coauthored the original version of *Franchising For Dummies* and whose insight and understanding is as fresh today as it was when the first book was published. Dave started out as one of the early franchisees of Kentucky Fried Chicken and later founded and built Wendy's into one of the franchising giants. Dave was known as a leader in the operation as well as the innovator of the quick-service restaurants industry, and he left behind a culture at Wendy's that lives on today. Many of the innovations that Dave pioneered are now the foundation for successful franchisors and restaurant operators around the world. Dave passed away a few years back, but he left a business and personal legacy that few of us will ever achieve.

It was Dave's and my desire when we wrote the first edition of *Franchising For Dummies* to return to franchising just a few of the many blessings that franchising has bestowed upon us. This new version of the book adds such a wealth of new material that it may be unfair to call it a revision of the original book. In addition to updates of all the information in the original text, this book has new and expanded chapters on how to become a successful franchisor. It also contains a bonus CD-ROM, which provides a wealth of new information for franchisees and franchisors on a variety of subjects, including the law, franchise sales, international franchising, and real estate (to name a few), and it even has an employee handbook and a spreadsheet to help you decide whether you are picking or have picked the right franchise. The workbook in the CD's bonus material section — "Making the Franchise Decision" — is an essential tool for anyone looking to invest in a franchise. And in case you prefer to deal with small chunks rather than a comprehensive mass, we include the individual checklists and forms that make up the workbook as separate files, all strategically referenced and explained in Chapter 4.

It is with gratitude and respect for Dave's contributions both to *Franchising For Dummies* and to the franchise industry that I, Michael, update our original title to provide fresh material and a new bonus CD-ROM to get you started or to push you further in franchising with all the information you could possibly need.

About This Book

When Dave and I started writing *Franchising For Dummies,* our goal was to help prospective franchisees make the right decision on whether to become franchisees. We wanted to give useful information and advice in a nonthreatening, maybe even fun, easy-to-use format that would help you pick the right franchise and understand what you were getting into. As we progressed, we expanded our goals and decided that we wanted to provide information to help businesspeople determine whether franchising would be a good expansion strategy for their companies, and if so, how to design, develop, manage, and expand their new franchise systems. We also tailored the book (and now the CD-ROM) to help experienced franchisors improve their current operations with effective tools that should make them heroes with their franchisees.

Franchising For Dummies, 2nd Edition, is meant to be an essential resource for both novices and experts. Prospective franchisees can find out what to look for in a great franchisor; existing franchisees can take a peek at what great franchisors are providing their franchisees. Business owners can find out how to determine whether franchising is the right growth strategy for their company and how to become a franchisor, and experienced franchisors can pick up new tricks on how to improve their franchise systems. The material on the bonus CD-ROM has tools for every reader — no matter whether you're a spring chicken in the franchising world or whether you're an old hand.

Much about *Franchising For Dummies,* 2nd Edition, is written from the viewpoint of franchising as practiced in the United States. Modern franchising is a product of U.S. engineering and made its debut in the United States under the leadership of one of our founding fathers back in 1731. (You may be surprised who the first franchisor in North America actually was. Curious? Check out Chapter 1.) It has grown substantially from back in the days when it played a part in the birth of the U.S. and now is emerging all over the world, creating jobs and wealth in places where, not so long ago, entrepreneurship was practically illegal. Whether you're located in the U.S. or anywhere else in the world, know that the basics of what makes franchising successful are universal.

Conventions Used in This Book

To help you navigate easily through this book (because every franchisor/-ee knows the franchising rules are complex enough on their own!), we've set up a few conventions:

- ✔ We use *italic* for emphasis and to highlight new words or terms that we define in the text.

- ✔ **Boldfaced** text indicates the action part of numbered steps and links we're directing you to on Web sites.

- ✔ Monofont is used for Web addresses and e-mail addresses.

When this book was printed, some Web addresses may have needed to break across two lines of text. If that happened, rest assured that we haven't put in any extra characters (such as hyphens) to indicate the break. So, when using one of these Web addresses, just type in exactly what you see in this book, pretending as if the line break doesn't exist.

What You're Not to Read

Sidebars contain extra information, so you don't have to read them. However, they often explain some franchising issue in more detail than in the regular text, and you may find the information helpful.

We also won't threaten treachery if you don't read the text marked with a Technical Stuff icon — although we put our hearts and souls into providing every ounce of information you may want or need pertaining to this book's topic, some of the info just isn't read-or-die. So, skip over these paragraphs if you want, but know that you may be missing some gold nuggets of additional info if you do.

Foolish Assumptions

We may not be foolish in the business sense, but while writing this book, we made some assumptions about you. Our notions? You may be reading this book for any number of reasons:

- ✔ You work for someone else and have dreamed about getting into business for yourself, being your own boss, and charting your own destiny.

- ✔ You're nearing retirement because 30 years have passed since you met your first boss or because you've been downsized, right-sized, or outsourced.

- ✔ You're looking over the fence and seeing that the grass is greener on the other side — the grass grown by the folks who own their own businesses.

- You're retiring from the military and you've heard about VetFran, a program available from many franchisors that lowers your cost of becoming a franchisee.

- You're the head of a sophisticated investor group or management company and you want to improve the return on investment that the bricks-and-mortar opportunities in your portfolio have been achieving for your investors.

- You have a terrific product or service business that's burning up your local market, and everyone — starting with your mother, your Great-Aunt Rose, and your Uncle Harry — thinks that now is a perfect time for you to spread your wings and start a new national franchise program.

- You're already a franchisor, maybe even experienced in a few countries, and you want to challenge some of the assumptions under which you've been operating. Maybe you want to look at new or fresh techniques and score yourself against the best practices in franchising. Maybe you're having difficulty with your franchisees and you want to understand what they're thinking so that you can improve your relationships and your system's performance. That information may be all you need to take your business to the next level — whatever that level may be.

Whatever your reason for reading this book, we hope that *Franchising For Dummies,* 2nd Edition, meets your needs.

How This Book Is Organized

Franchising For Dummies, 2nd Edition, is organized into seven parts, each covering a major aspect of franchising, as well as the standard *For Dummies* Part of Tens and a couple of appendixes with some extra information. The chapters in each part cover specific information in detail. You can read each chapter (and even each section) independently, which is useful if you have other things to do at the moment. In each chapter, we note other areas of the book that explore in greater detail some of the information you see.

You can also sit back and read this book from cover to cover. We hope that you do, because it's designed to give you information in a logical progression. Here's a summary of what you can find in each part.

Part 1: Franchising Basics: Separating the Myths from the Facts

Part I gives you an overview of franchising and insight into the relationship between franchisors and franchisees. It tells you about the types of opportunities available within franchising and helps you determine whether you're cut out to be a franchisee.

Part II: So You Want to Be a Franchisee?

Part II gets you thinking introspectively; it provides sources of information about franchise opportunities to guide your way as well as a process (and corresponding checklists and forms on the CD-ROM for deciding which franchise to get into).

Finding the money to become a franchisee is also important, so we help you determine how much you can afford to invest and where you can get the money. For prospective franchisees, this section is important because it helps you decide whether becoming a franchisee is in your best interests and shows you how to choose which franchise may be right for you.

Before you sign on the dotted line, though, you'd better understand what you're signing! Part II explains the Franchise Disclosure Document (FDD), the disclosure document provided to franchisees in the United States. It also talks about how to evaluate a franchise agreement, what you can negotiate with a franchisor, and how to find pros who can help you through the process. Although franchising is a method of business expansion, a significant body of law also surrounds it. This part helps you navigate the legal process of investing in a franchise, so even if you're not one of the pros, you can look like you are.

Part III: Operating Your Franchise like a Well-Oiled Machine

Part III starts you down the path of establishing and operating your business. It begins by looking at what you likely need first — the location from which your fortunes will be made — followed by the two other most important parts of running your business — your labor and the ingredients and supplies you need.

Every franchise system has a different personality. By that, we mean that they offer different services to their franchisees and provide them with different types and levels of support. Even the way that you, the franchisee, and the other franchisees work together will differ. Part III walks you through some of the most important elements of the franchise relationship and the types of support you're likely to receive. These include training and other support services; assistance in finding and developing your location; how and where you get your inventory and supplies; marketing to your customers; merchandising your location; and hiring, firing, and training your employees. Part III also gives you a glimpse of how you can interact with your franchisor and fellow franchisees. This part begins your process of understanding the difference between a great franchisor and those that may not be ready for prime time.

Part IV: Times Change: Deciding What to Do Next

Part IV talks about the life cycle. The first three parts of the book give you information on selecting the right franchise. Now it's time to talk about your growth options: investing in additional opportunities with the same franchise system and even investing in opportunities that other franchisors may have available. Many franchisees find that owning one franchise just isn't enough. This part explains the opportunities and some of the pitfalls of multi-unit ownership, as well as a reality of business: At some point, the relationship is likely to end. We discuss how to prepare for this end and what to do when it happens.

Part V: On the Flip Side: Building Your Own Franchise

Ever wonder where big franchisors come from? They come from companies that have chosen to expand by offering franchises to other people. Part V examines what it takes to become a franchisor, whether your business has what it takes, how to develop a franchise system, how to set fees, and, most important, what not to do. This part also looks at how franchisors expand, both domestically and internationally; what it takes to support a growing franchise system; and some of the mistakes you can avoid.

Part VI: The Part of Tens

In two chapters, we give you insight into what we've learned in franchising — what we consider to be the keys to franchise success. We also share ten questions you should ask yourself before buying a franchise.

Part VII: Appendixes

The appendixes are where you find the definition of that word or two (or ten) that you may not quite understand. This part also welcomes you to the amazing world of bonus material located on the CD-ROM that helps you find the right franchise, establish that franchise in just the right place, and set up rules for your management team and staff. It's also the place to look for information on what goes into an FDD and why. We asked some of the leading legal and business experts in the world to help us bring to you an advanced education in franchising, so enjoy delving into the best from the best.

Icons Used in This Book

To help you along as you read *Franchising For Dummies,* 2nd Edition, we include useful icons to alert you to important matters.

If you skip the paragraphs marked by the Dave's Wisdom icon, you'll miss out on an opportunity to learn from the master. This information gives you insight into what made Dave one of the leading franchisors in the world and why Wendy's is regarded as the franchise system to emulate.

This icon directs you to a document on the CD that gets you more involved in the franchising process; it's the place to go to get more information on the subject you're reading about in the book, as well as where you find checklists and forms to guide you personally on the road to and through franchising.

The Remember icon is a friendly sign noting facts that we think you should tuck away in your long-term memory.

These items, though not essential to your basic understanding of the subject, give you an edge. After you become familiar with the basics, it makes sense to glance at paragraphs marked by the Technical Stuff icon, to get your advanced degree.

The Tip icon flags helpful information about the topic being discussed — ideas to note and good actions to take.

Watch out! The Warning icon alerts you to common mistakes that people make in franchising and dangers to avoid.

Where to Go from Here

You've embarked on a journey. Neither of us can be with you in person as you make this journey, but we try to be your trusted guides throughout this book. With that in mind, you can consider *Franchising For Dummies,* 2nd Edition, to be your road map. In a simple, straightforward, and (we hope) entertaining way, we provide you with guideposts, options, and our opinions.

To make the journey, you have to read this book. If you're new to franchising, start at the beginning and read it all the way through to the end. Flag those sections that you think are the most important to you or that you may not have understood fully. Then go back and read them again; with a broader knowledge of franchising, they may start to make better sense to you. If you're experienced in franchising, skim the book and focus on the subjects that interest you most or on which you need additional guidance. Make certain you take advantage of the material on the CD-ROM. Much of it you've probably never seen, unless you invested substantial money in having your lawyer or consultant prepare it for you. Either way, this book contains a wealth of information and practical advice. We hope that this book gives you a jumping-off point as you make your franchise decisions. Simply turn the pages and begin.

Part I
Franchising Basics: Separating the Myths from the Facts

The 5th Wave   By Rich Tennant

POOR FRANCHISE LOCATION

Let 'em out a little more, Stan.

BALLOONLAND

LOONLAND
PARTYS
BUSINESS
SPEC.OCCASIONS

SKEETERS
OUTDOOR RIFLE RANGE

In this part . . .

Have you ever dreamed of becoming a franchisee and owning one business location, or maybe more, and operating under a nationally recognized brand? Hold on to your dreams for a bit, because before you make that life-changing decision, you need to understand what franchising is all about — and what it isn't. In this part, we give you an overview of franchising and the types of opportunities that are available. We also explain how to select a franchise that's right for you.

Later in this part, we spend some time looking at a franchise agreement and discussing the types of information you'll find in the Franchise Disclosure Document, the disclosure document you receive from the franchisor. Along the way, we tell you how to separate a good franchisor from the pack and let you in on the secret of what a franchisor may be willing to negotiate with you.

Chapter 1

The Power of the Brand: Franchising and You

- -

In This Chapter

▶ What is a franchise?

▶ What are the roles of the franchisor and the franchisee?

▶ What are franchise wannabes, and why should you avoid them?

▶ Does the franchise agreement grant ownership and a guarantee of profitability?

- -

Franchising is the engine that drives much of the world's entrepreneurial train, but it's more than just fast food. Today, you can't drive down a major street anywhere in the world and not pass by some business that is part of a franchise network, and those businesses can be in any of more than 120 distinct lines of businesses today. This chapter begins your exploration of franchising, not by looking at any particular franchise but by looking at how well you will fit in as a franchisee or maybe as a franchisor. We explore with you what franchising is and what the franchise relationship is all about.

The Birth of Franchising

Franchising has a long history stretching back to ancient China. The crowns in Europe even used it to control their lands and to explore and conquer the globe. The history of franchising is pretty interesting. But, before we jump right into the thick of things, we want to share the story of Benjamin Franklin.

Now, every grade-school student knows about one of the most important of our founding parents — the bifocaled inventor of seemingly everything, including the lightning rod, the flexible catheter (we don't want to know what they used before), swim fins, the odometer, daylight saving time, the Franklin stove, and even a library chair that converted into a stepladder. Old Mr. Franklin even invented a musical instrument called the armonica for which Beethoven and Mozart both composed music. Ben Franklin gave us our first understanding of the properties of electricity, founded the nation's first hospital, charted the temperatures of the Atlantic Ocean, drafted the Albany Plan, cowrote the Declaration of Independence, and on top of all that found time to create the first franchise system on these pre–United States shores.

It was back on September 13, 1731, 45 years before the United States was even a nation, that Benjamin Franklin and Thomas Whitmarsh entered into the first franchise, or what they called a "Copartnership for the carrying on of the Business of Printing in Charlestown in South Carolina." The printing shop published *The South Carolina Gazette* and was the local printer of many of Franklin's writings, including his *Poor Richard's Almanack*. Franklin went on to establish other franchises in the colonies in the years before the revolution.

Without Ben Franklin, the French likely never would've entered into our War of Independence against the British. Without the income Ben earned as a franchisor, he may not have been able to support himself while living in France. So, have a celebration each September 13 to honor the first franchise because it and Ben were important contributors to the birth of this nation.

So What Is a Franchise, Anyway (And What's the Big Deal)?

Franchising is a system for expanding a business and distributing goods and services — and an opportunity to operate a business under a recognized brand name. It's also a relationship between the brand owner and the local operator. For example, Wendy's doesn't franchise hamburgers, and Midas doesn't franchise car mufflers. They franchise business systems that provide hamburgers and mufflers to customers — with consistent delivery of products, services, and customer experience.

A franchise occurs when a business (the *franchisor*) licenses its trade name (the brand, such as Wendy's or Midas) and its operating methods (its system of doing business) to a person or group (the *franchisee*) who agrees to operate according to the terms of a contract (the *franchise agreement*). The franchisor provides the franchisee with support and, in some cases, exercises some control over the way the franchisee operates under the brand.

In exchange, the franchisee usually pays the franchisor an initial fee (called a *franchise fee*) and a continuing fee (known as a *royalty*) for the use of the trade name and operating methods.

TECHNICAL STUFF

Franchising: Method of distribution, or industry?

We, your coauthors, use the term *industry* when discussing franchising. Purists may remind us that franchising is really a method of distribution used by a variety of industries, and they're right. But continually describing franchising as a method of distribution is cumbersome, and so we beg forgiveness for this slight literary allowance.

The effects of franchising on modern business

Consumers everywhere love the consistency that comes from shopping in a franchised business. From the cleanliness of the rooms at a Courtyard by Marriott to the fun that children will have at a Kidville, people know what they'll get when they purchase under a franchisor's brand. The number of industries bringing goods and services to customers through franchising is growing, limited only by the imagination of the businesspeople who are beginning to understand the potential of this ancient method of distribution. Franchising creates opportunities for business ownership and personal wealth — both part of the foundation for the growth of peace and democracies.

What most people don't understand is the sheer size and impact franchising has on the economy in the United States. According to the 2010 Franchise Business Economic Outlook, prepared by PricewaterhouseCoopers for the International Franchise Association Educational Foundation (IFAEF), business-format franchising — before including product-distribution franchises, such as automotive and truck dealers, gasoline service stations, and beverage bottlers — is projected to generate in 2010 more than 9.5 million jobs in the United States and account for over $8.6 billion of the economic output in the United States.

Franchising is becoming an increasingly significant force in the overall U.S. economy — take a look at the economic impact of franchised businesses on the U.S. economy shortly after the turn of the millennium on the bonus CD-ROM (CD0101).

Today, even in the current economic downturn, it is projected that more than 900,000 business-format franchised businesses exist in the United States up from 847,000 when the recession began in 2007. PricewaterhouseCoopers is now completing for the IFAEF its most current study of "Franchising in the Economy"; it will be available on the International Franchise Association (IFA) Web site at `www.franchise.org` later in 2010.

Although industry facts and statistics are fun and somewhat useful, the only truly meaningful statistic when you're examining a franchise opportunity is how well the franchisees in that system are doing. Think of it like looking at the stock market. Do you really care whether the market went up if your stock lost six points?

The success of franchising for business owners

For years, the IFA kept statistics on the success of franchising. However, many of the studies that those widely published statistics were based on — including those claiming that franchisees have a success rate of 95 percent versus a failure rate of 85 percent for nonfranchised start-ups in their first five years in business — turned out to be inaccurate and usually misleading. The IFA no longer publishes those statistics and has asked its member companies not to refer to them any longer. You should be wary of any franchisor or franchise broker that still uses these claims of franchise industry success statistics.

What's the Big Deal about Brand?

Brand is the franchise system's most valuable asset. Consumers decide what and whether to buy at a particular location based on what they know, or think they know, about the brand. Unless they have a relationship with the local franchisee, they probably don't give any thought to who owns the business. In their minds, they're shopping at a branch of a chain.

In the consumer's mind, brand equals the company's reputation — the experience they expect to get. Franchisors spend a lot of time, energy, and money developing their brands so that consumers know what to expect before they even come in the door. A good brand communicates a message to the customer. When you see an advertisement for a Wendy's hamburger, you immediately associate it with your experience of ordering and eating a Wendy's hamburger. You may think of a Cheddar Lovers' Bacon Cheeseburger or maybe a baked potato or the freshness of the product. Maybe you think that the line moves just a bit faster, that the service is better, or the staff is friendlier. You may remember seeing Dave in that last commercial or think back to Clara Peller and her sidekicks, Mildred Lane and Elizabeth Shaw, in the "Where's the Beef?" ads. ("Where's the Beef?" registered the highest consumer awareness levels in the advertising industry's history. It stole the show at the 1984 Clio Awards, winning three of the industry's highest honors, and was voted the most popular commercial in America in 1984.) The experience of visiting a Wendy's, supported by the message in its advertising, communicates to the public just what Wendy's is. You can visualize and almost taste the experience.

The same can be said for other companies, such as Meineke. When you see an ad for the brake services that Meineke offers, you can almost feel your car stopping safely at the light. That's the power of a brand.

Brand recognition is part of what a franchisee hopes to get when purchasing a franchise. A good brand is immediately familiar in consumers' minds. With a well-known brand, you don't have to build brand awareness in your market. The franchisor and the other franchisees have taken care of that for you. This is one of the major advantages of investing in a larger, well-established franchise system. Smaller systems with limited brand recognition can't deliver that until you help them grow.

Ongoing advertising and marketing programs help ensure that the brand remains strong and growing. And if the franchise system is successful in making the brand mean something positive to the consumer, that success means possible increased sales for you.

Brands are not born fully grown. Almost every start-up franchisor begins with some local brand recognition (it may be only a neighborhood) and has to grow that brand to achieve regional or national status.

A company can provide the best dry cleaning in town, have a system for one-hour service, be loved by its customers, and yet be known only locally. For start-up franchisors with limited brand recognition outside of their home markets, this is an issue. Franchisees in markets where the franchisor's brand has little or no consumer recognition use advertising and promotions provided by the franchisor to build brand recognition in their markets. Those franchisees that must build brand recognition need to spend more on advertising and promotion and may require a different message than franchisees who enter a market in which the franchisor's brand is well known.

The Franchise Siblings: Two Types of the Same Blood

Two types of franchises exist: product-distribution franchises and business-format franchises. In *product-distribution franchising,* the most important part is the product that the franchisor manufactures. The products sold by a product-distribution franchisee usually require some pre-sale preparation by the franchisee before they're sold (such as you find with Coca-Cola, where the franchisee manufacturers and bottles the soda) or some additional post-sale servicing (such as you find at a Ford dealer with your periodic maintenance programs). But the major difference between the two types of franchising is that, in the product-distribution variety, the franchisor may license its trademark and logo to its franchisees, but it typically does not provide them with an entire system for running their businesses. Providing a business system is the hallmark of *business-format franchising*.

Product-distribution franchises represent the largest percentage of total retail sales coming from all franchises, but the majority of franchises available today are business-format opportunities. More than 80 percent of franchises in the United States are the business-format type.

Because most franchisees buy a business-format franchise, this is the type of franchise we focus on in this book. However, we give you a glimpse into the world of product-distribution franchises in the following section.

Product-distribution franchises

In a product-distribution franchise, the franchisee typically sells products that are manufactured by their franchisor. The industries in which you most often find product-distribution franchising are soft drinks, automobiles and trucks, mobile homes, automobile accessories, and gasoline. For example, Coca-Cola, Goodyear Tire, Ford Motor Company, and John Deere distributors are all product-distribution franchises.

Product-distribution franchises look a lot like what are called *supplier-dealer relationships* — and they are. The difference between a product-distribution franchise and a supplier-dealer is in the degree of the relationship. In a product-distribution franchise, the franchisee may handle the franchisor's products on an exclusive or semi-exclusive basis, as opposed to a supplier-dealer who may handle several products — even competing ones. With the growth in auto dealerships that sell multiple brands, this distinction is getting just a bit clouded. The franchisee in a product-distribution franchise, though, is closely associated with the company's brand name and receives more services from its franchisor than a dealer would from its supplier. Supplier-dealer relationships often exist in business opportunities relationships (which we discuss in the following section).

Conversion franchising

Although not truly a third type of franchising, conversion franchising is a modification of the standard franchise relationships. In *conversion franchising*, an independent operator in the same business as the franchisor adopts the franchisor's service marks or trademarks, and its system. In many cases, the new franchisee, who is likely an experienced operator, is reluctant to make all the changes or conversions required to make it identical to all other locations in the system, and the franchisor may not be able to require those changes. However, the franchisee adopts the system's service marks or trademarks, the advertising programs, the buying relationships, the training, and the critical customer service standards. Examples of industries that have used conversion franchising extensively are real-estate brokers, florists, and the trades (home remodeling, plumbing, electricians, and so on).

Business-format franchises

The business-format franchisee gets to use the parent company's trade name and logo just as the product-distribution franchisee does, but more important, it gets the complete system for delivering the product or service and for doing business. This system is what produces consistency — and consistency is a franchise's foundation for success. Wendy's, Kidville, Dunkin' Donuts, The UPS Store, Meineke Car Care Centers, and Maaco are all great business-format franchises. The business structure of a business-format franchise offers a detailed plan that explains how to do almost everything from the ground up. A franchisee is trained to manage the construction of the building, order the right equipment, and even hang the signs.

The confidential operating and procedures manuals (the how-to guides of every great franchise) generally give such specific information as how to market and advertise; open the front door; recruit, hire, train, and dress the staff; and greet customers. To ensure quality and consistency, most franchisors provide business-specific information in the manuals on how and where to order inventory, how to prepare products, and how to present them to customers. The franchisor sometimes even includes procedures for taking out the garbage, turning out the lights, and closing up at night. All these components are part of a business-format franchise's unique system. The franchisor may provide the system, but the franchisee is responsible for managing all the day-to-day affairs of the business. The goal is for customers to get the same brand experience each and every time they shop in one of the franchise's locations.

Each franchise system is different, each franchisor does not prescribe identical levels of controls, and each does not strive for the same level of consistency. But most franchisors do have standards that define the minimum levels of service and operations required from the franchisee. Every location — whether it's owned by a franchisor or a franchisee — no matter where it is in the world, should look and feel the same; in restaurants, the food should taste the same. Ever wonder why every Courtyard by Marriott room has a coffeepot, and a bar of soap and bottle of shampoo in the bathroom? It's one of the brand requirements set by the franchisor. In other words, with some minor variations, and even if the menu is a bit different in different areas of the country or the world, your *experience* at every location should be the same. Every well-managed franchise system strives to achieve a high degree of consistency so that the buying public knows what they'll get just by looking at the brand.

The Roles and Goals of Franchisors and Franchisees

The owner of a franchising company — the entity that grants the franchisee the right to operate their business under the franchise system's trademarks and service marks — is called a *franchisor*. The *franchisee* is the person or entity that becomes the licensee of the franchisor. The franchisee runs the day-to-day business using the franchisor's brand and the franchisor's system of doing business.

In this section, we lay out both sides of the coin for you; however, because most readers will likely be looking to buy into an already established franchise, we focus on the franchisee's point of view throughout most of this book. (For the nuts and bolts of the franchisor's business process, check out Part V.)

Looking at the world through franchisor lenses

Franchisors can be companies founded by individuals with a great deal of experience (such as Dave Thomas) or by individuals with little or no experience and who are just concluding an arrangement with the company's first franchisee. Consider the following points regarding franchise sizes and franchisor levels of experience:

✔ Often, the owners are large public or private companies with their founders still at the helm, such as John Schnatter of Papa John's.

- ✔ Sometimes, the franchisors are former franchisees who bought the companies from the founders (as Tom McDonnell did with U-Save Car & Truck Rental, Jack Hollis did with Computer Renaissance, and Abe Gustin did with Applebee's).

- ✔ Sometimes, the franchisors are huge conglomerates (such as Yum! Brands, which owns Pizza Hut, Taco Bell, KFC, A&W, WingStreet, and Long John Silver's, and operates restaurants all over the world).

- ✔ Sometimes, the franchisors are small and relatively new to offering franchises (such as Firehouse Subs or Oogles n Googles).

- ✔ Sometimes, the franchise system is large but seems almost brand new (such as Quiznos or Panera Bread Company).

A good franchisor gives its new franchisees the system and training they need to run their business without having to figure out everything on their own. The franchisor has already made most, if not all, of the mistakes. Franchisees get the benefit of the franchisor's experience, so they can take a shortcut through the minefields that start-up businesses usually face. The franchisee purchases the right to use the franchisor's expertise, brand name, experience, methods, and initial and ongoing support.

Businesses don't usually fail because their products or services are of low quality — they usually fail because the owners aren't prepared and make mistakes from which they can't recover. Great franchisors have already made the mistakes — and have survived. Their survival is the basis for the road map they provide, and that map is part of what franchisees pay for when they buy a franchise.

You have to remember, though, that the franchisor isn't providing all this assistance out of the kindness of its heart. The franchisor wants the whole system to grow, prosper, and turn profits. So the goal of a great franchisor is to provide a great system. If it does, the franchisees make money, stay in business, expand, and pay fees. And the franchisor's brand value grows as more people shop at its branded outlets and more people want to become franchisees. The franchisor is relying on the franchisee to manage the local business well so that each location will contribute to the entire system's success.

The franchisee's end of the bargain

You need to understand the following distinction: When you buy a franchise, you don't own the business. You own the rights to do business using the franchisor's trademark, brand name, product or service, and operating methods. What you typically own are the physical assets, the land, and the building and equipment, but not the brand or systems. In many systems, in fact, the franchisor may even have the right to buy the assets you do own if the relationship ends.

Doesn't sound like much of a deal? Here's what you do get when you join a well-established franchise system:

- A proven and successful way of doing business

- A nationally known brand name

- A complete training program with advanced training and updates

- Research and development into new products and services

- Professionally designed local, regional, and national advertising and marketing programs

- Often, a chance to own more than one franchise

- A shortcut around the common mistakes of start-up businesses

- Frequently, a buying cooperative or negotiated lower costs from suppliers for many of the things you need to run and operate the business (ingredients, advertising, insurance, supplies, and so on)

- Your fellow franchisees as a network of peer advisors

- Thorough and ongoing field and headquarters support

- Often, a protected market or territory

Franchisors often give their franchisees an area around their location in which no other company-owned or franchisee-owned location is allowed to operate. This is called a *protected market* or *protected territory.* Protected territories may be defined by the following:

- The radius or area around the franchisee's location

- The number of households or businesses in an area

- The number of people who live in an area

- Zip codes

- Boundaries using highways and streets

- Any method that defines the area in which no other same-branded location may be established

If the territory is too large, the total market won't contain enough locations to achieve brand recognition. If it's too small or if other locations are too close, there may not be enough customers to support the business. The goal in a good franchise system is to establish the right number of units in the right locations to ensure that consumers see the brand frequently, which is known as *brand penetration.* When too many units are close by, and that proximity negatively affects unit sales, it's called *encroachment.*

Not all territorial rights are permanent, and the franchisor may be providing you with those rights for only a limited period of time. You may also have to reach certain levels of performance to keep those rights. Also, when a franchisor provides you with a radius around your location, your radius and another franchisee's radius may and usually will overlap. The franchisor will not, however, establish another location within your protected area. Make sure you read and understand your contract, and consult with a lawyer to make certain that you do.

The Nuances of the Franchisor/ Franchisee Relationship

Franchise systems are built on the relationships that the franchisor establishes with its franchisees. *Remember:* Just as every franchise system isn't the same, the relationship between franchisor and franchisee in every system isn't the same. And this relationship may change as business conditions change.

Lately, more and more franchisors and franchisees share some of the decision making — but in limited circumstances. According to Rupert Barkoff, Partner, Kilpatrick Stockton LLP, of Atlanta, Georgia, "Holiday Inn, for example, is contractually committed to submit certain proposed changes in its system to its franchisee association before they are implemented, and the franchisees of Sylvan Learning Center have a veto right over marketing programs." At both Arby's and Subway, management shares marketing decisions with their franchisees.

Following are a few of the terms franchisees use to describe their relationships with their franchisors.

Franchisor as partner

In a certain sense, although not a legal one, a franchisor and franchisee are partners. After all, they're in this business arrangement together. Each partner has a role, and each partner depends on the performance of the other. But are they equal partners? No.

Both partners have their roles in the relationship; the success of the relationship rests on their interdependence. Only one, though, can make the systemwide decisions, and that is the senior partner — the franchisor. As part of this "partnership," the franchisor provides the system, and the franchisee supplies the capital, the labor, and the day-to-day enthusiasm that makes the brand live. In great systems, the partners discuss individual issues both one-on-one and communally through franchisee advisory councils (FACs; see Chapter 9), but the franchisor ultimately makes the brand decisions.

Most great franchise systems that work as partnerships have FACs in place to assist the franchisors in evolving and improving their systems. Often, one of the FAC's functions is to review ideas for new products and services, whether the ideas come from the franchisor or from a franchisee. FACs also work with franchisors to review system advertising and cooperative-buying arrangements, and they help to make other changes to improve the system for the benefit of both partners. When you're looking at franchisors, look for a system that has an active and participatory relationship with its FAC and one in which the FAC plays a constructive role.

Don't read too much into a franchisor's use of the word *partner*. Legally speaking, you aren't a partner. You can still have a good working relationship with your franchisor, but remember that a franchisor has a responsibility to look out for its — not necessarily your — best interests. Of course, over time, a franchisor can't succeed without successful franchisees, so your interests do coincide to some degree.

Franchisor as parent

Just like parents and their children, franchisors provide the early guidance necessary for their franchisees' healthy growth. A franchisor provides franchisees with a safety net in the form of training and nurturing during the franchisees' early days in the system. Like parents, the franchisor offers a support mechanism that franchisees can turn to for help when they're off track. The franchisor provides a set of training wheels to keep new franchisees balanced until they can pedal on their own. And, like real parents, the franchisor is usually a continuing source of advice, ideas, and wisdom as franchisees mature.

But franchisors aren't parents, and franchisees aren't children. Children don't get to choose their parents; franchisees do get to choose their franchisors, and franchisors get to choose who is allowed to join the family. And unless parents today are a lot different from ours, parents usually don't make their children sign a lengthy agreement at birth, spelling out the obligations each party has to the other, when the relationship will end, and what you need to do to keep it going. Franchising is a business relationship.

Franchisor as dictator

Ask some franchisees to describe their franchisor, and they may use a word such as *dictator* or *tyrant*. Why? A lot of reasons.

Some franchisees find the franchise relationship too constricting. They see themselves as entrepreneurs — someone who starts a business and can make all the decisions about how the business should operate. Almost from the day they become franchisees, they want to find a way to break free from the constraints that franchise systems impose on them. After all, don't they own their own businesses? Entrepreneurs have a lot more flexibility than franchisees. In a franchise situation, the franchisor owns the concept and the name, and the franchisor determines how the franchisee's business deals with consumers. Indeed, some true entrepreneurial franchisees have difficulty comprehending that the reason customers come to the location is because of the franchisor's brand. The customer, after all, is a customer of the brand.

The restrictions of a franchise can be overwhelming — like a dictatorship — for a true entrepreneur. So, if you see yourself as more of a true entrepreneur than as someone who can be satisfied following someone else's system, start your own business. You probably won't be happy as a franchisee.

Watch out for franchise wannabes

What's a franchise wannabe? It's a business opportunity (or *biz-op*) that looks an awful lot like either a business-format franchise or a product-distribution franchise. It masquerades at many franchise and business-opportunity trade shows. The most common types are rack jobbers, supplier-dealer distributorships, and vending-machine routes.

Although every franchise is a license, *not every license is a franchise*. The difference is in the definition of *franchise* established by the Federal Trade Commission. This definition requires the following elements to be in place before a license is classified as a franchise:

✔ The franchisee needs to distribute products or services that are identified or associated with the franchisor's trademarks or service marks.

✔ The franchisee is required to meet the franchisor's quality standards when using the marks; the franchisor has significant control over the business or provides significant assistance to the franchisee.

✔ The franchisee pays $500 or more to the franchisor.

Business opportunities have several advantages over franchising, most notably far more independence and flexibility. Business opportunities usually cost less to start up than franchises and don't require you to pay continuing royalties.

The biggest drawback of a business opportunity is that you seldom receive any significant help in setting up the business, in training, or in marketing, and you don't get much in the way of ongoing support, either.

Franchisors like to say that, in a franchise, you're in business *for* yourself but not *by* yourself. In a business opportunity, you're not only in business *for* yourself, but you're also usually in business *by* yourself. For most people looking for the support that comes from a franchise system, our advice is to stay clear of biz-ops and buy a real franchise.

Every order of Biggie fries should be the same. Every hotel room at Courtyard by Marriott should have a coffeepot, a couch, and high-speed Internet. That's consistency. To ensure that consistency, a franchisor has to make decisions about how the business operates globally. Franchisees may think that they have the next great idea, and often they do, but the franchisor must look at those great (and sometimes not-so-great) ideas and make systemwide decisions. Sometimes, the answer is no. But if the only reason a franchisor says no is that the franchisor didn't come up with the idea, the franchisor is not only a dictator but also a poor businessperson. On the flip side, if the franchisor lets the franchisee try every idea, the franchisor isn't a good parent, either; good parents protect their children from making unnecessary mistakes.

In most cases, however, franchisors aren't being dictatorial when they say no, and they're not being bad parents, either. They're usually looking at the big picture, deciding what's right for the brand, and acting as a senior partner should.

A Reality Check Before You Dive In: Franchises and Profits

If you buy a franchise, you get rich, or at least financially secure, right? We hate to burst your bubble, but that's a myth. Not all franchises are successful, not all franchises are profitable, and many fail.

Owning a franchise — like owning any small business — is hard work. Even though you get proven systems and training when you hook up with a solid franchisor, no one guarantees your success. Often, the variable in this equation is you. Business ownership is not a passive investment. It requires long hours and dedication. Even with the best franchise system and the most popular brand name, the franchisee is often the key ingredient to making the business successful.

Even with hard work, if you make the wrong choice and buy a franchise that you end up hating, chances are good that you won't be successful — or very happy.

Have we discouraged you? Scared you? Confused you? Don't worry. Franchising, when done right and entered into with eyes open, can be a profitable, highly enjoyable way to spend your future.

What makes a hamburger great isn't the sizzle or the smell — it's the taste. The same goes for great franchises. The brochure may be hot and the salesperson may be persuasive, but you're not buying the sizzle — you're investing in the steak.

Chapter 2

Franchising Is More than Just a Food Industry

In This Chapter

▶ Understanding the kinds of franchised businesses

▶ Recognizing the importance of brand

▶ Exploring franchising arrangements

---

*T*he number of available franchise opportunities is growing all the time and is limited only by the imagination and skills of the franchisors that create them. More than 120 distinct lines of business, including hotels, car rentals and washes, hair care, lawn care, water and mold detection, and everything in between, use franchising to get their products and services — and their brands — to market. One of the wonderful things about franchising is its wide variety of opportunities and its never-ending evolution into new products and services.

As you begin to explore franchising, you need to cast a wide net into the pool of franchise opportunities to see what interests you. Although running a restaurant is one of the most popular types of franchising, it's not the only — or necessarily the best — way for everyone. (Of course, you would've had a hard time convincing Dave of that!) In fact, restaurants make up only about a third of the available opportunities.

In this chapter, we introduce you to the main pools of franchising, because diving into the vast ocean of them is just plain overwhelming. But if you're just starting, this information is all you need — so wade in, dear reader, and get your feet wet.

Oh, Industry!

Many people look at restaurants and food-related franchises first (probably because of the number of opportunities available in those segments), but non-restaurant opportunities deserve a look, too. In fact, don't be surprised if many of these other opportunities actually do better financially than some of the better-known restaurant concepts.

Letting source guides drive your train

The *source guides* (a printed compendium of different franchise opportunities with information about each company) and Web sites that profile franchise opportunities (see Chapter 4 for a discussion of where to look for lists of available franchises) categorize franchise opportunities into different industries. The most popular franchise industries today include the following:

- Automotive
- Building, construction, and water and mold remediation
- Business services
- Fast casual restaurants
- Child-care and senior-care services
- Consumer and commercial maintenance and other products and services
- Lodging
- Quick-service restaurants (fast food)
- Retail

The list of successfully franchised industries is much longer than the preceding categories. You can find a list of industries that offer franchises on the International Franchise Association's Web site at www.franchise.org.

If you decide to get involved with a franchise, we recommend that you first select something that you want to do and then find a company that has a great reputation as a franchisor in that industry.

Unfortunately, the industry classifications used by the different source guides aren't standard; source guides don't use a universally adopted classification system. You may think that companies in a category are similar, but that's not always true. Take "Food — Pizza," for example. Some pizza franchisors provide a system in which pizza is delivered to customers' houses; others don't. Some have only eat-in facilities; others do both, and still others do neither — you only can pick up your pie. All these businesses are pizza franchises and may show up in some source guides under the same category. But the feature of delivery or non-delivery makes them significantly different types of franchise opportunities. The investment varies widely, as do the types and number of employees you need, the types of real estate, and, certainly, the amount of money you can earn. Although franchise opportunities may be listed in the same category, they truly are different opportunities.

Now take "Hair Salons & Services." Some franchises are geared to cutting only men's hair; others focus on women. Some provide perms, coloring, and manicures; others don't. Some franchises, such as Cartoon Cuts, specialize in children's haircuts, while Sport Clips cuts hair in a salon based on a sports theme with TV screens tuned to sporting events. All hair salons work on hair, but how they segment the market and approach their customers differ from company to company.

So much information about franchise opportunities is available today that you can easily get overwhelmed. Add to that the fact that information about direct competitors sometimes is categorized by different reference guides in different industries, and you're in an even tougher spot. The easiest way to work is to find one great source of information that you feel is clear and understandable and written in a style you understand (sort of like this book). Put the other source guides aside and do all your research using the one guide. After you get your list of possible opportunities down to a reasonable few, you can research those companies by name in the other books. It's much easier, and usually you won't miss much information that you'll need at this early stage of your investigation.

Paying attention to what's hot

So, what's hot? That question is usually the first one a reporter asks anyone involved in franchising. With all the industries involved in franchising, it's hard to give a decent answer — besides, by next year, the situation may change. Look for the trends and see who's capitalizing on them:

- If you see a movement toward healthier, fresher, and upscale grown-up food, then the new brands populating the casual fast-food segment may be hot for you.

- If you think that having dad and (increasingly) mom working longer hours outside of the house has created an opportunity for saving the family time and helping parents better bond with and care for their children, take a look at franchise systems that provide children's education and entertainment. You may also think that companies that do your shopping or let you assemble your meals with their ingredients look like the right trend to bet on.

✔ Paul McCartney wrote "When I'm 64" when he was 24, and in 2006 when he reached that magic number, he was glad to learn that today's 64 is yesterday's 44. That just may be your magic ticket — servicing the senior citizen who's living longer and healthier.

Every year, a new trend unfolds because of changes in technology, medicine and science, the economy, and geopolitical events. Follow the trends, look through the fads, and somewhere on the other side, you'll find an entrepreneur who's started a franchise system to capitalize on the opportunity or an older brand remaking itself for the same reasons.

We don't recommend it, but if you simply must have a franchise in one of the popular industries, consider a newer or smaller franchise system, which may be more flexible than the larger, more established ones. You may want to go down the less-worn path and look closely at opportunities in less-popular industries. Keep in mind, though, that the smaller systems, while possibly more flexible in working with you, may not have all the benefits and services of the larger, better-established franchisors.

Franchise Relationships: From the Single Soldier to the Whole Battalion

Franchising is an ideal way for individuals, investor groups, and business entities to become business owners because of the variety of opportunities. (For more on the advantages of franchising, see Chapter 1.) The number of franchisors, the variety of industries represented in franchising, and the range of investments available create opportunities for the smallest single-unit mom-and-pop operator to the large multimillion-dollar investor group looking to add a franchise investment to its portfolio.

Flying solo: Single-unit franchises

A *single-unit* or *direct-unit franchise* is just what it says it is: A franchisee obtains the rights from a franchise system to operate one franchise. This franchise relationship is the simplest form.

Most franchise systems have grown, one franchise at a time, over the years. Owning one franchise is the classic and, until recently, the most common type of relationship in franchising. As people looked for a way to get to their dream of independence through business ownership, franchising became their vehicle. In a single-unit franchise, the franchisee generally supervises the business.

Although a single-unit franchise is the classic method for franchise system growth, it does have some weaknesses for franchisors:

✔ Franchisors generally experience slower growth, and the growth can be more costly on a unit basis because they have to locate a new franchisee for each location.

✔ The franchisor has more franchisees to work with, and those franchisees may be less sophisticated and more wary of taking business risks than larger, multi-unit franchisees.

✔ Because an individual owns and operates each location, servicing a franchise system dominated by single-unit franchisees tends to be more expensive for the franchisor than if the same franchisee owned and operated multiple locations.

Figure 2-1 displays the single-unit franchise relationship tree.

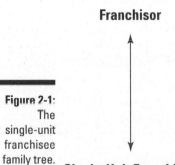

Franchisor

Figure 2-1:
The
single-unit
franchisee
family tree.

Single-Unit Franchisee

Growing a family, one franchise at a time

More and more often, as classic single-unit franchisees prosper (see the preceding section), they acquire another franchise from the same franchisor. They know their franchisor, have established a relationship with the franchise system, and can predict what they can earn from investing in additional units. Because they already know how to operate the business, the initial training they took when they opened their first location may not be necessary, and some of the key employees they have in their first location may be perfect to become managers in their second and third locations.

Acquiring additional franchises is a terrific way to grow, because the franchisees' knowledge of the business and the franchise system makes their risk lower than when they made their initial franchise decision.

Except for the added burden — or, possibly, joy — of operating additional locations, the franchise relationship between the franchisor and franchisee is substantially the same (see the preceding section). A franchisee who acquires one location at a time is a bit different from the franchisee who planned to operate multiple locations from the beginning. Generally, single-unit franchisees don't obtain any reduction in fees and often have to share a market with other franchisees. The franchisee simply has multiple single-unit agreements. With more units and more money invested in the franchise system, a single-unit franchisee who establishes additional franchises tends to be noticed more often than a single-unit operator would be by the franchisor and its staff. The franchisor is hoping that the franchisee will continue to grow and grow and grow.

Franchisors periodically update their franchise agreements. The franchisor may modify some of the fees, require additional equipment or investment in new technology, change some of the obligations between the parties, or make other significant and often material changes. Franchisees who, over time, acquire additional franchises are likely to find variations between their original contract with the franchisor for the first unit and the new franchise agreement for later units. Additionally, many franchise agreements provide for what is called a *cross-default*. This provision allows the franchisor to consider a violation of one of the agreements to be a violation of all the agreements.

As with all franchise agreements, you should have a franchise attorney review the franchise agreement and other documents provided to you by your franchisor. (We discuss how to select advisors in Chapter 6.)

Having twins, maybe sextuplets, or even more: Multi-unit or area developers

A *multi-unit* or *area development agreement* is a relationship that grants a franchisee the right *and* the obligation to open more than one location. It differs from a multiple single-unit relationship primarily because the multi-unit franchisee agrees upfront to open a specific number of locations during a defined period of time and usually within a specified area.

For example, say that you want to open ten haircutting shops in your town. You can go to the franchisor and buy one franchise at a time (see the preceding section), but you have certain risks. By waiting, you risk the following:

✔ You may have to share the market with other franchisees from the system.

✔ The franchisor may have sold all the other available franchises for your market before you were ready to invest in them.

✔ Other franchisees who came after you may already have opened in the best locations.

To avoid these risks, you can enter into a multi-unit or area development agreement. This agreement means that you agree to open and operate the ten units over a defined period — say, five years — and the franchisor grants you exclusive rights for the development of locations in your area.

Make sure that your development agreement gives you *market exclusivity,* which ensures that you're the only one using your brand looking for locations in your area. In some franchise systems, a development agreement may not give you market exclusivity.

When you go this route, you typically pay the franchisor a fee for the development rights and sign an area development or multi-unit development agreement obligating you to open the ten locations during the five years (in following with the hair-salon example). The opening dates are usually specified, so you may have staggered dates — such as January 1, July 1, and so on — to open each location.

When it comes to applying the fee you pay for the development rights, nothing is typical; it varies from company to company. As you identify each location, you usually sign a single-unit franchise agreement. What you pay and how the franchisor applies the fee vary, depending on the agreement:

✔ You may pay a full, initial franchise fee for the new location.

✔ The initial franchise fee for the new location may be a reduced fee from the franchisor's standard fee.

✔ Your franchisor may have a different royalty fee for multi-unit developers than it does for single-unit operators.

✔ A portion of the fee you paid for the development rights may be credited to the initial franchise fee you owe for each location.

Each franchise system is different. As with every contract you sign, you need to review the agreements with your lawyer. (See Chapter 6 for information on how to select your advisors.)

This type of relationship usually has significant advantages for both the franchisor and the multi-unit franchisee, including but not limited to the following:

- Because each multi-unit franchisee is opening more than one location, the cost of acquiring a franchise on a per-unit basis is lower.

- Because fewer franchisees exist, the cost of serving a multi-unit franchisee is generally lower on a per-unit basis.

- A multi-unit franchisee is obligated to grow the market, and controlled growth leads to better planning for advertising and better leveraging when negotiating with suppliers and other vendors.

- The area developer franchisee can often control the market he's in, so coordination of local advertising and promotions is easier than having to work with all the other franchisees.

- The franchisee often can shift personnel from one location to another depending on where the staff is needed.

- If the franchisee is in a food industry, he can often combine some of the preparation of products into a central commissary or kitchen.

- The franchisee may save on freight and other costs by buying in greater quantities at a lower cost and storing his inventory in a centralized warehouse.

Figure 2-2 depicts the multi-unit franchise relationship.

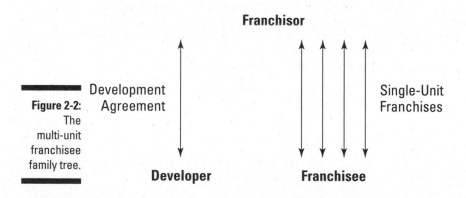

Figure 2-2:
The multi-unit franchisee family tree.

Why have two agreements — an area development agreement and a franchise agreement? Because the agreements serve two different purposes. Simply put, the area development agreement gives you the right and the obligation to open all those units and obligates the franchisor to allow you to complete your development schedule. The franchise agreement gives you the right to operate each location as a franchise of the system.

Keep in mind, though, that if you fail to meet the development schedule, the franchisor typically has the right to cancel the development agreement and keep the area development fee. So, make sure that the market you select can handle the number of locations you've committed to opening and that you have the financial backing to live up to the agreement if the first store gets off to a slower start than anticipated.

Playing in the big leagues: Master franchising

A *master franchise relationship* is similar to an area development agreement (see the preceding section), with one significant variation: The master franchisee, in addition to having the right and obligation to open and operate a number of locations in a defined area, also has the right — and sometimes the obligation — to offer and sell franchises to other people looking to become franchisees of the system. You become sort of a franchisor to those people who buy franchises through your master franchise.

As a master franchisee, you'll probably be required to own and operate at least one or two locations yourself. After you open those locations, you can then sell the rights to open additional locations to other franchisees — often called *subfranchisees* — who want to open and operate your franchise in your market.

When you sign the master franchise agreement, you pay a *master franchise fee.* Your subfranchisees then pay a franchise fee and a royalty, both of which you typically share with the franchisor. The percentage of each that you share with the franchisor varies widely depending on the system and the type of master relationship you enter into.

The master franchise relationship comes in several variations:

- ✔ The subfranchisee may execute a franchise agreement directly with the franchisor or with you as the master franchisee.
- ✔ The franchisor may have the right to approve the new subfranchisee, or you may hold that right.
- ✔ The subfranchisee may receive training and continuing support from the franchisor, the master franchisee, or a combination of both.
- ✔ The subfranchisee may pay fees directly to you, to the franchisor, or to a combination of both.

Each master franchise relationship may vary from others, and again, you should enlist the help of a qualified franchise attorney.

Of all the types of franchising relationships, the master franchise or subfranchise relationship is the most complex for all the parties — the franchisor, the master franchisee, and the subfranchisee.

Figure 2-3 shows the master franchise relationship.

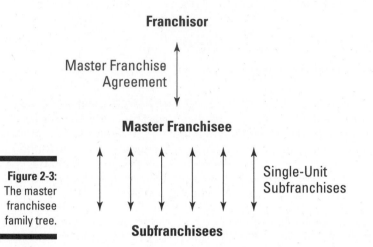

Figure 2-3:
The master
franchisee
family tree.

Master franchising is less popular in the United States today than it was in years past; however, it's still the most prevalent method used by U.S. franchisors entering other countries. Internationally, though, the trend is shifting to multi-unit and area development relationships for U.S.-based franchisors.

Conversion franchise (see Chapter 1) is a variation of a typical franchise relationship in which an independent operator, in the same business as the franchise system, converts the operation substantially to the franchise system.

Other variations of the standard franchise fall into a broad category usually referred to as *nontraditional locations.* These include mass-gathering locations — including airports, train stations, hospitals, college campuses, sports stadiums, ballparks, food courts, portable kiosks in parks, and so forth — where traffic to your business is generated by someone else's customers. Also included in this area are locations found in host locations, such as convenience stores, big-box retailers, and so on.

The hired (commissioned) gun: Area representatives

The role of an *area representative* in a franchise system is fairly unique. This person is the commissioned franchise salesperson and also the commissioned field support person for the franchisor in a geographic area. For each franchise that the area rep sells, the franchisor pays her a commission (usually based on a percentage of the franchise fee paid to the franchisor). Then the area rep provides opening and continuing support to the franchisees, earning a percentage of the royalty paid to the franchisor.

Just like a master franchisee, the area representative pays the franchisor a market development fee for the opportunity of developing and servicing a specific minimum number of units, during a specified time period in a defined territory. The difference between the two relationships is that the master franchisee signs an agreement with his subfranchisee, whereas the area representative doesn't enter into a contractual relationship with the franchisees. Those franchisees sign their agreement with the franchisors as in the normal single- and multi-unit development agreements.

Figure 2-4 displays the typical area representative relationship.

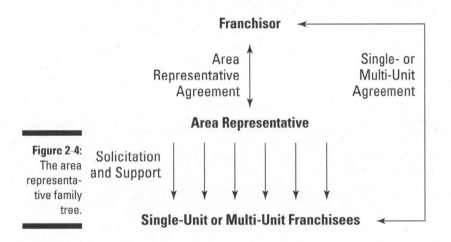

Franchisor

Area Representative Agreement

Single- or Multi-Unit Agreement

Area Representative

Figure 2-4: The area representative family tree.

Solicitation and Support

Single-Unit or Multi-Unit Franchisees

Buying Used (But Promising) Goods: Retrofranchising

The growth in the use of retrofranchising and refranchising is increasing. *Retrofranchising* refers to locations that were company owned and may never have been franchised; *refranchising* refers to locations that once were franchised but were acquired and operated by the franchisor.

Franchisors have many reasons for wanting to sell these locations:

✔ Operating company-owned locations may no longer fit the company's strategic plan.

✔ The company may still want to operate company-owned locations but wants to consolidate the number of markets in which it directly operates. It uses the capital from the sale of owned locations in some markets for the development of new locations in other markets. In essence, the company is adjusting its inventory of stores to better suit its strategy.

✔ To facilitate the growth of franchising in a market, the company may offer the sale of company-owned locations to franchisees to stimulate their development of additional units in the market.

✔ The company may have financial difficulties and need the capital from the sale.

✔ In some situations, franchisees are better at operating locations than the franchisor is. This success may be due to the distance from headquarters to the local operations, the skills of management and other personnel, or other reasons. In those situations, franchisors may sell locations simply because they believe the locations work better under the control of a franchisee than under the franchisor's own personnel.

Be on the lookout for retrofranchising and refranchising opportunities. Buying an existing location from another franchisee is also a great opportunity.

Acquiring an existing location has many advantages:

✔ The time it takes to get the business up and running is shorter because you don't have to find the location or work through constructing and equipping the business.

✔ Bank financing may be easier because the business is already up and running.

✔ The franchisor or the current owner may be willing to help you finance the location and also cut you a good deal on the purchase price. Franchisors are, after all, motivated sellers.

✔ You're buying a business that is currently operating, has existing customers, and has an established cash flow.

✔ You know what the performance of the operation is and can base your investment and operating decisions on facts rather than projections.

✔ The location may have trained staff and management.

Refranchising can be confused with *churning,* which occurs when a franchisor takes back a location from a franchisee, resells it, takes it back again, resells it again, and so on. This scenario often occurs when the original franchisee can't make a go of the location, the location isn't economically viable, or the location can't operate to company standards and is terminated. If a non-franchisor owned the location, it would probably be a candidate for closure. However, some franchisors take back the poorly performing location and, to protect themselves from having to disclose a failure in their disclosure document or to make additional income or recoup their investment, simply sell the business to another franchisee.

These "opportunities" need to be examined carefully. Don't assume that you're a smarter or better operator than the last guy. Also, a company that has a high percentage of churning may offer little chance for success and so may not be a sound franchising investment — even for franchisees not buying these recycled locations. Always ask how many owners have run the operation before you sign on the dotted line. Thankfully, not many franchisors churn their locations, but you still have to be alert to the possibility.

Chapter 3

Mirror, Mirror, on the Wall: Am I to Be a Franchisee?

In This Chapter

▶ Assessing whether franchises are right for you

▶ Understanding the advantages and disadvantages of investing in a franchise

▶ Recognizing the differences between franchisees and entrepreneurs

This chapter is all about self-evaluation. We won't lie to you: Being brutally honest with yourself is difficult when you're caught up in the excitement of striking out on your own. However, the results of this self-assessment are especially important when the franchise salesperson tells you that you're perfect for the opportunity. (News flash: Franchise salespeople and franchise brokers want to sell you a franchise, because they get a commission when you buy a franchise.)

So, you need to take this part of the process seriously. Making a decision to become a franchisee isn't just about numbers. This part of the decision is about you — your lifestyle, family, likes and dislikes, work rhythms, values, ethics, and even dreams. Keep in mind that this is the real world. Franchising won't make you a new person, and it isn't a self-help game. You need to define who you really are. Your future depends on your honesty.

This chapter helps you define who you are and whether you're the type of person who should invest in a franchise. Most individuals looking to buy a franchise have an emotional reaction to the process of selecting one. You may be the type who can stay above the emotional fray and make investment decisions based only on the merit of the offering. If so, congratulations. But, based on our experience, emotions have a lot to do with selecting a franchise — and sometimes not in a healthy way.

You may come away with the feeling that buying a franchise isn't necessarily the answer to your dream of economic independence. On the other hand, you may find that franchising is your ticket to economic security. You need to take the time to find out.

Deciding Whether to Start from Scratch or to Join an Established Team

Operating a franchise is a cross between business ownership and employment. On the one hand, you invest in the right to use the business system and the hard assets necessary to start and support the business. On the other hand, even though you're the only one responsible for day-to-day operation, you're working under a system provided and, to some extent, controlled by your franchisor. This duality can cause difficulty for some individuals.

You have a choice: You can be an independent business owner, or you can invest in a franchise opportunity. Which option you choose depends on a lot of factors: your personality, finances, motivation, experience, market niche, product or service longevity, business acumen, and level of tenacity. No universally correct choice exists.

If you're the independent type who always wants to run every detail of a project, perhaps you should look into starting your own business instead of buying a franchise. If you need the personal satisfaction of knowing that you created every element in your business, maybe franchising is not right for you.

Keep in mind that most franchisors — such as Dave Thomas — started out as independent small-business owners before franchising their concepts. They plowed every spare nickel and most spare moments into their businesses — not just for a few months but for a number of years. A dedicated, independent small-business owner never gives up and is willing to put everything on the line to see the business succeed. This approach to business offers few safety nets, and the only one making mistakes along the way is you. The support system you have is whatever you can create and sustain on your own.

If you have an innovative product or cutting-edge service that is currently not being offered to consumers, or maybe just a better way than is available elsewhere in the market, you may want to look into striking out on your own. Business groups, local banking institutions, universities, and area chambers of commerce offer a wide range of support seminars and other group benefits.

Before All Else, Consider the Pros and Cons

For many years the U.S. Department of Commerce, the U.S. Small Business Administration, franchisors, the trade press, and the franchise associations fueled the perception that franchising was a surefire method of expansion for business and a safe investment for franchisees. Although a well-designed franchise program *can* be an exceptional method of expansion, poorly designed and cookie-cutter franchise systems or businesses that are not well managed are not. This isn't just a franchise reality — it's a business reality.

Before you consider whether you're cut out to become a franchisee, you need to understand some of the advantages and disadvantages of franchise ownership.

Advantages of franchise ownership

Your chance of success in franchising can only be as strong as the franchise you select. Mature, well-operated franchise systems generally offer the following benefits.

Overall competitive benefits

The public has become accustomed to a certain level of quality and consistency from branded locations (see Chapter 2). What we mean by a branded location is a business that the public thinks of as a chain because each location has the same name, décor, products, services, menu items, and so on, and the customer experience is the same regardless of the location. Whether a company's product is superior or mediocre, if its locations are successful, the secret for its success will likely be in its consistency.

One of the secrets of being a good businessperson is not accepting a poll of one: Just because *you* find a product or service outstanding or mediocre doesn't mean the rest of the world does.

Regardless of where they are, consumers believe that they understand the level of quality they'll receive when they shop at a branded location. Because of this perception about branded chains, new franchisees often have an established customer base on the day they open. Branding enables franchises to compete with the well-established, independent operators and even against other franchised and non-franchised chains.

The advantage of brand recognition also extends to national accounts. Companies look at a system that has a network of locations and trust that each will operate at the same level of consistency and commitment. That type of system can service their needs wherever the franchise has a location.

Pre-opening benefits

Although the cost of entrance into a franchise system includes a franchise fee, which is often cited as a disadvantage, the franchisee benefits from the franchisor's having tested operating systems, initial and advanced training for management and staff, operations manuals, marketing and advertising programs, site-selection tools, store design, construction programs, reduced cost of equipment, and other necessary support required to successfully launch his business. Additionally, franchisees can ask their franchisor — a seasoned partner — questions, and they have a network of other franchisees in the system who also can be of assistance.

Ongoing benefits

Franchisees benefit from the home-office and field-consulting assistance that most franchisors provide. Franchisees enjoy the purchasing power that comes from joining with others, which often results in a reduced cost of goods. They benefit from professionally designed point-of-sale marketing material, advertising, grand-opening programs, and other marketing materials that independents could never afford. Franchise systems also can afford to modernize through ongoing research and development and by test-marketing new products and operating systems.

Each franchisee's spending power is combined with the spending power of all the other franchisees in the local market and in the rest of the system. This combined spending power — on advertising, for example — coupled with targeted strategic growth can result in market critical mass. Establishing critical mass enables franchise systems not only to dominate local markets and the established independents but also to compete effectively against large, established chains.

Disadvantages for franchisees

Franchising is not right for every person, and you need to understand some of the disadvantages in a franchise relationship.

Loss of independence

For some people, one of the most serious disadvantages of becoming a franchisee is loss of independence. If you want to make all your own decisions, franchising may be the wrong choice. Franchise systems are structured in such a way that the franchisor sets many of the rules; the franchisee is required to operate the business according to the franchisor's manuals and procedures.

Overdependence on the system

Loss of independence, if taken to extremes, leads to a further disadvantage: overdependence on the franchise system. Franchising succeeds when financial and emotional risks motivate franchisees. When franchisees rely totally on the system for their success, their overdependence can cause problems.

Franchisees have to balance system restrictions with their personal ability to manage their own businesses. For example, when a franchisee depends on national advertising exclusively and doesn't invest in local marketing, she's shortchanging her business by relying too greatly on what the franchisor is bringing to the party.

Other franchisees who are "bad apples"

The principal reason for the success of franchising is the public's perception of quality and consistency throughout the system. When the public receives great service at one location, the assumption is that the system has great service. This consumer expectation is also one of the potential major frailties of any chain, including franchising. Franchisees are judged not only by *their* performance, but by the performance of other franchisees. Poorly performing fellow franchisees or company-owned locations damage a franchisee's business even where they don't share the same market. If the hotel room is dirty in one location or, even worse, if the press were to report that the hotel had rodents, the public assumes that the problem exists throughout the system.

Elevated income expectations

Although good franchisors try to prevent it, some franchisees have unrealistic expectations about the income they're going to earn. If their expectations are unrealistic, they'll regret their investment in dollars, time, and effort and may become a negative influence on the system. Having realistic expectations is important to any investment decision.

Franchising inelasticity

Franchise systems are bound together through legal agreements between franchisors and franchisees. Often, these agreements contain restrictions that potentially impact the franchisor's ability to make strategic decisions. For example, if a non-franchisor finds a perfect location for a new store, it's free to do so. In a franchise system, the franchisor must first look to the legal agreements between itself and the franchisees in the market. If the franchisor has granted the franchisees protected territories, and the potential location is in one of those territories, the franchise system loses that market opportunity — and often to a competitor who doesn't have the same restrictions. A similar situation can arise with e-commerce sales over the Web if the franchisor has provided the franchisee with those rights in the agreement.

Because of the potential loss of market opportunities, many franchisors are reducing the size of the territory they're granting franchising today, and others are granting exclusivity for a short period of time or eliminating protected territories altogether. In the long run, having a market fully developed is a benefit to the franchisee and the franchisor, although it may have an impact on a particular unit's sales.

The restrictions of franchising can be a double-edged sword sometimes — they can make franchising successful but can also be disadvantages to some franchisees. The restrictions may be on the product and services they're allowed to offer; limitations on size and exclusivity of their territory; the possibility of termination for failure to follow the system; the added investment often required for reimaging, remodeling, or new equipment as a condition of renewal; the cost of transfer and renewal; and restrictions on independent marketing. Also, the added costs for royalties, advertising, additional training, and other services potentially reduce a franchisee's earnings.

Making Sure You're Realistic about Your Role

When you own a franchise, you become your own boss, right? Maybe.

Many media stories on franchising use the words *entrepreneur* and *franchisee* interchangeably, so newcomers to franchising may be confused by the reality that being a successful franchisee is usually not the same as being an entrepreneur.

Even in great franchise systems, some franchisees do better than others. Believe it or not, even great franchise systems have franchisees who are dismal failures. If one of the elements of successful franchising is about franchisors providing great systems that can be executed consistently, how is failure possible? The human factor.

Franchisees are not robots or computers that can be fed a string of commands that they execute flawlessly in every situation. Nor are franchisees true entrepreneurs with the flexibility to make every decision for themselves. If an independent operator is an entrepreneur, a franchisee is an "entrepreneur lite."

True entrepreneurs are their own bosses, free to make turn-on-a-dime decisions that are full of risk and often full of reward. True entrepreneurs are like captains of their own ships, and sometimes they have a "reefs-be-damned, full-speed-ahead" attitude. If that statement describes you, you may not be franchisee material.

In other words, when you become a franchisee, you give up some, but not all, of your freedom to run your own show. It's still your business and still your responsibility to supervise your management and staff, but you do so while applying the system that the franchisor licensed to you. A clear understanding of that relationship is important.

Consider these potential advantages and disadvantages of the franchising arrangement and gauge your reaction:

- ✔ The franchisor's standards on products and services may seem restrictive, but they provide the public with assurance on the consistency of the brand.

- ✔ Providing you with a limited or no protected territory may reduce your market, but doing so allows for the development of other franchise and company-owned locations in the area. These locations can contribute with you to the advertising fund, which will enhance the local name recognition of your business.

- ✔ Additional locations close to yours may seem like they're competing with you for your customers. But by working together with other franchisees, you can increase your effectiveness against the competition by reducing the costs of goods through buying cooperatives, jointly recruiting personnel, and creating improved brand awareness because customers see the system's trade name more frequently.

- ✔ The possibility of being terminated for failure to follow the system may seem unfair, but those same penalties may be imposed on other franchisees who may not perform as well as you. Because franchisees are part of a branded system, customers may view you in the same light as those poor operators, which can have a dramatic effect on your success (or lack of it).

If you can't let go of the need to run the show, you need to reevaluate your plan to become a franchisee.

Franchisees execute the system that the franchisor provides. Great franchisees take that system and improve it by providing excellent customer service; by hiring quality people and providing them with training; and by creating an atmosphere in their businesses that is palpably better than expected by their staff, their customers, their vendors, and the franchisors. Great franchisees enhance the basic system by simply executing the basics better each and every day.

Staring Hard at the Mirror: A Self-Evaluation

Only you can tell whether becoming a franchisee is right for you. It's a personal decision. But we ask you to look at yourself and answer the questions we pose in this chapter before you make that decision. You don't need to score yourself; no one element is more important than any other. You also don't need to get 100 percent to be the perfect franchisee. The questions are for you to ponder and use to make the correct decisions for yourself and your family.

These questions are some of the basic ones we think you need to consider before making a decision to become a franchisee. Other questions will come from those you trust for advice and from that little voice inside your head that wakes you up at night. That little voice deserves to have its questions answered, too.

Are you willing and able to learn new skills?

The first thing you find out as a franchisee is that you have a lot to learn. The second thing you find out is that every day you're going to have to be a teacher, a mentor, and a monitor. Teaching your employees how to operate the business, motivating them to succeed, and then monitoring how well they're serving your customers is your responsibility every day. Your franchisors will set the standards, but they aren't responsible for how you run your business, serve your customers, or maintain the safety and security of your operations.

Most franchisors include a clause in their franchise agreement giving them the right to terminate the franchise if the franchisee can't pass the training class. Many require the franchisee to retake the training until he gets it right. Most franchisors even require training for any management personnel who will be operating the business so that they can evaluate their ability to learn and operate the system.

Part of what franchisors look for is your ability to set aside your preconceived notions of how to operate the business and for you to focus on how *they* expect you to operate the business. This notion can be especially hard for those operators converting established independent businesses to the franchisor's brand and operating methods.

Your eagerness to learn new skills is an important attribute of becoming a franchisee.

Would you rather give or take orders?

Everyone has her own ideas about giving orders — and taking them. If you bristle at the thought of having to report your sales and expenses monthly or even weekly, or being told how to set up your merchandise, what ads to run, and how to display advertising banners, you should think about how you'll feel when you're expected to follow an entire system every day. That's day in and day out — year after year.

Successful franchising is based on the principle that following a detailed structure is your best guarantee of success. As a franchisee, part of what you buy is the franchisor's system and knowledge. Your role is to follow the formula that the franchisor has developed and to look for ways to improve your operation within the system. That means following the rules, working within the system, and running your business according to the agreed-upon plan. Ask yourself these questions:

- ✔ Can you follow somebody else's rules, even when you think you have a better way? And are you prepared to accept coaching and advice on how you run your business from a franchisor's field and headquarters staff? If not, independent business ownership may be a better fit for you.

- ✔ Are you willing to use the advertising and promotional material provided by the franchisor, or do you have to be the creative genius? If the latter, you may need to go solo.

- ✔ Do you think you can change the franchisor's system after you're onboard? If so, independent business ownership may be a better fit for you.

- ✔ Do you think that your local market is different from all others in the system, and that the franchisor will modify the system just to suit your needs? It may, but if you're counting on it, independent business ownership may be a better fit for you.

- ✔ Can you trust (with some honest skepticism) that your franchisor is working for the benefit of the entire system — even when its decisions don't necessarily go your way? If so, franchising may be your ticket.

- ✔ Are you willing to share financial information and provide required reports each month? If so, franchising may be for you.

- ✔ Do you have the personal drive to be a great operator? If so, franchising may be a good fit.

You won't be a robot doing only what you're told. There are great franchisees and less-than-great franchisees. Everyone starts with the same system. The great ones add their personal skills and personalities to the business. They invest themselves in the job. They successfully manage their personnel (their most important asset). They provide a better atmosphere for their customers (their most important marketing tool). They love what they do, and it shows.

But great franchise brands require consistency from location to location. Consistency means that you must follow the system and not make it up for yourself. So, if serving wings, fingers, sandwiches, and shrimp, all sauced in any of Wing Zone's 25 Signature Flavors, leaves you wanting to add a 26th flavor you made up for yourself in the kitchen — don't become a franchisee of Wing Zone. One of the reasons that Wing Zone is successful is that each customer can rely on consistency each and every time, regardless of the location.

Are you ready to say goodbye to corporate perks?

Oh those corporate perks: retirement plans; stock ownership and option plans; paid sick days; paid vacation days; expense accounts; company cars; and health, vision, and dental insurance plans. When you lose the comfort of working for someone else, you may start to miss those perks.

Perhaps you made the decision to leave your company, or the company's downsizing, right-sizing, merging, or early-retirement programs have left you with cash and more free time on your hands than you really want. If so, this section is about you.

The former corporate middle manager who wants to be a franchisee is a unique breed. This person has a broad understanding of business, knows how to work within a system, knows how to motivate staff, certainly is no stranger to long hours, and now has the capital to make a franchise investment.

In many cases, these former midlevel managers are missing only one key ingredient for running a business: They may never have started one from scratch — without corporate support and corporate financial backing.

Perhaps the biggest adjustment middle managers face as franchisees is the loss of many of the support services they've grown accustomed to. Their secretaries probably didn't come with them when they left the 22nd floor. And the copy machines, fax machines, filing systems, payroll clerks, legal department staff, computers, and travel services are probably also at the office where they left them. Although they're not in business by themselves, they may sometimes feel as if they are.

Success is no longer measured by the rapt attention that staff or superiors give to those fine PowerPoint presentations. Success is measured each day in performance. In other words, operating a business requires more self-reliance than many middle managers have had to possess.

A structured franchised system replaces some of the support that middle managers have relied on for their success. The system, the branding, and the franchisor support, coupled with the talents of the former corporate employee, make the transition to business ownership through franchising a success.

Franchising for veterans

Franchisors always have recognized that military veterans often make very successful franchisees. Because of veterans' frequent franchise success, and also to thank the men and women who have bravely served our nation, the International Franchise Association (IFA) established a program called VetFran. Today, approximately 200 companies participate in VetFran, and veterans who invest in those companies' opportunities are rewarded with financial support not available to others. Support for VetFran is also provided by the U.S. Department of Veterans Affairs, the U.S. Small Business Administration, and the Veterans Corporation.

The IFA Education Foundation has also established a veterans scholarship to assist veterans who are leaving the military and want to enroll in a business or entrepreneurial course of study. The first annual veterans scholarship was funded by Michael H. Seid & Associates (MSA) and was awarded to Marine Captain Nathaniel Fick, who commanded a special operations reconnaissance platoon in Afghanistan and Iraq. Since establishing that first scholarship, several other franchisors and suppliers to the franchise industry have joined with MSA in establishing additional scholarship opportunities for veterans. For information on VetFran and the Veterans Scholarship program, go to www.franchise.org.

How's your health?

The demands on a franchisee often require that you have an extraordinary level of staying power. Even when an extra ten minutes of sleep in the morning is what your body craves, you must get up, open your business, and serve your customers. To achieve that level of endurance, you have to be in good health. So, be brutally honest when answering this question: Do you have the physical ability to meet the needs of operating your own business?

Can you handle stress? Especially during the early days as a franchisee, as you learn your new craft, things won't always go exactly as you expect them to. On an almost continual basis, as a business operator, you'll need to deal with crisis issues and deadlines that will become stressful. How's your coping mechanism? Do you have the mental ability to meet the everyday needs of operating your own business?

Do you like people?

Do you *really* like people? This question may sound silly. You're probably thinking, "Of course, I like people. Who doesn't?" Keep in mind that we're talking about people relationships, because franchising is based on relationships between and among people. As a franchisee, you need to maintain relationships with your franchisor, staff, customers, and vendors. In addition, your various personal and family relationships can influence your franchise's performance.

You have to handle a lot of relationships at once. You need the ability to communicate and to listen, because every franchisee must interact with a wide array of people during the course of every business day. This essential personal characteristic is simple: You have to like to deal with people every day. A franchise is not a suitable environment for someone who prefers working alone! Your ability to interact positively with fellow franchisees, your franchisor, your staff, and your customers is important every day of your company's operation.

Consider these questions:

- ✔ Do you like people? Do you have patience when working and interacting with others?

- ✔ Do you communicate well? Do you listen? Can you be a leader and a trainer for your staff and a front person for your business?

- ✔ Can you maintain a positive relationship with the people who work for you?

- ✔ Can you meet the needs of your customers by staying open and managing the business during the key hours of the day?

- ✔ Do you have the ability to sell — yourself, your products, your services?

How much can you dish out and take on?

Many franchises have an initial investment of less than $100,000 and others can take you up to the multimillion-dollar big leagues. So, remember that franchising offers investment opportunities that fit anyone's needs, no matter how small your pocketbook is or how diverse your views on what will be successful in the future. However, having just enough money to invest in your franchise and to purchase the necessary equipment and stock is not enough. Even if you're prepared to invest what the franchisor predicts is required, you need to prepare yourself to invest some more, just in case things don't go by the book.

You've probably heard stories of successful businesspeople who have funded their franchises by maxing out their credit cards. These tales are part of the mystique of success and entrepreneurship. But, more often than not, this choice is really a path to disaster.

Don't risk all your financial resources, because all may not be enough. Look at your finances, determine what you need to live on if the business can't support you and your family in the early days, and set aside that amount. Make sure that you cover the important things, such as food, housing, and college funds for the kids. Franchisees with adequate resources can weather the hard times and have the extra funds available when they need them.

You need discipline to know what your limits are. Working with a financial advisor or an accountant is essential; these professionals can help you determine how much you can invest. Ask your friends and neighbors if they know a good Certified Public Accountant (CPA) who can help you through the process. You can also contact the local CPA association for recommendations. (See Chapter 6 for a discussion on how to find professional advisors.)

How are your family and friends responding?

Buying a franchise is a life-changing decision. Operating a business is more than a full-time job. During the start-up phase, a franchise can *become* your life. That commitment requires carving out time normally spent with your family and friends and pouring it into the business. If they resent the time you must dedicate to the business, business ownership may not be your thing. Stay an employee. However, we don't know many successful corporate executives who aren't currently putting in 70-hour workweeks. Even for those who punch a clock, between overtime and second jobs, 70-hour weeks may be the norm. Still, you, your family, and your friends must clearly understand and accept the demands on your time before you commit to any business.

Select an industry that meets your personal needs and likes. If you'll be embarrassed to tell friends and family that you own a janitorial business or a moving company, even if such businesses are highly lucrative, don't buy one. If working 12-hour days, seven days a week is not your idea of fun, make sure that the franchise industry you select offers better hours. Whether you need $50,000 or $200,000 a year to support your family, make sure that the other franchisees in the system you select make that type of return. And if you're getting groans from family members at the mere mention of franchising, stop right there. Work out the reasons behind the groans and get your family's support before you proceed. Business ownership is demanding — even within a well-developed franchise system.

Personal happiness is the most important factor in buying any business, including a franchise. However, with over 85 different industries and thousands of franchise opportunities available — both in product- and service-related areas — one of them may suit your needs. Examine your feelings toward each one before making a selection.

Include your family in all your preliminary and ongoing investigations into franchising. Get their support for your choice. That way, they'll feel invested in the process and can give you the support you need.

Fact: We were both franchisees. We worked hard. We dedicated more time than we wanted to the business and less than we liked to our families. Neither of us would change a thing. The investment was worth the effort. But that's us — and it may or may not be you.

Part II
So You Want to Be a Franchisee?

The 5th Wave   By Rich Tennant

4 Food Franchises to Avoid Buying Into

INTERNATIONAL HOUSE OF BROCCOLI

SQUID-ON-A-STICK

LiverLand
The Best in Balkan Cuisine

McOffals
HOME OF THE
Flame Broiled Tripe

In this part . . .

Becoming a franchisee is a big decision to make, and it's one you have to invest time in if you're going to do it right. Before you sign on the dotted line, you need to understand what you're signing and, more important, whether you're signing with the right franchisor.

In Part II, we let you in on how we'd begin to explore franchising today if we were prospective franchisees. We tell you where you can find the information you need as well as the tricks of the trade so you won't get burned in the process.

Part II also explores the law and gives you a detailed understanding of what goes into a Franchise Disclosure Document, the rather thick legal document you receive from each franchisor you meet with to discuss your becoming part of its franchise system. It tells you how to evaluate a franchise system, understand the agreements, know a bit about what can and won't be negotiated by franchisors, and, along the way, even question whether you should be considering being a franchisee at all.

By the time you finish with Part II — although you still need the assistance of knowledgeable lawyers to get into the end zone — you'll no longer be an amateur. You'll be able to run, block, and tackle with the professionals. Well, almost.

Chapter 4

Making the Choice: Deciding Which Business Is Right for You

*B*ecoming a franchisee within a solid franchise system removes much of the guesswork of running a business. It also allows you to avoid most of the mistakes that independent start-ups make. That's part of what you're buying when you purchase a franchise from a mature franchise system. You should expect to receive a proven system of operation with the kinks already worked out for you.

But which franchise system should you invest in? Don't ask us — we're not you. All we can do is provide you with some tools, give you advice on the process, and hopefully steer you away from some of the dead ends. Research is the single most important activity in making your franchise investment decision — and you're the one who has to do it. We can give you some guidelines, some questions to ask, and the bases to cover. But, in the end, you must put in the time, get the information, assess it, reassess it, and make an informed decision. Without adequate information, you may end up making the most expensive decision of your life.

In this chapter, you can stop kicking the tires and put yourself behind a franchise wheel or two. Don't get too excited, yet. *Remember:* Franchisees fail, but many franchisees could have avoided failure if they'd conducted more thorough research at the front end of the franchise selection process. Take your time — don't cut corners. Sure, you want to save money, but at times you need to spend money to ensure that you're making the right decision. **Remember:** A small investment in getting the facts could save you the pain and expense that comes from making the wrong choice — and possibly losing it all.

Here's a simple and effective way to find out whether a franchise is right for you: Try to get permission to work at a location for a while just to see if you like the business. Your investment is your time — what's three or four weeks if it shows you that you love, or hate, the business?

This chapter helps you get the information you need to make the right choice — for you. Nothing can substitute for good, old-fashioned research when you're looking into a particular franchise. Research means getting past the sales hype and getting at the systems, manuals, training programs, headquarters and field support, advertising, and financials. You must also talk to other franchisees in the system.

Most good franchisors stand ready to share this information. They want franchisees who have done their homework and are making informed decisions. That's why spending a few weeks in a franchised operation before signing the contract is a good way to find out whether you and the franchise were meant to be together. Words and numbers are fine, but you need to actually get into the business and try it on for size.

Finding Good Sources of Information about Available Franchises

Choosing and buying the right franchise takes time, money, and lots of information.

We've found that the best way to gather information is to make lists of questions, write down answers, and set up a method for cross-referencing and cross-checking facts as you proceed. Ask detailed follow-up questions. For example, the franchisor says it provides three weeks of training. "Gee," you say, "that's a lot." However, unless you find out what's included in the curriculum and who's training you, you may simply be working the service counter at a franchisor's company-owned location for 21 days. Or perhaps the franchisor says it has a fully qualified field staff assigned to work with you. Unless you ask, that fully qualified field staff may be a new hire and may visit you only twice a year — possibly only by telephone.

For each franchise system you consider, write down the names of the people you talk with. Jot down the information they tell you so that you begin building a body of information that eventually gives you a pretty clear picture of the business you're considering.

On the CD-ROM, we provide a workbook you can use in making your franchise decision, called, of course, the "Making the Franchise Decision" workbook. This file is a simple tool to guide you through some of the key issues you need to evaluate and is a way for you to keep track of that information. If you've ever bought a house, you may remember that by the third house you saw, you probably couldn't remember which house had the big kitchen and which needed the new roof. Selecting a franchise is pretty similar. The workbook helps to remind you which franchise system was the one with the great training program and operating system and which was the one with the 30-page operations manual. *Note:* To give you a choice on how to use the workbook materials, we provide the whole thing in one file (which is quite long) in the `Chapter 4` folder on the CD. In case you want to print out each part of the workbook individually so you have fewer papers to deal with all at once, and also so you can easily find the forms, checklists, and so on we're discussing throughout this chapter, we broke up the workbook into individual documents, which we reference throughout this chapter.

Okay, so where is all this research and information? Fortunately, you can choose among many different ways to get the goods on franchising. In order to get a complete picture of the franchises you're investigating, we suggest that you take advantage of every resource you can find.

Print directories

Several different franchise directories list most of the franchise companies currently offering franchises. These guides are among the best places to begin your examination because they give you a capsule of information on each company listed:

- ✔ *Franchise Opportunities Guide:* Published by the International Franchise Association (IFA), this guide lists the trade association's member companies, franchise lawyers, consultants, and other suppliers, as well as descriptive sections on franchise statistics, other publications, and educational affiliates. In addition, the publication contains helpful articles written by professionals in the industry. This guide is a particularly good source of information because the members of the IFA tend to be the strongest franchisors in the industry. The cost is $20 plus shipping and handling, and you can order the guide by contacting the IFA at 800-543-1038 or through its Web site at `www.franchise.org`.

- ✔ **Franchise Update Publications:** This magazine publishing group prints a variety of franchise guides, including *The Executives' Guide to Franchise Opportunities, Food Service Guide to Franchise Opportunities,* and *The Guide to Multiple-Unit Franchise Opportunities.* It also publishes *Franchise UPDATE* magazine, a leading trade and management publication targeted to professionals in the industry. For franchisors, franchise attorneys, and franchise consultants, Franchise Update's publications are must-reads. Prices vary, so contact Franchise Update directly for pricing and ordering information by calling 408-997-7795 or visiting www.franchise-update.com or www.franchising.com.

✔ ***Bond's Franchise Guide:*** This guide, published by Robert Bond, is updated annually and offers a comprehensive listing of franchise companies operating in the United States and Canada. It includes detailed profiles of more than 1,000 franchisors listed by name, address, and contact person. Robert Bond offers a number of other useful books, including *How Much Can I Make?* (a compendium of earnings claims included by franchisors in the Franchise Disclosure Document [FDD], the disclosure document that franchisors are required to provide to prospective franchisees). *Bond's Franchise Guide* costs $29.95, and you can order by calling 800-841-0873 or visiting www.worldfranchising.com. Much of the information contained in *Bond's Franchise Guide* is also available on the Web site.

Just because a franchisor is included in one of the directories doesn't mean that the information is complete or accurate. Many of the directories don't independently verify the information that the franchisor provides. Directories are the starting place for your examination, a place to get very basic information, such as who's offering franchises today and what industries may interest you. We discuss later in this chapter how to fine-tune the information so that you get a more accurate picture before you invest.

On the CD-ROM, we include a list of questions (CD0401) for you to ask the franchisor when evaluating the franchise's financial and local operational issues.

Consumer business publications

A number of magazines and newspapers regularly publish franchising-related sections that contain articles and advertising on franchising. They include

✔ *Entrepreneur* (www.entrepreneur.com)

✔ *Franchise Times* (www.franchisetimes.com)

✔ *Franchise UPDATE* (www.franchise-update.com)

✔ *Franchising World* (www.franchise.org)

✔ *Inc.* (www.inc.com)

✔ *Nation's Restaurant News* (www.nrn.com)

✔ *The New York Times* (www.nytimes.com)

✔ *USA Today* (www.usatoday.com)

✔ *The Wall Street Journal* (www.wsj.com)

Trade shows and expositions

Trade shows and expositions give you an opportunity to meet face-to-face with representatives of many franchise companies at one time.

The IFA sponsors the International Franchise Expo (IFE), which is a production of MFV Expositions. The IFE shows are the largest gatherings in the world of franchise companies actively seeking new franchisees. Usually, three big shows take place each year in the United States, including the following:

- ✔ **Washington, D.C.:** Spring to early summer
- ✔ **Los Angeles:** Fall to early winter
- ✔ **Miami:** Winter

The IFE is a great place to educate yourself about franchising. Some of the top professionals in the industry regularly conduct educational programs on franchising. For information on when and where the next Franchise Expo will be held, call MFV Expositions at 201-226-1130 or go to www.mfvexpo.com.

Another set of franchise trade shows is the National Franchise & Business Opportunities events, which are held in various cities throughout the year in the United States and Canada. These shows combine both franchises and business opportunities. For information on show schedules, you can go to www.franchiseshowinfo.com.

At trade shows, franchisors usually offer you a sense of their business on the exposition floor. You'll have a chance to ask a company representative questions and, if you're interested, give them some information about yourself as a step toward further discussions.

Trade shows are wonderful sources for brochures on franchise opportunities. Most franchisors give you their brochures and then follow up later by telephone or in writing. At the shows, some franchisors even hold seminars (often called *discovery days*) on their franchises and may give you a copy of their FDD, which contains a wealth of information on the franchisor.

Don't be surprised if a franchisor asks you to sign a receipt for the FDD given to you. Not only are franchisors trying to keep track of whom they give the books to so that they contact them later, but franchisors are also required to keep track of when they gave you their FDD.

Franchisors like trade shows because the shows give them a chance to strut their stuff, as well as do some on-site prequalification of interested parties. So, don't be surprised if they ask you as many questions as you're asking them. Good franchisors want to know as much about you as possible as quickly as possible, so no one ends up wasting anyone else's time.

Finally, under no circumstances do you actually buy a franchise at a trade show. Franchisors must follow certain rules regarding the offer and sale of franchises, and one of those rules requires that the franchisor give you a copy of its FDD and give you time to review the information. (See Chapter 6 for a discussion of the FDD.) The franchisor can't legally sell you a franchise — even if you want one — at a trade show. Trade shows are simply another tool for you to use in your research.

The Internet

The Internet provides a showcase for franchise companies and can be a useful avenue of basic information. Most franchisors have their own Web sites and list their Web addresses in their advertisements and their franchise brochures or, if they're members of the IFA, on the IFA's Web page, with links to their Web site. Many franchisors also are included in various online franchise directories. The online directories feature basic information, including company history, total investment, liquid capital needed to invest, areas currently developing, and descriptions of the business. Some directories offer an analysis of particular industries and organize franchisors for easy navigation and comparison, becoming the best source of information about any franchise.

You can find information about franchise opportunities on more than 40 lead-generation and broker sites used by many franchisors. To give you a head start, we include a complete list of franchise-opportunity Web sites (CD0402) on the CD-ROM.

Of all the franchise-focused Web sites, the IFA's site (www.franchise.org) likely offers the most franchise-only information in one location. Each of the 1,100 companies listed is a member of the IFA and subscribes to the IFA's Code of Ethics; plus, you can contact the companies directly through www.franchise.org. This site also includes hundreds of free articles, including the "FTC Guide to Buying a Franchise." You can browse the supplier directory to find a franchise consultant, an attorney, or any other business partner to assist in the discovery and due-diligence process.

Other popular sites are

- Entrepreneur (www.entrepreneur.com)
- Franchise Bison (www.bison.com)
- Franchise Gator (www.franchisegator.com)
- Franchising.com (www.franchising.com)

You can use the links on these Web sites and those we provide on the CD to directly communicate with the franchise sales department for more specific questions. Many of these online directories even allow you to complete a simple online application that can speed up the process of getting additional information from franchises.

Working with a Franchise Broker

Franchise brokers are individuals or companies that offer to help you find the franchise that's right for you. Some brokers will work with you to develop your individual profile that reflects your background, interests, lifestyle expectations, and financial qualifications. Based on that profile, the broker will refer you to up to four franchisors that meet those expectations. Some brokers, such as FranNet, will act as a liaison in your investigation process, helping you get answers to your questions and make an informed decision. Other brokers will merely make the referral and collect the fee if you become a franchisee.

Most franchise brokers no longer refer to themselves as *sales brokers* and now refer to themselves as *consultants* — as you can imagine, using a broker may increase the pressure on you to buy. Most brokers don't charge the prospective franchisee a fee; instead, brokers are paid by franchisors to introduce prospects to them. Franchise brokers usually receive 40 percent to 50 percent of the initial fee you pay the franchisor. A few of the franchise brokers also are paid a percentage of the continuing royalty payments you make to the franchisor, and others may earn equity in the franchisor if they sell a lot of franchises for that franchisor. Some franchisors also pay the broker additional fees (or *spiffs*), which are an additional incentive for that broker to steer you in that franchisor's direction.

Good and competent brokers provide a valuable service to someone looking to invest his life savings into a franchise. But, unfortunately, some brokers may not have your best interests at heart. Some will push you to purchase a franchise from one of their clients because the best opportunity for you is not on their client list and they won't earn a commission if you buy from a non-client. Some will push you to buy a franchise from one of their clients, even if the psychological test they give you (which they claim is meant to find you the perfect opportunity) points you away from any of their clients. Even if you decide to use a broker, you still need to explore franchising on your own. After a broker identifies a company for you, make sure you explore other franchises independently in that same industry segment.

Here are some of the better franchise brokerage firms you can work with:

- The Entrepreneur Authority (www.entrepreneurauthority.com)
- Franchise Solutions (www.franchisesolutions.com)
- FranChoice (www.franchoice.com)
- FranNet (www.frannet.com)
- Sunbelt (www.sunbeltnetwork.com)
- VR Business Brokers (www.vrbusinessbrokers.com)

We're aware of other franchise brokerage companies, some of which are good, but some of which have been involved in litigation and also have been subject to regulatory review. So, make certain you complete thorough due diligence on any of the professional advisors you choose to work with.

Will it pass the test of time?

You won't find a single franchise brochure, Web site, or advertisement that says, "We're part of a new fad that may only last a few months." Every franchisor you meet will tell you its opportunity is based on solid market demand that will continue well into the next millennium.

Take a close look at the industry. What's the track record for franchisors and non-franchisors? What does the business press say about the future? What impact will technology likely have on consumer demand?

Remember the days when automobiles needed a tune-up every 15,000 miles? Now that many cars need a tune-up every 100,000 miles, we bet the single-service tune-up franchisees are remembering the good old days.

Look at how the Internet is changing how people make their buying decisions. In Economics 101, they tell you that the weakness of a banana republic (a country, not *the* company) is that it has only one product to offer. When consumer tastes change, or technology makes the product less of a requirement or less attractive, these economies suffer. They have nothing else to sell. It's the same for single-product

franchise systems — but worse. Even if the demand for a single-product franchise system's products stays strong, other companies often add the product to their offerings and strip from those companies their major strength — uniqueness. That's what happened to the frozen-yogurt industry in the '80s and '90s as ice-cream chains and quick-service restaurants added frozen yogurt to their menus.

Look at the companies in the industry you're researching. Have they added new products and services or changed the way they deliver products and services to consumers, or is their location design about as old and out of date as the products and services they sell? What have the historic sales trends been? How are current sales? Are they increasing? Is the company taking advantage of the opportunities that e-commerce may provide the system?

Is the company focused on going international, or is it focused on supporting existing domestic franchisees? The hype of international expansion often strips resources from smaller, less-developed domestic franchisors, which is increasingly a problem.

If you decide to use a broker, ask a few questions upfront. On the CD-ROM, we include a list of questions (CD0403) for you to ask a broker before you agree to work with her.

After you have the answers to your questions, you'll quickly be able to identify the brokers who are genuinely interested in helping you, rather than the brokers who are interested only in notching a commission. ***Remember:*** Whether you decide to use a broker or not, any franchise investigative work is your responsibility. You must invest the time and energy to determine whether any franchise is a good fit for you. If you're working with a good broker, he'll help guide you in the process, but in the end, the final decision must be yours.

You're making a life-changing decision — don't look for shortcuts. Do the legwork yourself. Regardless of whether you're working with a broker, you need to invest in outside expertise as your advisor. The broker works for the franchisor, so make sure you hire your own professional advisor such as an accountant, an attorney, or a reputable franchise consulting firm to help you in the process. (We cover finding professional advisors in Chapter 6.)

On the bonus CD-ROM, we include a list of questions (CD0404) for you to ask a franchisor when evaluating its consumer research and marketing.

Deciding whether to Buy Old or New

Suppose you've narrowed your choice to one industry, and within that industry you've further narrowed your choice to one or two franchise opportunities. One franchise company offers brand-new store locations only. The other offers new locations but also a selection of existing franchises. What do you do — buy new or used?

Sizing up an existing franchise

Franchise companies often have existing company-owned locations for sale or keep a list of franchisees that are looking to sell their franchises.

Buying an existing operation from the company or from a franchisee may offer advantages over starting from scratch. Instead of evaluating a potential business, you're evaluating one that's already up and running. It has a history of performance, a reputation in the community, and an existing clientele. You know what the historic profit and cash flow have been and what the trends are for that store. The site is fully developed, and you avoid the burden of looking for a location, negotiating a lease, hiring a contractor, and building and equipping the location. (See Chapter 7 for a discussion about establishing a location.) The operation may have a trained staff, so you can avoid the hassle of having to immediately recruit new employees and train them before you service your first customer. On the other hand, their staff may be poorly trained or, worse, may need to be replaced entirely. You can be in business months sooner than if you start the franchise from scratch.

You have a lot to consider when buying an existing franchise, and on the CD-ROM, we provide many questions for you to ask (CD0405).

From a franchisor's perspective, your buying an existing location makes sense, too. The franchisor may have made a strategic decision not to operate a company-owned store at that location and may be looking for a franchisee to buy it. The franchisor may have had problems finding employees or a good manager to operate the business and may be hoping that a franchisee can do the job better. However, and this unfortunately happens, the store may be a dog that the franchisor took back from a failed franchisee and is looking to move quickly — we call that *churning*.

As we discuss in Chapter 6, not every franchisor provides unit financial information to prospective franchisees before they invest in a franchise. Even those franchisors that don't do so are allowed to provide potential franchisees with information on specific, company-owned locations that they have up for sale. If you're interested in an existing company-owned location, make sure that you get the financial information about that location.

Franchisors also benefit from franchisees selling their franchises to new franchisees:

- ✔ If the existing franchisee is unhappy, getting a new, enthusiastic franchisee is a good swap.

- ✔ Franchisors typically require new franchisees to sign the then-current franchise agreement, which allows the franchisor to alter the terms of the franchise for that location sooner than it probably would have if the franchisee had stayed and operated under the old contract.

- ✔ The franchisor can establish a selling price for individual locations. If franchises are selling at a high price, that news will get out quickly and will increase the franchisor's ability to sell new franchises.

Note that we left out the collection of a transfer fee as a benefit to the franchisor. Most franchisors charge a fee for the transfer of an existing location. This fee is usually a percentage of the existing franchise fee or a set amount. Although the franchisor doesn't have to incur the costs of recruiting the new franchisee or helping him find the site, it still incurs the costs of evaluating and supporting the new franchisee and bringing him up to speed through training. Transferring a franchise also involves legal costs for the franchisor. If the franchisor earns any profit on the transfer fee, it's usually negligible.

Before you buy an existing operation, do some digging for information. Find out why the owner wants to sell. Did the market dry up? Is the location no longer desirable? Did the owner simply want to move on to other things? Is the owner retiring? Look at the store location as if you were starting fresh. If the business is on the decline for any reason, buyer beware. Don't assume that you're smarter or a better operator than the existing or previous owner.

Don't assume that just because you're buying a franchise, you have a full term, with renewals available to you. Some franchisors allow the transfer of franchises with only the remaining term of the agreement. Others give you a full term plus renewals. Make sure that you understand not only the business you're buying but also the franchise you're buying.

Getting some details before you start from scratch

Most new franchisees enter franchising by buying a franchise and opening a new location. You get help from the franchisor with site selection, store construction, signage, inventory, grand-opening events, training, and ongoing support during the start-up phase of the business.

The helping hand may seem to be there, but be sure to do some extra pre-purchase research to discover the quality of that helping hand.

Ever think about buying a house without seeing it first? How about getting married without meeting your future spouse? When Junior went off to college, did you just hope that the school had everything the glossy brochure told you it had, or did you get in the car, board the bus, or hop on a plane and see it firsthand?

Franchising is no different. You need to see the franchisor's headquarters, meet its staff, and evaluate its capacity to deliver the services that it's promising.

Before the franchisor invites you to visit its headquarters, it will probably have done some preliminary research on you. Most franchisors require you to complete a preliminary application that provides information on who you are, your background, your employment and education history, and your financial capabilities. Some franchisors run credit checks to verify your finances, as well as criminal background and litigation checks. Good franchisors are as careful in selecting who they award franchises to as good franchise prospects are in selecting which franchise to buy.

Some franchisors may invite you to a one-on-one tour of their headquarters; others may invite you to a group session — called a *discovery day* — where you have the opportunity to meet with the franchisor and maybe other prospective franchisees. Whichever format you experience, this is the time to get to know the people and the organization that will be your support team. Don't be bashful about your questions. Like your grade-school teachers told you: The only stupid question is the one you don't ask.

During your discovery day, the franchisor may take you on a tour of its stores. Plan some extra time before the program begins so that, after it's over, you can go see some of the stores that *aren't* on the tour.

Use the questions in the comprehensive "Making the Franchise Decision Workbook" on the CD-ROM (in the `Chapter 4` folder) as a starting place for evaluating a franchisor.

When professionals in the franchise industry get together and socialize at educational and trade functions, we often talk shop. Who's doing what and when, what's working and what's not. Almost always, somewhere between the first beer and the end of the night, someone uses the phrase *passing the mirror test,* which refers to franchisors that have only two criteria for selecting their franchisees: (1) The prospect's check clears, and (2) the prospect is breathing — and can fog the mirror. Being considered a franchisor in this category is *not* a badge of honor. (Some franchisors don't even meet their franchisees face-to-face until they get to training. Their only requirement is the check clearing. We won't even think about what *their* standards are.) If your franchisor doesn't insist that you visit with them at their headquarters or their regional support centers, beware. If they don't care how well you're going to do as a franchisee, how much care do you figure they took in selecting the other franchisees in the system that will be sharing the brand with you? Making the trip to the franchisor's headquarters may be expensive — especially if you're looking at several franchisors — but it's essential.

If you're married or going to operate the franchise with a partner, bring your partner along. Your partners need to get to know the franchisor. Bringing them along shows the franchisor that you're taking the visit seriously. Most good franchisors will insist on this if your spouse is going to run the business with you.

On the CD-ROM, we include a list of questions (CD0406) for you to ask the franchisor in determining who currently owns the operating locations.

Expect to receive a copy of the franchisor's FDD if you don't already have one. Also, expect to be asked to sign a receipt. Franchise rules require the franchisor to provide you a copy of its FDD at least 14 days before you sign a franchise agreement. It's a good idea to request a copy of the franchisor's FDD even before you go to discovery day, and review the FDD with a franchise lawyer.

Evaluating a Franchisor's Services

Every franchisor is different — and the services that franchisors provide their franchisees vary widely, based on a company's philosophy, maturity, and fees.

On the CD-ROM, we include a list of questions (CD0407) for you to begin to capture basic information about the franchisor and some of the preliminary questions you should be asking.

The franchise agreement defines the services that the franchisor provides. The services are usually divided into those that the franchisor provides pre-opening, such as initial training, and those that continue throughout the life of the franchise, such as field staff support.

On the CD-ROM, we include a list of questions (CD0408) for you to ask the franchisor when evaluating its continual services.

If the franchise salesperson makes a promise that you're relying on, make sure that promise is contained in the franchise agreement. (For more on franchise agreements, see Chapter 6.)

This section mentions just some of the services you can expect to receive in addition to training.

Knowing what to expect before you open and beyond

Before you even open the doors of your franchise, franchisors help by providing services and information to new franchisees. Your franchisor may

 Determine that you have the financial resources and other requirements to become a franchisee.

   On the CD-ROM, we include a list of questions (CD0409) for you to ask the franchisor when evaluating its financial requirements.

 Register, protect, and provide you with the use of registered trademarks, service marks, and, if appropriate, defined trade dress.

 Provide site-selection criteria, selection assistance, site-approval visits, prototype plans, construction assistance, interior and exterior design, and layout.

   On the CD-ROM, we include a list of questions (CD0410) for you to ask the franchisor when evaluating its site-development service.

 Provide sources of demographic information and an evaluation of the market where you'll be establishing your business.

On the CD-ROM, we include a list of questions (CD0411) for you to ask the franchisor on how it evaluated your market or area.

✔ Provide specification and sources for equipment, fixtures, furnishings, signs, products, materials, and supplies required for the operation of the franchised business.

✔ Provide or license a point of sale and other system software.

✔ Loan you a library of operations manuals for unit operations, multi-unit development and operations, staff training, and so on.

✔ Train you and your management, staff, and training personnel (if any) prior to the opening of the business.

On the CD-ROM, we include a list of questions (CD0412) for you to ask the franchisor when evaluating its training program.

✔ Provide information on the required or authorized merchandise and services, which you must or may offer in your locations to the public.

On the CD-ROM, we include a list of questions (CD0413) for you to ask the franchisor when evaluating the franchise's products and services.

✔ Provide plan-o-grams that give instruction on where and how to display merchandise. Plan-o-grams also provide information on promotional displays, seasonal displays, and even the *end-caps* (merchandise displayed at the end of a row).

✔ Provide information on conducting a grand-opening marketing and public-relations program and continuing advertising and marketing.

On the CD-ROM, we include a list of questions (CD0414) for you to ask the franchisor when evaluating its marketing and advertising support.

✔ Help with coordinating store-opening activities.

Throughout the life of your franchise, you can expect your franchisor to provide some services on an ongoing basis. Here are examples of some of the services you may receive:

✔ Updates, from time to time, to the confidential operations manuals.

✔ National, regional, and local advertising programs and materials.

✔ Establishment of a local Web page for your location, linked through the franchisor's Web site, to provide information to the public about your business and location.

✔ Intranet-based training, chat rooms, and forums. Many franchisors include their manuals and some training programs on their *intranet,* which is like an Internet newsgroup, but private to the franchise system.

✔ Research and development of new products and services and system enhancements.

ON THE CD

- Recommended, approved, and required suppliers for equipment, products, services, and supplies.

- A franchisee advisory council (see Chapter 9) and other methods of communication.

- Field and headquarters support in the operations of the franchised business.

   On the bonus CD-ROM, we include a list of questions (CD0415) for you to ask the franchisor when evaluating its field-support services.

- Continuing, advanced, or replacement training.

- Group purchasing programs for inventory, supplies, insurance, equipment, and so on.

- Group meetings including conventions, regional meetings, and conferences.

- Periodic upgrades and changes to site design and décor.

- Enforcement of system standards and protection of the trademark.

Your prospective franchisor should have systems in place to instantly communicate data on inventory, personnel, and financial reports — such as point-of-sale (POS) systems and management information systems (MIS). Look for monthly newsletters and/or an intranet to transmit company news, industry information, and local market data. Some franchisors use voicemail to reach you personally.

Although the franchisor provides you with services to support your business, keep in mind that the primary purpose of any continuing service is to enhance and protect the value of the franchisor's trade name and related trademarks and service marks. So it's important that you work with the franchisor and its personnel to seek out and use the services that the franchisor provides. The support, after all, benefits both of you.

Finding out about the training program

Training is one of our favorite topics because it's one of the most important aspects of a healthy and profitable franchise relationship. The key to a good franchise business is training, training, training, and more training.

A point worth making here is that all franchisee training is not the same. Some franchisors emphasize a strong training effort at the front end — to get you rooted in the basics of the business. Other franchisors believe not only in offering a helping hand in the beginning but in standing by you in the years to come. Clearly, hooking up with a franchisor who wants to stand by you for the long haul is the better choice.

Also, franchise systems vary widely in their use of technology in training. If you're considering a new or recently launched franchise, you may find use of online training to be very limited because more-sophisticated online training requires large investments by the franchisor. A hard copy of the operations manual and a new franchisee training class are commonly the only training vehicles (and may be adequate depending on other support) in a start-up franchise company.

Modern franchising is a complex business, and franchisees require continuous updating and retraining to keep them up to speed and at the top of their markets.

On the CD-ROM, we include a list of questions (CD0416) for you to ask the franchisor when evaluating the operations manual.

Tapping others' firsthand knowledge

Talk to other franchisees in the system and find out exactly how much support they received from the franchisor's home office when they first opened their stores. You're trying to eliminate any surprises down the road. Did the franchisor deliver on the promised support before, during, and after the opening? What about the basic training — was it adequate, or did the franchisees feel they needed more training before opening their doors? How was the sales performance for the first six months of the business? For the first 18 months?

A list of franchisees is provided in Item 20 of the franchisor's FDD. Call as many of them as you need to until you're satisfied that all your questions have been answered. Also call some of the former franchisees listed in the FDD. Remember that they may have left on a less-than-positive basis, so you may have to filter what they say. But if they all have the same story to tell, the phone calls will be a worthwhile investment of your time. If you're purchasing a franchise outside the United States, and your franchisor is not required to give you a list of franchisees in the system, ask for one. You can also speak to an existing franchisee in the system and see if she has a list of franchisees you can copy.

The franchisees you call are not obligated to talk to you or give you any information. Even the ones who are willing to give you the information may be too busy running their businesses to spend the time to chat. Some may have signed a non-disclosure document with their franchisor and may not be allowed to talk to you about the franchise system (this is also disclosed in Item 20 of the FDD). When you call, ask if this is a good time. If it isn't, see if you can schedule a better time to speak on the phone or come to their locations and visit with them. They probably get calls from prospective franchisees all the time, so be honest with them about why you're calling. Not so long ago, many of them were probably making the same calls to other franchisees.

If you want, give the franchisor a list of franchisees you want to call, and they can alert those franchisees that you'll be reaching out to them.

Don't be bashful in the questions you ask. All they can say is no. Ask them about the required investment — especially the working capital. The franchisor will provide you with an estimate of the total initial investment in the FDD; ask how close it is to reality. Did it take three months, six months, two years, or longer to begin making a profit? When were they able to take a salary from the business?

We don't include every question you should ask here — we just want to get you started. The "Making the Franchise Decision" workbook on the CD-ROM gives you more.

Going Back Home and Eyeing Locations

From your research and from the information you receive visiting the franchisor, you should start to get a sense of what type of location you need. If you're set on opening a franchise in your hometown, you need to make sure that the appropriate real estate is available.

On the CD-ROM, we include a list of questions (CD0417) for you to ask the franchisor when evaluating the territory it may provide you with.

Conduct some preliminary market research. Most franchisors have fairly sophisticated support mechanisms that will assist you later, but you need to know some things before you make the decision to become a franchisee for a particular company.

Get an idea of the traffic patterns around the sites that you feel meet your needs. Call the city zoning board and planning commissions to get a heads-up on future road developments or other significant real estate plans for the area that may end up cutting into your customer base. Check with other merchants who have a customer base similar to the franchise business you're considering, and determine whether you have the right traffic at that location. For example, if you're looking at a franchise that markets upscale women's hair care, check with other merchants who sell products to a similar clientele, such as better women's dress shops. This research can give you a good indication of a site's future performance potential.

Don't sign a lease or buy a location for your future franchise just yet. In all likelihood, your franchisor will have to approve the location before you sign the lease.

On the bonus CD-ROM, we include a list of other questions (CD0418) for you to ask the franchisor when making your evaluation. We also give you information from the Federal Trade Commission's (FTC) "Consumer Guide to Buying a Franchise" (CD0419), which tells you what the FTC believes is important for you to consider when purchasing a franchise.

Chapter 5

Raising Capital: Wowing, Wrangling, and Winning

In This Chapter

▶ Taking a look at your current finances

▶ Determining what a franchise is going to cost

▶ Raising the money to buy a franchise

This chapter is where you begin to feel the financial reality of franchise ownership. When you decide to invest in a franchise, you have to come up with the money, or the deal won't fly. You need to determine whether you have the funds for your franchise investment and also to support yourself and your family (if you have one) for the first year or two of start-up.

This chapter helps you paint a realistic picture of whether you can afford to become a franchisee and, if you can, find financing. So, sharpen your pencil, get out your calculator, and go digging for dollars.

Examining Your Current Finances

Putting pen to paper and taking a good, hard look at your finances can be sobering. You may be tempted to cut corners and gloss over the realities of your financial picture, but having enough capital to get off the ground is not just important; it's vital. If you're heaving a heavy sigh right now, think about this statistical truth: The single most common reason new franchisees (and all other types of new businesses) fail is that they didn't have enough money going into the investment.

We didn't make up this statistic. The U.S. Small Business Administration (SBA) and a host of banks and lending institutions have tracked franchisee loan failures for years. Their combined findings show that when franchisees fail, the cause is often that the franchisee was financially stretched during the critical start-up phase of the business.

You won't know whether you have enough money until you start examining your finances. Use an organized approach to your research; make lists of information as you go along. Just to get your financial juices flowing, answer the questions on the checklist (CD0501) on the CD-ROM. This isn't a test with right or wrong answers, but it will help you in determining what your resources are, where you can get some help, and whether you're able to make a franchise investment.

So, what do you do after you've made your self-evaluation? The first thing is to realize that you likely have some limits in the type of franchise you can afford to invest in because of your available investable capital. This is an important milestone in your search for a franchise and one you should take seriously. Not all franchises are successful, and even when they are, they often take longer and require more capital to reach that point of success than anticipated. Give yourself a cushion.

The second thing you should do is begin your investigation of which franchise is right for you, using the investment parameters you've established. It's an easy trap to start playing with the numbers and convince yourself that you can afford to risk more. There are likely so many opportunities with good returns on your investment in your range that this really isn't necessary. Stay within your parameters at first.

Look for franchise opportunities that support your efforts by assisting you in obtaining loans and other forms of financing, such as equipment leasing. However, remember that even if you can borrow the money or obtain the financing, it may not be the smart thing to do. You still have to pay back that money, and if you've depleted your reserves, you'll be resting all your hopes on paying those obligations out of cash flow. *Remember:* Your franchise's cash flow also needs to pay for the little things that your family may be expecting — such as food, housing, tuition, and even the possible vacation.

Then expand your horizons just a bit. Make up a short list of opportunities that are a bit past your limits and talk to the franchisors on that list. In today's economy, several franchisors are finding creative ways to help their franchisees find financing; often, a franchisor can look at your numbers and see a mistake you've made in your calculations or an opportunity you may not have been aware of, such as company-owned units available for you to buy or even a retiring franchisee who has listed his business with the franchisor to remarket. Those opportunities usually come from a motivated seller who is willing to work with you with some self-financing or another creative arrangement. With these opportunities, you lose some of the speculation on future performance because you can analyze the business's historic performance. These types of opportunities also can be more attractive to bank lenders because the normal delays in starting your franchise are substantially eliminated.

DAVE'S WISDOM

Asking for proof of expertise

After Dave started Wendy's, lots of financial advisors wanted to offer him advice on how they could make him more money. So, he developed a rule: When an advisor came to him with a plan, he'd ask to see the advisor's balance sheet. If the balance sheet was better than Dave's, he'd listen to the advice. Most of these advisors didn't have money but were eager to tell Dave how to spend his.

Finding Out What a Franchise Costs

Opening up a business costs money, whether you go it alone as an independent or as a member of a franchise system. Having enough money to get the business up and running and through the cash-sponge period is life or death for a small-business owner.

If the only benefit you received from joining a franchise system was an accurate estimate of the costs of developing the business, sources for equipment and suppliers, and the knowledge of how much working capital you needed until the business could support itself, the investment in a franchise may still be worthwhile. Because of this helpful start-up information, an experienced and mature franchise system is worth its weight in gold to a new franchisee.

The big picture: What your start-up costs may look like

Franchisors reduce your time and costs on the learning curve. Without a franchisor, for example, you must research equipment options, work with designers on décor packages, independently research which vendors to use, and so on. Franchising succeeds because the franchisors take care of the details you may not even think of. In the franchisor's Franchise Disclosure Document (FDD), the franchisor provides you with a list of start-up expenses that will make up your initial investment.

Total start-up costs vary dramatically, depending on the franchise you select, varying from $20,000 (or less) to $1 million (or more). A typical investment for a single-unit franchisee is usually in the $100,000 to $300,000 range, including the franchise fee and all start-up costs. The FDD details the average investment you need to make. (For more information about the FDD, see Chapter 6.)

Most franchisors and bankers want to see a *liquid* (cash) capital investment of 35 percent to 50 percent of the total franchise cost (the franchise fee plus all start-up costs). They want to make sure that you have enough money not only to get started but also to pay your bills, including any principal and interest payments on your loans.

Start-up costs may vary dramatically depending on whether you need to own or lease real estate to operate the business. Fixed-base franchises, requiring bricks and mortar, almost always cost more than, for example, a franchise operating from a van or over the Internet.

The following sections give you a sense of the overall costs you'll face in developing your location.

Regardless of whether you're going to open a franchise or start an independent business, the spreadsheet (CD0502) on the CD-ROM, with the addition of franchise fees, helps you project the costs you'll incur in starting your business.

Projections are based on assumptions about events that haven't happened yet. Even if all your assumptions come true — and they won't — you'll experience differences between the projected and actual results, and those differences are almost always material. Expect the worst, and be prepared.

Initial expenses to set up shop

You'll incur many costs in the development of your franchise. Some, such as the franchise fee, you've likely thought about. Others, such as travel and living expenses while you're at training as well as pre-opening labor, may not be so obvious. Although this book includes a companion CD-ROM that helps you project your costs and potential income statement, this section notes many of the costs you should anticipate.

The franchise fee

First and foremost, be prepared to pay a *franchise fee*. A franchise fee is the price of admission to the game, but not the price to suit up and play — that's extra. The franchise fee is the amount you pay the franchisor to offset the franchisor's cost of locating, screening, negotiating with, and training you. It may also cover the costs involved in site selection and development, promotions, grand-opening events, and ongoing support during your first months of operation.

Franchise fees vary, depending on the franchisor. They can range from $0 (which is very unusual) to more than $100,000. The franchise fee for most franchisors is between $20,000 and $35,000. Rupert Barkoff, partner at Kilpatrick Stockton LLP in Atlanta, Georgia, offers this advice: "When comparison-shopping, pay particular attention to what services you will receive for your franchise fee and what other necessary services have separate charges. The lowest, most appealing franchise fee may not be the best value."

As you identify a location, you'll usually sign a single-unit franchise agreement. What you pay and how the franchisor applies the fee will vary, depending on the agreement. Your franchisor may have a different royalty fee for multi-unit developers.

Each franchise system is different. As with every contract you sign, you need to review the agreements with your lawyer. (See Chapter 6 for information on how to select your advisors.)

Other start-up costs

When planning for your franchise, you need to be aware of a number of other items and costs — in particular, make note of the following:

- ✔ Civil and architectural drawings and professional fees
- ✔ Contractor fees
- ✔ Costs for finding the right location
- ✔ Décor packaging and signage
- ✔ Equipment and fixtures
- ✔ Freight and sales tax
- ✔ Improvements and construction
- ✔ Insurance
- ✔ Landscaping
- ✔ Opening inventory
- ✔ Real property and occupancy charges
- ✔ Zoning expenses

In Item 7 of the FDD, a franchisor provides you with a chart and notes concerning your start-up costs for that particular franchise.

The CD-ROM includes the details regarding each type of start-up cost (CD0503), so head there when you're ready for more information.

The upfront and ongoing costs of hired help

Before you open up your business, expect your franchisor to require you and some of your key employees and management to attend training. Most franchisors take training seriously, and, depending on the complexity of the business and the philosophy of the franchisor, you can expect to spend as little as a few days and sometimes many months being trained in how to operate your new business.

Most franchisors will include the cost of providing you and your staff with training in the franchise fee; however, your costs for travel, lodging, food, and entertainment are costs you'll pay out of pocket. Also, don't forget the salaries and benefits for your staff attending training with you. You should anticipate other costs as well, including the ones in the following sections.

Training costs

Although the cost of tuition for initial training is usually included in your franchise fee, you'll probably have to pay for airfare, hotel accommodations, local transportation, food, salaries, and employment benefits for yourself and your staff who attend training. These expenses are on top of any salary you'll lose from your current job while you attend training. Find out more about training in Chapter 8.

Pre-opening labor

Before you even open your doors, you must pay your manager and staff. Your employees will help you set up and will need to learn how to run the business before that first customer comes in.

Professional fees

In addition to your architect and the professionals you hire to help you get through that zoning matter, you need the services of an attorney to help you negotiate your lease and do all the other legal work required to set up a business. You also need an accountant to help you set up your books and records.

Working capital

Working capital is the amount of money you need to support your ongoing expenses that aren't covered by your *revenue* (the money your business brings in). Depending on your business, you may need as little as two or three months or as much as two or three years of working capital.

If you're an independent business owner, you and your accountant had better ensure that your estimate of working capital is sufficient to get you through the early days. If you're a franchisee, your franchisor will provide you with an estimate based on experience.

When planning for your initial investment, remember that projections — especially regarding working capital — are not a guarantee of what you'll actually need. Projections are educated guesses based upon the best facts available at the time.

Doing Your Homework before Holding Out Your Cup

Before you start out on any trip, you need a destination and a map telling you how to get there. Even with a GPS device, you still need to tell the computer where you want to go. You choose when to follow or veer from the directions, and you choose where to stop along the way for gas, food, and rest.

Finding your way to a successful business really isn't that different, except that you need to do your own research on possible roads to choose and plot your own course. This section helps you begin the process of creating a business plan for your franchise. Although a lot of the information will come from the franchisor, you still need to adapt it to your business and situation.

It may seem logical that, after you complete your business plan, you send it to your franchisor for them to review, edit, and comment on. Don't be surprised if your franchisor is unwilling to review your plan. Rules govern a franchisor's pre-sale activities, and one of them deals with making an earnings claim. As strange as this may sound, if you send your business plan to the franchisor and they comment on it, they may be violating the rules they need to follow in making earnings projections. Speak to your franchisor regarding their policies. After you become a franchisee, the franchisor usually won't have any problem helping you create or fine-tune your plan.

Creating a business plan

Regardless of where you ask for money (your local bank or your Aunt Edith and Uncle Fred), anyone providing you with funds will want to know something about your business and how you plan to operate it. In other words, they'll want to see a business plan.

Think of a business plan as a road map. It gives you and your lender the lay of the land, some directions, and an idea of where your business is headed. You're the mapmaker and the tour guide. You're responsible for helping your lender see the destination and how you plan to get there. Don't fake any of the information — especially the numbers. Lenders and investors hate surprises.

Keep in mind that a business plan may be a pain to write, but writing one forces you to focus on setting goals and figuring out how to reach them. Take your time and don't be afraid to rewrite. You can be optimistic, but only if your optimism is based on reality.

The best business plan is a living document — you continually update it. It also is creative, reflects your enthusiasm, and includes solid information.

Among other details, a business plan defines the reasons you need financing, the way you're going to spend the money, and the method you'll use to repay it. It should explain to the reader everything about your location and how you intend to operate it. If you believe that your location will be better than the average location in your franchise system, let the reader know why you think so. Have facts available to support your assumptions.

Your franchisor should be able to assist you with information specific to the business. If you hire an attorney and/or an accountant, ask him or her for input, too. Many, but not all, have experience preparing business plans and can offer valuable advice.

After you have a plan, follow it — don't file it away. Update it as you learn more.

A business plan should include the following elements:

- ✔ **Executive summary:** This is a description of the franchise, products and services, opportunities, risks, strategies, target market, competition, competitive advantage, investment and financial overview, and projected return on investment. Bruce Schaeffer of Franchise Valuations, Ltd., in New York notes that the executive summary may be the most important part of your business plan: "We often refer to it as the 'elevator pitch.' In the executive summary, you get those two elevator minutes to convince a lender or investor of the virtue of your proposition. The executive summary should never be more than two pages long, and if you can fit it onto one page, that's even better." Experience shows that if the introduction to your business plan is not exciting and enticing, the proposed investor or lender often won't read any further and won't provide you with the funding you need.

✔ **Mission statement:** A mission statement defines the culture of your business. It should describe the fundamental reasons for the company's existence and establish the scope of its activities. The mission statement is a reflection of your philosophy as it relates to such things as the franchisor and the system, profitability, professionalism, customers, employees, vendors, and your community.

✔ **Overview of the business structure:** This section provides the reader with information about the business, including the date the business began, who the founders were, and whether the founders are presently active in the business. It also includes whether the business was acquired from the founders and when, as well as present financing equity ownership, loans, mortgages, overdrafts, debentures, and so on. Discuss any of your outstanding accomplishments and any setbacks that you've experienced and overcome.

✔ **Industry analysis and background:** After the executive summary, the industry analysis and background section is the most closely read section. In order for the company to have a clear direction, you must understand the industry you're in, your competition, and your position in the market. For clarity and comparison purposes, use charts where appropriate to compare your company and its products and services with those of the competition. Describe the industry in which you operate by answering the following questions:

  • What is the size of the industry? The reader will want to understand how large the industry is and whether it's growing.

  • Who are the major participants in the industry — in other words, who are your competitors, market leaders, franchisors, and suppliers?

  • Do a few companies dominate the segment, or is the market fragmented among a lot of smaller mom-and-pop businesses?

  • Is the market made up of a large number of potential customers, or do a handful account for a high proportion of sales?

  • What factors are important to success in your industry?

  • What do published forecasts say about the future growth and profile of the industry?

  • What legislation and environmental or business trends will affect your industry?

✔ **Market analysis and strategy:** In this section, you talk about your potential customers, the size of the market, trends in the industry, the existing and emerging competition, the type of location you need, and how the franchisor wants your location to look. It tells the reader that you know about the business in which you'll be operating.

✔ **Description of day-to-day operations:** People are your most important asset in any business. In this section, you describe your staffing plans for recruiting and paying personnel and the training programs you or the franchisee will provide. This section also deals with having the proper products and supplies to offer to the public and operate the business. You should also include issues dealing with your suppliers, how they'll distribute to you, and how you'll deliver the product and services you'll offer to your customers.

✔ **Marketing plan:** Every investor, lender, or member of management is interested in how you intend to attract customers to your franchise. In this section, you describe the overall franchise system's strategy for marketing, including any neighborhood and local marketing strategies. Most franchisors also will help you plan your grand-opening marketing programs. Let the reader understand how you intend to launch the business. Finally, deal with your pricing strategy. Do you intend to offer everyday low prices, or is your strategy to offer high prices as a standard practice with low promotional pricing for sales?

✔ **Management and organization structure:** Describe the day-to-day management required to operate the business; if you know who they are, include some biographical information about your managers. Describe the number and type of staff you need to recruit, as well as your compensation plans, employee benefits, and recruiting and retention plans. If you intend to work in the business, make sure to include information about yourself and the compensation you plan to take out of the business. To savvy investors, the experience and abilities of management is often the most important element they consider when evaluating whether you and your idea are worth the risk.

✔ **Financing:** What is the total start-up investment you require? Will the business require additional funding down the road? Provide the reader with information about your profit-and-loss forecasts and cash-flow analysis for five years. Provide a detailed examination of the amount of sales you'll need to break even and turn a profit.

✔ **Implementation plan and timetable:** In the business plan, not only do you need to deal with the *what*s of everyday operation, but you also need to include a detailed description of the *how*s. If yours is an existing business, what changes do you intend to make to meet the plan? What is the cost of implementing those changes, and when do you expect to recoup those costs? If your business is a start-up, define the investment, the timeframe until opening, and how long before you expect to break even and get some return on your investment.

✔ **Appendix:** The appendix is the place to provide the reader with copies of your tax returns, articles about the company, articles about the industry, information about the community you'll be serving, and any other information that will help the reader understand the business.

For details about creating a business plan, check out Chapter 14 and the corresponding CD file, "Planning for Growth: Creating and Using the Business Plan" (CD1403).

Creating a business plan may sound very scary, but if you truly want to go into business, doing so is a must. In fact, you should find preparing your business plan a welcome challenge. If not, perhaps you don't have the discipline to own your own business. Often, a franchisor will help you prepare or review your business plan, although the franchisor must be careful not to violate federal and state requirements that regulate its ability to make earnings claims. (See Chapter 6 for a discussion of earnings claims.) When seeking investors, you should also consider whether your attempt to raise money will be considered the offering of a security. A knowledgeable attorney can help in these circumstances.

Projecting income and cash flow

Most franchisees would rather run their businesses than spend time crunching numbers. Franchisors understand this, and many provide user-friendly accounting programs for the *front of the house* (customer sales) and the *back of the house* (bookkeeping, payroll, inventory management, and financial statements).

Unfortunately, bankers and investors want to see a projected income and cash-flow statement before they'll invest in your business. The statement reassures them that you've thought through the realistic growth of your franchise. The numbers may not be absolutely on the mark, but they reassure bankers and investors that you're thinking like a person who plans to be in business for a long time.

Where do you begin? A good place to start is to add up all the costs of staying in business for the first 60 months. You want to develop a cash-flow statement by month for the first and second years and at least by quarter for the third through fifth years.

Other franchisees already in the system may be sources for accurate information about actual costs.

Be very careful when you review information that other franchisees provide. Some franchisees may be reluctant to share information with you because you may buy a competitor's franchise and then go into competition with them. Although it doesn't happen frequently, on the rare occasion, the franchisee may be a *shill* — a person the franchisor directed you to call to get bogus information about the franchise that helps the franchisor make the sale. Get your information from several sources.

Most important, is the information you're getting relevant to analyzing your proposed business? Some franchisors today will provide you with annual cost information but are not allowed under the law to link those costs to unit sales. Remember, though, that the economics of selling ice cream in Fairbanks, Alaska, may be quite different from the economics of selling ice cream in Fort Lauderdale, Florida. Information about units that do match the demographics, size, and location of your franchise may be interesting, but it can also be misleading if you rely on it for projecting future results for your business.

Ask some of the local franchisees what accountant they use. An accountant who's experienced in the industry and who has a proven track record is your best bet. An accountant may be a source for projecting income and expenses if she has any experience in your business. Some franchisors require you to use their accountant for a period of time after you become a franchisee, but that requirement isn't typical.

Armed with both an annual cost figure and projected sales, you can forecast your needed cash flow. Your accountant can provide you with forms you can use to assemble the information.

The FDD gives you the projected initial investment. If profit and loss is in the FDD, it'll tell you how well the operating locations are doing. If your franchisor includes an earnings claim in the information it gives to you, it should be able to provide you with some of the detailed assumptions it used. This information is important — you need to develop your financial projections based on the market in which your business will be operating. (See Chapter 6 for a discussion on the FDD.)

If your franchisor doesn't provide earnings information, you may want to take a look at some of the competition. Robert Bond's *How Much Can I Make? Actual Sales and Profit Potential for Your Small Business* provides the earnings claims of more than 150 franchisors. You can order the book for $34.95 by calling 800-841-0873 or at http://tinyurl.com/mkkwrd.

Raising the Capital

Today, there are many ways to finance your new business. Some you know well because you grew up in their home — Mom, Dad, and your brothers and sisters are all good places to look because they know you best. Others exist as well, including angel investors and lenders. Your franchisor will be a good source of ideas and will tell you what has worked well in their system. The franchisor may even be able to introduce you to folks they've established a relationship with.

If you're the average prospective franchisee, you've pulled together all the financial resources at your disposal by combining your savings, the collateral in your home, bank financing, loans from family and friends, and possibly money from outside investors. Keep in mind that you can also cut your overall initial cash requirements by leasing your real estate and equipment rather than purchasing them. Most franchisors will walk you through the leasing options for their system.

Avoiding debt

Everyone aspires to avoid debt, but most people deal with it on a regular basis. Going into debt to buy a franchise is not something you should take lightly. Before you put your retirement fund on the line or refinance your home, look at a few ways to raise cash in order to minimize your debt:

- Use money you've put aside for a future project or a second home.
- Ask family and friends; they already know and trust you. They may want some equity in the business. Just keep in mind that family and friends are often more intrusive than professional lenders; also, you may damage relationships if the investment doesn't go well.
- Consider bringing in a partner who can offer money upfront or on a continuing basis.
- Sell your boat, cabin, second house, scuba gear, RV, jewelry, or any other toy or collectible you don't use.

Unless you live on the edge and like added risk, consider the following advice:

- **Don't use your credit cards to get ready cash.** Interest rates are too high, and you can run up your credit limit and get into financial difficulty too easily.
- **Don't use your 401(k), IRA, retirement funds, healthcare accounts, life insurance policies, or college funds to start up a franchise.** These accounts are for protecting your — and your children's — future.

Visiting the bank

In today's tight credit market, nothing can substitute for preparation. Neither Shaquille O'Neal nor Diana Taurasi would think of going into a game without first practicing and perfecting a few moves to guarantee a basket. That same attitude works when you approach lenders — except the ball is in their court, and your goal is to convince them to toss it to you.

Local bankers are in business just as you are, and they want to help you succeed. In order to do that, they need information about you, your plans for the future, your business, and franchising overall. Your business plan covers some of the information, but nothing is better than a personal visit to get started.

Just as franchising is based on relationships, so is banking. Establishing and nurturing an ongoing relationship with your banker is very important. That commitment means dropping in and visiting with them on a regular basis and sharing your progress as you get closer to signing your contract. In other words, your banker wants you to keep them informed. No banker likes surprises. The more you share of yourself — your business ideas, hopes, dreams, and goals — the better your banker can assess your loan application when it crosses her desk.

If you don't click with your local lender, shop around. Visit a few banks in your operating area and see which one is a good match. Make sure that the bank you choose has experience with small businesses. You should also visit your local credit unions — during the recent economic downturn, credit unions have emerged as some of the more flexible sources of franchisee financing.

Be smart in putting together your sales package for the banker. When you're presenting information for a loan, you're selling the bank not only on the business but on you as a businessperson. The banker wants to see that you understand what you're getting into and how you're going to pay back the loan. If you aren't able to put together a good presentation package — and it should be more than just the forms the banker gives you to fill out — work with a professional like an accountant to help you complete the package.

If you're in the United States, you stand a better chance of success with a certified SBA lender. These banks have government guarantees on the loans they make to small businesses, including franchises.

Getting a bank's support sounds pretty simple, doesn't it? But few franchisees take the time to establish relationships with their bankers. They show up when they want money. Sometimes they get it, and sometimes they don't. Because you may need to borrow expansion capital at some point in your business future, taking the time now to connect with your banker just makes sense. Consider your banker part of your business team, and keep the lines of communication open. Also, consider whether the borrowing will be a business loan or whether you'll be personally liable.

Check with other franchisees and find out who financed their businesses. A banker who has already financed a successful franchisee will be more receptive to your application and will need less education.

Finding an angel investor

After you've tapped all the available sources of conventional funding — friends, family, personal savings, franchisor assistance, and SBA bank loans — think about finding an angel investor. No, this isn't someone who arrives wearing wings. Typically, *angel investors* are individuals or groups who offer start-up funds in exchange for a direct role in a new business. They're people with high net worth who want to invest in businesses they know about. Although an angel is usually an individual, angels often form groups that commit larger sums based on the recommendations of one of the group's members.

National, regional, and local angel networks exist, and each functions a bit differently from others. The networks are usually fee driven, and you pay either to join the network or to present your plan. Depending on the network you select, you may be able to post information online about your opportunity for members to read, or you may need to provide it only upon invitation.

An angel investor often expects a direct role in advising the new company. This counsel can be an advantage for a new franchisee because, often, an angel can bring expertise to a new business that the owner can't get elsewhere.

A word of caution: Angel investors become your partners and may require you to seek their permission before you make decisions. You'll probably give up some control, and you'll certainly give up some of the profit if the angel takes an equity position.

You can find several directories of angel investors on the Internet. A new source for finding equity partners for franchisees is FranEquity (`www.franequity.com`).

The money you need is out there, so don't despair. Just be cautious in your enthusiasm, and don't put everything you have on the line. Spread your risk, combine your funding sources, sell the stuff you don't use, and build those relationships.

Seeking other financing strategies

Some franchisors offer a menu of other financing strategies to ease the financial bite. Although not every franchisor makes these benefits available, it doesn't hurt to ask. Here are a few examples of some of these financing strategies:

- ✔ **Deferred payments on your total franchise fee until after you're open for business:** The terms of the deferral can be a few months or sometimes a few years.

- ✔ **Out-of-pocket costs for training (except salaries and benefits) included in your initial franchise fee.**

- ✔ **A lease from the franchisor on the land and/or buildings.**

- ✔ **Joint ventures between you and the franchisor,** where you and the franchisor share in the investment and return on the business — like a partnership.

- ✔ **Supplier financing:** Some equipment manufacturers offer new businesses — especially franchisees — financing on the equipment you buy from them.

- ✔ **Credit systems:** Corporate employees who want to be franchisees can apply profit-sharing credits toward the franchise fee.

- ✔ **Reduced franchise fees for corporate employees who want to become franchisees:** This is a great employment benefit, which gives the employee an opportunity to invest in a franchise at a lower cost. The franchisor benefits by getting a new franchisee who probably knows the system and with whom the franchisor already has a relationship.

Franchisors often establish relationships with a group of approved lenders who are familiar with the business and will provide funding to qualified franchisees. On occasion, the franchisor may act as a guarantor of the franchisee's loans. Sometimes the franchisor provides the loans directly.

The SBA has a program called the Franchise Registry (www.franchise registry.com), which lists names of franchise companies whose franchisees can get a streamlined review process for SBA loan applications. The SBA already has reviewed the franchise agreements for those franchisors, and prospective franchisees in those systems can get an expedited review of their loan applications. Keep in mind that this process streamlines only the acceptance of the franchisor's concept — it isn't a guarantee that you'll be able to borrow any money.

Chapter 6

Signing on the Dotted Line: Legal Issues

*I*n this chapter, we talk about the Franchise Disclosure Document (FDD). You need to understand the FDD because it's where the franchisor discloses information about the franchise system and the franchise relationship they're offering. The FDD is designed to give you some — but certainly not all — the information you need in order to make an informed decision about investing in a particular franchise.

The FDD was known as the Uniform Franchise Offering Circular (UFOC) before the law changed in July 2007. It's also sometimes referred to as a *disclosure document* or simply the *offering circular*.

The Laws behind the Franchise Disclosure Document

Franchising is governed primarily by laws that require franchisors to inform prospective franchisees about the system. This information is contained in the FDD. Under federal and state rules, a franchisor cannot offer a franchise until the franchisor has prepared an FDD.

The history behind the Franchise Disclosure Document

Following World War II, franchising entered its modern era. Franchising boomed, fueled by pent-up consumer demand, returning veterans with great ideas and ambition to become franchisors, a G.I. bill that provided loans to fund new franchisees and franchisors, and a change in the trademark law in 1946 called the Lanham Act. The Lanham Act assured a franchisor of the safety of licensing its federally registered trademarks and service marks to others — an essential element for the local operation of a nationally established franchise system.

Do you remember where you were when you had your first hamburger from a franchised operation? The novelty of a hamburger (still warm and wrapped in paper) and some skinny, salty french fries jammed into a small white paper bag is something many of us still remember fondly. Ray Kroc began franchising McDonald's and single-handedly captured the imagination of a generation of consumers — securing a guaranteed market base for decades to come. Such was the magic of franchising in the 1950s. The franchising boom in the 1950s and 1960s achieved almost a mystical stature. Companies became household names, as integral to everyday life as homework and housework. Convenience stores started popping up, and the name 7-Eleven became part of the lexicon. Dairy Queen, Kentucky Fried Chicken, Texaco, Hilton Hotels, Marriott, Budget Rent A Car, Duraclean, Midas, and a host of other brand-name franchises were offering their products and services to American consumers who were ready to start spending.

To think that franchising matured smoothly and without problems would be foolish. By the late 1960s, the bloom had left the rose. Some franchisors began to focus more on selling as many franchises as they could than on their existing operations. In the process, their existing franchisees often suffered from diminished support from the home office. Another serious problem resulted when some franchisors misrepresented their franchise offerings in an attempt to attract more franchisees. During these darker days of franchising, franchisors sometimes used unscrupulous tactics to lure potential franchisees into buying into a system. Some used celebrity names and endorsements to attract buyers. Some even sold franchises for concepts that didn't exist.

Such fraudulent practices caused several states to enact laws governing the disclosure of information to potential franchisees. California led the way. The laws required franchisors to deliver disclosure documents providing information on the franchise opportunity to potential franchisees. But franchisees got this protection only in the states that followed California's example and enacted franchise disclosure laws.

It wasn't until 1979 that the Federal Trade Commission (FTC) implemented a franchise rule requiring minimum disclosure throughout the United States. Since then, the format and content of the disclosure documents have undergone changes that further strengthened disclosure.

After reviewing the FTC rule for ten years, in 2007 the FTC made major changes to the FTC rule that became mandatory for all franchisors in 2008. Most, but not all, of the states that regulate franchising have subsequently adopted the changes made by the FTC in its new FDD.

Although franchisors don't need to register and get approval of the FDD by the federal government, 14 states do require franchisors to register their FDDs with the state or to notify the state that they'll offer franchises before beginning to conduct any franchising activity in the state. The registration states are California, Hawaii, Illinois, Indiana, Maryland, Michigan, Minnesota, New York, North Dakota, Rhode Island, South Dakota, Virginia, Washington, and Wisconsin. Other states — including Florida, Kentucky, Nebraska, Texas, and Utah — have business-opportunity laws that require every franchisor to file a notice with the state but don't require a franchisor to forward a copy of its FDD to any state agency.

The laws governing the FDD mainly deal with disclosure of the terms of the franchise and information about the franchisor. However, a second body of law — called *relationship laws* — gives added protection to the franchisee. Relationship laws give franchisees protection from certain actions of the franchisor, including arbitrary termination of the franchise or nonrenewal of the franchise at the end of its term, as well as the freedom to form franchisee associations.

Nineteen states, along with Puerto Rico and the Virgin Islands, generally make it unlawful for a franchisor to terminate a franchise relationship without "good cause" and also provide the franchisee with the opportunity to cure their defaults within a period of time that ranges from 30 to 90 days. Eighteen states restrict a franchisor's right not to renew the agreement at the end of the term. Although the majority of these states require that a franchisor have "good cause" not to renew the agreement, your protection varies from state to state, and you should always consult with a qualified franchise lawyer to find out more about your state's protections. For example, in California, Illinois, Michigan, and Washington, a franchisor may not have to renew your franchise agreement if the franchisor agrees to purchase your assets and waive your post-term, noncompete restrictions.

For a more complete understanding of the regulatory landscape, and an understanding of how a franchisor goes about having an FDD developed, check out Chapter 14.

Although we miss the days of the handshake agreement, franchising has been strengthened by the rules of disclosure. For the most part, the rules have avoided tampering with the relationship between the franchisor and franchisee. This restraint has enabled franchise systems to compete for franchisees based on the merits of their systems instead of being bogged down by excessive government interference in this vital part of the economy.

Under the disclosure rules, franchisors have to provide prospective franchisees with information about the system. This knowledge allows intelligent buyers to make intelligent decisions. We believe that the lack of significant government interference in the franchise relationship coupled with disclosure of the offering have been good for franchisors and franchisees and have allowed franchising to grow and maintain its place as one of the major economic drivers in the economy today.

Franchisors are required to update their FDDs within 120 days after the end of their fiscal year. In addition, franchisors are required to update the FDD on a quarterly basis if there have been any material changes to the information contained in the FDD.

Understanding the Franchise Disclosure Document

The purpose of the FDD is to provide prospective franchisees with information on the franchisor, the franchise system, and the agreements they'll need to sign so that they can make informed decisions. In addition to the disclosure portion of the document, the FDD includes copies of the franchise agreement and other agreements the franchisee will be required to sign, together with the franchisor's financial statements; these are known as the *exhibits*.

The registration states require franchisors to include some additional information in the FDD and in their state filings. In order to provide some uniformity among the registration states, most of the registration states follow guidelines set by the North American Securities Administrators Association (NASAA). You'll find the state-specific changes to the FDD and the franchise agreement in the exhibits of the FDD.

To get a better understanding of the role NASAA plays, check out the letter from Dale Cantone, Assistant Attorney General, Maryland Securities Division, featured on the CD-ROM (CD0601).

What you'll see in the FDD

What appears in the FDD? In a nutshell, it includes information on the franchisor, the company's key staff and their experience in franchise management, the franchisor's bankruptcy and litigation history, and the initial and ongoing fees involved in opening and running a franchise.

Also included is information on the required initial investment, purchases you'll be required to make from the franchisor or from approved suppliers, and any territorial rights you'll receive. You also find information about your legal responsibilities as a franchisee and the responsibility of the franchisor to you. The franchisor will also include in the FDD copies of its audited financial statements.

In addition, the FDD presents information about system-wide growth, the company-owned locations, and the franchisees in the system (including the number of franchises opened, closed, and reacquired by the franchisor; franchisee-to-franchisee transfers by state; and, most important, a list of existing and former franchisees and their contact information).

You need to fully understand the franchise agreement and any other agreements you sign. If you don't understand what you're signing, you may find yourself locked into a business relationship that doesn't wear well for you. Make sure you have a competent lawyer who specializes in franchise law to help you review all franchise agreements. (See "Enlisting the help of an attorney or a financial advisor," later in this chapter.)

The waiting period between getting an FDD and signing an agreement

"I've completed my research, visited the franchisor, received a copy of the FDD, read and understood the agreement, and made my decision. I want the franchise now. Why can't I sign the franchise agreement today?" The answer: The law requires a waiting period.

Included in the regulations governing the sale of franchises is a cooling-off period called the *14-day rule,* which requires franchisors to wait a minimum of 14 calendar days after giving a prospect the FDD before allowing the franchisee to sign the franchise agreement or pay any money to the franchisor. If you'd like to receive a copy of the FDD prior to the date required by the FTC, you may request a copy from the franchisor. The purpose of the 14-day rule is to give you time to think about your decision.

The regulations also require a seven-day waiting period for the franchise agreement under some circumstances. If the franchisor makes unilateral changes to the form of the franchise agreement provided in the FDD or includes information in the final agreement that you haven't had a chance to review, then the franchisor must provide you with the completed franchise agreement at least seven calendar days before signing. This gives you time to review and consider the revised terms of the agreement.

These rules are great. When you initially make the decision to buy a franchise, your enthusiasm for the deal runs high. The 14-day and 7-day delays allow you time to reflect.

The FDD, point by point

Not counting the cover page, the FDD contains 23 areas of disclosure — referred to as *items.*

Franchisors are required to use "plain English" in drafting the FDD so that it's easier to read and understand. Although FDDs may be written in what attorneys consider plain English, it's still written by skilled attorneys who work for franchisors. Experience tells us that many of the terms used in the FDD can be confusing to a franchising novice. Get yourself a qualified franchise lawyer to help you understand all the terminology in the FDD.

The cover page(s)

The cover page(s) of the FDD contain interesting information that every prospective franchisee should read and understand:

- It summarizes the franchise offering and the initial investment the franchisee is required to make.

- It states that no government agency has verified the information in the document.

- It reminds you to carefully read the entire document and all the accompanying agreements.

- It suggests that you show the FDD and the franchise agreement to an advisor, such as a lawyer or accountant.

- It recommends that you learn about the franchising laws in your state.

It also contains information on some of the risks a franchisee should know about before signing a franchise agreement, including the following:

- **Choice of law that governs the franchise agreement:** The franchisor will likely select the laws of its home state to govern the franchise agreement, not the laws in your home state. Not all franchisors pick their home-state laws, though. Some states don't allow a franchisor to pick its home state or any other state and require the franchisor to use the home state of the franchisee.

- **Choice of where the franchisee may sue the franchisor:** If a dispute occurs, the franchisee may have to sue the franchisor in the franchisor's home state, requiring the franchisee to incur the cost of travel and other added costs. Some franchisee advocates believe this gives the franchisor a home-field advantage.

- **The inclusion of arbitration as a method to solve disputes:** In some systems, a franchisee may not be able to sue a franchisor but must instead bring the dispute to an arbitrator or use some other method of dispute resolution. The benefits and faults of the use of arbitration in franchising is an issue of fierce debate today between franchisor and franchisee advocates.

- **Information regarding the franchisor's financial condition:** This information will refer you to the franchisor's audited financial statements, where you can learn more about the franchisor's ability to meet their obligations to you and other franchisees in the system.

✔ **Electronic disclosure of the FDD:** Delivery of the FDD by CD-ROM, e-mail, and Internet download is now commonplace. Keep in mind that most FDDs will exceed 200 pages and 6 megabytes in size; if your computer system can't efficiently download such a large document or if you just can't bear to read the document on a screen, you have the right to request a paper copy from the franchisor. The cover page of the FDD will identify the contact person at the franchisor's office from whom you can request the paper copy.

Just because the state has registered the FDD doesn't mean that the state has verified the information or is making a recommendation about the company. (This reminder is included in the cover pages of the FDD.) Although franchise regulators will require franchisors to meet certain regulatory standards, require franchisors to answer questions about the offering, and even require certain changes to franchise documents before allowing a franchisor to offer franchises in their state, you need to remember that regulators don't generally set the terms of the relationship between the franchisor and franchisee. The franchisor establishes the terms, and you can agree with them or reject them.

The 23 items

The following are the highlights (not all the subtopics are included) of the 23 items required for disclosure.

Item 1: The franchisor, its predecessors, and its affiliates

In this section, the franchisor provides a description of the company and the franchise being offered. In Item 1, the franchisor is required to disclose the following information:

✔ The name of the franchisor, its parents, predecessors, and affiliates

✔ The name under which the franchisor does business

✔ The franchisor's address

✔ The state of incorporation of the franchisor or the type of business organization (partnership and so on) of the franchisor

✔ The franchisor's business and the type of franchise to be offered

✔ The prior business experience of the franchisor, its predecessor, and its affiliates

✔ Information related to any governmental regulation of the franchisor's industry

The FDD includes information related to the franchisor's parent company, but you may only see the name and address of the parent company unless the parent is a franchisor of another franchise concept, guarantees the performance of the franchisor or sells products or services to franchisees of the franchise system. Then you'll learn more about the parent company's operation and its role in the system.

Item 2: Business experience

Here, the prospective franchisee gets biographical and professional information about the franchisor and its officers, directors, and executives. This section tells you who you'll be going into business with.

Item 3: Litigation

In addition to providing a ten-year history of litigation that has been filed against the franchisor, the FDD includes a look at cases that the franchisor has filed in the past year against its franchisees.

This is the section of the FDD that gives you insight into the state of the franchisor-franchisee relationship in the system. You'll find a listing of cases filed by the franchisor for royalty or fee collection issues and cases against franchisees that aren't following "system standards" or, in other words, franchisees who aren't following the franchisor's rules in how they operate their units. This one-year snapshot of cases will give you insight into the franchisor's practice of initiating litigation, as well as the types of relationship issues that exist in the system.

Item 4: Bankruptcy

Sometimes franchisors or members of their management teams have gone through a bankruptcy. It's important information that every franchisee needs to know because it can tell you whether a pattern of bankruptcy exists by the people and company you'll be entering into a relationship with.

Item 5: Initial franchise fee

Item 5 provides information about the initial fees you'll pay to the franchisor prior to opening the business. It also tells you whether the fees are not uniform to all the franchisees and discloses the range and factors that determine the amount of the fees.

Item 6: Other fees

This item provides a description of all other recurring fees or payments that the franchisee must make to the franchisor during the course of the franchise relationship, including

- ✔ **Royalties:** The continuing payment the franchisee will make to the franchisor for the franchisee's continued participation in the system.
- ✔ **Contributions the franchisee will make to the system's advertising fund.**
- ✔ **Requirements for the franchisee to participate in any local or regional cooperative advertising programs.**
- ✔ **Additional training fees the franchisor may charge.**
- ✔ **Additional fees the franchisee must pay for services or other benefits the franchisor or their affiliates provide.**

✔ **Transfer fees the franchisee pays to the franchisor when the franchisee sells the business to a third party.**

✔ **Audit costs the franchisee may have to pay if the franchisor audits the franchisee's books and records and finds discrepancies between them and the information the franchisee provided the franchisor.**

✔ **Fees the franchisor charges at the end of the franchisee's current term for continuation of the relationship for another term.** You'll notice that we didn't say "for renewal of the franchise agreement." Franchisors will usually have made changes to their franchise agreements since the time the franchisee signed the original franchise agreement. In order to enter into a *successor agreement* to continue the relationship, the franchisee usually is required to sign the then-current form of franchise agreement. The new agreement could have minor or substantial changes from the original agreement.

Item 7: Initial investment

Item 7 is in a table format. The table includes all the expenditures a franchisee is required to make to establish the franchise. In addition to a range of amounts that the franchisee must invest for each start-up expenditure, the franchisor discloses the method of payment, when the payment is due, who the payment will be made to, whether the payment is refundable, and whether it's financed.

You can find the initial investment items that are usually included by checking out a helpful spreadsheet in the `Chapter 5` folder on the CD-ROM.

Item 7 typically has extensive notes, which give prospective franchisees additional information about the initial costs included in the table. Read the notes carefully so that you have a fuller understanding of your initial investment. As with everything else, make sure you understand what the notes say.

Item 8: Restriction on sources of products and services

The franchisor may have restrictions on what the franchisee can buy for the business and from whom the franchisee can purchase those items. A franchisor restricts sources for many reasons, including a desire to ensure consistency and quality. The franchisee may be obligated to purchase or lease products and services from the franchisor or from suppliers approved by the franchisor. The franchisor may also provide the franchisee with specifications for any of the goods, services, supplies, fixtures, equipment, inventory, computer hardware or software, or other items the franchisee uses in the business. The franchisor usually has the right to approve or revoke approval of a supplier, or to make changes to its specifications for products and services the franchisee uses.

The following tells you the methods the franchisor will use:

✔ **The franchisor is sometimes the only approved supplier.** This section tells you whether and in what categories the franchisor is the only approved supplier you may use.

✔ **The franchisor may earn income from its franchisees' purchases, regardless of their source.** This section tells you the amount the franchisor earns from franchisee purchases.

✔ **Where the franchisor requires the franchisee to make purchases based on approved suppliers or specifications, this section tells you the estimated proportion these required purchases are of the initial investment and the continuing operating expenses of the franchise.**

✔ **If the franchise system uses any purchasing or distribution cooperative, you'll find that information in this section.**

✔ **If the officers of the franchisor have an ownership interest in any of the suppliers to the franchise system, this section will alert you to that fact.**

Item 9: Franchisee's obligations

Item 9 provides a reference table that indicates where in the franchise agreement franchisees can find certain obligations they agree to. The list informs the franchisee of the obligation, where to find it elsewhere in the FDD, and where to find it in the franchise agreement. The details of the obligations are not discussed in Item 9.

Not all franchisees in every system have the same obligations. Some of these obligations may be the following:

✔ Site selection and acquisition fees

✔ Pre-opening purchases and leases

✔ Site development and other pre-opening requirements

✔ Initial and ongoing training the franchisee will be offered and may be required to attend

✔ Opening requirements — usually, how much time the franchisee has to get the business open and operating

✔ Fees the franchisee agrees to pay

✔ Requirement to comply with the system's standards and policies as included in the operating manual and elsewhere

✔ Trademarks and proprietary information provided by the franchisor

✔ Restrictions on products/services offered by the franchisee

✔ Warranty and customer service requirements

✔ Territorial development and sales quotas the franchisee must meet

✔ Ongoing product/service purchases

✔ Maintenance, appearance, and remodeling requirements

✔ Insurance requirements

✔ Advertising requirements

✔ Indemnification — the section that defines the franchisor's and franchisee's obligations or duty concerning their rights to seek compensation for losses, damages, or injury sustained due to the actions of the other

✔ Owner's participation in the operation, management, and staffing of the locations

✔ Records the franchisee must maintain and the reports the franchisee has to file with the franchisor

✔ Inspection and audit rights held by the franchisor

✔ Transfer requirements

✔ Renewal requirements

✔ Post-termination obligations of the franchisee after leaving the franchise system

✔ Noncompetition covenants that limit the franchisee's ability to go into similar — but unaffiliated — businesses during the term of the franchise relationship or after the relationship expires or otherwise terminates

✔ Methods the franchisor and franchisee will use to resolve any disputes

✔ Other obligations the franchisee may have

Item 10: Financing available

Some franchise systems provide financing assistance to their franchisees. Item 10 describes the terms and conditions of any financing arrangements offered directly or indirectly by the franchisor. The types of financing may include start-up costs (including the initial franchise fee), equipment, inventory, and so on. The exhibits to the offering circular will contain any financing documents, including loan agreements and promissory notes, that you'll sign if you accept the franchisor's financing assistance.

Item 11: Franchisor's obligations

When you invest in a franchise, you expect the franchisor to provide you with certain services. Every franchise system provides different types and levels of service to their franchisees. You need to clearly understand what you'll get. Included in this section is a description of

✔ The franchisor's obligations to the franchisee before and after the franchise opens.

✔ The methods the franchisor uses to select the location of the franchise.

✔ The typical length of time between signing the franchise agreement and opening the franchise.

✔ The franchisor's training program, including duration, outline of training, experience of instructors, charges, who is responsible for paying for travel and living expenses, whether the training program is mandatory, and whether any additional training and/or refresher courses are required.

✔ The franchisor's advertising program, including what media are used; who creates the advertising; the composition of the franchisee advertising council and cooperatives; the specific use of advertising funds, including payment to the franchisor or affiliates; and whether different franchisees contribute at different rates.

✔ Generalized description of the computer or electronic cash register the franchise uses, any required maintenance and upgrade costs and obligations and whether the franchisor has the right to directly access information held on the franchisee's computer.

✔ The table of contents of the franchisor's manual. Alternatively, the franchisor may elect to allow the prospective franchisee to read the manual before purchasing the franchise, although that rarely happens in the real world.

Item 12: Territory

Not every franchisor provides its franchisees with an exclusive territory. When franchisors do make that provision, the exclusive territory will vary for each franchise system and may vary depending on the circumstances within a system. Item 12 provides the prospective franchisee with the following information:

✔ A description of any exclusive territory granted to the franchise

✔ Whether the franchisor has established or may establish another franchise- or company-owned location in the territory

✔ Whether the territory is conditional on achieving certain sales volumes or other performance criteria

✔ Whether the territory is protected only for a period of time

✔ Whether the franchisor can modify the size of the territory

✔ The methods the franchisor will use to resolve conflicts concerning the territory

In this item, you'll learn whether the franchisor has the exclusive right to engage in sales over the Internet, through catalogs, telemarketing, or other similar channels of distribution or marketing (and whether you're prohibited from engaging in these kinds of sales). You'll also learn whether the franchisor has reserved a right to operate a competing brand in your territory and, if it does operate a competing brand, how the franchisor intends to maintain the distinct brands and what territorial rights franchisees in one brand have vis-à-vis units in the other brand.

Item 13: Trademarks

This section provides the franchisee with information about the franchisor's trademarks, service marks, and trade names that will be used.

Item 14: Patents, copyrights, and proprietary information

This section provides the franchisee with information concerning any patents or copyrights the franchisor may have and how they may be used by the franchisee. You'll also learn about any patent applications that have been filed by the franchisor and the status of those applications.

Item 15: Obligations to participate in the actual operation of the franchise business

Some franchise systems require franchisees to devote their full time to the operation of the business. Others may allow for absentee ownership, or management by a manager trained by the franchisor. Different franchisors have different requirements concerning the obligations of the franchisee to participate in the actual operation of the business.

Item 16: Restrictions on what the franchisee may sell

Item 8 discusses any restrictions by franchisors on suppliers and specifications of the products used by the franchisee. Item 16 deals with any restrictions on the goods and services that the franchisee may offer customers.

Item 17: Renewal, termination, transfers, and dispute resolution

This section provides the franchisee with information concerning the terms of the franchise agreement. Included in this section is information on the following:

- ✔ **The length of the initial term of the agreement.**

- ✔ **What hurdles you'll have to cross to renew your franchise agreement, and what your franchise agreement may look like during a renewal term:** For example, will you have to sign a new franchise agreement in order to renew? Will your royalty fee increase on renewal? Does the franchisor have the right to reevaluate your protected territory?

- ✔ **The number and duration of the renewal periods.**

- ✔ **Reasons the franchisor or franchisee may terminate the agreement, causes, and any** *cure period* **(the length of time a franchisee has to fix a problem).**

- ✔ **The obligations of the parties after the termination of the agreement.**

- ✔ **The rights of the franchisor or franchisee to transfer or assign the agreement to another person or company.**

- ✔ **The rights of the franchisor to purchase the franchisee's business.**

✔ **The in-term and post-term restrictions on competition with the franchise system.**

✔ **How the franchise agreement can be modified.** Usually the franchise agreement can be modified only in writing.

✔ **What methods are provided for resolving disputes between the franchisor and franchisee — litigation, arbitration, and mediation.**

✔ **What state's or country's law governs the contract.**

Item 18: Public figures

If the franchisor uses any public figure (celebrity or other public person) to endorse or recommend the purchase of the franchise or the public figure is used in the franchise system's name or symbol, the franchisor needs to disclose the amount the person is paid, the extent to which the public figure is involved in the actual management of the franchise system, and the public figure's total investment in the franchisor.

Item 19: Financial performance representation

This is one of the most important items to franchisees. If the franchisor provides any information that you can use to estimate what you can earn from the business, it needs to be disclosed in Item 19. This may include specific levels or a range of actual or potential sales, costs, income, or profit for a franchise or non-franchised location.

The franchisor may provide cost information outside of Item 19, as long as the information is not designed to tie back to overall sales revenues. For example, even if a franchisor doesn't provide a financial performance representation in the FDD, the franchisor may directly tell you how much it will cost to purchase a particular product from an approved vendor. The franchisor may also provide financial performance information that relates only to a subset of its units. For example, you may find performance data that relates to units that have been recently remodeled, that are reporting sales under a new point-of-service system, or that have drive-thrus.

Financial performance representations are a particularly sensitive area in franchising. We cover them in the "How much can I make? The Financial Performance Representation" section, later in this chapter.

Item 20: List of franchise outlets

This section provides information regarding the locations operated in the system. It includes

✔ A summary of system-wide growth and franchisee-to-franchisee transfers by state

✔ The number of franchises and company-owned locations by state

✔ The names, addresses, and telephone numbers of franchisees

- ✔ The estimated number of franchises to be sold in the next year
- ✔ The number of franchises transferred, canceled, or terminated
- ✔ The number of franchises that haven't been renewed by the franchisor or that have been reacquired by the franchisor
- ✔ The number of franchises that are known to have ceased operation

The franchisor is required to provide you with the names and last-known addresses and telephone numbers of every franchisee who has had an outlet terminated, canceled, or not renewed, or who otherwise ceased doing business under the franchise agreement during the past year. The franchisor also must disclose any confidentiality agreements signed by franchisees within the past three years that would prohibit them from discussing their experience with prospective franchisees.

In addition, Item 20 includes the contact information of any independent franchisee association of its franchisees that has requested inclusion in the FDD. If you're interested in purchasing a franchisor-owned unit, you'll also receive the names, addresses, and phone numbers of each owner of the unit for the past three years and the reasons for the ownership changes. This change should facilitate your due diligence on the unit.

Item 21: Financial statements

Franchisors are required to include financial statements for the past three years, or for a shorter period if the franchisor hasn't been in business for three years, prepared in accordance with generally accepted accounting principals (GAAP). Foreign franchisors may submit financial statements in a format permitted by the Securities and Exchange Commission (SEC) if they're prepared according to a comprehensive body of accounting principals. You'll find an explanation in Item 21 if the franchisor is not using GAAP for its financial statements.

If a franchisor's parent company performs post-sale obligations for the franchisor or guarantees the franchisor's performance, the parent company's financials must be included in the FDD along with a copy of the guarantee of performance.

Start-up franchisors that don't have audited financial statements are allowed to phase in their audited statements over a three-year period. Despite this change in the rule, several state franchise regulators still require start-up franchisors to present audited financial statements in their first FDD.

Item 22: Contracts

Item 22 provides you with a list of agreements you'll be required to sign, including the franchise agreement and any ancillary agreements like a confidentiality agreement, area development agreement, or software license agreement. These agreements must be attached as exhibits to the FDD.

Item 23: Receipt

You'll be required to sign a receipt that you received the FDD. Two copies of the receipt form are provided in Item 23. The FTC requires franchisors to identify the franchise sellers (including internal personnel and outside brokers) by name, address, and telephone number. This information will enable franchisees to later identify the individuals who worked with them during the franchise sales process.

Key elements in the FDD

Although your attorney can help you make sense of the FDD, we think that a few items require additional attention.

- ✔ **Item 7 tells you how much it will cost to get into business as a franchisee — the initial investment.** Remember that some of these costs are averages or estimates and that the costs in your market or for your franchise may be different. The areas that may vary the most from the franchisor's estimates are the estimated working capital and the cost of buying or leasing a site.

  When you call the other franchisees in the system, get a sense of how much money they needed to support the business in the early days until they became profitable or had a positive cash flow. See how much they were able to draw from the business to support themselves and their families. Try to call franchisees who have been in the system for a year or two, so you'll know their information is current.

- ✔ **Item 11 lists the franchisor's obligations to you.** Be sure that you understand what services you'll get before you open (training, site selection, development assistance, and so on), what support you'll receive for your grand opening (marketing, advertising, and field support), and what services you'll receive after you begin operating the business.

  Pay particular attention to those services that the franchisor is obligated to provide and the services it may provide. You must receive what is required in the franchise agreement; you may receive the others. If the franchise seller makes a statement about services — such as additional training, additional field support, or special marketing programs, to name a few — and if these items are not included in the written obligations of the franchisor, you and your attorney may want to propose an amendment to the franchise agreement.

- ✔ **Item 17 discusses renewal, termination, transfers, and dispute resolution, which may be important to you only at the end of the relationship or when a conflict arises between you and the franchisor.** This section also includes topics such as severability, mergers, and amendments. Attorneys often refer to these items as the boilerplate part of the agreement.

Boilerplate refers to those sections of an agreement that attorneys usually already have written and stored in their word processors and include in the back of most of their agreements. (It's the stuff many people forget to read.)

Boilerplate sections may not necessarily be fair or meet your needs. Take your time to understand what rights you'll have and what rights you're giving up. Pay particular attention to any noncompete provisions and your other obligations when the franchise relationship ends. Even upfront, you need to know what exit strategies will be available.

✔ **Item 20 provides you with information regarding the number of company-owned or franchised units that are open and those that have closed or been transferred.** This section may be the most boring to read — all it contains is charts and numbers — but it can tell an important story.

Examine how many units the franchisor has taken back and resold and how many units have been transferred between franchisees. A high number of units acquired and then resold by the franchisor could indicate churning by the franchisor. *Churning* occurs when a franchisor takes back failed locations from franchisees and then remarkets them — over and over again — to new franchisees.

In addition to the names, addresses, and phone numbers of the franchisees currently in the system, Item 20 gives you information on the franchisees who have left the system in the past year. These are people you want to talk to. Of course, some of this group may be unwilling to speak to you because they're busy working or simply don't want to participate. Others who have left the system may have out-of-date contact information listed.

✔ **Item 21 contains the franchisor's financial statements.** If your personal balance sheet and finances looks better than the franchisor's, what does that tell you about your risk? Your franchisor will need the resources to meet its commitments to you. Item 21 gives you an idea of whether the franchisor can do just that.

✔ **Item 22 contains a list of all the agreements, including the franchise agreement you'll be required to sign.** Make sure that all the agreements listed are attached to the FDD — and read every one of them.

How much can I make? The financial performance representation

All prospective franchisees want to know how much money they'll make if they invest in a franchise. Who is better suited to tell them than the franchisor?

With the exception of cost information that doesn't tie back to sales revenue provided by franchisors outside of the FDD, the general rule in franchising is that the only place franchisors can provide you with any information on projected sales, income, profit, or costs of franchised or non-franchised locations is in Item 19 of their FDD. This statement of earnings is called a *financial performance representation.* Unfortunately, only 25 percent to 35 percent of franchisors provide you with this written information.

Some franchise salespeople will tell you that franchise law prohibits them from telling you how much you're going to make. That's not true. They're only prohibited from discussing the numbers with you if they've chosen not to include the information in the FDD. The FDD requires the franchisor to alert you to this fact in writing in Item 19.

Seeing the franchisor's side of the coin

If every prospective franchisee wants this information, why do so few franchisors provide it? Good question. Here are some possible reasons:

- ✔ **We live in a litigious society.** If the franchisor's financial performance representation contains inaccurate or misleading information, franchisees can sue to get out of the agreement and to recover their losses or obtain some other form of relief.

- ✔ **In some states, the franchisor's officers or directors may be considered guilty of a crime if they give you improper earnings information.** Rather than risk the penalties, they choose not to include any earnings information at all.

- ✔ **Franchisors may feel that their system's locations and markets are too diverse to provide the franchisee with any meaningful information.**

- ✔ **Franchisors may feel that their locations are all at different stages of maturity and that providing information based on averages and varying levels of operating success makes the information misleading — at best.**

- ✔ **Some franchisors fear that because the information that their franchisees provide about individual unit performance hasn't been audited or verified, it may not be accurate.**

- ✔ **A franchisor may rightfully worry that, because franchisees are often late in providing their financial information, the information may be incomplete.**

- ✔ **Some franchisors also worry that information their franchisees provide may not be uniform.** They think that there's a high risk that any earnings information they prepare won't accurately reflect the financial performance of units in the system.

- ✔ **Most systems have accurate information on the performance of their company-owned locations.** However, they may not have similar information on the franchisee-operated locations. These franchisors believe that providing information based only on company-owned unit performance may not give prospective franchisees a true representation of the performance they can expect.

✔ **Some franchisors feel that providing earnings information gives competing franchise systems an advantage because it may contain what they feel are system secrets.**

✔ **No uniform standard exists for how unit financial information should be provided to a prospective franchisee.** The type of information can be as brief as gross sales on the average location in a system. It may be as extensive as full profit-and-loss statements on every location. Some franchisors include helpful statistical information in their financial performance representations. Others don't feel that statistics are particularly helpful.

Because financial performance representations may differ from franchisor to franchisor, even when those companies are in the same industry, many franchise professionals don't think the information is particularly useful for comparing one franchisor to another.

✔ **In some systems, the numbers are so bad that franchisors don't want anyone to see them because, if they did, the franchisors wouldn't be able to sell a franchise.**

On the other hand, some franchise systems give detailed earnings statements for every kind of franchise arrangement in their system.

Rupert Barkoff, partner in the Atlanta law firm of Kilpatrick Stockton LLP and a former chair of the American Bar Association's Forum on Franchising, warns: "Even when intended to be helpful, [financial performance representations] can be misleading because there are so many factors that enter in the success or failure of a franchisee. For example, hard work and diligence may make one franchisee successful, but might never offset the consequences of a poor site selection."

Knowing where to go if you don't receive a financial performance representation

The debate about whether franchisors should be required to provide mandatory financial performance representations disclosure is still unresolved. Meanwhile, if the franchise you're investigating doesn't provide you with a financial performance representation, your next best source of information on earning potential is the franchisees in that system. After all, they have the most accurate information on how well their locations are performing and how well the franchisor is meeting its obligations.

Another good source of information on franchisors that are public companies are the reports they make to their shareholders as required by the SEC. These reports contain information that is not required by the FTC but that is required by the SEC. These reports, available from stockbrokers and often available on the Internet, can provide additional insight into the company. The Internet offers an abundance of information — from press releases to articles — that can help you determine the potential earnings of the franchisor of your choice.

Even if a franchisor doesn't include a financial performance representation in the FDD, plenty of information is available in the FDD to help you start to project your earnings. You may need to dig out the information and combine it with information from some of the other sources we mention, but the process is worth the effort. Here are some steps you can take:

- ✔ **Examine the franchisor's financial statements contained in the FDD for information on company-owned unit performance.**

- ✔ **Look at Items 5 and 6 (initial fee and continuing fee).** Often, the franchisor has formulas on how the fees are calculated; these formulas can be helpful.

- ✔ **Look at Item 7, the initial investment — especially the notes.** Besides telling you the approximate size and type of location of the franchise (from which you can determine what your local rent will be), it often gives you information on the amount and type of staff you'll need, the frequency with which the inventory of locations is sold and replaced (inventory turns), and how the franchisor calculated the required working capital.

- ✔ **Item 8 is a gold mine.** It discloses the required purchases and the percentage of your operating expenses they represent.

Even if the FDD doesn't include a financial performance representation, the franchisor is allowed to provide you with information on company-owned units that are for sale, if you're interested in buying one. Ask the franchisor whether a company-owned location is for sale in your market; if one is, ask to see the books and records. In addition to getting information relevant to your market, you may find a great opportunity to buy an existing location. However, this exception to the rule isn't a license for franchisors to show you information on locations you're not actually interested in purchasing.

A franchisor who has made a financial performance representation is allowed to provide you with a supplemental financial performance representation that is different from the one in the FDD. These are often prepared when the information is about a particular location or if other circumstances require it. The information must be in writing, must explain why and how it departs from the information contained in the FDD, and must be prepared in accordance with the FTC Compliance Guidelines. Further, the franchisor must give a copy to the prospective franchisee. However, if the salesperson makes financial performance representations outside the FDD — sometimes orally, and sometimes on cocktail napkins or scraps of paper — these aren't supplemental financial performance representations. Don't rely on that type of information in making your purchase decision — but you should save it. You never know whether you'll need it during a dispute with your franchisor.

Surveying the Paperwork: Evaluating a Franchise Agreement

Remember that the disclosure section of the FDD describes the relationship between the franchisor and the franchisee, but the *franchise agreement* — the written contract — governs the relationship. This section introduces you to the franchise agreement and helps you evaluate the contract.

The franchise agreement is more specific about the terms of the relationship than the FDD is. After reading the FDD, prospective franchisees often believe that they understand the relationship, so they just scan the franchise agreement. This is a terrible idea. Make sure that you read and thoroughly understand the franchise agreement. Unless you're an experienced franchise attorney, you may misunderstand the impact of some of the terms included in the agreement. Generally speaking, if there's a difference between what the FDD says and what the franchise agreement says, then the language in the franchise agreement will be what you're going to live with.

Hire an experienced franchise attorney to help you understand the franchise agreement. Although Uncle Alex, who did your last house closing, is cheap, his lack of experience in franchise law and the customs and practices in analyzing franchise documents may be costly later on. An attorney who is inexperienced in the nuances of franchise law may be unprepared to help you understand the franchise agreement. In the "Lawyers" section, later in this chapter, we discuss how to locate a qualified franchise attorney.

Comparing the agreement with the verbal promises and the FDD

During meetings with franchisors, the franchisor's sales agents often make statements and promises about the franchise relationship and the way their franchisees operate the business. If those statements and promises affect your decision to invest in the franchise, make sure that they're included in the franchise agreement. Unless they're included, they won't be part of the legal relationship. Marisa Faunce, a partner with Plave Koch PLC in Reston, Virginia, notes that "Most disputes that arise between franchisors and franchisees during the early stages of the franchise relationship arise out of a franchisee's misunderstanding of their legal obligations under the franchise agreement. Franchisees should take their time to review the FDD and the franchise agreement. If you don't understand something you read, don't be shy to ask for clarification."

Regarding the importance of fully evaluating a franchise agreement, suppose, for example, that you buy a terrific franchise in a great location and your customers love you. As a new franchisee, you completed all the training your franchisor offered and finished with flying colors. You have a sharp staff, which you trained, and right now your monthly sales are strong. The future looks good.

Then a problem pops up, and you need your franchisor's help.

At this point in the game, you find out that what you thought were promises of future hands-on support from headquarters were nothing more than part of the sales sizzle. You may find yourself alone in a very nasty business situation. It's too late to amend the franchise agreement to force the franchisor to respond. For example, suppose that a key member of your management team quits without notice. Back when you were buying the franchise, the franchise seller told you about a great program in which the franchisor provides temporary replacement managers to franchisees should just this type of event happen. When you need such a program, you find out that it was only a test program and the franchisor no longer offers that service. If that service is not in your agreement, the franchisor may not have any obligation to provide it.

The time to find out whether you can depend on your franchisor through the bad times as well as the good is *before* you sign the agreement. When the unexpected happens in a good franchise system, franchisors may not have a legal obligation to help the franchisees, but they help anyway. Wouldn't it have been nice for the franchisee in the preceding example to find out that, although the program had been canceled, the franchisor was going to help out anyway? That's why we continually remind you to check with other franchisees before you buy the franchise. Make sure that when you call for help, your franchisor will answer the phone and take action to see you through the rough spots.

Enlisting the help of an attorney or a financial advisor

As you get closer to making a decision to buy a franchise, getting the right kind of help takes some research on your part. Perhaps you have a good lawyer who handles your current business and private dealings. You may also have a Certified Public Accountant (CPA) who works with you on your income tax preparation. If so, you have a good starting point. If you don't have a lawyer or a CPA, don't worry. Connecting with qualified help isn't difficult.

Lawyers

Making your way through the legal language of franchising can be daunting. A qualified franchise attorney can not only help you understand the terms you're considering but also protect you from taking a wrong turn.

Franchise law is a specialty; your franchise attorney should have substantial experience. Attorneys who are unsure of franchise laws and standard practices may review the agreements as they would a lease, thinking that they can make substantial changes to the provisions contained in the agreement. Experienced franchise counsel understand why certain terms are in the agreement and recognize when others are unusual. As a result, their comments tend to be on the important issues and usually on those issues that have the best chance of being changed during negotiations.

For example, the franchise agreement may provide for little or no protected territory. An experienced franchise lawyer may know that most of the franchisor's competitors have protected territories, and she could negotiate such an arrangement for you. The same goes for additional training or support that would be beneficial to you but isn't provided for in the agreement.

If you're looking for a franchise attorney, check out the following resources:

- **Your personal lawyer:** He may refer you to a partner or an associate or may be able to get recommendations from professional colleagues. You can also contact the local bar association, the American Bar Association (ABA), or the International Franchise Association (IFA) for a reference.

- **This book:** You may try to get a referral from one of the lawyers quoted in this book, or e-mail co-author Michael Seid at mseid@msaworldwide. com. We generally can steer you to a qualified franchise lawyer who can assist you.

- **Other franchisees:** Don't be afraid to ask for references.

- **The American Bar Association's Forum on Franchising:** It can provide you with sources for articles, papers, and information on franchising.

  For $35, you can also order a membership directory of all attorneys who are members of the forum. The directory is broken down geographically. ABA members can access the ABA Forum on Franchising by going to www.abanet.org, clicking Forums, and then scrolling down to Franchising.

- **IFA's Supplier Forum (SF):** The SF (the professional arm of the industry association of which co-author Michael Seid and his partner Kay Ainsley are past chairpersons) publishes a list of firms that specialize in franchise law both in the United States and internationally in the IFA's *Franchise Opportunities Guide.* Although some of the firms listed represent only franchisors, they usually can refer you to competent lawyers experienced in representing franchisees. You can access an online copy of the *Franchise Opportunities Guide* through the IFA's Web site at www. franchise.org.

- ***The Directory of Franchise Attorneys:*** This directory is published online by Franchise Update. You can find it at www.franchise-update.com.

Consider your franchise lawyer to be a member of your business team and someone you'll want to work with in the years to come. For now, though, she'll walk you through the FDD and advise you on the overall desirability of the franchise offering. Expect your lawyer to review the franchise agreement and flag any items or issues that could be concerns. Your lawyer is your frontline defense against signing up for a franchise relationship that may not be in your best interest.

Financial and business advisors

For crunching numbers in an unemotional way, who could be better than a professional financial advisor? We're talking about a banker, CPA, or chartered accountant (CA) — someone you trust and are comfortable sharing your financial information with. You can get directories of qualified CPAs or CAs from their local associations.

Other professionals who can provide you with assistance are franchise consultants. (Make sure you're working with a franchise consultant and not a broker or franchise seller calling himself a franchise consultant.) Although most franchise consultants work primarily with franchisors, several can be of assistance to franchisees. You can locate franchise consultants who are members of the IFA's SF at the IFA's Web site at www.franchise.org.

When you're seeking out professional advisors, ask them if they've completed the course of studies offered by the IFA's Educational Foundation and are Certified Franchise Executives (CFEs). The CFE designation is a relatively new but important industry standard for franchise professionals. It's an important enough designation that co-author Michael Seid and his partner Kay Ainsley both have completed the requirements and have been awarded their CFE designation.

Negotiating with a Franchisor

After you've digested the FDD, you may think that the next step is haggling with the franchisor. After all, haggling — or negotiating — is the business way, right? In most situations, we would agree. But *striking a bargain* is not a phrase in the vocabulary of most franchisors.

Franchising's strength is its consistency. It's what the public depends on. It's also what you depend on. Can you imagine being in a room with other franchisees who'd signed their agreements at the same time you did and finding out that they got a different deal than you did, simply because they negotiated better? Think about the franchisor trying to manage a system with everyone operating under a different deal.

Older, more-established systems may be less flexible about negotiating terms, and newer systems may be willing to consider certain points as negotiable.

If franchisors are willing to negotiate with some franchisees on the significant issues, they're likely to be willing to do so with others. This flexibility may not be a good sign. You should be concerned if the franchisor is willing to negotiate freely about the product or services you'll offer to the public, or if the company offers you lower fees for signing immediately. If a franchisor is willing to negotiate freely with you, what has it agreed to with others? You and the public are relying on the system's consistency.

A franchisor's reasons for negotiating may be based on its need to sell you a franchise to meet next week's payroll. Even if the need for immediate cash isn't the reason, the franchisor's flexibility can be a sign of inconsistency.

You should never sign a franchise agreement without clarifying any points you don't understand. Where possible, you should attempt to negotiate the terms of the agreement to fit your needs. (For more on franchise agreements, flip to the "Surveying the Paperwork: Evaluating a Franchise Agreement" section earlier in this chapter.)

Here are some of the common terms that franchisors may negotiate (these changes have little effect on the system's consistency; some even provide benefits, such as additional support from the franchisor):

- **A change in the size of your protected territory — or even the granting of a protected territory, if the franchisor doesn't typically do so in its standard franchise agreement.**
- **Additional grand-opening support.**
- **Further training for you and your staff.**
- **Extra field support.**
- **Intra-owner transfer:** The transfer to another franchisee without incurring transfer fees or changes to the agreement.
- **Payment terms for the franchise fee.**
- **Default cure periods:** The time you'll have to cure a default in your operation of the franchise. This item is important, because if you don't cure a default in a timely fashion, you could lose your franchise.
- **Start-up date.**
- **The formula for calculating the franchisor's purchase price for your business on termination.**

- ✔ **Lower fees for** *conversion franchisees* **(independent operators converting over to the franchisor's system and brand):** Conversion franchisees may be able to negotiate lower fees, or a longer time to liquidate existing inventory or switch to the franchisor's computer system.

- ✔ **Right of first refusal:** A franchisor may be willing to give up or modify any right of first refusal it may have if you try to sell your franchise before the term of the agreement expires. A *right of first refusal* refers to a franchisor's right to match a bona-fide offer you received from someone to purchase your business.

- ✔ **Guarantees and limited liability:** Although you may form a corporation to own the franchise rights for tax or liability purposes, the franchisor is relying on you personally to meet the commitments contained in the franchise agreement. One of the documents you'll be asked to sign will probably be a personal guarantee for performance under the franchise agreements. On occasion, a franchisor may be willing to waive the requirement that you personally guarantee the agreement, or the franchisor may be willing to limit your liability under the guarantee.

Part III

Operating Your Franchise like a Well-Oiled Machine

The 5th Wave — By Rich Tennant

"Ahhh, Mr. Dorfman. Already I can tell you're just the sort of person we're looking for to own a McFee Detective Agency franchise."

In this part . . .

Franchising, as you probably know, is all about relationships and your ability to work with people. So, in this part, we examine four key relationships: your relationship with your franchisor, your fellow franchisees, your employees, and your customers. We look closely at how franchisees and franchisors relate to and communicate with each other — during the good times and the bad. We discuss methods you can use to attract and maintain customers, and, most important, we talk about how to recruit your staff, which is the most important asset for any business. We also get you started in the process of opening up your business and establishing yourself as a franchisee.

Chapter 7

The Start-Up: Setting Your Franchise's Wheels in Motion

*F*ranchising is most successful when each and every location in the chain operates in a way that ensures customers a consistent level of quality and service, regardless of which location they're visiting.

But being consistent isn't an easy thing to do (in the business realm, that is). The location's design has to feel right to the customers, and the business needs to be placed where it's convenient for customers to shop. The quality of the products and services you deliver to the customers can't vary much at all from their last experience — they're coming for the experience of shopping with you, which requires your management and staff to be up to the task of delivering on your brand's promise to them. Giving customers that level of reliability is what franchisees do (or should, anyway) every day.

To reach that level of delivery you have to know where you should place your business and how to build it; find the vendors that have the products you need; and understand how to recruit, train, motivate, and manage your staff. Great franchisors teach you how to do all these things. In short, great franchisors share their formula for success.

Surveying Your Options for Locale

Depending on your franchise, you'll be confronted with a host of different types of locations in which to establish your business. Good franchisors look closely at successful operations in the system and provide franchisees with profiles of what they consider ideal locations. Some franchisees rent office space in high-rise office buildings; others work from home; but most select from an ever-growing list of options, which we cover in this section.

Common site options

Here are some of the types of locations you typically will be looking at for your franchise:

✔ **Malls:** Malls are large, enclosed shopping facilities anchored by two or more major retail stores and servicing a large geographic area. A mall is typically easily accessible by automobile via major arteries or interstate highways and surrounded by parking.

Selecting a well-developed mall requires a franchisee to balance the benefits and the drawbacks. The principal drawback is the cost, which includes not only the rent but a host of additional expenses, such as common-area maintenance — your share of caring for the public space. Malls also charge merchants association fees, which are used for advertising for all the tenants in the mall. You also usually have to operate during the hours that the mall is open. On the plus side, malls are natural draws and attract large numbers of potential customers from as far as 25 or more miles away, depending on traffic patterns and competing malls. You can expect that some malls will include a percentage of your sales as rent in addition to your base rent. In addition to your franchisor having a say on what your location looks like, the better malls may restrict your ability to reimage. You should discuss with your franchisor any restrictions that the mall may place on you.

✔ **Neighborhood centers:** A supermarket typically anchors a neighborhood center with a variety of convenience-oriented small retail and service stores. These centers usually provide the most reasonable rents, and they draw from a trade area of from 1 to 3 miles, depending on population access and concentration. Most neighborhood centers have few restrictions on signage — although the upscale centers or those in upscale towns can be as tough as the regional malls on signage and décor and are the type of location that many retail and service franchise systems target for their franchisees.

✔ **Community centers:** These centers are also convenient for local populations. They usually have two or more anchors, a supermarket, a drugstore, and other general merchandise retailers. They serve local populations up to 6 or 7 miles away, depending on ease of travel and accessibility. They have appeal similar to the neighborhood centers but are much larger and, hence, may have more signage limitations for their on-street pole signs.

These are the types of centers that most often have available *out-parcels* (spaces for smaller, free-standing buildings out on the parking lot). The quick-service restaurant business uses out-parcels, as do other businesses that need to be closer to the street to be seen by passing motorists.

✔ **Lifestyle centers:** Usually found near affluent residential communities, these open-air centers feature upscale national specialty chain stores, dining and entertainment, and fountains and other ambient design elements that make browsing the internal, uncovered walkways enjoyable — whenever the weather permits. In these setups, traditional anchor stores typically aren't dominant the way they are at the malls. Multiplex cinemas, small department stores, large bookstores, and large-format specialty retailers are usually the biggest individual draws. These centers combine some lower-priced, impulse-purchase vendors trading off of the high traffic counts along with higher-priced, destination-type merchants.

Often, these centers have parking at each of the retail stores and sometimes larger parking lots as well. They draw from up to 12 or 13 miles, depending on traffic patterns and convenience.

Be careful in choosing a site in a lifestyle center. They're excellent venues for compatible concepts, but they can be expensive mistakes if your concept isn't a good fit with the lifestyle of the majority of the center's visitors. Most of the time, your franchisor will know whether these centers are a good bet for you.

✔ **Power centers:** Power centers are open air and usually located near a regional or super-regional center. They include at least three big-box stores (or "category killers"), such as Walmart, Target, and Home Depot. Power centers draw customers from a 5-mile radius. A trend in many markets is to convert some of the underproducing regional centers to power centers, because people like the convenience of the regional centers but prefer the option of parking in front of the store of their choice.

✔ **Other centers:** Constantly evolving variations of developments exist where retailing, entertainment, employment, tourism, bargain hunting, and other activities come together. Theme/festival centers are heavy on entertainment and restaurant businesses for leisure and tourist activities. Outlet centers have great bargains and sometimes draw busloads of people from very far away. Mixed-use centers combine many activities in the same area: retail, restaurants, employment, transportation, sports, recreation, office, hotel, cultural, and other activities in various integrated combinations. Specialty centers can focus on restaurants, car care, off-price, and other specific types of businesses on a planned development parcel.

As with the more typical centers just listed, you want to be part of or nearby these centers to take advantage of the customer flows that they create.

✔ **Shopping areas:** A concentration of stores serving a local community is considered a *shopping area.* Downtown, also know as a central business district (CBD), is a shopping area that benefits from the traffic from office workers, visitors to downtown, and people who live in the downtown area. Because of the traffic and their prime locations, in some cities, these sites can be expensive and often suffer from lack of customer parking. Because most of the traffic in the downtown areas is usually created by office workers, the hours during the weekdays are busiest, with most customers coming in before work, during lunch, and after work. This inconsistent traffic pattern makes staffing a bit problematic. Except for a few cities that have re-created their downtowns as entertainment destination areas or festival marketplaces for residents from the suburbs — as Baltimore did — these areas are quiet in the evenings and on weekends and holidays.

✔ **Off-street sites:** Airports, universities, ballparks, and co-branded locations are all types of sites that usually aren't easily accessible to customers just driving or walking down the street. These locations represent significant opportunities for many franchisees today and have been a growing trend in franchising.

✔ **At-home sites:** Although home locations aren't sites in the traditional sense, more and more franchisees are choosing this option, where the franchisor allows them to work out of their homes.

Working from home

Many franchise systems, especially smaller service franchises that never have customers coming to their offices — for example, carpet cleaning, janitorial, maintenance, and repair services — not only allow their franchisees to work from their homes but actually encourage it.

Working from home reduces a franchisee's cost of doing business and is convenient. For many franchisees, working from home is perfect. They can get up early, do their paperwork, and plan their day — all before taking a shower and getting dressed. In the evening, after dinner, they can relax in their offices, watch some TV, and prepare for the next day. And because they don't have any other office, they can deduct the costs associated with their home office on their tax returns. (You should check with your accountant and tax preparer to determine what is deductible.)

Opting for alternate, or off-street, sites

Many franchisors are able to expand their systems by opening locations in off-street venues or captive-audience venues. These locations are popping up wherever people congregate — gas stations; convenience stores; hospitals; airports; train and bus stations; colleges; large department stores; offices; factories; and movable kiosks at seasonal and recreation locations, sporting arenas, parks, and malls. The idea is to provide your products or services to customers where and when they may want them. Franchisors and franchisees have gotten pretty creative in developing variations of their concepts to fit into more and more venues where people gather.

The strength of captive-audience locations is that the operations benefit from customers drawn to the location by something other than the product you're offering, such as the baseball game at the stadium or to college students between classes. The biggest drawback is that your business success is tied to the ebb and flow of people in the host environment. In other words, when the ballplayers go out on the road or when the season ends, you're out of luck. Colleges are governed by the academic calendar, so get ready to twiddle your thumbs a bit during summer vacation, unless many students attend summer school.

If you visit a convenience store when you purchase gasoline, you are also visiting a captive-audience location. Gas stations operated, for example, by ExxonMobil often share space with quick-service restaurants. Some may even have a small branch of a service franchise, where you can cash checks or mail packages, for example. The traffic from customers buying gas helps the franchise sell more product and services, and the traffic generated by the franchise helps sell more gas.

Single- or multi-unit operators can operate from these locations. The franchisees can be either the dealer who operates the gas station or another person or entity that simply is renting space from the dealer. Sometimes, the operator may even be the franchisor.

So has a captive-audience site caught your eye? Many of the same criteria you use to check out an on-street site apply here — and then some. Are there signage restrictions? Is it heavily traveled? Is it visible to patrons? If an airport location opens up, you'll see a lot more road warriors in a main terminal, concourse, or food court as opposed to a terminal for the smaller, less-traveled carriers, in small regional airports. Not every mass gathering opportunity is the same — you need to do your homework. Where would you rather be, in a sports stadium where the home team fills the stadium each game or in a sports stadium where the home team can invite the spectators to share the bench with them — and still have room? You get the point.

Landing near another franchise: Dual branding

Another type of arrangement you see frequently where more than one business uses the same premises is called *dual branding:* two or more franchises with different concepts that set up shop next to one another or within the same location, offering customers a one-stop shopping experience.

In this setup, your franchise shares common space with another brand — for example, in a food court at a mall. If your business brings in traffic in the morning hours and is less busy during the afternoon, partnering with another brand that has a heavy afternoon business but a weak morning business may make sense.

Yum! Brands, the parent company of KFC, Pizza Hut, Taco Bell, A&W, and Long John Silver's, often places two or three of its brands in one location. So does ExxonMobil, which often combines its gasoline stations with its On the Run convenience stores with various sandwich, doughnut, other food, quick oil change, or car wash businesses (often with multiple brands all at once).

A dual-branded location may be able to use labor and real estate more efficiently because, if done well, it expands a location's *daypart*. (In the restaurant industry, breakfast, lunch, and dinner are called dayparts.) For example, doughnut chains usually are busiest during the breakfast daypart and slow down during the lunch and dinner dayparts. Other concepts are slow during the breakfast daypart but busier during the lunch or dinner daypart. By dual-branding a location, the operator hopes to capture traffic generated by the other product offering and use the location more fully.

If you choose one of these dual-branded sites, you're still paying an initial franchise fee, paying royalties, and remaining accountable to the same standards. Make sure that your franchisor offers equipment, signage, and design specifications to fit these new locations. Compare the costs — and sales/profit potential — with those of single-branded locations. These sites are usually tucked inside another location and take up less square footage. The smaller space usually means less staff and possibly lower overhead. Some of these franchises operate seasonally. But just because they're smaller doesn't mean they're cheaper. Some — such as limited-access highway travel centers — are on prime properties, and the bidding can be fierce.

Setting Up Shop: Finding Your Franchise's Habitat

We won't kid you: Finding a good retail or restaurant location in today's market isn't always easy. Many of the best spots already have been taken, and competition for the available real estate is brisk. Given rapidly changing consumer traveling patterns, opening your franchise in the right location matters, because if your operations and your location are great, you have the best of both worlds.

Keep in mind that although a good location is important, a good or even great location won't make up for a bad operator. Given the choice between that old tired chant of "location, location, location" and an equally one-dimensional chant of "operations, operations, operations," we opt for neither — but lean toward the latter.

Exploring your location options is a big part of your franchise research. Start-up costs for a home office versus a free-standing site — and everything in between — can vary by hundreds of thousands of dollars. How's that for hitting you in the pocketbook? Defining your location is also a vital part of your business plan. Anyone who's financing your venture — even your moneybags uncle — will want to know where the cash is going, what the site will look like, why it will attract customers, how much customer traffic will pass the site, and who your competitors will be. This section can help you find a site to suit your fancy.

You may luck into a site just by driving through town on the lookout for for sale or for lease signs. Or you may opt to use a commercial real estate broker. You'll find that many, or most, of the better sites never have for sale or for lease signs on the property. The local brokers will become aware of them or dig them out for you based on their business networks and experience. Another resource is the exhibitions where shopping center developers lay out their construction plans. Contact the International Council of Shopping Centers at 212-421-8181 or `www.icsc.org`.

Finding out what constitutes a good site

First, you need to establish the criteria that are important for your type of business. You may think the best place to open your doors is where the crowds are right now, such as in a shopping mall or adjacent to a busy highway. You may be right — for now. But with all the acquisitions, mergers, and market pullouts happening with major retailers and grocers, that major draw your business is dependent on may go away and take with it your customers.

No one can offer a stock definition of a good site, because different businesses require different kinds of locations. Some generalities do hold up, however. If you're investing in a retail franchise, focus your search on a location that gets in your customers' faces. If it's in the path of people commuting to work, near an entertainment arena, or in an office complex, customers can see your business, recognize your brand, and more easily come in to buy your products and services.

For some businesses, however, getting the best corner in town, with high visibility and terrific customer access — in a strong, anchored shopping center, for example — is not only unnecessary but also the path to rapid disaster. Carpet cleaners, janitorial services, building-repair services, direct-mail companies, lawn-care services, pest-control businesses, moving companies, tool-delivery services, and home-inspection services, among other service providers, don't usually need high-visibility retail space (and can't afford it, either). Their needs run more to good-looking trucks, delivery access, access to postal facilities, highway access, warehouse facilities, and good telephone service than to locations where their customers shop. After all, most of these service providers go to their customers — the customers don't come to them. Bottom line, if you don't need to be at the corner of State and Main, you'll most likely have more options to choose from, lower rent, and a more accommodating landlord.

Using the franchisor as your compass

When you're dealing with location issues, most franchisors can offer one big advantage: experience. The staff at a mature franchisor can help you identify the kinds of locations that usually work — and those that don't. For example, staff members know whether a franchise can be effectively home-based initially or even long term, whether an office attracts more business in a generic, white, two-story building or with a Park Avenue address, or whether a retail franchise fares better tucked inside a mall or flaunted center stage on a main thoroughfare. So, your first step in the process of selecting a location is to discuss viable options with your franchisor. The company may allow a variety of locations, or it may stick to only one type.

You still need to double-check any information the franchisor supplies against your own research. Think of this as a check-and-balance. You check on the accuracy of the data, and your information provides a balance to what the franchisor offers.

A good franchisor points you in the right direction. The franchisor's staff can fill you in on demographic secrets, especially the chain's target market — the profile of your potential customers. How many customers do you need, say, of a particular age and income that can drive to your business in a certain amount of time? How long are customers willing to travel to buy your goods or services? How much are they willing to pay for what you sell?

Many franchisors bombard new franchisees with site criteria — a list that spells out specifications for a particular franchise — inside and out, so that the site meets the franchise system's standards. You may be required to have x number of parking spaces, x number of seats, x number of grills, and so on. Retail and restaurant franchisors, especially, expect their franchisees to comply with their design standards — without variation. On the other hand, an office-based franchise may not care whether you have wood floors or carpeting, mahogany desks or oak. A consistent look at each of the locations may not be important to franchisors, as long as the locations meet their overall quality standards.

Will your franchisor ultimately help you find this crown jewel of a site? Typically, a franchisor will educate you about its site criteria, provide you with site criteria forms, and ask you to find the location and do the required research — before you present the site package to the franchisor for review. Then the franchisor will evaluate your information and possibly visit the location before approving or disapproving your choice.

Check your franchise agreement to see whether and how the franchisor must approve a franchisee-selected site and the time limit for the franchisor to render a decision. (See Chapter 6 for more on franchise agreements.) Standard contracts allow a franchisor to accept or reject your request to open at a particular location. This decision, like everything else in franchising, reflects the need for consistency.

In almost every franchise agreement, the franchisor is only approving or rejecting a site, not guaranteeing it. This is true even if the franchisor found the location for you — you didn't have to accept it, did you? The franchisor's approval indicates only that the site is acceptable. Ultimately, the selection of the site is your responsibility.

As for actually finding the site, some franchisors provide considerable help, some provide guidance only, and some leave you on your own. The more hands-on support the franchisor provides in site selection, the better your chances of finding a successful site. Look at your franchise agreement to find out what your franchisor will do for you. Ask the other franchisees in the system how good the franchisor's site-selection assistance actually was.

Typically, the franchisor will approve a general area for your location and expect you to search within those boundaries for a location, unless the franchisor already has a site in mind. After you find a site, the franchisor's role is to accept or reject it. Other franchisors — especially start-up franchisors — may physically accompany you on your site hunting; the staff may jump in the car with you, plot demographics, and talk to landlords. Some franchisors may already have located the site, built the building, outfitted it with equipment and fixtures, and made it available for you to buy or lease.

Using specific data to evaluate a site on your own

Investigating a site for your franchise is very much like following the scientific method. Suppose you hypothesize that a given site may be a good location. You need facts to support your hypothesis before you can reach any conclusions.

Most demographic studies today can present information based on census tracts, block groups, zip codes, a radius measured in miles from a center point, drive-time polygons, and many other configurations. For retail and restaurant franchises, the drive times are usually best (except for walk-up locations) because most people will drive to your business — either coming from someplace or going to someplace else. Given a specified amount of time (3 minutes, 5 minutes, 20 minutes, and so on), a computer program can draw an irregular polygon based on vehicle speeds on the various roads and highways and then provides demographic and employment information for the contained area. These polygons usually vary dramatically from the comparable circles of 1, 5, 10, or 20 miles. The size of an area you should measure is most important. If your customers are quick-lunch types who typically drive no more than three or four minutes each way to get lunch and return to work, measuring the employment population ten minutes out won't help you. The franchisor usually can give you assistance in determining the size of your *trading area* (the area where you draw the majority of your customers).

The factors that influence site success fall into four primary categories: demographic and employment, activity generators, physical and traffic, and competition. For a breakdown of each category, what you need to know about each when searching for a site, and where you can get that information, see the checklist (CD0701) on the CD-ROM. We also provide some content on the CD to guide you in your market research (CD0702).

As you look for a site, keep your eyes peeled for any red flags. A location that keeps turning over or that has been on the market for a long time should raise your eyebrows. If anything — and we mean *anything* — smells fishy, investigate further before you sign a lease. Don't let your desire to find a site and open your store trap you into selecting a substandard location. Jim McKenna, president of McKenna Associates, Corp., a Milton, Massachusetts, consultant specializing in franchise real-estate issues, says that you need to be aware of other site detractors, too. If your customers would be turned off by odors from neighboring businesses (perhaps *literally* smelling fishy), loud or annoying sounds, or any other negative factors, you may have to reject an otherwise strong site. Consider whether you would leave your children at a beautiful landscaped and convenient day-care center if a halfway house for criminals were next door.

Avoiding encroachment

One thing that gets people talking in franchising is *encroachment.* You'll hear the term, and we suggest that you understand the concept before, not after, you sign your franchise agreement.

Suppose that your franchisor has granted you a protected territory stretching 1 mile around your location or for a specific trade area outlined on a map. The franchisor then is prohibited from allowing another franchisee- or company-owned location from opening closer than 1 mile from your store or within the boundaries. But the franchisor isn't necessarily prohibited from selling over the Web, depending on the language in the agreement.

Suppose that you open a franchise on the corner of Fifth and Main. A year or five years later, another franchisee from the same system opens a franchise on Fourth and Main. The new franchise is so close that you can see your customers going in and out of the new location. That's what we call encroachment.

Getting a landlord on board

Many times, a landlord may be unfamiliar with your business. Worse, he may have a negative perception of your business. He may simply be naïve, have bad information, or possibly have had a bad experience with a past tenant who offered similar services or goods. Explain why your business is different, who your customers are, and the benefits the other tenants will receive from your business. If your concept is national in scope, give the landlord a sense of the prestige his center will receive by being part of the system.

When you're looking for sites, think of yourself as the seller, not the buyer. Your job is to sell the potential landlord on the merits of your business. Your franchisor should provide you with marketing materials to give to landlords. Give landlords a reason to pick you over other businesses competing for the same space.

As in this example, encroaching can come from another franchisee- or company-owned location opening in your protected territory. But it can also happen if the franchisor begins to sell products in other locations — such as a supermarket or a convenience store within your protected territory. It can also happen if the franchisor allows others to offer the same services you sell in your neighborhood. Encroachment can occur through catalog sales (from catalogs mailed into your market) or through the Internet, if customers can buy through e-commerce the same products you sell in your location. It depends on what the franchise agreement says about your protected territory.

Encroachment is like someone stepping on your toes — only the person doing the stepping is your franchisor, who you thought was your partner. Ouch, that can hurt!

On the other hand, you don't want to be the only one of your brand in the market. Left all alone, you'll be vulnerable to competitors who will have no problem with opening next door to you, especially if you're part of a weak brand with little penetration and you're unable to advertise sufficiently. Good franchisors try to achieve a balance to create brand recognition in the marketplace and, therefore, more demand for the products and services of the franchised brand so that everyone in the chain can benefit.

Obviously, encroachment can potentially have an adverse impact on your business. Carefully examine the language of your franchise agreement. Are you getting a protected territory, or do you have no territorial rights? If your franchise grants you only a site address franchise (your protected territory is no bigger than the four walls of your store), the franchisor could conceivably establish other locations nearby that will compete with you. Some contracts specifically state that a franchisor may establish other units and/or sell items through other channels of distribution in direct competition with a franchisee. Because Internet sales don't require the establishment of a location, e-commerce may not legally be encroachment, unless specified in the agreement. Don't assume that you have rights not provided in the agreement.

You need to know — before you sign the franchise agreement — whether the franchisor will be able to open locations in your market area. Joyce G. Mazero, lead franchise attorney at Haynes & Boone in Dallas, Texas, cautions, "Contracts normally tell you what the franchisor is granting, such as the right to operate a site, but don't always plainly tell you what it is not granting — such as no right to exclusivity outside of the site, no right to conduct business on the Internet, and no right to prohibit the franchisor or another franchisee from operating from a site close to your site. What you are getting is just as important as what you are not getting."

Don't rely on a franchise salesperson's statements about what the system generally does or doesn't do regarding its locations. Even if the salesperson makes sense when saying that the franchisor would never open a location so close to you that it would adversely affect your business, get the necessary language in writing in the franchise agreement (as with everything else that's important).

Even where the franchise agreement allows the franchisor to establish new locations close to an existing franchisee, some franchisors establish procedures — adopted internally or with their franchisee advisory councils (see Chapter 9) — to review the impact of encroachment on existing units. If it seems that the encroachment will cause a prolonged and material adverse impact, a franchisor may decide not to allow the development of the new location. If it appears that the encroachment will cause a minor or temporary impact, the franchisor may allow the unit to be developed but may also assist the affected franchisee to make up for the lost sales.

Other franchisors simply cite the terms of the affected franchisee's agreement and allow the unit to open — regardless of the extent of the impact.

Find out what the franchisor's policies and practices are concerning protected territories and encroachment impact before signing the franchise agreement. Read your franchise agreement. Speak to other franchisees in the system, and talk to your attorney.

On the CD-ROM, we provide you with information on how to look for and secure real estate for your business (CD0703), as well as a site-selection support tool for new franchisors (CD0704), to help you support your new franchisees in obtaining real estate.

Securing Your Space after Finding Your Piece of Heaven

After you find the perfect location, the real work begins: convincing the landlord to give you a lease you can live with, and then selecting contractors who will build out the location.

Understanding and signing a lease

When you're about to sign a lease, you've already decided on a location. You should be in the process of contacting the real estate or mall management company that manages the property to determine space availability and specific occupancy costs and lease terms, and to complete your site review package for your franchisor.

Does the center have an adequate amount of space available for your business? Although you don't want to squeeze into a space that's too small, you also don't want to pay for space that you'll never need. Square-foot costs can vary with overall size; often, the larger the space, the lower the square-foot cost. However, even with a lower per-foot cost on a larger space, the maintenance and development costs will be higher. Evaluate size based on your needs.

In order to determine specific leasing costs, you need to understand their many components. We provide a detailed list and explanations (CD0705) on the CD-ROM.

Building a location

Sometimes the only site you can find in the area that is perfect for your franchise is an empty lot. What do you do now? Build.

Building your own location can be tedious and demanding. But if you select the site based on your franchisor's criteria, plan the job, carefully select your contractor, and closely monitor the job, you'll have the exact location that you need.

If building a site is going to be your choice, make sure you touch base again with the local zoning board and building department before you even close on the property and certainly before you move that first shovel of dirt. You want to be in compliance with everything — down to local ordinances that set the hours you can hammer and saw to your heart's content. You also want to determine whether the town needs to approve any *variances* (which give you permission to do something on the land that's different from what the zoning rules allow) for the property and whether the site will support your needs for utilities, parking, and the like. Early discussion with the municipality is important. Even where your use is permitted, the planning board can have some unusual requirements that could make the site unworkable for you. Sometimes green-space setbacks or water-retention basins, although nice for the ducks, can push your building out of sight of approaching traffic. If your business relies on impulse purchases, you're in a tough spot.

Although your contractor or architect usually does the pre-groundbreaking legwork, seeing that it all gets done is your responsibility — not the franchisor's.

Your contractor needs to obtain the following:

- ✔ **Permits:** For construction, utilities, signs, *curb cuts* (those indentations in the sidewalk that let the cars in), and environmental matters
- ✔ **Variances:** If you need the town to approve some specific violation of the zoning requirements for your site
- ✔ **Certificates of occupancy:** To allow you to occupy the location

You also have to prepare preliminary plans and specifications for site improvement and construction, and usually — big surprise! — submit them to your franchisor for approval. Your banker or lender will also want to see these plans.

Understanding the layout

Every retail and restaurant franchisor has a floor plan (footprint) that is excruciating in its exactness. Even if you think that a counter should be 2 inches longer on the left side, you have to follow the franchisor's plans — or get the franchisor's permission for a change. Even if you know for a fact that menu signs are more readable if they're placed 12 inches closer to the floor than the required 90 inches, you still have to follow the plans. You need to get these specifications and standards so that you can review them with your architect and contractor.

Franchisors usually provide prototype plans for every location. Your architect must develop plans for your site that meet local ordinances and codes as well as the franchisor's standards. Don't assume that you can add improvements to the design, such as a bigger *back of house* (the kitchen and storage area). Check with your franchisor before making expensive changes that you may have to reverse.

All these specifications from the franchisor are intended to ensure consistency, which is great, but what if your particular community has some type of restriction that runs counter to your franchisor's building plans? Make sure that you notify your franchisor so that you can discuss the required changes. If the changes are important, the franchisor often personally contacts the builder or city planner to discuss the changes.

Selecting the contractor

You're probably groaning by now, remembering the last time you hired a contractor to fix up your family room or enclose the patio. But selecting a reputable commercial contractor who has experience with meeting deadlines and the quality requirements of a franchisor isn't difficult. And doing so is only common sense.

To help you in your search, we include a checklist for selecting a contractor (CD0706) on the CD-ROM.

Getting the Goods: Merchandise and Supplies

In this section, we look at the way franchisees purchase and maintain inventory and supplies. One of the main benefits you're looking for in a good franchise system is the ability to combine your purchases with those of the franchisor and the other franchisees. Working together, you hope that you can get the best price, the best products, the best equipment, and the best service from suppliers. A good franchisor has also made certain that the suppliers want to participate in this beneficial relationship simply because it's good for their business, too.

Probably no benefit is more important to a franchisee than the potential strength in numbers that the system brings to controlling the quality, consistency, availability, and exclusivity of the equipment, supplies, merchandise, and raw materials used by its franchisees.

All franchises need merchandise and supplies of some kind. Some franchise systems require franchisees to buy certain goods direct from the franchisor. Some systems specify that franchisees must purchase from approved suppliers. And some systems allow franchisees to choose their own vendors. The method or combination of methods depends on the type of industry, the products or ingredients the franchise uses, the size of the system, the size of the region the franchisor serves, and the available delivery methods.

The benefits from the buy

When you're looking at different franchise opportunities, you can tell in advance what methods the franchisor uses by reviewing the franchisor's Franchise Disclosure Document (FDD; see Chapter 6). The FDD tells you which methods the franchise system uses and whether the franchisor earns any income on the franchisees' purchases. Finding out in advance is important, because some systems with a lower royalty rate may actually cost you more money than a system with a higher royalty rate, because the difference may be more than offset by the income the franchisor earns from your purchases. (In case you're wondering, the *royalty* is your payment to the franchisor that allows you to continue in the franchise system — it's usually based on your total sales.)

Nothing is wrong with a system that earns money every time you purchase goods from a supplier. After all, setting up and maintaining these supplier relationships costs the franchisor. And franchisees need to have a financially strong franchisor that can provide them the services they need and want. However, in a perfect world, you want to find a franchise system in which the "blended" costs of being a franchisee (royalty and other costs) are the lowest, and the services provided by the franchisor are the highest.

Knowing who to buy from when your franchisor is involved

Suppose that you've purchased a maid service franchise. You've hired a first-rate staff, and they're ready to get busy scouring, wiping, dusting, and polishing. But elbow grease isn't enough — they need cleaning products. You may not have the option of hopping over to the local warehouse store and loading up a cart. Your franchisor may require you to purchase products directly from the company. Or your franchise agreement may specify that you use only franchisor-approved suppliers or authorized products. These rules ensure that the supplies you use meet the franchisor's standards. A bonus to you is that, because the franchise system may buy in large volume, prices may be lower.

In this section, we explore some of the more common arrangements on how franchisors can enforce system standards by ensuring consistent ingredients and supplies for the franchised network.

Buying goods direct from your franchisor

When franchisors elect to be the exclusive suppliers to their franchisees, the requirement usually extends only to items that are proprietary (secret recipes) or that contain certain key ingredients. These products may be ordered directly from the company, or in most systems, the franchisor provides the products to the distributors that serve the system.

Nonproprietary merchandise and supplies are another matter. Even if the franchisor distributes the goods, it usually isn't the exclusive supplier, and franchisees have the option of making their purchases either from approved suppliers or from their own chosen vendors. (Sometimes, the purchases must meet standards or specifications set by the franchisor.)

Many of the legal disputes over the past two decades have resulted from franchisees' perception that they're getting gouged — that is, the products they must purchase from the franchisor are excessively marked up, making the franchisee less competitive. Rupert Barkoff, Partner at Kilpatrick Stockton LLP in Atlanta, Georgia, warns, "Beware of franchisors who require that certain products be purchased through them. It is easier for a franchisee to digest the franchisor's decision that products must be purchased from the franchisor when the product sales are not a profit center for the franchisor."

Although the methods the franchisor uses for supplying products are in the FDD (find out more in Chapter 6), the franchisee usually gets additional information on supplier relationships at training.

Getting merchandise and supplies from approved and required suppliers

Rather than inventory all the merchandise required for a network of franchisees, some franchisors give franchisees a list of approved suppliers from whom they can buy their items directly. As long as the approved suppliers sell only the merchandise approved by the franchisors — without unauthorized substitutions — franchisors can maintain control over the quality of the products sold under their brands.

A good franchisor is the keeper of the brand. In that role, the franchisor's representatives identify, screen, and approve suppliers to the system. Suppliers come in all shapes and sizes, and your franchisor has hopefully sifted through the best of them for you. Before you chafe over having to use only a franchisor's choice of suppliers, curb your entrepreneurial spirit and read on.

A good franchisor wants to keep your operational costs as low as possible to help you make as much money as you can. If a franchisor has gone to the trouble — and expense — of finding good suppliers for you, take advantage of that effort! Of course, ask your fellow franchisees whether they're happy with their suppliers. (Make sure that you ask this question before you buy the franchise. You don't want to be surprised.) If they are, be thankful that finding good suppliers is one less item on your to-do list.

Supplying goods the Wendy's way

Wendy's franchisees can take advantage of arrangements the franchisor makes with suppliers. Programs set up by the purchasing department can help make sure that products meet their quality standards and are available when their franchisees need them. At the same time, their franchisees can buy at a lower price because of volume buying. The franchisor provides the purchasing service free of charge to its franchisees — it's not a profit center for the franchisor. It's another way that the franchisor ensures consistency in the Wendy's brand. A good franchisor should offer this service for franchisees, simply because it's the right thing to do.

Wendy's has a whole staff of people who go into the suppliers' operations and audit their facilities. Staff members check on the entire production line and make sure that the company is doing everything the way they want it to. They even check their products by pulling them from the suppliers' facilities and the distribution centers around the country and sending them off to an independent laboratory for evaluation. Wendy's wants to make sure that all the food safety measures are in place and being used. With all the recalls in the food industry, you have to be aware of exactly what the suppliers are doing, what's going on at their production facilities, and what environment your products are being produced in.

Franchisors worth their salt negotiate with manufacturers for the lowest net prices on goods, for marketing support, and for other benefits. Check with your franchisor about the way rebates are handled in your system. The procedure is far from uniform among franchisors or among suppliers. Also, if you discover that a supplier in your area meets your franchisor's criteria and is less expensive than the franchisor's authorized suppliers, make sure to pass the information on to the franchisor's headquarters.

Buying products authorized by the franchisor

All franchisors — big, small, or in between — require consistency in the products sold under their brands. Product standards and specifications are one of the keys to controlling product consistency.

Franchisors set product standards and specifications, which means that they tell their franchisees what type and quality of products to buy. As long as franchisees follow these rules, they can choose their own vendors. This practice is common in small franchise systems, but even big franchisors often allow franchisees to buy items locally, as long as those products meet the standards.

Buying goods through cooperatives

Several franchise systems use *cooperatives* (buying groups) to purchase products, marketing, advertising, insurance, leasing, credit, and other goods or services.

Cooperatives are by no means uniform in how they function and who they represent. Many are started by franchisees, and the franchisor isn't part of the buying group. Other cooperatives include both company-owned and franchisee-owned locations. Still others represent members from several franchise systems.

The value of joining a cooperative is that group purchasing lowers prices. This method gives you a competitive advantage over those who can't buy as cheaply. Also, large buying groups often get better access to new products, better allocation when products are scarce, and better service from suppliers when things go wrong.

Franchisees and/or franchisors purchase membership in the cooperative and commit to buying a certain percentage of their requirements through the cooperative. Cooperatives are controlled by the members, typically on a one-member, one-vote basis, with members determining the officers, directors, policies, and procedures adopted by the cooperative.

Cooperative members may also share in what are called *patronage dividends,* which, like stock dividends, are distributions of the earnings of the cooperative. However, patronage dividends differ from stock dividends in one major way: Stock dividends are based on the number of shares you own, whereas patronage dividends are based on the amount of your purchases from the cooperative. The more you buy, the more you get back in patronage dividends.

Of course, when you purchase through a cooperative, you still must meet the standards and specifications your franchisor has set for your location.

Finding your own suppliers and goods

One key advantage of buying a franchise is that you can be part of a larger network that includes your franchisor, fellow franchisees, and regional support staff. But if you're one of the first franchisees in a system, or your franchisor isn't large enough to have national or regional distributors, you may have to do some of the relationship building with suppliers that a franchisor in a larger system would do for you.

If your franchisor doesn't provide you with a list of authorized suppliers, you're going to have to choose your own vendors.

Work with your field consultant and your franchisor's purchasing department to see whether they can help you identify suppliers in your markets. Visit other similar businesses and ask what suppliers they use. Your local chamber of commerce may also have a list of suitable suppliers.

When you review bids and quotations from vendors, make sure that you understand the total charges. Some vendors quote a low price on a product but make up the loss with additional handling and delivery charges. Look for these hidden charges when you compare pricing.

Price is certainly one of the prime considerations in selecting a vendor. However, basing your decision solely on price can be a mistake. A good price on items constantly out of stock or a good price from a vendor who is continuously trying to dump outdated merchandise won't help you build your business.

If your franchisor offers a supplier-evaluation questionnaire, get it — and use it. If not, you need to make one up yourself. Check out the CD-ROM for a couple of checklists (CD0707) to get you started finding and evaluating vendors.

Receiving Merchandise

If you own a franchise, the first thing you have to figure out is how to manage your *receipt of merchandise.* You must properly check, log in, and store all merchandise entering the store. You can negotiate lower prices for your merchandise, but you won't save any money if you don't notice unacceptable quality or shortages in shipments. To avoid these losses, you or the store manager must establish a regular receiving routine for your store. Having a routine helps to monitor vendors and reduces the chance of shortage.

Your franchisor should provide you with a list of recommendations and procedures for maintaining your inventory. Follow it. If your franchisor doesn't provide inventory procedures, the following sections offer useful guidelines.

Receiving deliveries

Suppose that you've just purchased a convenience-store franchise. The new site has been built, and you're standing inside your brand-new building. The only problem is that the shelves are empty. Soon you'll need to begin scheduling and receiving deliveries, but you may not have any experience in this process. Follow these general tips for receiving merchandise at any type of franchise:

✔ **Make sure that suppliers schedule their deliveries in advance.** Accept deliveries only during specified hours. When the location is open and operating, you want the merchandise to come during off-peak hours so that you can concentrate on accepting the delivery.

✔ **Don't allow vendors to park in front of your business.** Require vendors to park in an out-of-the-way spot. The front of your business is for customers.

✔ **Have the delivery driver bring all products into the building before you check the items.** Some systems want their own employees to bring merchandise into the store.

✔ **Make sure that the merchandise you receive is for your business.**

✔ **Check all vendors in and out.** Be sure to physically see every item — don't just take the driver's word. Check all cartons and boxes when the vendor is leaving to make sure that they're empty and that no merchandise is being carried out of the store. Unless absolutely necessary, vendor check-in should be done away from that vendor's display and away from merchandise you already have on hand. Don't allow a vendor to both stock shelves and remove boxes unless you check both before the vendor leaves.

✔ **Watch helpers.** Some vendors have helpers whose main job is to distract you during the check-in process.

✔ **Immediately put away all perishable products.**

Checking the goods after they're in your location

A truck pulls up at the back door of your franchise, and a flurry of activity follows. Suddenly, you're surrounded by boxes. The driver is completing the paperwork for your signature. This situation doesn't have to be scary if you know what to do. Check the quality and condition of the merchandise before accepting it. Here are some additional tips:

✔ **Examine every box for obvious signs of damage.** Look for things like tears, broken or crushed cardboard, signs of tampering, rattles, damp or wet cardboard, bad odors, dented cans, substitutions of standard items, and so on.

✔ **Before signing for the boxes, open any cartons that have been opened and resealed or that you suspect have internal damage.** Note any damages on the receiving record.

✔ **Always check the date code on the product when it's delivered.** Make sure that the product is within the code and that you can reasonably expect to sell it before the code expires.

Verifying invoices

Attending to paperwork may be the least entertaining part of franchise ownership, but in the case of delivery receipts, it can be rewarding. You can avoid financial losses by ensuring that you're getting what you pay for. Check out these tips:

- ✔ **Before accepting delivery, check each item on the delivery receipt against the product that has been delivered and then compare against the product ordered.** Check quantities received against quantities ordered. Count the number of cartons delivered and compare this number to the number on the driver's record or freight bill. Never sign for more cartons than you receive. Note any discrepancies on the freight bill or receiving record, or correct the errors before the vendor leaves the store.

- ✔ **Never give the delivery receipt back to the vendor.** Obtain the delivery receipt when the vendor walks in and under no circumstances return it to the vendor. Manipulating the delivery receipt is one of the most common ways that some vendors steal from franchise locations.

- ✔ **If the vendor made a substitution, call your franchisor's field consultant to verify that the substitution is valid and acceptable.** Inform the driver and note on the invoice that substitutions not approved by your franchisor are subject to return for full credit.

- ✔ **If you don't receive an item appearing on the delivery receipt, have the driver clearly mark the item "short" along with the quantity not received.** The driver must then sign the delivery receipt before you sign it.

Maintaining Inventory

Your franchise training manuals teach you all about maintaining your inventory. Procedures vary widely, depending on the type of franchise you own. Your franchise may not even have any inventory, and in that case, you can skip this section. (Nobody but you will know — you don't have to take a test at the end of this book.)

Back of the house

The back of the house is also known as the stockroom. It's literally in the back area of your business, and it's where you keep all the items not currently in use. If you need more vitamins, you go to the back of the house — or the back room or stockroom — and get them. Back of the house is also where you store perishables or frozen items, which means that it also can be the location of a refrigerator or freezer. You'll be expected to know what you have in the back, too. But again, franchisors already do a lot of the work by providing a plan-o-gram for the back of the house, just as they do for the front.

Your franchisor should provide detailed back-of-the-house storage procedures. Follow them. If your franchisor doesn't provide information on back-of-the-house arrangements and procedures, the following sections provide some procedures to consider.

Dry storage

Dry storage may actually be wet — sorry. The term *dry storage* is used for items that don't require refrigeration. If you're a health-food franchisee, your vitamins and sports drinks are both dry-storage items. The following are some dry-storage practices:

✔ Store products at least 6 inches off the floor on clean, nonporous surfaces to permit the cleaning of floor areas and to protect from contamination and rodents.

✔ Don't store products under exposed sewer or water lines, or next to sweating walls.

✔ Store all poisonous materials — including pesticides, soaps, and detergents — away from food supplies, in designated storage areas.

✔ Store all open packages in closed and labeled containers.

✔ Keep shelving and floors clean and dry at all times.

✔ Schedule cleaning of storage areas at regular intervals.

✔ Date all merchandise upon receipt and rotate inventory on a first-in-first-out basis. Place the oldest products in front of the newly received merchandise.

✔ Locate most frequently needed items on lower shelves and near the entrance.

✔ Store heavy packages on low shelves.

✔ Don't store any products above shoulder height.

Refrigerated storage

If you have items needing refrigeration, place them into your cold storage as soon as you can. Here are some tips for storing your refrigerated items:

✔ Enclose any food or other product removed from its original container in a properly identified, clean, sanitized, and covered container.

✔ Don't store foods in contact with water or undrained ice.

✔ Check refrigerator and freezer thermometers regularly.

✔ Store all foods to permit the free circulation of cool air on all surfaces.

✔ Never store food directly on the floor.

✔ Make certain that the temperature setting is appropriate for the product(s) you're refrigerating.

✔ Schedule cleaning of equipment and refrigerated storage at regular intervals.

✔ Date all merchandise upon receipt and rotate inventory on a first-in-first-out basis, placing the oldest products in front of the newly received merchandise. This step is particularly important with refrigerated products because their shelf life is usually short.

✔ Establish preventive-maintenance programs for equipment.

Front of the house

The front of the house is everything that's not the back of the house. This is the area that customers see when they enter your store. Obviously, how the front of the house looks is more important for locations that are frequented by customers and less important for locations that customers never see.

If you're a retail location, you'll handle your merchandise differently than you would if you were a restaurant. Still, at all times, the front of the house is your showcase — it's what customers see every time they visit your store.

Retailers need to place merchandise on shelves so that it's attractive to customers and induces them to buy. Restaurants and other businesses that sell food also need to keep their locations attractive. If you have reach-in refrigeration accessible to your customers, or if you have items on display, how you display them is just as important to you as it is to a retailer. Your franchisor should provide you with a plan-o-gram for that purpose.

In order to keep the front of your store in tip-top shape, make it a priority to

✔ Follow your system's plan-o-gram.

✔ Keep your shelves and *merchandisers* (displays for your merchandise) stocked, clean, and dust free.

✔ Use proper product rotation by placing the oldest product in front of the newly received merchandise (first-in, first-out).

✔ Price identical items the same. One benefit of modern point-of-sale (POS) technology is that you don't have to reprice each item when prices change — all you have to do is change the price in the computer and on the shelf's price tag.

✔ Allow adequate space between displays, as required by your local code.

✔ Use only signage that is acceptable in your system. If your franchisor requires you to use professionally prepared signage, don't use hand-written signs. Equally important, make sure that you keep your signage current. (Remove the Christmas posters before Labor Day!)

✔ Keep your floor area free of empty boxes, unless they're part of your design concept.

The Americans with Disabilities Act requires that you keep your store arranged in a manner that makes it usable for individuals with disabilities. As a general rule, provide enough space for easy passage of a wheelchair throughout the store, make sure that the lines to your registers are accessible, and don't display merchandise in a way that makes it difficult for people with disabilities to shop. If you have no choice about how you merchandise the store, make sure that your staff is actively available to any customers who may need assistance. *Remember:* Complying with all federal and local laws is the franchisee's responsibility.

Getting Good Training before and after You Open Your Franchise

A good franchisor insists that you learn the business and that you keep learning as the system changes and market conditions evolve. Most franchisors train at their offices, at established operations, or at franchisee locations. Follow-up support is usually handled through the area field representative, who acts as the liaison between you and the home office.

A right way and a wrong way

Training your staff is the most important thing you do. And the training never ends. You even need to teach them how to clean the tables. Believe it or not, there's a right way and a wrong way to teach even these mundane tasks. Dave knew that the art of teaching and learning goes on forever, and he devoted a lot of time and money to making sure that his franchisees had the best information to help them succeed.

Also, franchise systems vary widely in their use of technology in training. If you're considering a franchise that is new or recently launched, you may find use of online training to be very limited, because more sophisticated online training requires large investments by the franchisor. A hard copy of the operations manual and a new franchisee training class are commonly the only training vehicles (and may be adequate depending on other support) in a start-up franchise company.

Getting good initial training

Expect to cover a lot of ground during your initial training. Initial training should be aimed at teaching you and your staff how to produce and deliver the franchisor's product or service the same way every time. But good training is more than simply learning how to make the product.

Franchisees should learn

- Standards and operating procedures
- Food safety and storage (if the franchise is a restaurant or a store selling food products)
- Technical operations on products and services (for nonfood franchises)
- Leadership and business management
- Problem solving
- Tips for understanding the customer experience
- *Brand positioning* (how the franchisor wants the public to think and feel when they hear the brand name)
- Merchandising and pricing methods
- Marketing and advertising
- Labor management, including recruitment, supervision, and motivation
- Techniques for training staff
- Cleaning and maintenance
- Safety and security
- Vendor relations, purchasing, receiving, stocking, and inventory management
- Financial management and business plan development
- The *management information system* (MIS; the computer system used to manage business matters, such as accounting, payroll, and so on)
- The *POS system* (used to manage sales activities, such as cash registers, pricing, and inventory)
- Communications, both internal and external
- Site selection, construction, landscaping, and store design

Good training instills in the franchisee the franchisor's brand philosophy, teaches franchisees everything they need to know (from opening the business in the morning to closing at night), and gives them the sources for additional or emergency support.

Most franchise systems begin training after you sign the franchise agreement and pay your initial fee. Many provide training in segments such as the following:

- ✔ Initial training to assist you in site selection and development
- ✔ Training for both you and your management personnel
- ✔ Training for your initial staff
- ✔ Continual training that introduces your staff to new products and services
- ✔ Replacement staff training when employees leave the franchise

How much training you can expect depends on the industry, the complexity of the business, and especially on the franchisor.

If the industry historically has high staff turnover — and the franchisor requires you to send your staff to the franchisor's training program and then charges to train your replacement staff — you'll incur additional training costs. These costs are a good inducement to recruit and *retain* good employees.

In some systems, you can expect only a few days of training; often, this time is spent working in operating locations. In other systems, you can spend months in training — both in class and on the job in training locations — and then the franchisor provides continual training for innovations, new products, and your replacement personnel. The FDD (see Chapter 6) details the length and scope of the training you'll receive. Make sure you feel confident that the training is sufficient for you to operate your business.

Ensuring that you receive effective ongoing training

In larger franchise systems, field support is usually provided from one of the franchisor's regional offices. Smaller franchise systems may use the headquarters staff to provide you with your training and ongoing support.

Operating a franchise in today's economic climate means staying on your toes all the time. You can't do that by yourself. As a franchisee, you should expect the franchisor to provide you with more than initial training. After your franchise is open, expect the franchisor's field staff to show up armed with operational, marketing, and organizational support. You should also expect the company's help with the rollout of innovations, such as the preparation of new products or the operation of new equipment. The hallmarks of great franchisors are offering new products, updating research, implementing new-product development, installing state-of-the-art technology, introducing better methods of customer service, and repositioning franchises in the market. These services keep a company more than one step ahead of the competition, like Wendy's Service Excellence program (described in Chapter 8).

Chapter 8

Hiring, Training, and Other Staffing Decisions

- -

In This Chapter

▶ Hiring talented employees

▶ Following EEOC guidelines

▶ Interviewing applicants

▶ Managing, training, and keeping your staff

▶ Ensuring workplace safety

- -

*Y*ou're about to add the last spoke to your franchise's operations wheel: staffing. Every employment decision you make has far-reaching implications — on your franchisor's brand, your budget, your competition, your aggravation level, and, of course, your customer satisfaction. Human resources executives and business owners agree: If you want to be customer-focused, you have to be employee-focused.

In this chapter, we give you tips on how to hire employees, how to train them to the *n*th degree, and how to motivate them with incentives.

Finding Folks Who Fill the Bill

As desperate as you may be to staff your business, hiring anyone who walks through the door doesn't make much sense. You want to hire only the best. By developing the reputation of offering a great place to work, you'll attract quality candidates. The result will be better customer service, less employee turnover, reduced cost of recruiting new employees, and reduced cost of training new employees — in short, more profit.

As an employer, you also need to be conscious of one more thing: the law. You have the right to be very fussy, but you also have to be fair.

The following sections help you find and attract potential employees and stay within the laws while wooing them.

Finding the right employees

Are you resourceful? Good. You have to be for this job. Finding employees boils down to putting in time and effort, thinking creatively, and, usually, spending some money. In a tight labor market, you have to try everything and anything once, and then four more times to see what works.

Before you start recruiting, do a little planning:

- **Have an idea of how many employees you need and when you need to bring them onboard.** Your franchisor's operations and training manuals should help with this process; you're a step ahead if your own business plan spells out these guidelines.

- **Make sure you have clear job descriptions.** Franchisors typically help you out here; they also usually provide you with information on employee profiles to look for and to avoid. Although not perfect in every situation, the employee profiles can provide you with a good tool to work with as you learn the business.

After you write up the job descriptions, decide how many employees you need, and figure out when you want them to start, you're ready to go out and find your workforce. Your recruiting options are many — some pricier than others (and some are even free!):

- **Use word of mouth:** Spreading the word is a great way to start your search. Just as with marketing, talk up your business to friends, relatives, neighbors, and other businesspeople. People are often in the market for new jobs or know someone who is.

- **Begin a referral network:** When you hire your employees, you've begun a referral network. Happy employees are your best marketers; they love to bring in others — especially when they have an added incentive. Many franchisees offer rewards — such as cash, concert tickets, or other prizes — for every referral who's hired. Advertise the program on bulletin boards, in newsletters, and at employee meetings.

- **Recruit at your site:** You can also use your site to give customers a heads-up; they're the perfect captive audience! Wendy's uses outdoor billboards, counter cards, crew buttons, tray liners, job posting centers, and recruitment messages on carryout bags. You may want to put a sign in your window — help wanted, homemakers: spare cash for your spare time, or students: spare cash before and after classes are just a few ideas.

✔ **Tap into the community:** Churches, community organizations, schools, and colleges are all good recruiting sources. In some areas, employers can claim a tax credit for hiring at-risk youth and other hard-to-employ residents. Contact the Department of Housing and Urban Development at 202-708-0380 or online at www.hud.gov to find out whether you're in a federally designated zone. Government agencies, local chambers of commerce, and nonprofit groups can help you locate senior citizens and the developmentally disabled.

✔ **Check out the classifieds:** So far, with the options in this list you've probably gotten away cheap. Now get ready to open your wallet. Classified ads are the most popular hiring tool. See whether your franchisor offers recruitment ad slicks you can use; they can also guide you on the appropriate media.

Recruitment ads, just like every other advertisement you use in your business, need to be professional and well-designed to be effective. Many franchisors produce advertising material you can customize for your location.

You can also look beyond the "help wanted" sections of your local newspaper. Other possibilities for classified placement include school publications, senior-citizen newsletters, trade journals, hospital and other employers' internal newsletters, as well as Web sites such as CareerBuilder.com (www.careerbuilder.com), craigslist (www.craigslist.org), and Monster (www.monster.com).

✔ **Use employment agencies and executive recruiters:** Agencies and recruiters, which typically charge a flat fee or a percentage of salary per hire, may be a good option for some positions, such as management or other staff that require certain skills or licenses.

✔ **Network within your franchise system:** Consider this: A wonderful employee at a franchise in Florida is relocating to Tempe, Arizona — exactly where your franchise is located. You've just hit the jackpot! You get someone who not only has glowing references but also knows the system.

✔ **Try several other methods:** Host open houses or so-called "discovery days," contact your local department of labor, and/or participate in career fairs. You can also contact vocational and trade schools, college placement offices, religious advisors, community agencies, and other neighborhood stores or retailers.

Don't forget to review any applications you have on file from the last time you had a job opening. Who knows? Maybe someone who didn't quite make the cut last time is available and interested.

Job opportunities may come across as more inviting if you convey a personable image. As a job seeker, which would you choose: a mega-supermarket that has a stark white sign in the window with help wanted printed in black ink, or a full-color poster or billboard with pictures of happy workers that says join our team — it's not a job, it's your future.

Remember that your franchisor has rules about how you use the franchise's logo in advertising, and those rules don't apply only to the ads you use to attract customers. Many franchisors provide franchisees with advertising for the recruitment of personnel, but if they don't and you need to create your own, check with your franchisor for permission before you use the franchise's marks in your recruitment advertising.

In addition, emphasize — go ahead, even boast about — how you stand out from the crowd. People like to work on a winning team. Perks such as bonuses, child-care reimbursement, and career advancement could make you the employer of choice.

Following equal opportunity guidelines

The one word you don't ever want to hear while operating your franchise is *discrimination*. We urge you to become extremely familiar with the employment laws designed to prevent discrimination. Discriminatory practices include bias in hiring, firing, promotion, and job assignment. The U.S. Equal Employment Opportunity Commission (EEOC) enforces the federal labor statutes; you'll want to be in touch with this agency to find out about the laws.

These are the major statutes:

- **Title VII of the Civil Rights Act of 1964** prohibits employment discrimination on the basis of race, color, religion, sex, or national origin. Sexual harassment and harassment on the basis of race and/or color or national origin violate this act.

- **The Age Discrimination in Employment Act (ADEA) of 1967** protects job applicants and employees who are 40 years of age or older from employment discrimination based on age.

- **Title I of the Americans with Disabilities Act (ADA) of 1990** bans employment discrimination on the basis of disability.

✔ **The Equal Pay Act (EPA) of 1963** prohibits discrimination on the basis of gender in compensation for substantially similar work under similar conditions. It applies to most employers.

✔ **The Immigration Reform and Control Act of 1986** makes it unlawful for an employer to hire any person who is not legally authorized to work in the United States. Employers must verify the employment eligibility of all new employees.

For more information, contact the EEOC headquarters at 800-669-4000, contact any of its 50 field offices in the United States, or visit the EEOC at www. eeoc.gov. Also, check with your local Department of Labor or state attorney general's office for local rules that may affect you.

Make sure that the language you use in your recruitment materials is in compliance with EEOC guidelines. For example, to avoid discriminating against older job candidates, nix words like *young, recent graduate, boy,* or *girl.* Your message makes all the difference.

Conducting the Interview Process

When you're interviewing candidates, you're not only representing the brand but also making an important investment decision. If the interviewee becomes an employee, you want that person to understand your passion for your business and the way you expect him to perform as an employee. Even if a candidate doesn't join your team, he can still talk about you and your operations from an insider's viewpoint. *Remember:* Candidates can influence others — both potential employees and potential customers.

Before you don the suit and tie

An interview presents the perfect opportunity to discover the human being whose name tops a résumé or job application, which is a challenging process. Many of today's job candidates are very well polished, including those who have been coached by outplacement firms or how-to books. Your job is to understand the position you're looking to fill, ask fair questions, maintain control of the interview, and project a sense of confidence. You may want to ask for guidance from human resources personnel at your franchisor's corporate or regional headquarters.

Most franchisors include a human resources section in their operations manuals and training programs. Make sure that you have the most up-to-date version. The manual should have information on the following:

✔ Applications and other hiring tools

✔ Guidance on how to anticipate your management and staffing needs (which vary depending on your volume, the type of location, and the maturity of your business)

✔ Hiring evaluation

✔ Human resources paperwork

✔ Interview preparation

✔ Interview questions and techniques

✔ Job descriptions and staff responsibilities

✔ Job features and benefits you can use in recruiting candidates

✔ Profiles of the types of candidates you should be looking for

✔ Recommended pay plans and bonus plans

✔ Recruiting sources

✔ Recruiting techniques and strategies

✔ Recruiting tools — brochures, ad slicks, letters, in-store signage, and so on

✔ Reference checklists

✔ Telephone techniques for recruiting

If your franchisor doesn't provide this information to franchisees, ask the franchisor to begin the process of developing a human resources guide.

As you approach the interview process, remember that you need to select — not just hire. You want the best candidate for the job. Having just any warm body filling a position places your investment in jeopardy. Invest the necessary time and money to put together a team of employees who take your investment seriously. Before you interview a candidate, make sure you

✔ **Have the right tools.** These tools may include the following:

   • **A prototype application form:** If this form is included in your operations manual, photocopy a big stack.

   • **Information about your franchise and the brand:** Give this information to the prospective employee. Many franchisors produce information brochures that you can use for this purpose.

- **A document listing the questions you want to ask:** The purpose of an interview is to get the information you need, and the best way to do that is to know in advance what you want to ask.

- **The rules of employment:** If you're going to offer the candidate a job, provide her with the rules that you may include in an employee handbook.

  We provide you with a sample employee handbook (CD0801) on the CD that accompanies this book. You can use it as a guide in developing your own employee policies.

✔ **Know the days and hours you have available or want the candidate to work.**

✔ **Review the candidate's application.** Look at all the answers, placing the greatest emphasis on dates of employment, reasons for leaving, salary history, positions held, and references. Review the applicant's work availability and decide whether it matches your scheduling needs. You'll have time before you make the job offer to verify all the information. During the initial interview, simply accept the answers as facts that you can use to ask probing questions.

Asking the right questions

Running a business is like being onstage, and you're the stage manager. You control the environment. During the interview process, remember the following guidelines:

✔ **Set the tone for the interview.** Conduct the interview in a quiet location with limited disturbances. Your goal is to establish rapport with the applicant so that you can gather information to guide you in making your decision. Always give candidates your undivided attention. They deserve this courtesy. Job seekers are eager to please and may give you answers they think you want to hear, but you can avoid feeding them answers if you ask your questions first.

✔ **Introduce yourself and explain your function within the business.** Always refer to "we" rather than "I" to instill a sense of belonging. Making sure that candidates know "we" includes them if they join your team makes them feel that they're joining an inclusive organization that cares about them, the team, and their work environment.

✔ **Make sure all your questions are specifically job related.** Consider the value of each question and ask questions accordingly. Base hiring decisions strictly on the requirements of the job and the behavior and personality necessary to perform it — according to your standards, of course.

During an interview, don't ask questions that the law forbids you to ask. If you're not sure whether you're crossing the line, double-check with your attorney, your local Department of Labor, or your state attorney general's office. Your franchisor likely also has a do's and don'ts list in the operations manual.

✔ **Ask open-ended questions whenever possible.** Open-ended questions are ones that interviewees can't answer with a simple yes or no. They encourage the candidate to talk and provide a basis for interaction, expressing her ideas, goals, values, and feelings. An interview featuring primarily open-ended questions is more lively than an interview that goes from one staged question to the next. Open-ended questions usually begin with action words, such as *why, who, where, how, in what way, describe, tell me about,* and so on. For example:

- Tell me about yourself.

- Describe what you liked most about your last job.

- In what way would you provide great customer service?

Often, candidates will tell you about their families and their hobbies. This information offers hints about what excites and motivates them and whether they'd be happier, say, behind a desk or out on sales calls. Reading between the lines can give you a sense of their interpersonal skills, strengths and weaknesses, and willingness to be team players.

If the candidate tells you that he didn't learn anything on his last job and that his supervisor was constantly on his back for not coming in on time, you have to look further to see whether the candidate understands the meaning of working as part of a team. If the candidate thinks that petty theft is okay, do you think you can trust her? Look past the surface answer and probe until you get an understanding of who the person is and how well he'll fit into your team.

✔ **Avoid closed-ended questions, except to gather factual and objective information.** Closed-ended questions provide specific information about such things as skills and experience. For example:

- What was your title in your previous position?

- Did you graduate from high school?

- Do you have a driver's license?

✔ **Determine the applicant's wish list.** Figure out what she wants in terms of position, shift, part-time or full-time work, pay, and opportunities for advancement. Do the applicant's needs concerning pay and hours match your needs? If not, the applicant probably won't take the job; if she does, she'll be unhappy.

✔ **Ask about availability.** Often, class schedules, second jobs, a spouse's or partner's job schedule, or child care affect an applicant's availability, so asking about it may identify a candidate suitable for split shifts or part-time hours, which can reduce your payroll costs. (Make sure, however, that your questions don't violate EEOC guidelines.)

✔ **Assess the applicant's demeanor.** Pay attention to appearance, attitude, character, and desire for the job.

✔ **Determine the applicant's potential.** What is the candidate's education background? Has the person had a career that shows progression in responsibility? Do the applicant's speaking ability and demeanor command respect? The answers to these questions can identify traits you should be looking for.

✔ **Make a decision.** Either continue or close the interview.

Continuing an interview

After you've covered your preliminary questions, if you decide to continue with the interview, your next step is to run through all the details of what you're looking for in the ideal candidate so that the candidate can make a decision:

✔ **Provide the candidate with a complete job description.** Include duties, available shifts, hourly wages, benefits, training, and so on.

✔ **Let the candidate know your policies and expectations.**

✔ **Discuss your dress code and grooming requirements.**

✔ **Let the candidate know your scheduling requirements.** What shift will she be on? When does she need to be at work? Does she need to be on call? Do you need to tell her times of the year she can't have vacation or time off because it's your busy season?

✔ **Stress that the atmosphere is one of teamwork and why this is important.**

If an applicant is worth considering, he'll have questions. Respond to them. The candidate needs to make an important decision and, just like you, wants to have all the relevant facts. Allowing the candidate to ask questions may open up a line of thought you hadn't considered before. By making sure that a candidate understands what's what, you reduce the risk of turnover due to misunderstandings and unrealistic expectations.

After all the interviews

After you find a qualified applicant, check references — personal and business — before you make an offer the applicant can't refuse. Background checks go beyond job skills to reveal other qualities. Is the applicant conscientious? Does she have integrity? Is she arrogant? Is she a perfectionist?

Obviously, some people will get cut. You may, however, want to keep their applications on file for a year in case a job opens up that fits their skills.

You represent the brand in everything you do. Just because some candidates don't fit your needs today or you don't fit theirs doesn't mean you have to part as enemies. Candidates may have friends who need a job and fit your requirements better. They may know co-workers at their current jobs who are perfect for your opportunity. They may love your product or service and tell their family and friends. Even in a job interview, you represent your brand.

Leading the Troops Effectively

In any business, effective leadership is critical. Franchising includes another layer: Effective franchisors lead to effective franchisees, which lead to effective employees.

Franchisors shouldn't pass the buck here; they should give you intensive training and operations guidelines to help you hire and train your staff. You can read Chapter 7 to find out about franchisors' training programs.

Regardless of what a franchisor suggests in their manuals or procedures, your employees are your employees. Your actions are your own — not the responsibility of the franchisor. Carefully verify all your employment procedures and policies with your attorney or other advisors.

Next, a franchisor should clearly communicate its corporate culture so that you can transmit it down the line. The corporate culture must be the central focus of the system. It defines your brand and is included in your promotional messages, in your local and community image, in your quality and consistency. It's also evident in how your employees interact with each other and with consumers, vendors, and everyone else who comes in contact with your business.

A good manager

A good manager is flexible enough to help out with whatever is needed in the restaurant — lending a hand at the window, cleaning tables in the dining room, or greeting customers. The manager has to be very observant of what's going on — and keep the lines moving. It's really a lot of fun. If you stand behind the grill all the time, you're not being a good manager.

A good manager thinks. It's not how hard a manager works — it's the manager's ability to get other people to work hard. Is he a good motivator? Does she know her people? I mean, you've got to have the right person at the cash register. You have to cross-train, of course, but you'll still have some people who are better at certain tasks than others — at making sandwiches, for example. You have to be very fast to do that, and only certain people are good at it. The manager really has to say, "Okay, this person is best and happy at this job." That's part of management — you've got to know your people.

Dave liked to work the grill. He didn't like the cash register at all. If Dave had to go in and take over something, he wanted to go in and take over the grill.

Familiarity with the corporate culture can help your staff make decisions. For example, suppose that you have a store manager who has never met the franchisor and is wondering how to handle a certain situation. That manager may find the answer by asking "What would the franchisor do in this situation?" Your leadership will convey to the staff what the culture really means. It must be the rallying point or, better yet, the "fabric of the system" that transcends the manuals, the forms, and the written procedures. It generates in every staff a level of ownership in the brand and loyalty to the system. The power of the culture is there.

Finally, a franchisor should lead by example. If a franchisor maintains high standards, that tone is set for franchisees. Then — you guessed it — you'll be the role model for your employees.

One more thing: Until now, you've been relying on your franchisor a lot. But employment is one area where franchisors have to step back a bit. From a legal standpoint, how much franchisors can tell franchisees what to do in regard to human-resources issues is unclear, so many franchisors steer clear of making certain requirements. These are *your* employees, and you're responsible for selecting them and managing their day-to-day conduct.

There's a silver lining behind this cloud, though. Franchisors can make suggestions, and when they own corporate units, they can show actual case histories — of recruitment strategies, wages, bonuses, training, promotions, work schedules, filling out government forms, and so on. Many operations manuals contain EEOC policies, interviewing guidelines, and sample recruitment materials. (Some don't, because franchisors are sensitive to the potential liability of looking like co-employers to your employees.) Plus, you can always tap your fellow franchisees to see what's working for them. That's plenty more information than you'd get as an independent business owner.

Grabbing the torch: Training your team

We suggest that you face the music now: You can be the best-trained franchisee in the system, but if your full-time and part-time employees don't know how to provide the product, ring up sales, keep the store clean, and offer a positive shopping experience, you're not going to get happy — and repeat — customers.

Keep in mind too that training is like a song that never ends. It keeps playing on and on because you'll always have new employees, new things to learn, and information to reinforce.

Employee training is part vocational, part philosophical. Sure, your employees need to know their specific tasks, maybe even be cross-trained in several roles. But they also need to understand the chain's vision and culture, especially its thoughts on customer service — the lifeblood of any business.

The next question worth asking is this: Who trains the employees? It depends on the system and often on the specific job. Check your Franchise Disclosure Document (FDD; see Chapter 6) to see whether the franchisor offers initial or ongoing training to any of your employees. Is a limit in place regarding how many, say, managers, assistant managers, and shift leaders they'll train over time? Is only a certain level of employee included? Are you responsible for additional training costs? In any event, expect to pick up transportation and lodging costs if you and any of your staff have to go to the franchisor's training facilities. And unless you're obsessed with racking up frequent-flier miles, find out whether continuing training is available at a closer, regional office or through the franchisor's intranet site or on CD so that you and your staff don't have to trek to corporate headquarters.

Most franchisors provide some training at your site when your franchise first opens so employees can get in on the act. Later on, ongoing training may be available at your site, probably for a fee or by the field consultant during her periodic visits. Many franchisors include training programs on their intranet sites, and many include train-the-trainer programs so you and your managers have the skills to train your own employees.

Taking responsibility for getting your gang in gear

What's the best way to train your employees? You won't find one right answer to that question. Some franchise systems work best if franchisees handle all the training. If you're buying that kind of franchise, make sure that your franchisor teaches you how to train your employees. That advice may sound convoluted, but think about it: How can you teach your employees about their job duties if you've never been taught how to teach?

If your franchisor takes training seriously (like a great franchisor should), you'll be loaded up with training manuals, pamphlets, checklists, and audiotapes to ensure consistency. Tech tools such as CD-ROMs or training programs on the franchisor's intranet sometimes lighten the training program with everything from music to interactive games; the best part is that you can continually pop onto a computer to train new employees or refresh memories. Many are reinforced with printed materials and online training on the franchisor's intranet through distance-learning programs.

Expect your franchisor to address some training issues at your chain's annual meeting. Franchisors usually welcome managers and employees at continuous training, including some national and regional training seminars.

Teaching someone how to do something is a skill — maybe even an art. Simply saying "Here, watch me" isn't adequate training. Therefore, if you're expected to train your staff, you need to receive train-the-trainer instruction. This training gives you the skills you need. Great franchisors also provide franchisees with training aids to make their jobs easier. If you're likely to employ staff for whom English is a second language, ask whether training materials are provided in your employees' primary language.

Increasingly, franchisors are using the Internet to provide training through distance-learning programs. Providing online training enables franchisees and their staffs to access the franchisor's training program when they have the time to devote to learning. Find out to what extent online training uses engaging visuals and graphics to convey content to your employees if you anticipate that they'll have low reading levels. Although online training may sound exciting, simply posting reading-intensive material may not help you train your staff.

Web-based training also can enable the franchisor to know who is being trained and how well franchisees and their employees are scoring on the tests that are often provided. A mature franchisor that uses learning-management systems also can monitor whether your team has completed required training, giving the franchisor a solid program to ensure quality and consistency from location to location.

Keeping the job diverse and interesting

Particularly in the restaurant business, the tasks that the staff performs are pretty much the same day in and day out, so it becomes important for employees' mental well-being that they're cross-trained so they can get diversity in their work; otherwise, employees will get bored and leave. The days of the assembly-line mentality are changing.

In times of labor shortages, employees need to understand how to work more positions. If you have a staff shortage in one area, you can easily slide employees over from other areas.

Now, some people will argue that an employee never becomes good at a task if she's constantly being moved around. Dave disagreed with that because there aren't 100 tasks to do — you may be moving around among 3, 4, or 5 tasks.

Find out whether you're on your own if an employee needs some extra training. A good franchise field staff can help with retraining and refresher courses, so check on that option, too.

Marla Rosner, Senior Training Consultant at Michael H. Seid & Associates, underscores the importance of your role in developing a team of competent and service-oriented employees. "Franchisees wear numerous 'hats,' from marketer to bookkeeper and in some cases chief cook and bottle washer (literally). They have to be prepared and committed to either execute staff training provided by the franchisor or create training regimens themselves. There will always be competing demands, but if staff training is ignored or compromised, the product or service and customer satisfaction will deteriorate. If a franchisee can't find the time to train, they should assign the training function to someone on their team."

The day-to-day follow-up and supervision of your staff belongs entirely to you. Your employees are your front line — they create the first impressions your customers have of your store. And those first impressions are lasting ones. So, your employees need your ongoing attention and input — they're an important part of the recipe for successful franchising.

Finding a method to the madness

When you're training a new employee, avoid a sterile, lecture-like approach. Encourage the new employee to ask questions and get involved. A new employee may have the right attitude but lack the experience and skills necessary to work effectively.

Manual skills are best taught by a simple four-step method:

1. **Prepare the employee.**

   Explain to the employee the task he'll be doing. The employee simply observes someone else doing the skill and asks questions.

2. **Present the information to the employee.**

   Let the employee do the task. Slowly lead him in the process while you explain how to do each step.

3. **Let the employee practice.**

   Have the employee do the task, but this time let him explain each step while performing the task at half speed. Provide the employee with coaching and advice as needed.

4. **Follow up to see what the employee has learned.**

   Have the employee perform the task at full speed, without any coaching or assistance. This step tells you whether the employee is ready to work independently and with your customers on that specific task.

   Congratulate the employee when he has mastered the new task. Doing so instills pride in doing a good job. Go back and observe the employee periodically to make sure that he's still doing the task correctly and hasn't picked up any bad habits.

Break down the skill into easy-to-understand portions. If the skill is to learn how to clean a restroom, work on sweeping and washing the floor separately from cleaning the mirrors, the washbowls, and other fixtures. The job may be cleaning the bathroom, but the task is the individual components of the job.

Holding on to your employees

Look at how much time you've already invested in rounding up and training your employees! Now you have to figure out ways to make sure that they'll stick with you. A paycheck alone isn't good enough. You have to motivate and offer incentives. Everyone appreciates a pat on the back.

The best approach is to make recognizing your employees a priority — throughout the day, not just at the end of the day. You have to delegate. You have to empower. You have to give respect. You have to relate well. Express your expectations to employees and communicate with them, via such methods as rap sessions, anonymous employee surveys, and information — positive only, please — posted on bulletin boards.

One of the greatest motivators is making employees feel that they contribute to your franchise. If they don't feel respected, they'll leave no matter what you pay them. Are you giving people responsibility? Do you recognize and reward good deeds? Do you bounce ideas off employees? Do you let them mentor newer employees? Do you encourage them to voice complaints?

Employees also get energized if you offer them some diversity in their responsibilities. That's a big reason to include cross-training in your training program. If employees feel skilled and confident at their tasks, they'll be more likely to stay on.

Here are some other tips on keeping good employees:

- **Rotate boring and routine jobs.** Job rotation will keep the staff fresh.

- **Be fair.** Don't show favoritism. Nothing is worse for morale than a boss who isn't fair.

- **Allow staff input in developing the schedule.** Give your employees some say in making the schedule. If employees informed you of hours they couldn't work back when you hired them, make sure that you don't pressure them to work those hours after they're on the job. If you have more hours available, and employees want them, give them the additional hours.

  If employees attend school, see if a split shift is better for them. (A *split shift* is when an employee comes to work for a few hours, leaves, and then comes back later to finish the day.)

- **Post the schedule.** Do it at least two weeks in advance. Let employees plan their personal lives.

- **Treat your employees with respect.** Don't allow any employee to be disrespectful to any other employee.

- **Keep employees informed.** Let them know, for example, when you're beginning a new marketing campaign or other promotions.

- **Remove the hassles of the day.** Ask employees which procedures are working for them and which aren't. If possible, change the conditions that are making them miserable.

- **Make their workdays challenging.** But also make the work fun.

- **Provide performance reviews.** Make sure they're timely and frequent and give wage or salary increases.

Obviously, even with your best efforts at retention, you'll probably have some turnover; someone may move or become a stay-at-home mom. Or misconduct, customer complaints, or poor job performance may be so severe that, despite warnings, you'll have to let an employee go. Even if you have a great staff and your turnover has been low, maintain a strong staff-recruiting program. You never know when you may need it.

DAVE'S WISDOM

Service Excellence

Wendy's has a program called Service Excellence. It's real simple. It's about cross-training people, motivating people, and giving people the best service and the best product so they'll come back. In the pick-up window, for example, they're running 100 seconds from ordering to delivering, and they've increased their percent of total restaurant sales coming from the pick-up window from 50 percent to 65 percent of the operation. That's where the gravy is.

Restaurants run so much better when you have incentives for your crew. Wendy's has parties, football tickets, concerts, and so on, and they consistently provide incentives so that when people come to work, it's fast, it's working, everyone's getting things done, it's cross-training, and it's fun.

Fostering a good work environment

Franchisees always talk about making customers happy, which is absolutely a top priority. But if your employees aren't happy, how can your customers be happy? A big step toward employee satisfaction comes from creating a good workplace environment. You can't create a good environment by simply plastering smiley-face stickers on every wall; you have to concentrate on those aspects of your operation that make employees feel they're being treated fairly and safely.

To create this feeling among employees, you have to do three things:

- ✔ Establish and enforce policies on antidiscrimination compliance.
- ✔ Follow the franchisor's safety and security guidelines.
- ✔ Encourage employees to speak up about any of their concerns on these issues.

Ensuring Workplace Safety

You run your location and control your staff. Safety and security is your responsibility, not your franchisor's. Smart franchisors, however, provide you with reams and reams of paper on recommendations for safety and security. You should be looking for this kind of commitment. You also need to review the Occupational Safety and Health Act, which is administered by the Department of Labor's Occupational Safety and Health Administration (OSHA). The act regulates safety and health conditions and may require employers to adopt certain practices to protect workers. All this material may be tedious to read through, but it's worth your time. Preventing mishaps directly corresponds to employee and customer retention — and profitability.

Safety concerns vary by business, of course. But some safety issues are pretty standard, such as properly using the equipment; correctly handling materials; knowing where you store fire extinguishers; and preventing burns, falls, and other accidents. Nobody wants to see an employee or customer fall on a sidewalk that should have been cleared of ice. You should have certain procedures down to an exact science — for example, how often you clean the bathrooms and mop the floors and how to lift heavy objects. In the restaurant business especially, food handling, storage procedures, and cleanliness are major priorities for safety and health reasons. Remember that you want to have happy employees. Well, no one will be happy working hard and long in a dirty place.

Regardless of whether the franchisor gives you guidelines, and regardless of whether it includes comments about safety and security on its field reports to you, operating your business in a safe and secure manner is *your* responsibility, not the franchisor's.

As an employer, you could face a wide range of problems, from employee theft to armed robberies. Find out what your franchisor, other franchisees, and local merchants recommend in terms of alarm systems, closed-circuit TV systems, and door controls. Check with local experts and the police on what you can and should do to make your location safe. Safety and security are your responsibility to your customers, vendors, and staff.

Also, carefully check out employees' backgrounds — to the extent that you're legally able to. Then train your employees to be on high alert. For example, instruct office or store managers to call the police immediately if they see a crime in progress or someone disturbing customers or employees. Educate employees in simple security precautions; for example, advise them to leave a restaurant after dark only if they're accompanied by another worker.

We know this advice sounds like common sense. Still, you need to have security precautions in place and procedures for reporting all crimes.

Chapter 9

Working with Your Franchisor and Fellow Franchisees

*T*his chapter, perhaps more than any other, talks about people. People will give you plenty of directions for operating your franchise. People will look over your shoulder to ensure consistency. And people — lots and lots of people — will make up the franchise team. You need to know how to deal with them and what to expect from them. This chapter provides that information.

Playing by the Rules

Franchisors and franchisees show confidence in each other by signing the franchise agreement and agreeing to work together. But others — the other franchisees in the system — are also part of this bargain. How well you operate has a direct impact on them. If you don't follow the system, your operation is likely to suffer, and you may fail. If you fail, the value they have built up in the goodwill of their businesses is reduced. The concept is really very simple. The whole team is counting on you to play by the rules.

Meeting franchise system standards

When you become a franchisee, good franchisors hope you'll do so with pride. Franchisors are going to show the same pride by drilling into you the chain's standards — at training sessions, during franchisee meetings, in the operations manual, and in franchise newsletters. Hopefully, they'll celebrate those in the system who execute the standards best of all. But, in all cases, franchisors will constantly be emphasizing the importance of standards — all in an effort to maintain the value of the brand and to support the pride everyone has in it.

Maintaining a system you can be proud of requires that everyone meet the system standards — at every franchisee operation and at every company-owned operation.

Violating system standards poses a threat to the system, and franchisors take violations very seriously. So do the franchisees who work hard every day to maintain the quality of their locations.

Violations occur. Most are corrected as soon as the franchisee becomes aware of the problem. If violations continue, most of the time (unless the violation is creating a public hazard or is considered extreme) a *field consultant* (the franchisor's employee assigned to a location) contacts the franchisee. The consultant gives the franchisee the right to fix the situation (or at least counsels him to stop any unapproved actions).

Typically, in mature systems, franchisors offer the franchisees assistance in returning to operating standards. Franchisors usually beef up the oversight of the location to ensure that the franchisee makes the necessary corrections. They also monitor the situation going forward to make sure the violations don't reoccur. This process goes on in every mature franchise system. If the violations continue, though, the remedies included in the franchise agreement kick in, an action that could ultimately terminate the relationship. Nobody benefits if a franchise contract is terminated.

Supporting and watching the system

In franchising, big brother (or sister), is watching. This oversight is for your benefit — and protection — and may take many forms, including those described in the following sections.

Field support staff

The *field staff* — sometimes called field representatives, field consultants, or regional managers — are the real troubleshooters in franchising. They're the members of the franchisor's staff who work directly with franchisees. Field consultants and franchisees must develop a relationship of mutual confidence and respect in order to maintain a positive working relationship.

If Dave were a franchisee

If Dave were a franchisee, he'd expect field consultants to help him, not hurt him. He'd want a field consultant to come in and tell him what's wrong with his restaurant. If he had a problem, he'd want the consultant to help him solve the problem. He'd want the consultant to be professional, and he'd want the consultant to treat his people with respect.

Field consultants are not dictators, and they're not reporters. They don't come in and "write you up."

If Dave had a problem with training, for example, he'd want a consultant to come in and explain what's wrong. That's part of what franchisees pay for. Wendy's franchisees pay 4 percent in royalties (the continuing fee paid to the franchisor that is usually calculated as a percentage of gross sales) to help them become successful.

Of the various names franchisors use to describe their field staff, *field consultant* is the most accurate because the major role of the field staff is to act as a consultant to the franchisee. A field consultant's primary job should be to help franchisees improve the performance of their operations. Field consultants stay in regular contact with franchisees by phone, e-mail, or in person to identify problems, answer questions, and hopefully bring solutions and new ideas directly to the franchisee. In some systems, field consultants are also involved in local training.

The field consultant's job is to conduct regular inspections of the franchisee's location, discuss any deficiencies, and make recommendations for improvements. Perhaps the franchisor's standards are not being met, the staff is not in uniform, or the merchandise displays are empty or dirty. Perhaps the franchisee's sales are down, and the location's payroll is up. The job of the field consultant — in good systems — is to help franchisees improve their performance.

In some systems, field visits are few and far between. Infrequent visits from field consultants are not a badge of honor for those systems, but they may be perfectly in line with the promises made in the franchise agreement. In some systems, every franchisee is visited on a set schedule. Others vary visits depending on a host of factors that may include the franchisor's analysis of the franchisee's financial and operational indicators. In mature systems, the franchisor obtains this information from reports and other information that the franchisee routinely sends (usually electronically), as well as from other sources. Depending on the industry, the ratio of field staff to franchised location could be as low as 1 to 8 or as high as 1 to 100, but the average is probably closer to 1 to 40.

Mystery shoppers

Mystery shoppers are usually employees of companies that specialize in shopping a chain's location and reporting back to the company what the customer experience is really like. Mystery shoppers are used not only in restaurants or retailers; franchisors rely on mystery shoppers to help them evaluate carpet cleaning, haircuts, gas stations, automotive repairs — just about every segment of franchising uses mystery shoppers.

That woman in the red dress may look like the other women in line, but she's really under cover to check out your staff and operations. The mystery shopping company and the franchisor work out a checklist about the shopping experience — and those reports are sent to the franchisor, who then discusses the reports with the franchisees.

To keep it fun, some franchisors have contests and give prizes — including trips — to the staff persons at system locations identified as doing an outstanding job. The hope is that all customers will be treated as if they were mystery shoppers.

Your customers

Have you ever noticed those customer comment cards in the front of a business? Franchisors take customer comments very seriously and work with franchisees to deal with complaints by the customer and to improve their operations. You should use the information you receive from a customer to better your operation because it may be the most important information you'll receive on how well you're really doing.

Some franchise systems' computer software randomly produces a coupon that the customer can use on another visit after they phone a toll-free number and answer a few key questions on the business's performance. These surveys, because they're generated randomly, can provide you with a wealth of information from your average everyday patron.

Fellow franchisees

Your fellow franchisees can also be the eyes and ears of the system. Don't be surprised if they approach you with concerns about how you're operating your business. The biggest enemy to a franchisee is a fellow franchisee down the road who's doing a poor job. Customers may not know and certainly don't care that each location is individually owned. They'll just assume that the product or service is bad all over.

Often a franchisee's best advisor is a more experienced franchisee. After all, franchisees are in the trenches together. Some franchises have "senior franchisees" or assigned mentors whose role is to assist franchisees in certain circumstances. Who better to get advice from than a peer who understands the reality of day-to-day operations and knows the tricks?

On occasion, one franchisee will report another franchisee to the franchisor if he sees that the fellow franchisee is not complying with the system's rules and standards. Franchisees don't think they're interfering in someone else's business. Each unit is part of the whole; they're just protecting their interests.

Franchisees are part of the support team. Look over your own shoulder. Periodically review the operations manual and any training materials to ensure that your business is up to snuff. Ask for help if you need it. The franchisor may not know that you have a problem unless you tell them.

Keep one thing in mind, though: All knowledge and assistance does not flow from the franchisor's well. The franchisor is licensing you a system, not operating your business.

If you need help, you can and should seek professional, outside advice: local accountants to help you improve your record keeping so that you can get a better handle on the business; marketing experts to help you create cross-merchandising opportunities with other merchants in the industry or to help you develop ways to target new customers; mystery shoppers who can tell you how well you're really doing — on a more frequent basis than the franchisor. Attend management classes at the local university. You can also send your manager and assistant managers to class — after all, they're running the show when you're not there. *Remember:* The responsibility for execution excellence is yours, not the franchisor's.

Attempting to change the system

Ideally, every system should encourage ideas from franchisees. After all, franchisees are the ones on the front lines, and they may see ways to tweak the system.

Newer chains may be most receptive and may say yes immediately or fine-tune the suggestion further before rolling it out system-wide. Older systems also embrace great ideas but typically use caution before rolling them out because they've refined their operating systems over a number of years. They may conduct focus groups to see how customers will perceive the change and test it for ease of preparation, cost, and other factors in their test facilities long before they bring it to market. Even then, they launch it conservatively in a few test markets before introducing it to all the locations.

DAVE'S WISDOM

The well of innovation

Many of Wendy's best ideas have come from the franchisees and from the franchisee advisory council (FAC). The Wendy's FAC meets regularly to discuss issues that affect the franchisee community. Members of the FAC are a sounding board for changes or improvements that Wendy's plans for its stores. For Wendy's to be successful, everyone must work together toward a common goal: to serve the best-tasting hamburgers in the business.

Franchisors want consistency, but they also should have flexibility in certain areas. Franchisors should develop a partnership relationship with their franchisees. (Franchisors may not be partners in the legal sense, but they should respect their franchisees' advice. Still, they're the senior partner, and they need to make the final decisions.) Franchisors have to remember that sometimes, to buy their franchise, franchisees have signed over their houses, taken out loans, put their kids' futures in jeopardy, and so on — so they must recognize that franchisees are a big partner in the business. Wendy's may have a basic menu, but different items are added from time to time, many of these proposed by franchisees.

TIP

You have a much better shot at having your changes accepted if the new idea improves the system, fortifies the brand, doesn't infringe on the system's goal of uniformity, and enhances a franchisee's profitability. You improve your chances for success if you present your proposal in a professional manner and garner the support of other franchisees and your field consultant before approaching the franchisor. Some franchisors have new product committees as a subset of their franchisee advisory council. In those systems, talk to members of the committee to determine what criteria they use for recommending approval of new products and services.

If you have what you think is a great idea, speak up. But don't be insulted if the franchisor says no. A franchisor has to look at the overall system and how it serves the customer. Your great idea may not fit into the overall scheme of things. Good franchisors are open to ideas that come from franchisees, but the franchisor's job is to make the hard decisions — and sometimes the decision is no. If, however, the idea is approved, most franchisors consider that improvement their property and reserve the right to use it in the rest of the system — without paying the franchisee any compensation.

WARNING!

Be wary of franchisors who willy-nilly approve all suggestions, especially those that compromise product lines and quality standards. That lack of discretion is evidence of a weak system and can destroy the basic concept you're buying into.

Building a Relationship with Your Franchisor

In franchising, as in any relationship, you're bound to have ups and downs. The key is to be part of a system in which the seesaw tips toward the higher end.

 We're not going to fool you: The love-hate relationship between the franchisee and the franchisor can turn nasty. You need to check out any past or present litigation involving the franchisor. The franchisor must disclose this history in Item 3 of the Franchise Disclosure Document (FDD; see Chapter 6). If the franchisor has been involved in a number of lawsuits, check out the lawsuits before you buy into that franchise system.

Being a team player

If you sign a franchise agreement, you're committing to a relationship for a long term. You're promising to uphold your end of the bargain (pay royalties, abide by the operations manual, and so on), and the franchisor is also promising to meet certain obligations (support services, brand identity, and so on). That's the relationship drawn on paper by the lawyers.

The real relationship begins from the very first moment you meet the franchisor and continues through initial training, the grand opening, field consultant visits, phone calls, e-mails, newsletters, continuing training, updates to the operations manuals, and annual meetings. Communication is a two-way street. Taking part in communication with your franchisor keeps you current, keeps the relationship fresh and open, and helps you move forward as the system evolves.

Base the relationship with your franchisor on mutual trust and respect. Don't worry if your relationship grows into a friendship — a franchise relationship is a long one, and working with people you like is always a good situation.

Some chains are so convinced that personality contributes to a successful relationship that they compile behavioral profiles on franchisees. So, don't be surprised if franchisors put you on the proverbial couch. Their assessments usually are based on the profiles of top-performing franchisees. (Yes, some franchisors may reject your franchise application if you don't meet their preferred profile.) The franchisors aren't therapist wannabes.

There's no "I" in Wendy's

Wendy's starts with "We," and "We" can do almost anything together.

Wendy's has staff who have been with the company for 25 years, and they still look at the company as a team. Everyone discovers what works best together. Nobody's an expert. They have a system; they know that we have a good product, and — if franchisees do it right — they know that the concept works. But they always have to ask, "How can we improve? How can we make the system better?" Wendy's is not unique in franchising. Great franchisors don't have I's — they have We's.

The best franchisors know what it takes to be effective in their systems, and they want to approve only prospects that will fit the system's culture. Scott Haner, VP from Yum! Brands, the franchisor of KFC, Pizza Hut, Taco Bell, and other brands, notes that embracing the Yum! culture and the focus on its Customer Mania philosophy is critical to long-term success. "We're talking about a working relationship that lasts 20 years, longer than many marriages in today's society. It's important that both parties have similar sets of values for the franchisor-franchisee relationship to be most productive." If the franchisor knows how you tick, it can best make a match. The support staff will also be in a better position to help you.

Being a team player usually tops franchisors' most-wanted list of franchisee traits, because they want you to be willing to abide by the premise of the ongoing franchise relationship. The franchisor is the coach — the designer of the plays, the person responsible for the whole team. You're the superstar — the one who makes all the plays work, the person whom the rest of the franchise team relies on to perform well. This basic relationship — in which everyone depends on everyone else — doesn't change even as you mature as a franchisee.

Don't overdose on support and expect the franchisor to manage your business from afar. The responsibility for your success or failure is yours, not the franchisor's.

Getting what you need from the relationship

As a consumer, you want to get what you pay for. We all do. So, even though, as a franchisee, you aren't really a consumer or customer, whether your business launches slowly or fires up like a rocket (we hope the latter is the case), you want to feel like you got your money's worth each time you mail your royalty check.

You aren't generally paying for services when you give your franchisor its royalty payment each week or month. What you really get for your royalties is the right to use the franchisor's trade name and membership in its system, factors that should translate into brand identity and consistency. If you believe that the franchisor's ultimate success is tied to yours and that of the other franchisees, then the services you receive are as much a benefit to the franchisor as they are to you.

As franchisees mature in a franchise system, their need for support changes; they certainly shouldn't need the level of hand-holding in year five that they received in year one. What doesn't change is that, every week or every month, they write their franchisor a check for their continuing royalty payments. And, as sales go up, usually so does the size of the checks. This could be a formula for dissatisfaction for the franchisee — they need less support as they mature in the system, yet the size of the check is bigger. They can ask, "What's the franchisor done for me lately?"

Some franchisors' royalty schemes make adjustments with lower royalty rates for franchisees with higher sales or multiple locations.

The hard answer you need to understand as a franchisee is that the fees you pay to your franchisor generally allow you to use its brand name and marks and gain access to its operating system as provided for in the franchise agreement. Unless that agreement provides for field support or other services, you may not be entitled to receive them. And, although most franchisors provide great service for the general well being of their franchisees, what your franchisor has done for you lately is allow you to continue using its brand and operating systems per the franchise agreement. That's the bargain you agreed to, and that's what you paid for.

Mature franchisees understand that they've prospered in the system in part because the franchisor is working in partnership with them. Franchisees may not like to admit it, but they may not be in the successful position they're in without the system, the brand, and the support they received from being a member of the franchise.

Pause every once in a while and look at your ongoing relationship with your franchisor. Ask yourself, for example: Is the franchisor telling me what I need to know? Is the franchisor listening to what I have to say? Am I getting what I need? Am I following the procedures and meeting the standards of the system? Am I available when the field consultant wants to meet with me, and have I established a good relationship with the consultant and the franchisor's headquarters staff? The franchise relationship should be give-and-take.

DAVE'S WISDOM

Timing is everything

Dave really believed in research and development. He also believed in letting the Wendy's organization take the time to do things properly. The timing would have been wrong for a lot of products that he would've rolled out.

For example, he would've rolled out their new bun six months earlier. But doing so probably wouldn't have been right because it wouldn't have been the best product they could've provided to the franchisees and may have raised their labor costs. So he let the R&D people do what they do best — work on improving it. You have to let the organization work.

Wendy's is totally committed to research and development, commits money to it, and has done so for years. Franchisors today who don't look at R&D as a major part of the future of franchising aren't focused on keeping their companies competitive. When Wendy's works on new products or product enhancements, they get all the other departments involved to understand how it affects the entire system. Wendy's includes the folks in charge of operations and training, the people responsible for sourcing and purchasing new equipment and ingredients, the people who will plan the marketing strategy, and the accountants who can explain what the financial impact on the system will be. The franchisee advisory council is involved in the process, too.

How can you tell whether your franchisor is looking out for your future needs? Ask yourself some simple questions about the franchisor's focus:

- ✔ Is the franchisor's staff doing research and development into new products and services?

- ✔ Is the franchisor working on new ad campaigns?

- ✔ Is the franchisor ahead of the technology curve to keep you competitive?

- ✔ Is the franchisor examining opportunities to expand business through e-commerce?

- ✔ Could the franchisor turn on a dime in response to changing customer demands and market conditions?

- ✔ Does the franchisor have an active franchisee advisory committee, empowered to help improve the business and look at new opportunities?

- ✔ Are franchisees involved in strategic planning for the franchisor?

A franchisor can't afford to be complacent about the system and the services it provides to its franchisees. In today's competitive environment, franchisors must be the active shepherds of their brands — committed by their actions and their resources to improving the competitive performance of their franchise systems.

The following sections discuss a few support services that franchisors typically provide.

Research and development

Great franchisors keep their franchisees one step ahead of the competition.

One function of a good research and development (R&D) department is to understand changes in the market, see opportunities for new products and services the franchisee can sell to the public, and introduce those new products and services to the marketplace.

Most franchisors use their company-owned stores as test locations before they try out new products or methods on their franchisees. Others, working with their franchisee advisory councils, also test new products and procedures with their top-performing franchisees.

In launching new products or services, good franchisors typically go through an elaborate process that includes the following:

- Gathering consumer research
- Examining other industries and competitors for ideas for new products and services or other uses for existing products and services
- Seeking franchisee input
- Lining up suppliers needed for the new product or service
- Testing products or services in test facilities to determine ease of preparation or assembly, ability to achieve consistency, time required to deliver the product or service, and so on
- Determining what existing equipment or technology will be used and what new equipment will be needed
- Developing training materials on the new product or service
- Determining inventory requirements
- Planning advertising and promotions
- Verifying economic viability
- Testing in company-owned or franchisee-run facilities

Even great franchises begin to lose market share when the public gets tired of their products, their look, or their services — or when the public just wants something new. They also lose market share when competitors introduce new products and services that are simply better or are sold in a way that customers prefer — including via e-commerce. Although many new products and improvements come straight from the franchisees (after all, they're on the firing line with consumers every day), the responsibility to keep the concept fresh rests with the franchisor.

Office support

At some chains, your royalty payments buy nitty-gritty back-office support. For example, some chains maintain a toll-free hot line for your customers or divert phone calls placed to your local franchise to a main switchboard. This way, a person — not a machine — answers the phone when you're out, making you appear much bigger than a one-man show. Other franchisors also take care of billing customers and handling employee payroll. Such administrative services are most commonly found in commercial/residential cleaning and employment franchises.

Other perks

Most modern franchisors have moved away from an a la carte–type support system where you pay for services as you go. The reason for this change is obvious: The franchisee who most needs the service, such as additional field support, may not be willing or able to pay for it.

Don't assume that all types of support are included in your royalty payments. Additional fees are common in many systems for a host of things, including further training of managers and employees, reservation systems (for hotel or car-rental franchises), proprietary software, marketing, and special field support.

At times, you may think that the franchisor should offer you more support. You may expect additional service because the franchise salesperson told you to expect it. The key is to look at your original franchise agreement (see Chapter 6). It lays out in black and white the franchisor's obligations. Strong franchisors, however, often go beyond their spelled-out obligations, doing more than they have to. In practice, the concept is really very simple: A franchisor's job is to help franchisees be successful.

The franchise agreement is the key to understanding the obligations of the franchisor and the franchisee. Just because one party to the bargain wants more services, or doesn't live up to the contract, the other party isn't obligated to perform those additional services or ignore the first party's contractual requirements. If you're getting more services from your franchisor than what the agreement requires, say thank you. Such support shows that your franchisor cares.

Dealing with Change

Time for a wake-up call. Does everything with your franchisor seem same old, same old? Or has something changed while you were snoozing? Just as people pass from infancy to adolescence to adulthood to old age, franchises go through stages, too. These phases can greatly affect the franchisee-franchisor relationship — for better or worse.

Changes in a company's growth, financial state, support staff, and even competition all can contribute to subtle or blatant swings in support services, communication, operating requirements, and other aspects of your relationship.

When the system's size or focus changes

Regarding a chain's size or focus, consider this: If a franchisor adds more and more units nationally and even internationally — or even begins to offer another type of franchise or begins an e-commerce business — but doesn't increase staff or services, the support you'll get from the franchisor will suffer.

Consider this example: You joined a franchise system that sells a product manufactured by your franchisor. Since the beginning of your relationship, your field consultant has visited your retail store each month, spending four to six hours with you, going over marketing, operations, scheduling, and other important matters. Then the company begins to offer franchises internationally, and your field consultant is assigned the added responsibility of overseeing the development and support of locations in a country you can't even pronounce. The consultant visits you quarterly rather than monthly and spends only 30 to 40 minutes with you before rushing off to another franchisee.

Here's another example — same franchisee, same system: Instead of going international, the franchisor begins franchising another product or diverts attention to the development of an e-commerce business or buys or starts another franchise system. The franchisor uses the training, operations, and field personnel from your franchise system to support the development of the new product or the new franchise system. Same results: The support you came to rely on is no longer there.

Read your franchise agreement. You probably were never promised weekly or monthly visits that lasted four to six hours; you just grew accustomed to them. Still, a reduction in the frequency and length of meeting with your field consultant is no reason to be complacent. You may want revenue from e-commerce activities, but you may not legally be entitled to it (see the next section, "When conflicts occur").

In looking at a franchisor, don't be overly impressed by its entrance into foreign markets or that new store that just opened on the other side of the country. Although a growing chain adds to the brand's value, it doesn't necessarily contribute much to what you should be interested in: franchisor support for your location.

Ideally, as a franchise chain grows, the size of the support organization also should grow. For example, if the optimum ratio of field consultants is 1 to every 30 franchisees in a system, and the franchisor doesn't add a new field consultant to service new franchisees, the number of units that that field consultant is responsible for will increase, and the consultant's ability to service each franchisee will decrease. Higher density of units also means that field consultants can get from store to store more easily. And, typically, multi-unit franchisees often need less hand-holding anyway.

Technology, however, can allow a field consultant to handle additional locations effectively. Many mature franchisors use cellphones; e-mail; automated sales reporting; Web-based training, distance learning, and CD-ROM-based training; videoconferencing; and so on to make their field consultants more efficient and effective.

But, absent changes in technology, as the number of locations increases, franchisors should add field consultants so that the ratios stay basically the same. That's franchising at its best.

When conflicts occur

Smart franchisors work hard every minute of every day to forge lasting partnerships with their franchisees. Franchisees need to have confidence in their franchisors, and vice versa. The recipe doesn't get any more wholesome than this: honesty, integrity, and open communications.

Communication has to flow in both directions to work. You may have a problem and be angry that the franchisor isn't helping you. Does the franchisor even know that you have a problem? If something is on your mind, call your field consultant. If you've spoken to your field consultant, and he hasn't taken care of your problem, call your franchisor's regional or headquarters personnel. Franchisors may not know something is broken unless you tell them.

Imagine this scenario: Despite your best efforts, sales have been down for the past two months, and you're looking at a potential cash problem in the coming few months. You're upset and worried about meeting your financial commitments to the bank, to your suppliers, and to your franchisor. Don't wait until you have no money in the bank and are in default to ask for help. Call your franchisor and ask for advice. But don't demand that the franchisor waive your royalties simply because you have a cash problem. The franchisor didn't sign up to be your banker or your guarantor.

What franchisors can do is look at your operations, see whether they can find the problem, determine whether a quick fix may work, help you prioritize your cash flow, lend you some other support, and maybe — but not often — work with you on a temporary deferral on your royalty.

When changes occur that affect you negatively, speak to your franchisor. Find out whether the change is permanent or temporary. See whether you can work out a compromise position that satisfies both of your needs. Talk to the other franchisees who are affected. Talk to the leadership of the franchise advisory council. Often, when franchisees come together to talk to a franchisor about a problem, the franchisor and the franchisees work it out together. Sometimes, however, they don't, and that's often when the relationship between the parties begins to experience difficulties.

Although working through the chain of command is the best way, don't be afraid to voice your concerns to a higher level if you've received less than legendary service or don't get a satisfactory response. Good franchisors need to know when their field consultants and other personnel are doing a good job and when they aren't responding or performing. Also, consider putting your serious concerns in writing. Your written communications don't need to be nasty or threatening, but a letter often helps you to convince your franchisor of its staff's inadequate performance.

Open communication between you and the franchisor may build your relationship and possibly avert or quash any friction. Your goal should be to resolve any disagreements in the least costly, least time-consuming, and least adversarial ways if you want to continue being a franchisee.

Disputes sometimes occur that the franchisor and franchisee can't work out. Before going to blows in a lawsuit, many franchisors require that (as provided for in the franchise agreement) franchisees first meet with them and an impartial mediator. Some franchisors, instead of going to outside mediation, set up internal mediation units that include other franchisees, and some appoint an *ombudsman* (an employee of the franchisor who is paid to be an advocate for the franchisees) to look into disputes.

Several franchisors in the United States have joined the National Franchise Mediation Program, which is a formal mediation program endorsed by the International Franchise Association (IFA).

Reaching Out to Your Fellow Franchisees

Your fellow franchisees are a big part of the team, and as the newest recruit, you want to hear their take on the game, the coach, and the other players. Think of existing franchisees as the live version of an operations manual; they live and breathe the system every day, so they know what playing by the franchise system's rules is like.

Go to the franchisees

If you came to Dave and wanted to know about Wendy's, he'd tell you to go talk to their franchisees. Let them tell you the story of Wendy's. Let them tell you whether Wendy's is doing its job as a franchisor.

In the early, early days of Wendy's, when the chain was just a handful of restaurants, Dave put prospective franchisees on a bus and drove them to an existing franchise in the city. He let them see all the lines, the store, and the lunch business — and he talked to them. After the lunch rush was over, the franchisee opened up the books and showed the group how much that particular franchise made. This was a real, live, working restaurant. And visiting this operating location — this living laboratory — was the fastest and most truthful way to sell a franchise to a prospective franchisee. Prospective franchisees saw not only the success but also how hard a franchisee really has to work.

Building a relationship with other franchisees goes beyond simply tapping their knowledge. They're also great sources of inspiration because they usually have confronted the same issues you may be facing. Finding out the success routines they use to drive execution excellence and how someone else has successfully dealt with a similar problem is not only helpful but also inspirational.

Franchisees who share a geographic area often get together to chat about common issues, including marketing, spending, training, or operations concerns. Good franchisors encourage this type of communication. When staff recruiting is difficult, they often work together by getting a booth at a local job fair. Need a cup of sugar — or is it a case of carpet cleaner? That's what neighbors are for. Franchisees get together to plan local promotions, create local buying cooperatives, or just to update each other on what is and isn't working in their businesses. In short, other franchisees provide a valuable support network.

The IFA has established a monthly networking group for franchisees, franchisors, and suppliers. These meetings are held in cities around the United States. The great thing about these meetings is that you get to meet franchisees and franchisors from not only your own system but other franchise systems. It's another place to build a support network of franchisees and learn from them. Even if a franchisee is not in your industry, they face many of the same challenges you face regarding staffing, retention, and employee motivation. Many of the suppliers who come to the meetings can also provide you with advice. Contact the IFA at 202-628-8000, speak to someone in membership support, and ask whether a networking group meets in your city.

Even if you don't make an effort to reach out to your fellow franchisees, they'll find you. You'll meet at regional meetings, annual conventions, franchisee advisory council or association meetings, perhaps even on the Internet, or maybe on the intranet the franchisor has set up for the system.

How do you go about getting to know other people who share your franchise name? Most franchisors will be happy to provide you with a list of your fellow franchisees. Ask for it. You should also attend your regional, area, or convention meetings, which is the easiest way to meet franchisees you may not know and a good way to see old friends again.

Joining advisory councils and associations

Franchisee advisory councils and franchisee associations (don't fret, we explain the difference) give order to the franchisee universe. They're communication vehicles — among franchisees, and between franchisees and franchisor. As a franchisee, you want representation. And you want a system that welcomes quality input.

Franchisee advisory councils

A *franchisee advisory council* is a committee established by the franchisor and composed of franchisee representatives. It may also have representatives from the franchisor-operated units.

Its purpose is purely advisory. Here are some of the ways a franchisor can use the council:

- To bounce new ideas off franchisees before rolling them out system-wide
- To solicit suggestions on improvements to products, services, and system support
- To review marketing and advertising strategies
- To assist the franchisor in looking at conflicts in the system

Franchisees can use the council to influence the company's direction, network with peers, and voice complaints. In a council, franchisees are heard more loudly and clearly than they're heard as individuals. Even if you don't sit on a council, you can raise your points by contacting one of the council's members, who can then speak for you.

Wendy's set up its franchisee advisory council because everyone has a role to play, and the franchisee's role is to give Wendy's guidance and relay what it needs to do better.

The structures of franchisee advisory councils vary from one franchise system to another:

- ✔ In some systems, the franchisees and franchisor jointly establish a council and agree on the membership, meeting dates, voting rights, and other rules. In other systems, the franchisor establishes the council and draws up the bylaws.

- ✔ Some franchisors pick up the cost of the franchisee's attending council meetings, some pick up a portion of the cost, and others pick up none. No hard-and-fast rules exist.

- ✔ Some councils have franchisor-operated locations represented; others don't.

- ✔ Some councils have franchisees elected by their peers, others are appointed by the franchisor, and some have a combination of both.

Often, a franchisor will establish criteria on who may sit on the council. If a franchisee is in default, for example, he's usually not invited to the big table.

Councils often spin off other committees, such as an advertising committee that provides input into advertising decisions and a buying committee that looks at cooperatives or other joint efforts for purchasing products and services for the system.

When you're speaking to the franchisees of a system, ask about their views on the advisory council. What does it do in their system? Do they get reports on the council's activities? Get the name of the head of the council or the local representative and give them a call. You want to understand if the council is well run and empowered by the franchisor to have a meaningful role in the system.

Franchisee associations

Unlike franchisee advisory councils, *franchisee associations* are usually independent organizations, made up of dues-paying franchisees who come together when no franchisee advisory council exists or the council is not viewed as adequately promoting their interests. They may function like a council, but franchisee associations set their own rules, membership requirements, and agendas. Membership dues usually fund them, whereas the franchisor more often than not picks up the tab for its franchise advisory council.

Historically, many franchisee associations were started because of a systemic crisis. For example, the franchisor may have been on the verge of bankruptcy or introduced a radical new product or service into the system without adequate testing. Or a change in management may have occurred, or the franchisor may have dramatically revised the terms of its new and renewal franchise agreements. Franchisee associations were also frequently formed on the verge of system-wide litigation.

Today, many franchisors have recognized that an independent association is not a bad idea and may make a positive contribution to the system, as long as its leadership acts responsibly and listens to the legitimate concerns of its constituency. Although franchisors have no legal duty to recognize a franchisee association — like a company would recognize a union — many franchisors have cautiously developed procedures to include the associations as part of the process to maintain and grow their systems. In some systems — Holiday Inn and Sylvan Learning, for example — the franchisee associations are granted specific rights under the franchise agreements. Holiday Inn, for example, has agreed to run certain proposed changes past its franchisee association; the Sylvan Learning franchisee association owns 50 percent of an entity that controls that system's marketing fund.

For a franchise system to have both a franchisee advisory council and an independent franchisee association is not unheard of. Moreover, the lines between a franchisee association and a franchisee advisory council are not always clear-cut. Some groups have elements of both types of organizations.

Being number one in a class of one

All this concern about interacting with other franchisees is well and good. But what if you're it?

When you're the first franchisee in a new chain, you don't have another franchisee to check with about a franchisor's follow-through — or anything else, for that matter.

Some buyers find being number one exciting, anticipating a great surge in their franchise's value as the chain grows.

You have reason to be cautious, however. Just because a company has a Franchise Disclosure Document (FDD; see Chapter 6) doesn't make it qualified — in a business sense — to be a franchisor. (Chapter 14 discusses franchisability.)

Without the input of other franchisees, you need to scrutinize the company much more carefully, because the network you're joining — for the foreseeable future — may be just you.

If the management of the franchise system you're looking at also operates another franchise system, feel out the franchisees in the other system to at least get a sense of the company's management.

If you're thinking about being the first franchisee, you need to weigh the potential risks against the potential rewards. Support services may be lacking, systems may still be evolving, and buying cooperatives to give you lower prices may not be available. In fact, almost everything the franchisor will know about franchise system operation and franchisee performance will come from working with you. Unless your franchisor has done its homework and is experienced, you're about to pay for the privilege of being a guinea pig.

But as the first franchisee, you may be able to get your pick of location, negotiate a better franchise agreement, and get concessions that subsequent franchisees won't get.

You may want to consider a form of a prenuptial agreement. Part of what you're expecting is that the franchisor will grow and you'll be part of a franchise system — with all the benefits. But what happens if, a year from now, you're still alone or if, in five years, just you and one other franchisee are in operation? Not all new franchise systems grow — in fact, based on our experience, many don't. Negotiate a walk-away clause that gives you the option to leave the system before your franchise term is finished if the franchisor can't grow the franchise system. Pick a number — a good one is the number that the franchise salesperson has been telling you the system will grow to during the next year or two. Have your franchise attorney discuss other options with you.

Being a franchisee of a new system is a tossup. (Dave was an early franchisee of Kentucky Fried Chicken, and it worked out for him.) You may be getting in on the ground floor of a great opportunity, or you may be joining the crew of the *Andrea Doria.* (Everybody uses the *Titanic* as a metaphor for disaster; we thought that, as franchise executives, we should be more innovative.)

Chapter 10

Attracting and Keeping Customers

*Y*ou're probably familiar with the movie *Field of Dreams,* in which a starry-eyed Midwesterner transforms a cornfield into a baseball field so that Shoeless Joe Jackson can come back and play ball. Despite skeptics, the farmer believes "If you build it, they will come."

We bet you have that same twinkle in your eye. And that's great. Optimism is a necessary ingredient if you want to have success. But you have to build a foundation for your business to be successful. You have to fill your stadium — regardless of whether it's built on a concrete pavement in New York, on farmland in Iowa, or on the Left Bank in Paris.

This chapter explains how to attract customers in the first place and then how to give them a winning experience so they turn into real fans.

We begin with a few definitions. Many people use the words *marketing* and *advertising* interchangeably, but they mean different things. The savvy business owner knows the difference:

✔ **Marketing:** This is the big picture of selling your products and services. It involves all aspects of getting a product into the buyers' hands, which are often referred to as the four *P*'s: *product* (having the right products and the right quantity of products available to meet consumer demand), *price* (discount, competitive, or premium), *promotion* (getting your offer and message to consumers), and *place* (distribution and delivery to the customer).

✔ **Advertising:** A paid, non-personal communication that attempts to persuade, inform, or create an image. Advertising messages are distributed to consumers through various media (television, radio, newspaper, magazines, direct mail, Internet, and out of home).

Creating an Effective Marketing Plan

Common sense tells you that customers won't show up at your door unless they know you're there. A marketing method can be as simple — and as cost-free — as mentioning your new franchise to your golf buddies, former co-workers, or Grandma Frieda, who tells the women at the bridge game, who tell their hairdressers, who tell their clients, and so on. On the other end, a marketing plan can be as outrageous — and as costly — as parading a cavalcade of elephants draped with your company's banner throughout town. But to be successful, marketing has to be targeted to the right audience, planned in a way that the audience will see it, and made cost-effective so you can sustain it.

Successful marketing campaigns are a unique blend of science and art. They present the right product to the right audience in the right manner at the right time. They require research, planning, and creativity.

Here are some suggestions for developing an effective marketing plan:

- **Do your homework.** Learn everything you can about your product, your concept, your customers, your marketplace, and especially your competition.

- **Create an offer that features the attributes of your product that are in the most demand.** If you offer a deal emphasizing the features and benefits that your primary customers want the most, you provide them with an incentive to buy that is too good to refuse.

- **Create an advertising and promotion message.** Create a message that speaks directly to your target customers and clearly defines who you are and what you're offering with a sense of excitement. If your franchisor uses an advertising or marketing agency, those who work on your business must thoroughly understand your concept, your market position, and your goals and be able to create and communicate an effective message to your target customers.

- **Make sure to properly deliver your message to your audience.** Messages may be delivered through traditional media, including TV, radio, print, out of home (billboards and so on), and direct mail, or through community involvement, sponsorships, and public relations activities. Which method(s) you select depends on your concept, your offer, and your message. *Remember:* What works for one franchise may not work for another.

- **Keep your name in front of consumers.** Television is still the medium with the most impact — combining sight, sound, and motion with great entertainment value. Studies show that an average consumer has to see a TV commercial at least three or four times before having any recollection of the message. (Because consumers watch a variety of programming, your commercial must run many, many times to ensure that your target audience sees it three times.) Other media require even greater frequency. Use a combination of media in order to reach your target audience most cost-effectively.

✔ **Select media you can afford to use with adequate frequency.** Consider the cost of producing the commercial or ad and how much money you will have left to actually run your ad. A print campaign run every week in a local paper is more effective than a TV commercial that runs only a few times or late at night when your target audience is asleep.

✔ **Talk only to people who can buy your product.** We don't want you to be rude, but remember, broadcast media cover vast geographic areas. If your customers come from no more than 5 miles around your location, paying to advertise to a wider audience is a waste of valuable ad dollars, which advertising types call *waste circulation*. Talking frequently to those people who can benefit from your message is certainly much more effective.

✔ **Pool your resources with other franchisees.** By combining advertising dollars, you can afford a stronger advertising plan and get more bang for the buck.

✔ **Check out local media discounts.** As a local advertiser, you may be eligible for local advertising rates that aren't available to large, national advertisers.

✔ **Create cross-selling opportunities by aligning your business with a complementary business in your community**. Make sure that business shares the same target audience and its business values are in alignment with yours so that your cross-selling efforts don't backfire.

✔ **Consider business-to-business partnerships.** Most retail- and/or consumer-based companies focus their marketing efforts on their core customers, which makes all the sense in the world. The opportunity that many of these companies overlook is the formation of business-to-business partnerships that allow them ultimately to reach more of their core consumers faster. For example, Budget Blinds formed strong relationships with real estate agents. The real estate agents act as an additional sales force to market the Budget Blinds brand through the distribution of gift certificates to their clientele. The cost to do this is merely the production of the actual gift certificates; the return on investment compared to other forms of advertising is tremendous!

✔ **Monitor your results.** Do more of what works, and change what isn't producing the results you want.

✔ **Become a spokesperson to market your product or service.** Making a personal connection with customers strengthens the business. So the more you become identified with your company in your local community, the better off you'll be. (Someone may even ask for your autograph!) Check with your franchisor before you hire an outside spokesperson. This is the type of thing the franchisor may not want you to do unless they know and can check on that spokesperson's background.

Brand marketing often boils down to dollars and cents. Franchisees of larger chains gain an edge because their collective advertising dollars can support national ad campaigns. Smaller chains have to work harder because they lack the financial muscle. In either case, you, as a franchisee, have to do your part, too.

Evaluating National and Local Advertising Strategies

Don't worry if you're not the creative type. That's where franchisors come in; they'll help get the word out. Many chains spearhead regional and national advertising campaigns, organize advertising cooperatives with franchisees in your area, and provide a wealth of marketing materials. At a bare minimum, franchisors should offer marketing guidelines and suggestions — if not the materials themselves — to help with your own local advertising efforts.

Dawn Lawin, president of Hot Dish Advertising, states, "There is a common misperception that the brand image developed by the franchisor does not work in a particular market. The reality is that a different strategy may need to be employed to reach your target audience. However, the brand image should be one and the same."

When you look at advertising, divide it into national and local levels. We discuss the national picture first.

The franchisor's national ad campaign: Your fee dollars at work

Life would be easier if all advertising contributions worked the same way in every franchise system. Instead, what's likely is that you'll be bound in some way to contribute some dough.

Many franchisors — especially large ones — administer system advertising funds. They most commonly charge a national or system ad or brand fee based on a percentage of sales or revenues, ranging from less than 1 percent to 10 percent. Some franchisors charge a flat dollar amount or a fee based on each transaction; others don't impose any ad fees, or they collect only a regional/local fee. The requirements and recommendations often depend on a chain's size and industry. Make sure to ask the franchisor about your obligations and review them in the franchise agreement. And talk to other franchisees about the franchisor's approach, the effectiveness of the chain's campaigns, and the franchisees' individual marketing strategies.

Not all advertising funds operate the same way. Their structure, including decision-making power, could greatly affect the end result — and your bottom line. Ideally, franchisees should have input. Some companies set up national marketing/ad committees or councils, most commonly made up of franchisee and franchisor representatives. In other cases, franchisors make all the decisions. Funds can really get a boost when the system's vendors and suppliers also contribute. Consider whether your franchisor has that kind of clout.

Look for some safeguards to ensure that you're getting value for your money. The franchisor should use the advertising fund only for the purposes that it states. For example, if the fund's purpose is to market the brand, it shouldn't be used to recruit franchisees. However, because the franchisor is administering the fund and may have personnel working on the marketing, most franchise agreements allow the franchisor to charge the fund for its administrative costs, including fees paid to advertising agencies and public relations firms. You should be aware of how much and what kinds of administrative expenses the franchisor is charging to the fund. Also, if the franchisor is operating company-owned locations, do those locations contribute to the fund just as the franchisees do? You would hope so, but not all of them do.

Many franchisors don't provide audited financial statements to their franchisees on their advertising funds. Many don't provide even an unaudited report unless the franchisee requests it. Often, the request must be in writing. Read your franchise agreement carefully to understand what your franchisor is obligated to provide to you.

Be aware that franchisor policies can change. In their disclosure documents and franchise agreements, some franchisors specify an advertising contribution, but in practice, they may suspend collection (usually because of the chain's small size). Others reserve the right to impose an advertising fee and fund at some later date. The agreement should state the exact or maximum fee and the conditions upon which the fund can be established or changed. If the mandatory fees are described only as "reasonable" — or worse, not described at all — beware: You may find yourself in a potential bottomless pit. Franchisors may also ask franchisees from time to time to voluntarily boost their contributions or shift the national/local allocation. To protect yourself, look for fee caps and majority voting requirements should the franchisor want to increase your advertising contributions.

When dealing with advertising issues and budgets, use the checklist (CD1001) on the CD-ROM to make sure you ask all the right questions.

Times change, and so do franchise systems. When systems first start, franchisors often establish an advertising fee structure that turns out to be too small. Then they often need to go to their franchisees and request that they voluntarily increase their advertising contributions. The ad fund is set up for the benefit of the system. If the franchisor requests that you increase your contribution — and has a good case for making the request — work with your other franchisees to do so. Make sure, though, that if you're increasing your contribution, the company-owned locations are increasing theirs as well.

Getting in on the ground floor

Some chains don't have a system or national advertising fund because they don't have enough units to make national, or even regional, advertising efficient. Remember that the science of advertising is getting the right message to the right audience. Reaching an audience beyond your geographic or demographic profile is a wasted effort. People will travel only a certain distance to buy your product — no matter how good your offer. And people outside your target demographic group are unlikely to purchase as well — not many teenagers have a need for carpet-cleaning supplies.

If your chain isn't large enough to need an ad fund, stay tuned — you can still buy prime time on a local basis. And your franchisor may establish a fund as the need arises.

Local advertising options

Now we get to the local scene. Here's your opportunity to strut your stuff.

Often, a franchisor requires or recommends a level of local advertising expenditure — again, either a flat amount or a percentage of sales or revenue. It may organize — and you may be required to join — regional or local advertising cooperatives among franchise-owned and company-owned units. Pooling local money enables you to afford bigger buys on radio, TV, out of home, print, direct mail, and so on.

Pooling also helps to keep a consistent message in front of consumers. Imagine 15 franchisees in your city, each advertising a different offer in a different manner, as opposed to everyone's advertising sending the same message. Which approach does more to promote the brand?

Before you do your own thing, try to be objective and understand the importance of staying within your franchisor's policies. Do your materials maintain brand identity? Are you confusing customers by sending a message that's different from the national campaign? Does your campaign really sell your product or service? Can you afford to create new materials instead of using those provided by your franchisor? Spending local dollars to create advertising means you have less to spend on advertising time. Make sure that the local ad you want to make is worth the cost of making it.

In essence, the sky's the limit in promoting your franchise in your own market.

Most franchisors require some form of approval over ads that franchisees create. Check with your franchisor about the system's policy.

Here are some suggestions on how to promote your franchise:

- **Sponsor a Little League team.** Provide T-shirts with your name on the back. (Your parents probably still have your first Little League shirt in the attic!)

- **Reward students.** Hand out discount coupons, free products, or award certificates to students who earn high marks or record good attendance in school.

- **Send out newsletters or press releases.** Use these tools to announce new products or services or to highlight accomplishments of employees at your franchise.

- **Use telemarketing.** Telemarketing is more challenging today than in years past, but it still can be effective. Make sure that you abide by the Federal Trade Commission's Telemarketing Sales Rule, which requires certain disclosures and prohibits misrepresentations; call 202-326-2222 for more information.

  If you're calling consumers who may not be your current customers, you also have to comply with the Telephone Consumer Protection Act, which, for example, limits calls to between 8 a.m. and 9 p.m.; contact the Federal Communications Commission at 888-225-5322 for more information.

- **Do cross-promotions.** Hooking up with other local businesspeople cuts the advertising expense and adds credibility if you're the new kid on the block.

- **Participate in charity promotions.** As a franchisee, you'll find that participating in a community event or charity works wonders to promote your franchise. It builds goodwill, and it can build sales. Many franchisors encourage franchisees to support charitable causes that are most appropriate for their local communities. The key is that they suggest, not mandate. See whether your parent company offers guidelines. For example, steer clear of any controversial or political issues that could polarize a segment of your customer base.

  Even though you'll participate in charity promotions out of the goodness of your heart, check whether the cost of sponsoring a charitable event gets credited to your local marketing expenditure requirements. It probably does. Discuss this with the franchisor's marketing department.

"Nonpaid media placements are often more important and critical to the brand than paid advertising," says Brad Fishman, president of Fishman Public Relations. "Using PR to keep your brand in front of the consumers not only is cost-effective but can significantly increase your target audience's brand recall."

Be sure to let your staff know about all your promotions and marketing efforts. Consumers easily become frustrated when they visit your location looking for that great offer you ran only to find out no one working there is aware of it.

Before taking any of these steps, make sure that your plan is in compliance with your franchisor's policies. Any advertising or promotional materials that involve the franchised business and include the franchisor's trademark must almost always be submitted to the franchisor for approval. Franchisors are vigilant about protecting their trademarks.

Franchisors take local advertising seriously. Most likely, you'll have to document advertising expenditures. Your operating manual should specify what counts — and what doesn't count — toward these authorized expenditures. At Wendy's, local radio, TV, outdoor billboards, newspaper and magazine ads, coupon offers, direct mail, in-store materials, and sponsorship of community events all get a thumbs-up. Logo T-shirts? Nope. Hiring your nephew as a marketing assistant? No way.

Ask your franchisor for guidance on appropriate media (for example, whether to buy airtime or newspaper space) and analysis of marketing costs in your local area. Advertising on a talk show with a well-known but offensive host can be expensive and turn off customers, but funneling your dollars into a family-oriented channel may create the wholesome image you want to project.

All media representatives you meet with will tell you that their products are the *best* at reaching your target audience. Don't take their word for it. Ask to see the demographic breakdown and evaluate the information objectively.

In addition, the franchisor should help you evaluate the effectiveness of any promotions or campaigns. You don't want to wait until the end of the promotion to find out that it's a dud. If it's broke, fix it as you go. A minor adjustment to your offer or message could save the day.

Most franchisors also prepare advertising materials for use by franchisees — sometimes for an additional fee, sometimes not. These materials usually include the following:

- Advertising, publicity, and promotional kits for the grand opening
- Direct-mail pieces
- Newspaper, yellow pages ads, and coupons in modular form that easily can be adapted to your local market
- Outdoor billboards
- Point-of-sale (POS) materials, such as window and floor signs
- Promotional contests
- Public relations kits

Your franchisor may give you the actual materials needed for print advertising or provide you with the components on CD-ROM or via the Internet or intranet. Most often, print ad layouts are modular so that you can tailor your exact offer while maintaining the overall look associated with the brand. Usually, the layout will include space for your name, address, telephone number, and hours of operation. Your local newspaper or direct-mail house can handle the production for you.

Broadcast advertising is similar. Your franchisor will give you a tape of a radio spot or television commercial with time allotted for your local identification. Your local TV or radio station can take it from there.

Can't wait to get started? Hold on a minute. Before you start to market your location, you must make sure that your operations and management systems are ready for prime time. If you don't run your business right, telling people who and where you are won't do you any good. You'll just disappoint your customers, which means that ultimately you won't have any.

Your location must deliver to the quality standards of the system and give the consumer what the advertising campaign has promised. Suppose that a doughnut company promises the public that all its doughnuts will be hot and fresh and melt-in-your-mouth good. Mr. Smith hears the brand promise, but at the local gas station he finds that the doughnuts have been sitting under a heat lamp for hours, and instead of melting in his mouth, the doughnuts are greasy and taste stale. In his mind, the company's advertising lied, and the product didn't deliver on the promise made to him in the ads.

All Hail Customer Service

Take this simple test to find out whether your franchisor is a tad bit selfish: Who comes first in your franchise system — the customer or the franchise? If it's the customer, give your franchisor an A+ in customer service; if it's the company, watch out.

In today's marketplace, a franchisor must pay attention to the local customer first and the franchisor company second so that it can meet and then surpass the customers' expectations. Putting customers first means giving customers what they want — not what the franchisor wants to give them. Doing otherwise could be an expensive mistake.

Knowing your customers

Knowing your customers is a major step in customer service. Their wants, their needs, their buying habits, their ages, their genders, their lifestyles, their pocketbooks, their time schedules — all this information provides the clues you need to serve them better.

No doubt, this census sounds like a daunting task. But it really isn't. Keep in mind that you're part of a team. Your franchisor will help you capture this information — without your having to knock on every door in town. You can supplement this demographic information with a narrower study of your local area (see Chapter 7).

After customers storm your franchise (and they will, because you've done such a great job of marketing), you can cull even more insight. Tech-savvy franchisors require computerized POS systems that store customer profiles, buying habits, and other information. Some larger franchisors have private-label credit cards and frequent-buyer cards to track purchasing trends. On a more human note, be observant — and encourage your staff to be observant, too. Paying attention to your customers lets you know what they crave and helps you anticipate their changing desires.

A critical part of customer service is giving your customers a good and fair product or service. Customers want true value each and every time they shop at your store. We're talking about total quality, and you must — absolutely must — keep a keen eye on operations, every minute of every day. It's really a no-brainer: If you give your customers the best service and the best product, they'll be back.

Showing honesty and integrity

Honesty and integrity: These two traits are ones you wanted in a franchisor, remember? Well, what goes around comes around. Customers look for the same traits in you — in your franchise. If you don't demonstrate honesty and integrity, someone else will scoop up your customers. You're a step ahead of the game if your brand already portrays this image.

Customers expect consistency from franchises. They expect to receive the product or service your franchise is known for. And they expect to receive it in the way it's been portrayed to the public, through advertising or other means. Your job is to give it to them so that the reputation of the brand doesn't get tarnished.

For example, just imagine if all franchisees personalized their franchises — Dorothy's Wendy's, Alyssa's Wendy's, Charlie's Wendy's. What a mess. The public wouldn't know whether the product in each location was the same or whether Dorothy added a new ingredient to the chili to make it Dorothy's chili. Imagine trying to advertise a consistent message when the name isn't consistent. Dave never wanted to personalize Wendy's and make it Dave's Wendy's because doing so would weaken the brand.

Be careful about introducing new products. If your franchisor is constantly changing the operations and focus of your business, it's putting undue stress on your operations and may confuse the customer. The customer will forget what you really stand for. Work with your franchisor to introduce products that your *customers* want, not what your franchisor may like.

Your franchisor has most likely conducted consumer research that shows what customers are looking for. For example, at quick-service restaurants, patrons want economy, convenience, filling and satisfying food, and a familiar and predictable experience. If you don't fool with any of those factors, you're right on target in customer service.

Customers have good memories. They remember what ads say, and they remember what a business actually delivers. If they notice a discrepancy between the two, say goodbye. So when you make a claim, you'd better live up to it. Honor your fellow franchisees' coupons — to customers, you're all the same brand. If you're stingy, all they'll remember is that they couldn't get what your location advertised.

Keep this in mind, too: Customers tell twice as many people about a bad experience as they do about a good one. So, if you maximize customer satisfaction, you'll reap a positive domino effect. Customer satisfaction is the best advertising in town. Customers will visit again and tell others to visit, too.

Making sure customer experiences are positive (and fixing those that aren't)

You'll face all kinds of customers at your franchise. Some will look at the glass as half full, and others will look at it as half empty. Their perspective makes a difference in your franchise's success. Suppose that you run a computer-training franchise. One day, a customer comes in and finds the latest equipment working without a hitch and instructors who really know their stuff. The next time that student shows up, the computers keep crashing and the teachers are fumbling. If the customer views the glass as half full, he may remember the first experience more and give your franchise another try. If he sees the glass as half empty, you really have a lot of making up to do.

The message we're giving you is this: Be on your toes at all times, and try to change a customer's negative experience into a positive by correcting your franchise's mistakes and resolving any conflicts.

Any blunder is a signal to look inward. Strip apart your operations and see what needs improvement. Go back to the franchise operations manual — it most likely addresses your particular problem. Seek help from regional or corporate support staff if you need it. Maybe you need to retrain employees in customer service. (In Chapter 8, we discuss employee training.)

To salvage relationships with customers, your best bets are to

- Respond quickly.
- Listen to what they have to say — without interruption.
- Apologize and then apologize again for any errors.
- Be polite and make eye contact.
- Put yourself in your customers' shoes; think about how you'd want the problem resolved.
- Promise your customers a correction — free product or services, discounts on future sales, shifting employees, extra attention, and so on.
- Prove yourself the next time.

Be aware that very few customers verbalize their complaints to employees or management, especially if money isn't involved. Unfortunately, you find out about poor customer service when it kicks you in the stomach: Customers don't come back, and sales plummet.

There are two ways to check customer satisfaction — inexpensively and expensively. The cheap but effective approach, of course, is simply using your eyes and ears — listening to and watching customers and employees. Here are some additional ways:

- Read your mail — from fans and foes.
- Make comment cards easily accessible so customers can fill them out; using these feedback cards is low-cost and easy.
- Check with your franchisor; many franchisors solicit input from customers on the company Web site and can pass on that information to you.
- Periodically, speak directly with customers to make sure that all's well — or to identify a small problem before it becomes a bigger one.
- Perform informal one-on-one surveys and random phone surveys with your customers.
- Use the sophisticated tools you may already have at your franchise, such as cash registers that capture sales and customer information. These tools can facilitate customer surveys by providing the names of customers and what they've purchased.

✔ Go the extra mile and hire local research organizations to gather quantifiable research on your franchise's performance. If you want to hire outside experts, talk to your fellow franchisees about combining forces and splitting the cost.

Looking beyond your cash register

Every part of your business makes an impression on the customer. Sure, the customer can't wait to dip his spoon into a Frosty, or slip into a freshly detailed car, or find the perfect healthcare aide. No question, the end product or end service offered by your franchise is why customers come in the door to begin with.

But customers do notice things like the wallpaper, employee appearance and friendliness, equipment, and restrooms — most definitely, they notice restrooms. Paying attention to details is a big part of customer service — and a big part of employee service; nobody likes to work in a junky or dirty environment. The job of both you and your franchisor is to set tough standards — because customers do, too.

Obviously, franchisees in various industries have to inspect the premises a little differently in order to meet the needs of their specific type of business. Here are some general guidelines to make sure that your business is in shipshape:

✔ Are employees friendly, helpful, and well trained?

✔ Are problems resolved quickly?

✔ Is service prompt, dependable, and consistent?

✔ Is the location clean, welcoming, and in good condition?

✔ Can your customers see your quality as they drive by? What does the outside of your store say to your customers?

✔ Do customers or employees have concerns about security or safety?

✔ Is equipment updated?

✔ Are products in stock?

✔ Are you offering all the products the customer expects from your brand?

✔ Are you meeting the needs of the physically challenged customer?

✔ Are you available to answer questions or resolve your customers' problems if needed?

A perfect score is reachable — it just takes time and teamwork. And a big part of that teamwork must come from your staff.

The hands-on approach is best

Wendy's strongly encourage its franchisees to be on the front lines on a regular basis and to talk to their customers. Doing so is the best way to get immediate feedback.

In addition to not having enough money to fund their businesses, another reason franchisees fail that's equally relevant is absentee ownership. If you're going to be a franchisee and rarely show up at your location, you're an absentee. And if you're an absentee, you don't know what your customers are thinking and how they're interacting with your staff.

You must have hands-on involvement to truly understand the pulse of your business.

Part IV
Times Change: Deciding What to Do Next

The 5th Wave   By Rich Tennant

"Our customer survey indicates 30% of our customers think our service is inconsistent, 40% would like a change in procedures, and 50% think it would be real cute if we all wore matching colored vests."

In this part . . .

In this part, we talk about your growth options — buying additional units from your franchisor or investing in additional franchises with other franchisors. If you're successful as a franchisee, owning just one franchise may not be enough for you.

At some point, your relationship with your franchisor is likely to come to an end. This part also prepares you for that situation and lets you know how to exit your franchise system gracefully or leave it to your children, if that's what you want to do.

Chapter 11

Acquiring Other Franchises

· ·

In This Chapter

▶ Buying more than one franchise: The pros and cons

▶ Complying with your franchise agreement

▶ Evaluating personal and financial resources

▶ Exploring purchasing options

· ·

For some franchisees, jingling just one set of keys is fine. For others, one franchise is just the beginning.

Some franchisees open one location and wait for years before they approach their franchisor with a request for a second or a third. Others enter franchising intending to open multiple franchises so that every location in town carrying their franchisor's brand is a place they can point to as their own. Still others dream of becoming master franchisees — that's when they obtain the rights from the franchisor to recruit their own subfranchisees who will operate under the franchisor's brand. Their goal is to become sort of mini-franchisors. (For details on master franchising, see the "Acquiring an area" section, later in this chapter.)

This chapter shows you how you can buy another franchise — or even multiple franchises — and how to make sure that you're making the right choices along the way.

Considering whether Multiple Ownership Is Worth Your While

Suppose you're a franchise owner and from where you sit, everything looks rosy. Your franchise is doing great. Your franchisor loves you — your royalty payments are rising and paid on time. Your banker loves you — you're paying back your loan and meeting your payroll, and bill collectors aren't camping out on your doorstep. You love you — you're in the black, baby; you may even kick off your shoes and take that cruise to the Caribbean.

Just for a moment, stop patting yourself on the back (even though you really deserve to) and ask yourself the big question: Will expansion change all this? The reality is that acquiring more units can have advantages and disadvantages.

The high feats

You don't have to be a rocket scientist to figure out that the more businesses you own, the more potential you have to make money or lose money. You're building equity in your business — and possibly in real estate. Just as at the franchisor level, sheer size should bring you better prices on supplies and services. It may also yield favorable financing; the common wisdom is that lenders are more interested in multi-unit operators. Also, as you get a reputation for being a great multi-unit operator, expect the real estate community to notice. They'll start to offer you locations — even before you ask for them.

Remember that you'll have more at risk than a smaller franchisee with locations in your market. Their performance will affect yours. Make sure that you keep abreast of how neighboring franchises are doing.

Expansion can also help you with marketing. When you have only a few units, radio and television spots are difficult to justify, let alone afford. When you cluster your franchises in a regional market, however, the mass-media costs start falling into a realistic range on a per-unit basis.

Purchasing additional franchises has an impact on employees, too. With size, you'll likely attract higher-quality employees. They can envision career-growth opportunities. You may qualify for lower rates on insurance plans, enabling you to offer better benefits. You may not have to reject good job applicants; you have more placement choices now. A candidate who hails from a small town may not be happy in, say, Los Angeles but may thrive in a surrounding community where you own another franchise.

Having multiple units close to each other often lets franchisees float staff between units as the need arises. The same goes for unit management. Sometimes, one skilled manager can direct three or four units, while the day-to-day responsibilities are met by a less expensive, but still talented, assistant manager.

Perhaps the greatest benefit to multiple ownership is sharing. Multiple units are great for swapping employees in a bind. And imagine this scenario: The new manager at your pizza franchise makes a mistake with the cheese order and runs out of cheese on the very day that all the town's soccer teams are having pizza parties to mark the end of a brutal season. What does she do? She rushes to another one of your units to replenish the supply — and satisfies lots of little customers (who will grow into big customers someday). You can take the same approach with staffing. If one franchise is overstaffed and the other is understaffed, you can shift employees to meet your needs.

You may also be able to save labor or product costs by setting up a *commissary* (a central location where you can prepare some products for all the locations) and shipping products to all your locations in a prepared or semi-prepared fashion. This approach is acceptable in some franchise systems and taboo in others. Check with your franchisor.

Consider pricing, too. Because franchisors can't tell franchisees what to charge for their products and services, prices may be inconsistent in a region dotted with individual owners. If you own all the units, presto — uniform pricing and less customer confusion.

Remember those other franchisees in the market? Don't talk to them about pricing. Price fixing, whether it's between the franchisor and franchisee or between franchisees, may violate antitrust laws in the United States.

In general, the more franchises you own, the more clout you wield with the franchisor. That's not to say that chains don't have small, successful owners who aren't very influential. But listening most to the people with the loudest voices — those with the greatest economic power — is just human nature.

The downbeats

Although you may be enthusiastic about future development, you must weigh the cons along with the pros.

The greatest risk is not having the operational and financial capabilities to effectively be a multi-unit owner. Perhaps you're growing too fast. Without leadership, management skills, and a financial cushion, your new empire could sink — like the *Titanic*. That's why we again encourage you to really investigate yourself and your business before moving forward.

Think about bringing in partners or establishing a workable joint venture with another businessperson — or even the franchisor. This approach may make your financial share smaller, but a smaller share of success is a whole lot better than 100 percent of a loss.

Getting carried away by your business size is another potential drawback. You run the risk of thinking you don't have to have your hands in the business anymore because you've built an organization. That assumption is far from the truth.

As you purchase more franchises, you may conceive of new ways of doing things. You'll be more tempted to tamper with the system, only to get frustrated because, although you're allowed some room for change, you have to work within the franchisor's system.

You can turn these negatives into positives — just proceed with caution.

Checking Your Franchise Agreement: Can You Buy Another Franchise?

Before you get charged up about buying multiple franchises, make sure that multi-unit ownership is an option in your franchisor's system. Companies have different philosophies on expansion. Some franchisors say that one's the limit — period. Other companies encourage you to expand, expand, and expand some more. Still others embrace only multi-unit development, turning their backs entirely on the little guy.

Some franchisors have a set waiting period before you can open another location or another territory. (Population or geographic area typically defines territories.) These companies may want to make sure that franchisees can operate their first business to system standards and do so profitably before they'll consider letting them purchase number two. Make sure that you're aware of your franchisor's restrictions and requirements.

Your franchisor's policy may be spelled out in its disclosure document — the Franchise Disclosure Document (FDD; see Chapter 6). Even if it's not, check with your franchisor to determine what the franchise fees and other fees are for expansion. Some franchise systems charge lower fees — at least upfront — for franchisees who are willing to commit to opening multiple locations.

Reviewing Your Personal and Business Resources

Having 1 franchise unit is far different from having 2 or 10 or 20. Buying another franchise is like having another child — the entire dynamic of your family structure changes. You need to deal with issues on a whole different scale — including hiring staff, training, purchasing products, and marketing.

You may know the old adage "Small children, small problems; big children, big problems." But don't forget: Growth also can bring big rewards.

We hate to recommend more paperwork, but we suggest that you develop a tactical plan before you make a decision about owning multiple franchises. Don't worry — your plan probably doesn't have to be as grandiose as one that a Fortune 500 company would develop.

Being honest with yourself: Are you ready for multiple ownership?

Brace yourself — you need to take a look in the mirror. Do a thorough self-assessment to see whether you're ready to own multiple franchises, which is a totally different issue from whether your business is ready to expand. (We cover the latter issue in the "Taking a hard look at your business and finances" section, later in this chapter.)

Successfully shifting from a single-unit operator to a multi-unit operator depends largely on your personality and personal issues. Before jumping into multiple-franchise ownership, consider the following questions about yourself:

✔ **Are you a team player?** The more units you own, the more staff you'll need, including some in managerial positions. Be sure that you can handle coaching a much bigger team. Decide whether you're able to give up some decision making to employees whom you've hired and trained, and whom you trust.

✔ **Are you an operator or a manager?** Saying that you want 50 stores is easy; understanding what it takes to manage that many stores is another thing. Single-unit owners worry about opening the business in the morning, taking care of the events of the day, and closing at night. As a single-unit owner, you may be used to greeting your customers, training your employees, and taking care of many of the hands-on tasks yourself. Become a multi-unit franchisee, and you're forced to be even more of a manager. You'll have to build and rely on a support organization.

✔ **Can you delegate responsibility?** No question, letting go is tough; after all, the franchise is your baby. Being in two places at once (unless you know something we don't know) is impossible, so you must develop staff and delegate responsibilities — comfortably. You'll probably spend a lot of time nurturing each new unit, and then focus your attention — more or less — on your other franchises as different issues arise.

✔ **Are you organized?** You'll have to be. You may be at a construction site on Tuesday morning and a staff meeting at your existing location in the afternoon. Assuming responsibility over different locations, with different problems and somewhat differing obligations will make you feel like a juggler sometimes. Depending on the number of units, you'll have to set up internal support systems, such as hiring a general manager, a bookkeeper, and administrative support staff to free up your time to let you handle more than one location.

✔ **Is the timing right?** Look at your personal life, and determine whether you can devote time to another project and still maintain your desired lifestyle.

✔ **Do any family members want to get involved?** Perhaps your spouse wants in. Maybe you want your children to earn their own gas money, with an eye on succession. (In Chapter 15, we discuss leaving your franchise to your children.)

✔ **Do you think big?** If you do, you probably won't be content with a single site for very long. But you also have to know your limitations. You have to be *able* to expand, not just *want* to expand.

Taking a hard look at your business and finances

If you already own one franchise, hopefully you conducted some research before you made that purchase. Before you make the leap to multiple-unit franchising, we recommend that you examine your existing business and your finances.

Asking the right questions about your own franchise

Answer these questions before you move forward and become a multi-unit franchise owner:

✔ **Do you have the money?** Hands down, your existing unit should be profitable first. Many franchisees dip into cash flow from one franchise to fund part of their entire next unit, and then they finance the rest. No matter how many units you have, you can't make money if the individual locations are losing money. What are the costs involved? Will you have to pay additional franchise fees?

✔ **Are your employees ready?** We hope you've been grooming your employees for promotion, which is a great motivator. But right now, your highest-level employee is probably an office or store manager. Now that you'll likely need more managers — and perhaps even a district or general manager — responsibility goes up a notch. Can your existing managers move up to general managers? Is your crew good enough to assume new duties? Will you have to retrain or hire new employees? Can you let go a little and trust them to make decisions?

- ✔ **Do you have your operations perfectly down pat?** Are you carrying out operations according to the franchisor's rules and standards? Although you probably won't be an absentee owner (we never suggest that), you can't possibly be as hands-on when you purchase an additional business.

- ✔ **Are you feeling competitive pressures?** Perhaps a competing chain has steamrolled into town, quickly erecting one unit and plopping down construction signs elsewhere. If you don't catch up, your competitor may gain market share by its sheer number of locations.

- ✔ **Will expansion affect customer satisfaction?** Suppose you've harnessed a steady stream of regular customers, but recent highway construction projects are hindering your customers' access to your franchise. Rumor has it that some customers may take their business closer to home. If you open a second location in another part of town, maybe you can salvage the relationship. Conversely, if you're no longer at your current location all the time, will customers miss your personal touch?

- ✔ **Is another franchise location in your chain up for grabs?** This idea isn't so far-fetched. Consider this: The perfect site is available in your market, and your franchisor wants its name on it. Your franchise agreement doesn't give you an exclusive territory, meaning that anyone else — company or franchise unit — can move in. If you don't grab it, someone else will. Is this a prime site?

- ✔ **Does your franchise agreement restrict you in some way?** Make sure you check your agreement and contact your franchisor if you have any questions.

Crunching the numbers

How much you'll have to pay the franchisor for a second location varies according to your franchise agreement. Some chains charge the regular franchise fee for a second unit; some reduce the fee and slash it even further for subsequent ones.

The last thing you want to do is rob Peter to pay Paul. You don't want your second — or seventieth — unit to unduly or unexpectedly impact the ones that came before. So to plan for growth, you *must* look at your financial picture. (Be sure to review Chapter 5 to avoid financial pitfalls.) This section offers more tips for evaluating your financial readiness to expand.

First, review your franchise's overall financial condition, using the following list:

- ✔ **The balance sheet:** This document includes your assets (cash, real estate, inventory, depreciated equipment, and accounts receivable) and your liabilities (outstanding bills, including tax obligations and loans).

- ✔ **Return on investment:** Are you outperforming other investment opportunities? You need to calculate whether the return you're getting from your investment in your franchise is better than you could get from investing in something else. For example, if all you are earning on your investment in the franchise is 3 percent, and your bank is paying 6 percent, you have to decide whether buying more units is a smart decision.

- ✔ **Budget:** This group of numbers projects income and expenses for the coming year, which you can then compare to actual income and expenses.

- ✔ **Profit and loss statement (referred to as a P&L):** This document summarizes your income and expenses — your profitability or unprofitability.

- ✔ **Cash flow:** This figure tells you how much cash you're generating from your existing operations.

These tools can help you identify whether you can afford to expand — using your current cash flow or by seeking financing. Find out whether your franchisor will lend you expansion funds. (Chapter 5 guides you through financing options.)

You must weigh other money matters, too. Will your bank support your growth? If you need financing, what's the current interest rate? Rates may have been low when you took on a loan last time, but higher rates could dramatically alter your investment strategy. Also, escalating costs of real estate and construction mean you may need to borrow more money.

Consider all your initial costs — the franchise fee and other start-up expenses. Don't assume that you'll pay exactly the same amount as you paid the last time you bought a franchise. Some costs may be lower — such as a reduced franchise fee for subsequent units or diminished advertising costs because you can share promotional costs. But some expenses may be higher. The franchisor may have chosen a new design, décor, and equipment package making construction more expensive, or maybe a prospective site requires a zoning variance — which requires lawyers' fees and possibly more construction costs later.

Also, as you acquire more franchises, you may be able to buy inventory and secure other services at better rates because of volume purchasing. These savings should help boost profitability. You may incur additional expenses, though, because you may need to hire higher-skilled personnel.

If you're buying area development rights, remember that you typically pay a portion of the franchise fee upfront for unopened units — way before they pull in any revenues. This prepayment will not be earning you any immediate money, which could have a profound impact on your profits.

Just because you're operating a unit successfully, don't mistake yourself for Donald Trump. Review your financial state of affairs with your franchisor's development staff, your lender, your lawyer, and your accountant before making any firm decisions.

Understanding Your Purchase Options

You have to decide how you want to expand. Depending on the rules of your chain, you may be able to open up new locations only one at a time, or you may be allowed to go for multiple locations, acquire an entire territory, or convert an existing operation. Either way, you have to deal with where to establish your next franchise.

Go back to the drawing board and diligently pursue site selection with the same gusto you did the first time around. You may think that you know your market inside and out if you've already been operating a franchise, but you need to be aware of other considerations. For example, a location in a different neighborhood or even on a different avenue in the same neighborhood may have totally different dynamics than your current operations.

Traffic patterns will likely differ, your customer base could change, your competition will be different, and you'll even have to consider the side of the street a potential location is on. Your franchisor should help you with site selection guidelines. Check demographics, traffic patterns, zoning laws, competition, and so on (for more, see Chapter 7).

Starting from scratch

You always have the option of simply going through the same process you did when you opened up your first franchise: Purchase a franchise from the franchisor, locate a new site, and develop it fresh from the ground up. That's how most franchisees go from being single-unit operators to multi-unit operators — building one unit at a time.

Buying multiple units

Many franchisees decide right from the start that single-unit ownership is not for them. These franchisees plan for multi-unit ownership right off the bat. Many of these new franchisees are investor groups, and some are even public companies that are larger than the franchisor.

By the time a franchisee purchases four or five franchises, she'll probably start creating some of her own administrative and back-office operating systems. Franchisees often set up training stores; their trainers will probably be trained by the franchisor. They'll add supervisory personnel, such as store-level managers and a district or general manager. Ideally, managers will receive training similar to the training provided to franchisees when they first joined the franchise system. (We discuss training in Chapter 8.)

After purchasing several franchises, franchisees often begin to feel the need to increase or fortify their back-of-house support capabilities. They'll typically have an accounting department, human resources personnel, a training department, and a team responsible for developing local advertising. Even when they get this big, franchisees still need the franchisor. Besides getting the almighty brand, franchisees can take advantage of the franchisor's expertise in national marketing, research and development, and field support.

Buying a franchise from another franchisee in the system

Sometimes you want what you can't have — like your neighbor's location. Well, maybe you can have it.

She may be chugging along day after day, never thinking of selling until you bring up the idea. Or maybe your neighbor has her franchise on the seller's block because she's planning to retire or cash out while the business is thriving. Perhaps the business is failing, and you're sure that you can turn it around.

Don't rush headlong into the deal. Find out what the franchise contract says — yours and hers. Usually, the franchisor will consent to a transfer, but the company may reserve the right to disapprove a proposed transfer to an existing franchisee based on specific conditions. You need to read the fine print in the agreement and discuss expansion criteria set by your system. If your existing locations are not meeting system standards or are performing poorly, your franchisor likely will be reluctant to see you open another location. Maybe you're already in default under your existing agreements. Do you think the franchisor wants to see you possibly default on other agreements?

A franchisor may also have the right of first refusal over any location up for sale; that is, the franchisor can match any bona-fide offer and purchase the seller's interest. (See Chapter 13 for more information on selling out.)

Finding out whether a franchise is up for grabs

How do you find out if existing franchises are for sale? The first place is straight from the horse's mouth. Stay in touch with the other franchisees in your system — especially franchise owners in your market area. By doing so, you're likely to know what other franchisees are planning and which one has a location that may be up for sale.

Your franchisor may approach you about acquiring an existing franchise, but you don't have to wait for that to happen. Call the franchisor's headquarters or speak to your field consultant about possible opportunities they may know of. Many franchisors operate active resale networks, sometimes for a fee but usually for free. After all, the franchisor benefits from helping someone who wants out of the system to leave, especially when an existing good operator wants to expand.

Measuring proximity to yours

Buying an additional franchise takes analysis, perhaps even more analysis than starting from scratch. Before deciding to purchase, consider the other franchise's proximity to your current site. Is the site so close to your existing store that you won't get any real benefit, or is it too far away for you to properly manage? Maybe the area it's in has changed since it was opened, and the change is having a negative effect on the operation. You don't want to invest a great deal of money only to find that you're splitting, rather than adding to, your customer base.

Life is easier if you expand nearby, so you can still be a hands-on manager. Time spent driving long distances or even flying to a second location is time that you could better spend on operations. Of course, the location shouldn't be right next door, either. So how close is ideal? No hard-and-fast rules govern this decision. You could have one location 2 miles away that hurts your current business; another location that's ½ mile away could have no negative impact if it's separated by a river or a major street that divides the town or trading area. The bottom line: Look carefully at your trade area.

Remember, though, that the business is already in existence. If it's already affecting your existing operation — whether it continues its operation in your hands or someone else's — the impact will probably still be there.

Just because you have a unit in a mall doesn't mean you can't develop a successful location nearby — even right on the pad in the mall's parking lot. You may be drawing from a completely different population of customers.

Even in franchising — the king of duplication — your second site doesn't have to be an identical twin of your first. If you have a free-standing location now, perhaps a nearby strip center or a nontraditional site (such as a kiosk that sells the same merchandise you carry or in a food court) is a better choice for your next purchase. (Turn to Chapter 7 to find out more about nontraditional locations.)

Franchisors are not allowed to provide you information about unit financial performance in the United States unless they do so in the FDD. However, this restriction does not exist when you buy a location from another franchisee that's up and running, or even when you buy a company-owned location from your franchisor. You can, and should, always ask to see the actual operating results for the location you plan to buy from your franchisor or from another franchisee.

When you buy an existing franchise, you need to be aware of the issues and examine them closely before you make the purchase. We cover those details in Chapter 4 and direct you to a questionnaire on the bonus CD-ROM for you to fill out as you evaluate your prospects.

Retrofranchising: Buying a company-owned location

Often, franchisors own locations they operate themselves. Sometimes the franchisor will build locations with the intention of operating them for the long term; they may also build locations so they can sell them to prospective franchisees, and sometimes they buy locations or take them back from franchisees who may have left the system.

A franchisor may sell an existing operation for one of the following reasons:

- ✔ The franchisor needs the proceeds from the sale to pay down debt or for other corporate purposes.
- ✔ The franchisor wants to exit one market so that it can build additional units elsewhere.
- ✔ The franchisor changed its strategy and no longer wants to operate company-owned locations anywhere.
- ✔ The franchisor built the location with the intention of selling it to franchisees.
- ✔ The franchisor acquired the location from a former franchisee with the intent of selling it to a new franchisee.
- ✔ The location is losing money, and the franchisor wants to get it off its books.

Franchisors look for franchisees who are willing to buy the location and are willing to invest in additional locations in the same market.

DAVE'S WISDOM

Snapping up opportunities

If the financial deal is favorable, sometimes a franchisor develops a location that offers a unique opportunity — regardless of whether a franchisee is waiting in line to purchase the site. The franchisor may run the location as a company unit until a new franchisee buys it. Or the franchisor may offer the site to an existing franchisee. Getting the location is the first priority, and then the franchisor can work out who will operate it.

This situation happens often with nontraditional units because these opportunities are few and far between. There may be only one high-volume hospital in town. So, if a location becomes available in the hospital, you'd better grab it because another one may not be available for 20 years. If franchisors don't want to operate the location themselves for the long term, they have the option of offering it to new or existing franchisees.

Assume the franchisor determines that, in order for the market to be a success, it requires five locations — we call that *critical mass*. Critical mass is important because it gives the brand a stronger presence in the market and allows advertising costs to be spread over more locations; therefore, the franchisor can purchase more advertising. Critical mass enables the franchisor to more easily provide support to the locations in the market, because more franchisees bear the cost of the market visits that the field staff makes. (We call that *leveraging* the costs.)

By tying the sale of the company-owned location to an obligation to build out additional locations — and create the desired critical mass — the franchisor benefits the system.

Retrofranchising locations is often good for both the franchisor and the franchisee. For example:

- ✔ The locations are up and running, and you can see their track records and performance.
- ✔ Franchisors may be willing to sell these businesses at a discount or finance some of the acquisition costs if the franchisee is willing to invest in additional locations.
- ✔ The franchisor gets to use the money for other company needs.

WARNING!

Retrofranchising is different from churning. *Churning* occurs when a franchisor takes back a location from a franchisee and then resells it repeatedly, knowing that the subsequent franchisee is also likely to fail at that site. This scenario, while infrequent, can happen when the original franchisee can't make a go of the location or is not able to operate to company standards and is terminated.

Make sure that you look at the financial performance and ownership history of a location. If it was a bad location in another franchisee's hands — and if your franchisor has a habit of flipping bad units from one franchisee to another — even your great operations skills can't magically turn a failing business into a success.

"On the other hand," says franchise lawyer Arthur Pressman, co-chair of the Franchise and Distribution Team at Nixon Peabody, in Boston, "if you can buy a second location at a substantial discount from what its original owner paid, your *debt service* (the interest and principal you pay on a loan) may be less than the original owner's was, and even with no change in sales, you will have a much easier go of it."

Converting a competitor's location

If you're looking in your market area for expansion opportunities, but no available sites fit your needs, check out competitors' locations. Acquiring an existing location from a competitor that meets your requirements is a way of finding sites and knocking out the competition in one fell swoop.

Sometimes, this opportunity can be a no-brainer. An independent may beg you to buy him out. A lot of independents feel like David up against Goliath when franchises charge into town. If franchising is working right, your powerful name recognition, national advertising, and better prices (thanks to a chain's volume buying power) are pushing the competitor's customers to your doors. Consequently, he may be about to close his business.

Buying a competitor's site is another case where you won't be starting from ground zero. Hopefully, you can pick up the competitor's customers. You may be able to retain, but retrain, some employees. Who knows? The former business owner may want to be your new manager.

Making the transition, however, won't be easy. Because the competitor's location probably has a different design than units in your franchisor's system, you'll probably have to remodel the location to meet system standards. You'll have to hire an architect and a contractor to make the changes. If the location was being used for the same type of business, zoning probably won't be a problem. In addition, your cost for developing the location should be lower than the cost of building a new location, because the building is up and the electricity, water, and sewage are probably in operation. To convert the location to your system's brand, you'll be changing the layout, hanging new signs, changing the décor, and possibly adding new equipment.

Ask your franchisor's real estate and development department to work with you on this project. These professionals can help you determine whether the savings you expect from buying an existing location is likely to happen. For example, the site may have plumbing, but it may be in the wrong place, and you'll have to move it. The site may have electric service, but it may not be sufficient for your needs. The building may be zoned correctly, but it may not have enough parking spaces. Seeking assistance before you make your purchase helps you work out these potential issues.

If you're buying a location that has been operating under a different franchisor's brand, consult your attorney to make sure that you can acquire the location without violating the other franchisor's rights or the seller's lease; some leases have limited permitted uses. The existing operator's franchise agreement may prohibit or hinder the sale. Also, confirm that your own franchise agreement allows you to expand and that the competitor's location won't encroach on another franchisee's territory or — in the opinion of the franchisor — negatively affect sales at your existing location.

Acquiring an area

If, from the start, you have big dreams of being a franchise tycoon, you may want to consider franchisors that offer the whole package: area development rights. These rights allow a franchisee to expand exclusively within a specific territory, according to a schedule — *x* number of units within a certain period.

In a twist on this method, some chains sell an entire territory to a franchisee and, based on a schedule, allow the franchisee to open units herself or sell unit franchises to other operators, called *subfranchisees*. This approach is called *master franchising*.

The master franchisee recruits new franchisees into the system and often provides them with many of the services other franchisees get directly from the franchisor. In exchange for recruiting and supporting the subfranchisees, the master franchisee retains a portion of the initial fee paid by the subfranchisee (the *franchise fee*) and also retains a portion of the continuing royalty payments (a continuing fee paid by the unit franchisee to the franchisor, usually based on a percentage of gross sales). This arrangement is very common in international franchising but is becoming less so in the United States. (In Chapter 16, we explore international expansion.)

Some franchise systems expand only via area development or multi-unit development. Theoretically, by dealing with fewer but larger and hopefully more sophisticated franchisees, they can manage their systems with more ease and focus their efforts on support, new products, services, and other areas besides franchise sales.

Other chains use a multi-unit strategy only in their core or larger markets and sell single franchises only in their smaller markets. The method depends on the system and its growth strategy.

For franchisees, an advantage of acquiring an area is that you lock in a territory in which you can develop multiple locations without having to worry about how many other franchises are being developed and how close those locations are to your sites. In contrast, if you buy franchises one at a time, you risk getting closed out of parts of your area because other franchisees or company-owned locations have been developed.

Before striking a deal for area development rights, consider the following:

- ✔ The number of stores you ultimately want
- ✔ The amount of money you can invest or raise to develop those stores
- ✔ The number of locations the market can support
- ✔ The additional costs and savings you'll incur
- ✔ Your ability to manage multiple owners

Be prepared to pay substantial money upfront. Area development rights typically command either a flat fee — that could be even hundreds of thousands of dollars — or a fee per franchise you commit to develop. For example, if the franchise fee is $40,000, you may fork over the entire franchise fee for the first unit and a $15,000 deposit on each additional one; the remainder would be due upon opening.

If you default on the development schedule, you may lose your deposit — plus the exclusive rights to the area. Check to see how strict the franchisor is regarding the default option. Some franchisors will amend the agreement to accommodate late construction schedules or other problems. Franchisors may also extend the opening date. (Sometimes they charge the franchisee an extension fee.) The development schedule may include grace periods. Many franchisors don't have a set policy — how they respond often depends on whether the franchisee has been trying to get the units open and whether, despite their best efforts, unforeseen obstacles have arisen. The flexibility of the franchisor may depend on whether the franchisee and the franchisor have a good or bad relationship. Check with other multi-unit operators to find out what the franchisor does in a crunch.

Franchisors often offer a lower per-unit fee to an area developer than they do to a franchisee who is only committing to opening one site, primarily because of these two basic issues:

- ✔ **The franchisor reduces their costs by having one individual or company own multiple locations.** The franchisor saves on having to recruit additional franchisees to open the locations and on the time, cost, and effort of providing support to individual locations; with an area developer, a franchisor works with only one franchisee for all the locations.

- ✔ **The franchisor recognizes that the area developer makes a commitment to the system and takes a sizable financial risk.** Both franchisor and area developer feel that the commitment should be rewarded in some fashion — usually lower fees.

The amount of the fee discount depends on the franchisor, the number of locations being committed to, and the time it will take to get the units up and running. Franchisors usually limit any fee reduction to the initial franchise fee and rarely reduce the continuing royalty rate. From the beginning, make sure that the development schedule is reasonable. If it's not, and if you need to negotiate later with the franchisor for an extension of time, you may find that you have to make certain concessions, such as a reduced territory.

You're probably thinking that area development is for gamblers. In a way, it is. These franchisees are betting that their units — and the franchise chain — will strike it rich. The gamble is the same, but the stakes are higher than with a single franchise. Instead of going to the $2 blackjack table, franchisees who acquire areas are sitting at the $20 one. If they make the wrong bet, they're out of luck; but if they make the right bet, they're very happy that no one else can touch their entire franchise area.

Chapter 12

Acquiring Other Brands

After some folks discover franchising, they just can't get enough. If you want to own more than a single franchise of the same concept, head over to Chapter 11, where we discuss acquiring multiple franchises within the same chain. That's probably the most common method people use to expand and perhaps the easiest, because you're staying with a business — and a system — you already understand. But if you're after more than one unit and more than one brand, stay put. This chapter covers expanding outside your current franchise concept.

Don't feel guilty if you want a little variety. It's the spice of life, right? Touting multiple brands may seem odd, because we've compared the franchisee-franchisor relationship to that of a family. But in the franchising world, you're not cheating on your "spouse" if you marry into another system without divorcing the first. For the most part, you can step up to the altar repeatedly. (We discuss the exceptions in the section "Reviewing the Ties That Bind: Legal Issues," later in this chapter.) Given the thousands of franchise concepts, in your future relationships you may end up with new partners, but not likely from the same industry segment.

In most instances, franchisors don't allow you to acquire another business in the same industry — hamburgers to hamburgers, sneakers to sneakers, and so on. You may find that a franchisor will restrict what other businesses you may own or even the percentage of ownership. This is because the franchisor rightfully is concerned with the confidentiality of its system and trade secrets, among other good reasons. You may not be allowed to own any other businesses — read your franchise agreement.

Seek legal advice very early in the process of looking at other franchise systems. Even having discussions with other franchisors sometimes can lead to problems, especially if you discuss, or jeopardize in some fashion, any of your current system's confidential information or trade secrets. Chat with an experienced franchise law firm before you take any steps in this direction.

Really, the only way to effectively wear multiple hats is to focus. Be prepared to toil as you did the first time, and put all your energies into your new venture. But at the same time, be careful that you don't lose sight of your original concept — the one that brought you here. Having a start-up business that needs all your energy but being forced to deal with a formerly successful business that's on the decline because you weren't around to manage it is a guaranteed recipe for disaster.

Knowing What You're Getting Into

If you thought buying your first franchise concept was a big deal, here's a news flash: Buying multiple franchise concepts is an even *bigger* deal. Unlike round one, though, you have a head start this time. You already know how to be a franchisee, and you grasp the franchisee-franchisor relationship as an insider.

Round two is different. You're starting over with a new concept and, maybe, a different franchisor. (Read about companies that franchise multiple concepts in the next section.) This time, your decision can have a domino effect on your original business. Say you've worked your tail off, and your first franchise is humming along smoothly. Now you add a second brand, which steals some of your time, energy, and money from your first venture. Any expansion can hurt — just as easily as it can help — your other franchise or franchises.

So, before you diversify, do your homework. Explore the risks and rewards of tackling another concept, whether you're limited in any way from expanding, and which franchisor to hook up with.

Check your current franchise agreement (for more on this, see Chapter 6). Some agreements require you to spend 100 percent of your time on that business; others limit the types of other concepts you can operate or even invest in. Then get ready for a balancing act. If you've ever tried juggling, you know that keeping your eye on the ball when you're tossing more than one takes a lot of concentration. Mix different shapes and sizes and, boy, keeping everything in the air is difficult.

Even if you can legally become involved in another business, be prepared to answer concerns and questions your franchisor may have with your taking this step, including how you plan to successfully manage two different businesses, perhaps at separate locations. As a simple matter of good relations, discuss your plans with your current franchisor before you take any irreversible steps, and make sure your current franchisor hears about your plans from you, and not from someone else!

Taking a look at yourself: More self-evaluation questions

Before you start juggling, make sure that you can handle this new venture emotionally, operationally, and financially. Franchisees who expand within the same chain go through basically the same analysis, so turn to Chapter 11 to see what questions you should consider personally and financially.

With the added dimension of diversification, we've added the following bonus questions:

- What's your existing franchisor's philosophy on multi-concept franchisees?

- Does a strategic similarity exist between the concepts, and will the two concepts operate to help build each other's business (such as a pizza parlor and a movie-rental store, located next door to each other)?

- Will you be able to divide your attention between more than one concept, let alone more than one location?

- Who will operate your existing business while you're away at training for your new franchise?

- Can your existing business survive your absence?

- Can you use skills you learned at your original franchise (customer service, management, recruiting, and vendor relations) at the next chain?

  When you move from brand A to brand B, you certainly can use many of the skills you've mastered. However, confidentiality requirements may preclude sharing of proprietary information, which is particularly true if the concepts are not identical, but similar in operations, marketing, and customers, such as two fast-food concepts.

- Will you mind writing more than one royalty check each month?

- Can you deal with more than one franchisor and more than one set of rules?

- Will you play favorites?

- Are you willing to expend all that start-up energy again?

✔ Will you truly listen to and accept new ideas and training? (The operating methods you learned with the first concept may not be transferable.)

✔ Is one franchisor more mature than the other? Will the new franchisor meet your expectations on franchisor services?

✔ Do you have existing managers (or employees who have the capability to become managers) who would be perfect for the new operation? Who do you have to replace them if they move to your new concept?

✔ Are you better off selling your existing brand and focusing all your time and attention on the new brand?

✔ What happens if one of the concepts fails — especially if they're sharing the same location? This is another good reason to chat with an experienced franchise attorney; she may recommend that you set up separate corporations for each concept or unit.

✔ How do you intend to structure the ownership of the multiple franchise rights: one company, parent/subsidiary, holding company, brother/sister? Talk to your attorney and your accountant to find out which structure can work best for you.

✔ Can you realize any overhead or other cost savings by being affiliated with two or more brands? For example, will vendors combine purchases you use for both concepts for purposes of volume discounts or other benefits?

Smart multi-concept franchisees build up strong management teams. They oversee all their brands, and they assign managers to each entity, which requires two skills: shifting gears and delegating. With multi-concept operations, it's good to be smart if you want to be successful.

Weighing your reasons for branching out

So, you think you can be a chameleon, switching back and forth from one concept to another. The real question is: Why should you?

Just as you did when you bought your first outlet, look at general market trends and demand for a particular product or service. A few factors may prompt you to acquire other brands:

✔ **Silver bullet for a shrinking market:** You want to add franchises, but your territory already is saturated with your first format. So, if you want to keep all your businesses close to home — making them easier to manage — your only option may be to develop another brand. A newer concept, in particular, may have wide-open spaces.

✔ **No room for expansion:** Although the market may have room for growth, local zoning restrictions, or a tight real-estate market and a limited supply of appropriate locations, could make affordable or available locations hard to find, which may stunt or delay your growth with your first franchise system.

✔ **Defensive play:** You own the only chicken joint in town. Customers flock to your restaurant. But will they fly the coop if one of your competitors rolls into town? You decide that you don't want someone else clawing at your niche, and you open the other chicken brand yourself. Although you may cannibalize your own sales, you'd much rather divide sales between your own units than lose market share to a stranger. Keep in mind, though, that you may or may not be allowed to do this under your current franchise agreement. (We cover noncompete clauses in the section "Reviewing the Ties That Bind: Legal Issues," later in this chapter.)

✔ **Diversification:** Consider yourself lucky if your franchise always runs smoothly. More likely, your business goes on a roller-coaster ride every now and then. It may dip or rise according to competition, economic conditions, seasonality (ice cream and skis, for example), trends, or the state of your franchise concept. Operating more than one brand may get you through these cyclical flows. You may even be able to cross-train some of your employees to balance ebbs and flows in seasonal businesses. The bottom line: Diversifying spreads your risk and could give you better use of your staff. Of course, if the business cycles coincide, the result may be disastrous.

✔ **Economies of scale:** Adding units may bring economies of scale. Obviously, a lot depends on the synergies between the concepts. You're a big spender now. If product lines match up, and you're not restricted by the franchisor, you may net better deals from suppliers. The same goes for print, TV, and radio ads. You may be able to leverage an office, computer and phone systems, accounting departments, and warehouse space. And if you locate your franchises under the same roof, you may be able to slash utility, real estate, and other fixed costs. (See the section "Siamese Brands: What Co-Branding Can Do for You," later in this chapter, for details on operating multiple brands in shared space.)

✔ **Cross-marketing momentum:** If the multiple brands are complementary, you can pitch your marketing to the same customers. You already have a market base with one concept. Customers know and trust you, so sales may take off quicker with the next brand.

For example, say your original business is a carpet-cleaning franchise such as Rainbow International (a franchise offered by The Dwyer Group). Also, suppose that your choice for a second business is a plumbing franchise such as Mr. Rooter (also a franchise offered by The Dwyer Group). You may have a natural cross-marketing opportunity. Your Rainbow

International customers already know you and trust your work at cleaning their carpets. Now when you launch your Mr. Rooter franchise, you can let your existing customer base know about your new venture and possibly jump-start your sales. Better still, as customers use one of your business services, you can offer them a discount on your other services. That's one way to continually reward your customers of both brands.

✔ **Prime locations:** With more concepts, you can respond to more real-estate opportunities. Say a prime spot in a mall or strip center opens up. It may be too small for your original concept but perfect for brand B. Or maybe the center already has stores that compete with brand A, and the landlord won't allow any more direct competitors to have space in the center; you can put in (noncompetitive) brand B instead. For example, if you're a franchisee of Play It Again Sports and Once Upon a Child, both consignment-type franchises offered by Grow Biz International, you have flexibility when that perfect spot opens up.

✔ **Employee retention:** As a one-concept franchisee, you may not be able to satisfy an employee's desire for more hours, diversification, or career advancement. After you add units, opportunities open up. For example, the assistant manager at your auto-detailing shop does a bang-up job, but your manager is here for life; open up a brake-repair franchise, and the assistant manager is a perfect candidate to run it. It's a win-win situation: You retain a known commodity, and your employee gets to move up the ladder.

✔ **Pure excitement:** You feel like a kid in a candy store. A franchisor is marketing a hot concept, and you absolutely must get a piece of the action! You want a challenge. Or you've been successful, you've earned a bundle, and you feel primed to do it again. If this is really your core motivation, take a moment and be careful. This is often the warning sign of what may be an emotional decision rather than a well thought-out business plan. Frequently, someone who has been successful in one business concludes that he is a business genius and can succeed at anything. He opens a second, unrelated business in which he has no experience, and he crashes!

Any or all of these reasons may prompt you to speed ahead. We must flash a cautionary yellow light, however. Think twice if you want to acquire other brands. Doing so could

✔ Reduce your focus on your original business.

✔ Hurt your financial situation.

✔ Overtax, not leverage, management and existing systems.

✔ Cause friction between you and your current franchisor.

✔ Take time away from you and your family, just as your first franchise did when you got started.

Franchising is an inelastic business. By that, we mean that when franchisors grant territorial rights to one franchisee, they often preclude other franchisees or the franchisor from establishing new locations in the market — even when market demand exists and competition requires it. This inelasticity is considered one of the biggest weaknesses of franchising when compared to traditional, non-franchised businesses. Traditional businesses can deal with the market; franchisors also need to deal with the contracts they have with their franchisees — and those contracts can limit market development.

If you're satisfied with your current operation and you're looking outside the system only because no free territory is suitable for development, consider buying existing operations from other franchisees or the franchisor. Consider contacting your franchisor in advance and sharing your plans. You may be able to gain your franchisor's support in restructuring your agreement into an area-development arrangement. This allows you, after you acquire the other locations, to establish new locations in areas previously restricted from development because of other franchisees' territorial rights, assuming the franchisor is comfortable with your management skills and other resources, the possible new locations, and so on. (See Chapter 11 for more details.)

Reviewing the Ties That Bind: Legal Issues

Before you begin a double shift with another chain, sit down with an experienced franchise law firm, dust off your franchise agreement, and make sure that you can do so, legally. Lest you forgot, franchising includes ties that bind you.

Check out the discussion of dual branding and its legal issues (CD1201) on the CD-ROM.

Most important, review your existing franchise's and the new franchise's *noncompete clauses*. Typically, these clauses prohibit you or a member of your family (among others) from being involved in a competing business or in the same industry during the term of the franchise agreement. Geographic restrictions range from not competing anywhere to not competing in a specific market. Noncompete clauses that restrict you during the term of the franchise agreement are enforceable as long as they're reasonable.

Talk to an experienced franchise lawyer early and get her opinion. When you bought your first franchise, you probably weren't contemplating investing in another opportunity from a different franchisor.

A noncompete clause in the same business or industry is in the typical franchise agreement. Some noncompete clauses go to opposite extremes, however. Most liberal hotel franchisors don't restrict franchisees at all, so they can operate competing brands — even right next door. At the other extreme, a few chains forbid franchisees from participating in any type of business — competing or not — during the term of the franchise agreement.

In any case, don't try to be cute and attempt a ploy such as putting the new (competing) business in the name of a relative or friend. If the franchisor finds out, you can expect swift legal action in response, and courts and arbitrators don't look upon such conduct in a friendly way.

When you renew your franchise agreement, the new agreement may read differently from your current agreement in many ways, including the noncompete language, and a business that you legally acquired under the old franchise agreement may now be forbidden. If the noncompete clause changes or product lines differ, you have cause for concern: You may be holding a hot potato — another franchise that's now "competitive," even though it wasn't before. If you find yourself in this situation, you have three choices:

- ✔ Don't renew your original franchise agreement.
- ✔ Divest yourself of one of your franchise affiliations.
- ✔ Try negotiating with the franchisor.

Speak with your legal advisor to determine whether you have any legal rights that would preclude the franchisor from making these types of changes to the agreement.

Other contractual clauses may affect your acquisition plans. Franchisors may restrict the goods and services you can sell. And, typically, you can't use your franchise premises for any other purpose without the franchisor's okay. So, before you set up the sugar cones and sprinkles, check out whether you can add an ice cream business to your hamburger franchise.

You want to be familiar and predictable to the consumer. Wendy's doesn't allow its franchisees to open up, say, a Dairy Queen inside a Wendy's, because it's not their business. And it's confusing to the customers because they would see this Dairy Queen here and then they would go to a Wendy's 5 miles away and wonder, well, why doesn't this one have a Dairy Queen? The whole purpose of franchising is to be predictable to the consumer.

Even if you have clear sailing to jump aboard another chain, confess your expansion plans to your existing franchisor. You don't need their blessing; but your frankness avoids muddying the waters and is part of being a good team player and shipmate. You may also want to tell the new franchisor about your current business. (It'll probably be on the franchise application anyway.)

Investigating Endlessly — Again

Each time you expand, you need to get back to the basics: researching the franchise concept, the franchisor, its franchisees, and the competition. Franchises — even from the same franchisor or within the same industry — can be as different as night and day. So, even if some of the faces are the same, the old rules still apply: investigate, investigate, investigate.

Now that you're in the game, you do have some advantages: You know the ins and outs of being a franchisee. And you've purchased a franchise once, or more than once before, so you know what to look for in a chain. (See Chapter 4 for information about choosing a franchise.)

Because you're already a franchisee, feel free to tweak our formula a bit by investigating some areas more than others or asking questions based on your own experience. For example, if your franchisor offers great product discounts, see if you'll get the same royal treatment again. Or if franchisee-franchisor relations are rocky at your existing chain, you know how disruptive this can be on a franchisee's operations. This time, because of your experience, you're better able to dig into the issues that are important to you.

Don't get complacent if you're buying another brand from your existing franchisor who happens to also sell other concepts. Obviously, you know the franchisor. But now may be a good opportunity to take a fresh peek. And, of course, you still have to examine the individual concept. Think of each brand as a company within a company. Scrutinize the staff and support. Also, your core franchise concept may be tops in its industry, but another concept offered by your existing franchisor may be trailing, raising a whole new set of challenges. For the inside scoop, contact existing and former franchisees of the sister concepts and talk to headquarters employees assigned to this arm of the company. Also, ask whether the employees assigned to the new concept have the appropriate experience in that industry, are being spread too thin with responsibilities for multiple brands or concepts, and so on.

If you buy two different concepts from the same franchisor, watch out for the so-called *cross-default provisions*. For example, if you're behind in your royalty payments under one franchise agreement, this may be a default under your other franchise, exposing you to the loss of both if you don't cure the default. Check your agreements carefully. The easiest way to avoid this dilemma is not to buy into two concepts offered by the same franchisor if this cross-default provision could affect you.

Whether you're dealing with the same or a different franchisor, scout out a few multi-concept franchisees in your current chain and the new one. The more similarities to your situation, the better. The trick is to get the sharpest possible picture of owning multiple concepts. A good source for this type of information will be members of the franchisee advisory council of both systems. They're likely to know the players and who's doing what.

You're a franchisee — we know you're busy. But don't cut corners in your investigation. Being successful once doesn't guarantee success again.

Deciding whether to Mix Industries or Brands — Or Neither

If you're thinking expansion, don't just jump in the car and go. You need to be headed in a specific direction. One big decision you need to make is whether you want your second — or subsequent — venture to have any connection to your existing one. Here are some possibilities:

- **Do you want your franchises to be in the same industry?** Lots of restaurant franchisees add other food concepts, for example. A recent survey by Restaurant Finance Monitor (www.restfinance.com) shows that 76 of the nation's top 200 restaurant franchisees (by revenue) own and operate more than one restaurant concept.

- **Do you want the brands to be complementary so you can overlap some of your operations or marketing? On the other hand, do you want to run them separately?** Picture an automobile repair center where you own the franchise rights to a quick oil change franchise, a muffler or brake franchise, and maybe a body-shop concept. Your customers never have to leave your lot — except to drive home.

- **Do you want to stick with the same franchisor or switch to another company?**

Generally, franchisors won't be very happy if you jointly market brands of different parent companies; some companies don't even want you to link their own brands. Most franchise agreements expressly allow the franchisor to control all marketing that involves their brand. Franchisors control their trademarks, so they can police any such tie-ins. (Read about the do's and don'ts of marketing in Chapter 10.)

Buying more from the same franchisor

You're not the only one talking multiple concepts. Franchisors are, too. More companies than ever are franchising more than one brand. In 2005, of 1,555 systems, 79 systems had two concepts/programs, 9 had three concepts/programs, 7 had four concepts/programs, and 5 had five or more concepts/programs, according to FRANdata, a Washington, D.C., franchise information and research company. And some conglomerates have various separately incorporated entities that sell franchises — such as The Dwyer Group, which includes seven service-based franchising companies.

Your strategy — and the whole viability of taking on a second brand or second franchisor or becoming involved in a new industry — may depend on your willingness to return to the trenches. You'll need to learn new skills, operating methods, and industry and brand terminology; to retrain or hire new management; and to work with a new franchising partner. If that's not viable for you, then expansion within your existing concept may make the best sense.

Looking at your franchisor's other concepts

Multi-concept franchisors are starting additional brands from scratch, acquiring companies, or doing both, and their franchise agreements often give them the express right to do so. The trend of mega-mergers is hitting franchising, too. So, even if your franchisor has only one concept today, it may have more under its umbrella tomorrow. Keep your eyes open: Franchisors typically introduce new concepts to existing franchisees first, particularly if they've been team players and successful operators with the existing brand.

Usually, a multi-concept franchisor's brands are within the same industry or complementary industries; however, some are unrelated. Here's a glimpse of what's out there:

- Wendy's/Arby's Group, Inc., is the parent company of both Wendy's and Arby's. (Wendy's and Arby's merged in 2008.)

- Dunkin' Brands is the parent company of Baskin-Robbins and Dunkin' Donuts, which, combined, has over 14,800 outlets worldwide.

- Moran Industries sells several transmission repair brands and other auto-related services, such as Mr. Transmission, Dr. Nick's Transmission, Multistate Transmission, AltaMere, and Milex.

- The Dwyer Group offers six service concepts: Rainbow International (carpet cleaning), Mr. Rooter (plumbing), Aire Serve (heating and air conditioning), Mr. Electric (electrical repair), Mr. Appliance (appliance repair), and Glass Doctor (automotive glass). It also provides services to an associate company, DreamMaker Bath & Kitchen.

- The ServiceMaster Company offers several franchised opportunities: AmeriSpec (home inspection), Furniture Medic (residential and commercial furniture and wood repair and restoration), Merry Maids (home maid service), and ServiceMaster Clean (janitorial services, commercial carpet cleaning, disaster restoration services, and residential carpet and upholstery cleaning). It's a busy company. The ServiceMaster Company also owns Terminix (pest and termite control), TruGreen ChemLawn (lawns and shrub care), and American Home Shield, which provides home warranties. These companies operate primarily through company-owned branches.

✔ At Mrs. Fields Famous Brands, you find two brands: Mrs. Fields Cookies and TCBY.

You can check the International Franchise Association (IFA) Web site (www. franchise.org) for other companies that offer multiple franchise brands.

Considering the values of buying twice from the same guy or gal

Expansion opportunities may be right under your nose. If you're happy with your franchisor, looking to acquire more of its brands, rather than an outsider's, is natural — as long as the franchisor's other concepts make good business sense for you. You'll still deal with one company. You know its business philosophy, its business culture, its strategic plan, its management, its system functions, and its support services. The comfort factor and stability could shorten your learning curve tremendously. And you increase the odds of greater negotiating leverage with your franchisor when you have more units of its brand(s).

Another possible value is brand synergy. If a franchisor's multiple concepts complement each other, you could gain volume-purchasing discounts, central customer service systems, and cross-selling opportunities.

Some franchisors act on these synergies. For example, they may cross-market concepts, helping you move sales between the brands. But just as important, some *don't* capitalize on these synergies or even allow cross-merchandising. If you're buying a franchise from a diversified company because of its scope, make sure it doesn't just sit back. Otherwise, you'll be responsible for producing cross-marketing materials or hooking up with franchisees of sister chains; you can still use these synergies to your advantage — doing so just takes more effort.

Shopping well

Don't just assume that what succeeded once will succeed again. Not all concepts — even from the same franchisor — are winners; numerous multi-concept franchisors have divested themselves of some brands that didn't work out. And not all concepts get equal attention from a franchisor. Beware of so-called *franchise factories* — companies that spit out concepts with the sole intent of selling franchises rather than servicing franchisees and their customers. Also, be leery of those that spread limited resources (particularly human resources) too thin and fail to provide adequate support to each of their concepts.

Kay Marie Ainsley, Managing Director of Michael H. Seid & Associates, says "Many franchisors that choose to offer multiple concepts do so because they have the expertise as well as the resources required to support additional brands." She adds, "Many of the multi-brand franchisors find that there are synergies between their existing brand and their new concepts, and these create opportunities for efficiencies that would not be available otherwise."

What you want is a franchisor that pays attention to each of its concepts (or, selfishly, at least the ones you're buying). In other words, it doesn't play favorites. Does it have good management? Does it have dedicated staff for each brand? Are support services as mature for both? Is the franchisor actually cross-marketing and facilitating franchisee's cross-marketing opportunities with the appropriate programs and tools? A franchisor should maximize its management and resources, not stretch them as the franchisor adds to its family of franchises. The franchisor needs to concentrate as it expands, just as you do.

Be on the lookout for lower prices if you buy more than one brand. Not all franchisors give preferential treatment to existing franchisees, but some reward their own. For example, The Dwyer Group discounts based on a franchisee's years in business, up to 50 percent for seven years or longer.

One more thing: Just because you're an existing franchisee doesn't mean you're a shoo-in with a sister concept. Franchisors still give you the once-over, and some set even tougher qualifications for expansion. For example, in many instances, the ServiceMaster Company hasn't offered a second brand to franchisees because it wasn't "in their best interest," says Jim Wassell, vice president of marketing at ServiceMaster Franchise Services. "We want to make sure that the person with the original brand is really developing that brand aggressively and exploiting that brand as best they can before we encourage them to split their attention to another brand," he says. "It's certainly not for everyone."

Starting fresh with a new company

One big reason to join forces with a different franchisor is because it has the brand you're after. It's that simple. This concept is no different from switching to another pet store because it has healthier treats for your terrier or to a new clothing boutique because it has exclusive fashions from the next Calvin Klein.

You may also want to spread your wings to grab perks that your franchisor doesn't offer. Maybe another franchisor negotiates better discounts, and you can ride those coattails for both of your ventures. Perhaps another chain offers superior training, giving you a franchise MBA that you can apply to all your businesses.

Diluting your focus

Must a Wendy's franchisee have the head honcho's permission to open a franchise of a non-competing chain? No. Would the franchisor like to talk to him about it? Yes.

Wendy's has learned from experience about diluting focus. If you want to develop a second chain, how are you going to do it? Will you take some of your best operators from Wendy's and move them over to the new place? Will you run it yourself? Will you take 20 percent of your workday and go work on this other chain?

When you started Wendy's, you devoted your time — morning, noon, and night — to making it a success. Why would it be different when you buy into another franchise? You're still going to have to devote morning, noon, and night to making it a success. How will you do both?

Wendy's wants its franchisees to go in with their eyes open. The franchisor doesn't want them to dilute their focus and risk losing their success rate at Wendy's. It also wants to make certain they haven't forgotten what it's like to open the very first store and the time commitment and attention that are necessary.

By splitting loyalties, you may gain negotiating power with franchisors. Consider this: You have limited capital resources to develop more franchises, and a prime site emerges. Should you put in brand A or brand B? A franchisor, knowing that you're weighing the two concepts, may agree to lower fees or grant other concessions if you give priority to its brand. On the other hand, a franchisor may give preference to those it sees as most loyal; you'll simply have to make a judgment as to your franchisor's attitudes.

Finally, call us doomsayers, if you must, but you may want to diversify your risk. Say you've bought two or three brands from the same franchisor. If that company tumbles into legal or financial trouble, all your franchises may go down the tubes along with it. Stay diversified and, hopefully, some of your concepts will remain intact if the others crack up.

Tread gently when advertising multiple brands. Focus on maintaining brand identity for each concept. In cross-marketing, you don't want to confuse the customer.

Siamese Brands: What Co-Branding Can Do for You

If you flip through any directory of franchises, you quickly see that franchising responds to consumer demand. Pick a need, and a franchise probably fills it. Not surprisingly, then, when harried consumers began craving convenience — *voilà!* — a strategy called *co-branding* appeared on the franchising scene. Co-branding is when more than one brand operates in a single location.

It may be two brands (dual branding), three brands (triple branding), or any other multiple (multi-branding). For simplicity's sake, we'll refer to this tactic as co-branding.

No doubt, you've seen these kinds of partnerships. We bet you've probably dropped some dollars at them, too. The most visible are travel centers along the nation's highways, combining fast-food franchises, gas stations, and convenience stores. In one fell swoop, you can fill up your belly, your car, and your pantry. Shopping malls, airports, and stadiums host co-branded food courts — the ultimate smorgasbord of franchised concepts. And look around Main Street in your own town. You'll probably see some two-in-one franchises, perhaps a combination dessert/convenience store or sandwich shop/car wash. If none is there yet, believe us, they'll be coming soon.

Setting up a one-stop shop

You're reading this chapter because you want to acquire other brands, right? Well, co-branding certainly offers you the opportunity to do this in a couple of ways:

- **Buy the franchise rights to each of the concepts you bundle under one roof from either the same or different franchisors.** Taking this approach lets you control the whole operation. Expect to sign separate franchise agreements and pay separate franchise fees for each concept.

- **Stick with just one concept but take advantage of co-branding at the same time.** This tactic may sound contradictory, so listen up. You can

  - **Own a franchise and share space with a franchisor or franchisee(s), even an independent businessperson, who operates different concepts.** You could be the quick-service restaurant inside a convenience store operated by a major oil company. Just make sure enough profits are available to go around.

  - **Lease space.** You buy the franchise rights to a concept and lease space, say, in an airport or a hotel.

See whether the franchisor sets different fees or net-worth requirements for co-branded locations as opposed to traditional outlets. Also, find out if you get a break by buying more than one concept from the same franchisor.

So, where should you hang your multiple banners? Co-branding today occurs everywhere. You can find Yum! Brands' six brands (Taco Bell, Pizza Hut, KFC, A&W, WingStop, and Long John Silver's) sharing space in *pad locations* (freestanding locations in parking lots) outside of malls, just as other franchisors set up shop inside ballparks, arenas, and airports.

Wherever you choose to set up, check out the site just as you would for a single franchise, including demographics, traffic patterns, competition, and accessibility (see Chapter 7 for more on site selection). Then add the co-branding factor. With multiple concepts, you may be able to secure a better location. A landlord may have a prime 2,000-square-foot location, but you can only use 1,200 square feet for your brand. But if you co-brand with another concept, together you may be able to use the entire location. In addition, because the cost of developing two brands under one roof is typically lower than building two separate locations, you may be able to afford more-expensive land, because you'll be dividing the development costs.

In selecting a site for a co-branded unit, consider these issues:

- Is the site conducive to operating more than one brand? If you have a breakfast site, it had best be on the going-to-work side of the street in most neighborhoods. However is that location suitable to blend also with a dinner concept?

- How much will you save by developing one building, not two? (Consider the sharing of land costs, taxes, and maintenance fees.)

- Will your brand be front and center?

- Will you have adequate room for signage to maintain brand identity?

- Can customers easily gain access to, say, the counter space and cash registers for each brand?

- Are common areas large enough to accommodate customers of multiple concepts?

- Do both concepts benefit from the same traffic patterns?

You may not be lucky enough to get equal treatment for every concept in every location. (After all, doesn't someone always end up with the short end of the wishbone?) If you're the stronger brand, try negotiating a more prominent position. In any case, you don't want to be overshadowed or hidden by another brand, or be inaccessible to your target market.

Combining your resources

Co-branding is taking off because of strength in numbers. With more choices, customers have a reason to stay longer and buy more during each visit.

When co-branding is effective, you draw new customers, boost brand awareness, increase market share, and reduce start-up and ongoing costs.

Here's how to jump aboard this hot trend:

✔ **Find a partner.** But don't just pick one out of a hat. The other brand should complement your brand, not cannibalize sales. It should add value for a customer. Combine a breakfast concept with a lunch/dinner concept, and you have something for everyone throughout the day. (In industry lingo, this is called *balancing dayparts*.)

When picking a partner, you can look to brands from the same franchisor or different franchisors. Some multi-concept franchisors such as Yum! Brands and Wendy's are integrating their concepts into co-branded sites. Others are forging alliances with co-branding partners; in other words, they're doing the legwork for you.

Be aware that not all franchises belong together. Buddying up with another brand that is equal to or stronger than your brand sends good vibrations to consumers — and can steer sales your way. But a weaker brand or a concept that doesn't have your standards can pull your business down. You want to add, not take away, credibility. You also don't want to confuse a customer with too many concepts in a single location. The same advice is true for picking a location, by the way. If your franchise strives to give a wholesome, clean environment to your customers, and the center you select has dirty parking lots and filthy common restrooms, guess what? The site's appearance negatively impacts the customers' perception of your brand.

✔ **Look before you leap.** Make sure that your franchisor lets you add a specific concept on your premises (see the section "Reviewing the Ties That Bind: Legal Issues," earlier in this chapter). In fact, if your franchisor has not been previously involved with the additional concept, it may need to negotiate a "treaty" with the other organization dealing with a number of concerns each franchise system may have regarding co-branding locations. You may end up being part of a three-way negotiation! Although this can work out to everyone's advantage, make sure that you have experienced franchise counsel on your side to protect your interests. Also, think ahead: If you operate a single-brand unit, and your franchisor's new strategy is co-branding, you may be pressured by your franchisor to co-brand in the future.

✔ **Reconfigure the real estate.** You can either develop a co-branded location from scratch or retrofit an existing location. Obviously, size is essential. With some renovations, you may be able to squeeze another concept into an existing unit.

In arranging your co-branded unit, you should have two goals: to have each concept maintain its own identity and to reap economies of scale. So, with a co-branded food franchise, you'll want — or your franchisor may require — separate counters, signage, and cash registers. You ring in the overhead savings by sharing a parking lot, restrooms, and dining area. Be sure to configure the concepts to grab customers' attention, making it conducive for them to purchase brand B even if they only came in for brand A. These are the incremental sales at the root of co-branding.

Some franchisors may allow you to share space but not equipment or employees, so be sure to factor this in.

✔ **Work out the details.** If you twin with another franchisee (rather than own the multiple brands yourself), determine how you're going to split the cost of utilities, insurance, repairs, landscaping, snow removal, and cleaning common areas. And if the franchisors or the operators have different standards of cleanliness and service, you must address these issues, too.

Sometimes partnerships look better on paper than in reality. If you're sharing space with someone else, make sure that you can live with this stranger — and his habits.

✔ **Staff up.** Ideally, you want to identify separate staff for each concept to maintain brand identity and to assure that you meet adequate training and staffing standards. To save money, you may be able to have one manager oversee all the concepts. Franchisors have various staffing requirements at co-branded units. Some mandate entirely separate staff. Others have few standards and may allow an employee to throw on a branded hat and apron over a gas station uniform to make a bologna and cheese sandwich, and then run back to the pump. You need to be sure that the standards for each brand match up.

If you cross over employees between multiple concepts, you may be able to offer them more hours of work, which often helps recruit and retain better employees.

✔ **Decide on your "menu."** Depending on the concept, you may have some leeway to adjust your product offerings.

✔ **Cross-market.** Signage helps you cross-market various brands, so make sure your brands are clear to consumers. Do they get equal billing? In addition, many co-branding partners share the costs of traditional advertising and offer coupons that drive traffic from one concept to another. Through co-branding, you could also get a free ride on national advertising if, say, one chain does national advertising and the other doesn't. You could also consider training cashiers or other employees to recommend additional purchases from the other concepts.

Building an empire through the addition of other brands is becoming more popular. Markets are maturing, and franchisors are constantly developing new concepts that may just suit you. But remember: You have to do your homework. Ask yourself these questions:

✔ What impact will the new brand have on your current operations?

✔ What impact will expansion with the new brand have on you financially? Will other opportunities suffer?

✔ Are the operational, financial, marketing, or other synergies between your existing franchise and your new franchise real?

✔ Does either franchise agreement place restrictions on you that could cause you problems during or after the term of the agreements?

✔ How strong is the new franchisor you'll be joining? Does it have the support programs you've become accustomed to from your existing franchisor?

Chapter 13

When the End Is Nigh

The topic may seem odd to you, but we want to talk about ending a franchise when you're just about to begin one. As the expression goes, all good things come to an end. Bad things, too. In franchising, you're not locked in for life. When your franchise agreement expires, you may or may not want to renew. Or a time — any time — may come when you want to sell out. That's okay. The hope is that someone — your children, a fellow franchisee, your franchisor, or a complete stranger — wants to pick up where you've left off.

We want to be completely honest with you. Sometimes franchisees leave a system because their businesses have failed or because the franchisor terminates them for, say, withholding royalties or violating other aspects of the franchise agreement. But lots — lots and lots — leave the ranks because they want to, not because they have to. Perhaps your franchise caught on like wildfire, and you want to take the money and run. Perhaps your spouse got a great job offer out of state, and you want to ride her coattails. Perhaps you've brainstormed a new business (even want to become a franchisor), or this was your final hurrah before retirement. Or perhaps you've rolled one too many bagels, heard one too many complaints from customers, or butted heads with your franchisor one too many times.

Whatever the scenario, the end doesn't have to be as ominous as it sounds. It could be the start of a whole new world.

Going for Round Two (Or Three or Four)

On a franchise journey, you don't hold an open-ended ticket. You're leasing the right to use a franchisor's brand name and system for a specific period of time. Depending on your franchise agreement, your rights may last 5, 10, 15, maybe 20 years. The clock usually starts ticking on the day you sign your franchise agreement and not when your location opens for business. So, at some point, you'll have to — happily or unhappily — end the relationship.

At the end of the term, you have a few options:

- ✔ If you've had enough, you can simply thank the franchisor for the ride and move on. You'll relinquish the brand name, and the franchisor may resell rights to that particular area to a new franchisee. You'll also probably sell your building, equipment, and other assets, or return them to the lessor.

- ✔ You may sell the business to another person who could sign a new franchise agreement with the franchisor — that is, if the franchisor wants to sign a new franchise agreement.

- ✔ Depending on your franchise agreement, you may choose to stay in the game, but as an independent. You could take down the brand you've been leasing, put up your own brand, and continue as you did before. In most instances, though, this won't be an option.

- ✔ If you think the trip's been too short, you most likely can renew your franchise agreement and go around again. Usually, you have to notify the franchisor in writing within a specific time period of your intent to renew. You need to check your original franchise agreement, but you're usually required to give notice six months before your existing agreement expires.

In this section, we cover the last of these options — renewing your franchise agreement.

Knowing how much the fee will cost you

Just as with the first time around, when you renew, you obtain the rights to use the franchisor's trademarks and operating methodology in a certain area for another specified period of time. Each franchisor puts its own spin on successor agreements. Many successor agreements are for the same number of years as the original agreement (such as ten years with one ten-year renewal); others are for a shorter period of time (such as ten years with two five-year renewals). Some franchisors offer unlimited, continuing renewals (called *evergreen agreements*); others permit only one successor term. Don't assume that the brand is yours to use for life.

Be aware of the terms when you sign the original franchise agreement (see Chapter 6); fully understanding the agreement helps you plan your business — and your life.

Renewal or successor fees also are across the board. Some franchisors don't charge any fee. (Many franchisee advocates think that's the way it should be.) Other franchisors require either a flat amount — typically ranging from several hundred to several thousand dollars — a percentage of the then-current franchise fee, or the same fee they charge for new franchisees.

However the franchisor figures the fee, it shouldn't be anywhere as steep as your initiation dues, because you're not starting from scratch this time. The franchisor's job is a lot easier because you've already mastered operating the franchise. You don't need initial training, site selection, or inventory advice; you've already been there, done that.

Still, don't be surprised if you're required to undergo some training. For example, the franchisor may require you to install a new computer system and proprietary software upon renewal — and you may have to go to corporate headquarters for training. You may or may not have to pay for the training, but you can pretty much count on covering your travel expenses.

Putting together a brand-new agreement

Will the deal be the same as the original agreement? Not usually. A number of years — 5, 10, 20 — have passed since you signed the original agreement. The system and marketplace have evolved and changed — and, in most cases, so have the terms of the agreement. You should expect to sign a new franchise agreement — typically, the then-current franchise agreement for new franchisees. Logically, franchisors adapt over the years, which could mean a change in fee structure and operating system, new products or equipment, or different territorial rights.

The new agreement may differ substantially from the one in your hip pocket, which may work to your benefit — or detriment. An agreement that works to your detriment probably doesn't sound fair to you, right? After all, you've paid your dues all these years. But, as you know by now, franchisors want consistency, and renewal brings the old franchisees into compliance with the terms of the deal newer franchisees receive.

Many franchisees are surprised, and sometimes angry, at the differences between the arrangement they have and the one being offered when they want to extend the relationship. The royalty and advertising fees may have changed, the size of their territory — or even having a protected territory — may have changed, and the cost of bringing the location to the then-current design (a common feature of renewal agreements) may be high. You have to make a decision when the time comes, but be prepared for, not surprised by, the changes. During the term of your franchise, keep abreast of the changes your franchisor is making to new franchise agreements. Discuss them with your franchisor. Keep in mind, though, that times do change, and the needs of the system change as well.

A limited number of states have laws that limit a franchisor's right not to renew your franchise. Rupert Barkoff, a partner with Kilpatrick Stockton LLC, Atlanta, Georgia, says, "If your franchisor has informed you that your franchise will not be renewed, you should immediately consult with your attorney as to your rights. One way to avoid surprises is to try to negotiate limitations on the franchisor's ability to change the deal at renewal time before you sign the original franchise agreement."

Be on the lookout for changes in the following:

- Royalty and advertising fees
- Territorial rights
- Remodeling requirements
- New equipment and signage
- Training requirements
- Renewal or successor terms
- Material business terms of the relationship

You may face a hike in royalty and advertising fees — which may have swelled in line with the system's growth — especially if you got in on the ground floor of a franchise. These fee bumps aren't cut-and-dried, either; some franchisors carry over their existing royalty structure for renewing franchisees.

Very often, you have to make remodeling changes. Typically, franchisors require renewing franchisees to do anything that the majority of existing franchisees must do. Perk up your ears, however, if the franchisor requires excessive remodeling. Reasonable upgrades are understandable because, again, franchisors want consistency. You have to define *reasonable*. For example, would you like to live with the same bright purple paint for another ten years when the walls at new franchises are bathed in lavender? So, you may have to paint, lay new carpet, put up new signage, redo the seating area, install new equipment, or add a drive-through window. A franchisor may offer a cap on remodeling costs (limiting the amount of money a franchisee is required to spend) or a monetary incentive. Find out whether any offers are on the table.

Franchisors typically ask for some additional things upon renewal. They want evidence that you can continue to occupy the same or a different location — in other words, a lease, rental agreement, or deed. After all, they don't want you frying chicken in the middle of the street. And you typically have to sign a general release of liability of all claims under the prior franchise relationship. The concept behind that release is this: If you've got a claim against us, raise it now.

Watch for any substantial changes to the material business terms of the relationship. One big issue today is the method used to resolve franchise disputes. Perhaps a franchisor now requires mediation with a neutral party, which is a whole lot different from requiring you to bring legal action in the franchisor's home state. Another hotbed of controversy is *encroachment,* or when someone sells products or services in your operating area (read about this in Chapter 7). Make sure that the rules haven't changed — or that you can live with them if they have.

Times have really changed. When many franchisees originally signed their franchise agreements, alternative locations may not have been as popular, and competition from Internet sales certainly wasn't even considered. However, e-commerce doesn't require the establishment of locations, so the franchisor may require those Web sites to keep the brand competitive and may not include them in the franchisee's territory. Make sure that you understand the full impact such changes may have on your business. Understand, though, that in the age of the Internet, the idea of protected territory may start to seem as quaint as waiting for the town crier to give you the week's news.

Negotiating change

You feel like you've been a loyal soldier all these years. Shouldn't the franchisor cut you some slack at renewal? You'll never know unless you ask.

One area worth a try is *release of liability.* A typical agreement provides for a general release of all claims in favor of the franchisor. Many franchisees end up negotiating a mutual release of liability — claims against the franchisor and against the franchisee.

You also may try negotiating changes to territorial rights, training, renewal fees, changes in royalties, and remodeling requirements. Perhaps you can strike a deal that places a cap on refurbishing costs, if no such limit exists. Or maybe you can split the royalty increase.

Although negotiations in changes to territorial rights, training, renewal fees, and additional capital costs are not all that uncommon, changes to the then-current royalty rate and advertising fees are, which makes a great deal of sense if you think about it. When you entered the system, the costs for operating the system and supporting the franchisees were at one level, and time may have changed those realities. With advertising, *grandfathering* (giving a benefit to a defined group) older and often lower fees to renewing franchisees puts a strain on the system's advertising budget. Doing so could also have an ill effect on the franchisor's relations with other franchisees, who may be paying a different (and often higher) fee.

If your negotiating efforts foundered when you were a fledgling franchisee, take heart. The franchisor doesn't want to lose you or your location from the system — it doesn't want to incur the cost of finding a new franchisee and everything it takes to get a new franchisee started. So you may have more negotiating power now than when you first started.

Too often, franchisees make the mistake of hiring an attorney to do battle with their franchisor rather than simply sitting down with the franchisor, discussing their concerns, and coming to a negotiated resolution. The only people who benefit from unnecessary legal conflicts are attorneys and some of the advocacy groups whose only way of remaining in business is to ferment disputes between franchisors and franchisees. Discuss your concerns with your franchisor first. You can always bring in the legal troops later if you can't resolve your concerns.

Bowing Out at the Right Time

You open your store at 10 a.m. sharp, hire more employees to service the evening customers who pick up their vitamins or get their hair cut after work, and insist that your employees greet the customer within 20 seconds of their entering the door. You do these things for a reason: timing. Running your franchise according to the clock makes sense. The same goes for selling it: You'll discover right times and wrong times to exit. The time all depends on inner and outer forces.

Just like potential home buyers, potential franchise buyers want to know why you're selling. Your reason could affect the sales price. If a buyer senses urgency, you can bet your bottom dollar he'll try to squeeze out the lowest price. If a buyer understands that you're in an industry that's flying high, she'll pay extra for the privilege of taking over.

Getting personal . . . with yourself

If burnout is the culprit, can you do some things to rejuvenate yourself? Maybe you just need a long vacation to recharge your battery. Or are you so far gone that getting out is the only solution? If the burnout is real, you may want to get out sooner than later, before the telltale signs really start to affect the value of your business. *Remember:* Bad reputations spread faster than good ones.

Maybe you're just downright miserable. Everyone knows someone who unhappily dragged his feet to the same job day in and day out. After 25 years, he was rewarded with a gold watch. After another 25 years of dragging himself to work, he was treated to a blowout retirement dinner (with lobster and champagne, if he was really lucky). You vowed you'd never stay that long if you were unhappy.

Perhaps the business has outgrown you: You lack the skills and money to take it to the next level. Or maybe selling your franchise never crossed your mind until you became seriously ill. In both cases, it may make sense to leave now, before the business — and subsequently, the price — begins to suffer.

Say, though, that you want to sell because you're focused on the future — a new racket, relocation, or retirement. In these cases, financial factors are critical. Do you need to hold out for a certain price to fund the new venture or to secure a worry-free retirement? Do you have to sell within a certain time to kick-start your new life?

Of course, even the best-laid plans can go astray. Maybe you anticipate retiring in five years, but an unsolicited — and incredible — purchase proposal lands at your feet. That may be reason enough to hang your hammock now.

Examining the world around you

Begin by zeroing in on the economy because good times are conducive to buying and selling a business. When interest rates are low and financing is plentiful, more buyers jump into the pool. Even if you're thrilled by your business, if the right offer comes by, can you afford not to take it? Maybe with the proceeds from the sale of your existing business, you can relocate to a place where you've always wanted to live and invest in a new franchise — maybe even one from the same franchisor.

Also, look around the area in which your franchise is located. Are new businesses coming in? Is the area undergoing revitalization? Is the landlord beefing things up? If the answer to these questions is yes, that could bolster the price of your business. In contrast, if the surrounding neighborhood is starting to look shabby, you may have missed the boat. Try to get out before, say, a new mega-bookstore sets up near your little bookshop or before a business-unfriendly local law takes effect.

Then look at your industry. A thriving industry could be your ticket on the gravy train. You want to cash out before a market is saturated, before a fad fades, and before new technology makes your business obsolete.

Finally, consider the state of your franchisor. We know that you did all that due diligence about the company before coming into the franchise, but things change — for better or worse. If same-store sales are starting to get soft because new and innovative competitors are entering the market, maybe you should bail out before the news becomes generally known. Maybe, though, you learned that the franchisor has developed a new product line, and it's going to be a big hit. In that case, you may want to invest in more locations. Market leaders command higher value; declining systems get you less.

If trouble is brewing, or unknowns lie ahead with the franchisor, the situation could scare off buyers or drain the value of your business. Pay attention to such developments as franchisee lawsuits, uncontrolled growth, sagging systemwide sales, unprecedented franchise closures, unacceptable changes to the new franchise agreements, management shake-up, or an acquisition of the franchisor.

Passing On Your Business to Your Children

Little Johnny has swept the floors at your franchise since the broom was taller than he was. Little Jane has stuffed marketing coupons into envelopes since before she could write a complete sentence. Sound familiar? For your franchise to be your children's second home is not at all unusual. But have you ever thought of them not just as helping hands but as potential successors? Growing numbers of franchisees have that very mindset.

Your children have worked hard, love the business, and have helped you build up value. Who better to pass the business on to? Like any parent, you probably think that your kids can do anything. But because we're not talking independent business here, you have to convince your franchisor of their greatness. In a franchisor's mind, children aren't always chips off the old block.

Franchisors normally reserve the right to approve transfer of ownership — even to family members. If an owner dies, some franchisors allow assignment of the franchise to a spouse or heirs without approval; others require approval within a certain time period — say, 12 months — and others require approval immediately. Some franchisors waive a fee for transfer of ownership to a spouse, parent, or child; others don't.

Specific approval criteria usually aren't laid out in a franchisor's documents, so you may want to feel out the franchisor in advance to see what they'll likely require. Gradually acclimating your son or daughter to the franchisor may also help. Take your child, at an appropriate age, to franchise conventions and training, for example. Some franchisors "preapprove" your children or your spouse as future franchisees if they satisfactorily complete the required training program now.

Passing on or selling a franchise to your children isn't as easy as giving them a shiny new bicycle on their tenth birthday. You must plan to transfer a business, which takes time. Lack of planning can significantly affect whether a family business passes smoothly into a new generation. Don't assume that your franchise will be in your estate. Understand your rights contained in the franchise agreement by knowing the answers to the following questions:

- How much time is left on the franchise agreement?

- Do you have the right to transfer your franchise in the agreement? In most instances, the right to transfer is no different from your right to sell your franchise; check with your accountant concerning how you value the franchise and any tax consequences.

- What renewal options are available? Who has to execute them to get the most benefit?

- Does the franchisor require the new owner of the business to sign a new franchise agreement with terms that are different from the ones you're currently operating under? Will the franchisor allow the transfer for only the remaining time you have left under your agreement?

- Does your franchisor have a right of first refusal to buy your business if you try to transfer it to your children?

- Are your children acceptable franchisees to the franchisor? Usually, the franchisor has the right to approve who the new franchisee will be.

Before handing over the reins, you need to develop estate plans, which include the current fair-market value of the business; succession plans, which should include personal, financial, and business goals and time schedules; investment plans; and written strategic plans.

Transferring a family business has financial, legal, and tax consequences. You can pass down the business through estate planning or sell some or all of your interest, or a combination of the two. Consult with accountants, estate attorneys, investment advisors, insurance agents, and family business consultants. Your franchisor may offer succession-planning advice. Nationwide, about 100 family business centers that are affiliated with universities provide education on family business topics.

A successful transition depends a lot on your mindset as an owner. In order to tackle succession planning, you first have to recognize your own mortality. You also have to be willing to let go. Pass down your knowledge (although your kids will likely still have to go through training when they become franchisees) and recognize that they'll probably run things a little differently from the way you did. Let them learn from their own mistakes. And don't push the family franchise on your children; the decision has to be theirs. The feelings that you transmit about the business — from around the dinner table to when you're standing behind the counter — influence them from the time they're off the bottle. Moan, and they'll moan, too; be positive and watch the good feeling spread.

Your kids have to do their share, too. Oftentimes, they'll just work the family business and never have to go on job interviews or wear a suit to the office. But the lack of a well-rounded work background doesn't work well for succession. Outside experience adds credibility and kills a "boss's son" attitude among employees.

Selling Out

What you should *not* do if you want to exit your franchise is simply turn out the lights, lock the door, and vanish. Leaving in this way would be wasting all the sweat equity — and real equity — you've pumped into your business all these years. Even if you want to disappear, your business doesn't have to. Value is there, and you should reap it.

When you want out, you can sell (or assign or transfer — or whatever the legal language is in your agreement) your interest in the franchise agreement and sell your assets (such as the building, fixtures, and equipment if you own them). Doing so can add up to a big chunk of change.

Smart franchisees orchestrate their exit strategies meticulously, from the overture to the finale. They devise a personal business plan, plotting when and how they want out. In this way, they can continue to have one foot firmly in their franchise while the other foot is inching out the door.

Beginning to prepare several years before your target date makes sense. You want to take steps to boost the value of your business — and doing so takes time. You also need to investigate and then select an appropriate sales vehicle. After you put your franchise up for sale, it could get swept up right away, or it could take weeks, months, or even years to sell. You also have to insert another element in the timeline: the franchisor, who gets a voice on several items before the deal is done.

The word on the street is that 20 percent of companies on the market sell right away. The other 80 percent don't, because they're overpriced or the owner didn't get the company in shape. So, start preparing — and good luck.

Getting the most return on your investment

Selling a franchise is very much like selling a house. Obviously, you don't have to light a fire in the fireplace or fill the air with the aroma of freshly baked apple pie. Still, you want to make your business look, feel, and be its best before potential buyers cross the welcome mat. What you put into the selling process affects what you'll get out of it.

The first place to start is with your finances. Without question, a prospective buyer's biggest concern is your bottom line. Is your business profitable? The only way anyone knows for sure is if your books are in tip-top shape — clean enough to pass the strictest military inspection. Give yourself at least three years' lead time to start keeping accurate records. By "accurate," we mean bumping your Porsche, artwork, and other personal assets you used to minimize taxes off your financial statements (and by the way, they shouldn't be there in the first place). Your books should reflect only the business's true expenses and revenues. Set up your records by using generally accepted accounting principles and consider including audited annual statements. Try to settle any financial obligations, liens, and claims or lawsuits from suppliers, customers, or other parties. Also, talk to your accountant and your attorney this far in advance for financial-planning purposes — such as setting up charitable trusts — so that you don't get slammed in post-sale taxes.

Have other papers in order, too. Prospective buyers see value in such things as business plans, employee records, supplier contracts, operational diagrams, and, of course, organized franchise support materials. Keep all your operations and training manuals, as well as any additional information that may come in handy — such as materials from seminars or conventions, surveys, the title, and environmental information.

Next, cosmetic changes may be in order. You already should be in good shape because you've had to meet the chain's standards all along. Still, any business could probably use some spit and polish in some nook or cranny. Be your own worst critic; attack things that a customer — and, therefore, a buyer — would see. Low-cost, routine maintenance pays off here. You may want to get new blinds, paint some walls, and straighten the pantry.

Bigger investments take more thought. For example, should you upgrade equipment or remodel to meet current standards, or should you let the new franchisee deal with — and pay for — these requirements? Will your investment or non-investment impact the sales price or the sale? The answer depends to some extent on how far in advance you're starting to spruce up (will you benefit from the improvements before the sale?) and the extent of the franchisor's requirements upon transfer.

In the end, much of your preparation work in buying a franchise pays off when you're selling. Site selection was quite a chore, right? Here's the payback: Many buyers consider physical location a primary factor in determining value. Real-estate leases that have several years remaining and renewal options are selling points; leases on, say, obsolete equipment are not. Remember the amount of time you spent on employee training? Perhaps the prospective buyer is so impressed that she wants to keep some of your employees. And how about your devotion to customer loyalty? Supplying the new owner with an organized data bank of customer names gives her a head start.

Finally, you can sweeten the deal to make your business worth more at resale. One legitimate concern of a buyer is whether you plan to open a similar business nearby in the near future. His wheels are spinning, figuring that you easily can duplicate your success — and potentially cut in on his turf. The point is moot if you're bound by a noncompete agreement with your franchisor. Otherwise, calm the buyer's fears by striking your own noncompete deal. You may also offer some type of financing arrangement or help train the new owner for a specified period. These latter conditions tie you to the business a little longer, but if they help get you where you want to go, do it.

Figuring out how much your business is worth

At this point, you probably want us to talk dollars. Just how much can you get for your franchise? Answering this question isn't so easy. In the past, many business consultants and brokers were quick to rattle off formulas — usually, a multiple of cash flow. But they've wised up and realized that too many factors go into valuing a business to make it so generic. Every business has to be valued by itself.

Here's another reason why rules of thumb don't work. Say that you're basing a valuation purely on gross sales. Well, you'll notice a huge difference between a franchise that's sunk from $1 million to $500,000 in sales and a business that's grown from $250,000 in sales to that same $500,000. You'll also notice a big difference between a franchise with 3 years remaining on the contract and one with 23 years remaining on the contract.

Valuations are based on the financial facts of the business, the current state of the industry, the business's position in the industry, the location of the business, and timing. The key to valuation is that the numbers have to be accurate, and the ultimate value is based on cash flow, assets, and the return on investment anticipated by the buyer.

You can set a higher value on your business if you have time left on the agreement than if you're at the end of your last renewal period.

When you transfer the franchise, many franchisors require the new franchisee to sign the then-current agreement but may not provide them with a full-term and renewal period(s) as they would for a new franchisee. The agreement is modified to provide only the remaining time and renewal periods unexpired from the original agreement. The difference between 3 years and 23 years of remaining life can have a dramatic effect on the selling price of the business. Determine what your franchisor will do concerning the length of time available to the new franchisee. Franchisors often consider an early renewal, especially when only a short period of time remains on the franchise agreement, or they provide the new franchisee with a full term.

You can certainly ask the franchisor and other franchisees what comparable franchises have sold for, but don't expect your franchisor to help you set a price. Doing so could be a conflict of interest if the franchisor has a right of first refusal to buy your business. Doing so also could open the franchisor up to other potential liabilities should the selling price that the franchisor sets for you be lower than you could've reasonably expected.

Having your business appraised is worth the expense. Seek out an independent third party to do the valuation. The cost of a valuation depends on the company, the condition of its records, and the number of locations. The Institute of Certified Business Counselors offers this range: $1,500 to $4,500 for a company that sells for under $2 million. Figure that a valuation takes about 30 days — and plug that into your timeline as well.

Again, just as with selling a house, don't expect your asking price to be your selling price. Be prepared for negotiations, and be willing to compromise. Try to understand the buyer's motivations and to view things from the buyer's perspective. We know that letting go of something you've put your blood, sweat, and tears into is tough, but being calm, rational, and friendly throughout the selling process pays off.

Playing by the franchisor's rules

When selling a franchise, you're not a free agent. Even if a buyer tosses you a great offer, you can't officially catch it until you check out some details with your franchisor.

Most franchisors have what is called a *right of first refusal*. This term means that whenever a prospective buyer makes a bona-fide offer to purchase the franchisee's interest in the franchise agreement or assets, the franchisor has the right to purchase it on the same terms and conditions within a specific time period. Review your franchise agreement to see what rights the franchisor has reserved for itself, how you're required to notify the franchisor of the possible sale, the form of the notification, and how many days the franchisor has to respond.

In other words, your franchisor may end up buying your franchise. Many franchisees have a problem with this provision, and rightfully so. They feel that such a provision hurts their sales efforts. Consider a sophisticated buyer who spends months checking out your franchise and makes an offer — only to be pushed aside because the franchisor moves in, matches the price, and buys it right out from under them. Trust us, this person will not be pleased.

Some sophisticated buyers will not even begin to negotiate with you or do their due diligence on the business if they have to go through the expense while the franchisor will likely match their offer. Discuss this issue with your franchisor and determine what its intentions are before you begin to market your business. If your franchisor decides that it isn't interested in executing on its right of first refusal, get it in writing. Such proof allays the potential buyer's fears.

You also need to deal with the issue of approval. Most agreements give the franchisor the right to approve all transfers of ownership. Think of this right of approval as a prospective groom asking the father of the bride-to-be for permission to marry his daughter before he asks for her hand in marriage. Some provisions add that the franchisor can't unreasonably withhold consent. The word *unreasonable* can be open to debate, however.

Typically, a new franchisee must meet the franchisor's qualifications, fulfill ownership requirements — such as training and remodeling — and sign a then-current franchise agreement.

The franchisor also receives a transfer fee (usually to cover legal and accounting costs). Not all transfer fees are identical for all buyers, so be aware of the exact fee before you start negotiating the purchase price. Instead of charging a flat fee, some franchisors charge a percentage of the then-current franchise fee or even the sales price. Others reduce the fee if the buyer is an existing franchisee or an employee of the franchisor or franchisee.

Transfer fees, training costs, and even the cost of remodeling requirements all can be bargaining tools in the negotiating process — from your end or the buyer's.

Also, expect your franchisor to eyeball the purchase agreement between you and the buyer before anyone signs on the dotted line. Franchisors basically are looking for the following:

- ✔ Any inconsistencies between the purchase agreement and the franchise agreement

- ✔ Debt structure and leverage

- ✔ Overall viability of transaction

- ✔ Structure of ownership and operations

- ✔ Condition of the facility

Don't forget to get your attorney involved in drawing up a purchase agreement.

Franchisors also tend to put in their two cents about a seller's obligations upon transfer. They typically include three conditions of transfer — the franchisee must

- ✔ Pay all monies owed to the franchisor and their affiliates.

- ✔ Sign a general release of all claims against the franchisor.

- ✔ Sign a noncompete agreement. Sometimes the noncompete agreement has already been built into the franchise agreement.

In addition, some companies suggest, highly recommend, or mandate that the existing franchisee remain onboard for a certain amount of time to smooth the transition. They may also require the existing franchisee to stay on as a guarantor of the franchise if the company has concerns about the buyer. These stipulations have both pros and cons. The need for such requirements and how well they work out may depend on the expertise of the new buyer and the personality of the seller. Obviously, just as when you're asked to train a new replacement in corporate America, watching someone fill your shoes is a little awkward. The situation is even more awkward if someone starts messing with your tried-and-true methods. Also, both you and your employees may feel separation anxiety.

On the plus side, in-house mentoring, a consulting agreement, or personal introductions to suppliers and customers should raise the sales price. Purchasers may view your willingness to stay on as an admission that you're not hiding anything. And, you may gain some peace of mind if the new franchisee's a gem — seeing for yourself that your baby is in good hands.

Many franchisors are reluctant to get involved in the sale — especially regarding the selling price. The reason is that if the selling price is high, but the buyer is willing to pay, the selling franchisee may sue the franchisor for stopping the sale. On the other hand, if the franchisor doesn't tell the new franchisee that the price is excessive and the new franchisee is unable to meet his debt service, the new franchisee may sue the franchisor later on. These scenarios create a troubling aspect of the relationship. Many franchisors have worked out formulas concerning debt service–to–cash flow ratios, which they make available to their franchisees. Although not guarantees, specifying these formulas can avoid problems later on. However, several legal precedents suggest that as long as the franchisor is acting in good faith, the franchisor may refuse to approve a deal where it thinks the price is too high. Sometimes the franchise agreement specifically makes an excessive price an acceptable reason for the franchisor to refuse to approve a sale.

Selecting a sales method

Okay, this is it. You're ready to let go. You're convinced the timing is right, you know what your business is worth, and you're aware of your obligations to your franchisor. All that's left is actually putting it on the block.

We suggest that you don't try to market it yourself. Doing so is draining. Besides, you're a franchisee, not a broker or negotiator. Leave the selling to a professional, and concentrate on running your franchise so that you have something to sell.

The most logical place to start is to contact your franchisor. Because franchisors typically have the right of first refusal, checking whether they want to take the business off your hands just makes sense. Selling to a franchisor usually yields the fastest — but not necessarily the highest-priced — deal.

 From the moment you buy your franchise, be alert for signs that your franchisor may be interested in a sale when the time comes: Is the franchisor establishing a pattern of buying back units? Is it repositioning itself with more company-owned franchises? Is it selling pieces of company units to employees in lieu of stock? Is it looking to edge in on your particular market?

Here's another reason for going to the franchisor: If the franchisor isn't interested in buying, it probably knows who is. Potential candidates logically flow through corporate offices. These can be either existing franchisees or new candidates just dying for your territory or — in some systems — any territory. The franchisor considers these leads qualified if they're in its database, which should speed the process along.

Many franchisors are turning informal grapevines into formal resale networks. They've assigned salespeople exclusively or nonexclusively to handle sales of existing units. They market units through newspaper advertising or the Internet. Check whether the franchisor charges a commission for this service.

Sometimes, franchisors have an easier time selling an existing franchise than a new one. That's because an existing franchise is an open book. If a franchisor doesn't make an earnings claim in its Franchise Disclosure Document (FDD; see Chapter 6), buyers of new franchises may have some difficulty projecting earnings. But if a franchisor is selling a live business, the potential new owner can check out her financial health firsthand. As a result, someone who comes in thinking "new" may realize that "used" can work out just as well — if not better.

Here are a few strategies for shopping your franchise:

✔ **Don't rely only on your franchisor to get to existing franchisees.** Tap your chain's franchisee advisory council (see Chapter 9). Put out the word yourself on the chain's intranet forums, and talk up your franchise at conventions and other meetings. If you're active in your system — which you should be — you should know which franchisees are on the prowl for acquisitions. Usually, existing owners more heavily critique your operation and your books, but they also tend to pay more to corral another unit of the same chain.

✔ **Try marketing your franchise on a resale listing service on the Internet.** But be careful, because this sales technique also opens your information to your managers and staff. Owners and brokers pay to post franchises and other business opportunities for specific time periods. The big plus is that the networks — thanks to the power of the Internet — expose resales all over the world, 24 hours a day. Prospective buyers can search for free — by city, state, listing price, and category. They may be put in touch with a broker or the owner, or the listing service may pass the prospective buyer's name to the seller.

✔ **List your franchise with a business broker, the equivalent of a real-estate broker for businesses.** Use a business broker with a national and international network, because the buyer may not come from around the corner. If the business broker is familiar with franchises, all the better. Fees vary by location and sales price. For referrals to a broker in your area, contact the Institute of Certified Business Counselors (541-345-8064) or the International Business Brokers Association (703-437-4377; www.ibba.org).

Now That the Party's Over . . .

You've just completed Life as a Franchisee. Sounds like a movie title, right? Well, most great flicks usually spawn a sequel. Now you need to write yours. Will part two be more enjoyable, more adventuresome, more dramatic, more humorous? It can play out however you want it to.

Of course, you may just want to pocket the box-office sales — take the $100,000 or $500,000, or however much you've made from your franchise and head off to Cancun, indefinitely. But unless you're retirement age, most people get itchy after a while and are ready again to star in a more active role: Life after Being a Franchisee.

Reflecting on your experience

In order to look ahead, look back at your past. Rewinding your experience as a franchisee in your head helps you determine whether you want to do this again, do something similar, or do something entirely different.

So, hop on the couch for another self-analysis session. Before you bought a franchise, you asked yourself a lot of questions to see whether you were cut out to be a franchisee. (Turn to Chapter 3 to refresh your memory.) Now, based on your experience, revisit those questions and see whether your initial answers really held up. This exercise helps you determine what you've learned about yourself:

- ✔ Before you got started, you had to make sure that you weren't very entrepreneurial. Well, did it bother you to always be concerned about rules, standards, and consistency? Did you have to control many urges to do it your way? Were you devastated any time the franchisor flatly rejected one of your suggestions? Or were you thrilled that you had a system to follow — that someone was always there to lead the way?

- ✔ You also asked yourself whether you're a people person. Were you comfortable dealing with customers? Were you able to coach employees — motivate them, criticize them, teach them, and praise them? Or did you cower under the table when you had to confront someone or were confronted?

- ✔ We warned you going in that the franchisor wouldn't run the business for you. Were you able to keep up the pace and work those long hours? Were you annoyed when you'd get called back to the shop for an emergency just when you were settling in to watch a Sunday football game? Did you pitch in and mop the floor with a smile on your face when an employee called in sick?

- ✔ In addition, we stressed upfront the importance of the franchisee-franchisor relationship. How would you rate yours? Were you at loggerheads with the franchisor, or did things run pretty smoothly? Did you milk the system — get involved with other franchisees and tap into the franchisor's resources? Did the franchisor come through? Were you a good franchisee?

- ✔ Think about your particular franchise. Did it end up matching your interests? Did you have the right skills? Were you happy on the job?

- ✔ The most telling question of all is one you pose to existing franchisees during your due diligence: Did you have any fun? Would you do it all over again? Well, would you?

Making your next move

Football players have hung up their jerseys, lawyers have thrown out their law books, and doctors have put away their stethoscopes — all to become franchisees. No kidding. So, if you want to be an ex-franchisee turned football player, lawyer, doctor, or anything else, you should go for it. Don't be afraid to do something totally different (even if you're not going through a midlife crisis).

And just how do you go about plotting out a new path? Read on.

Considering your options

Based on your franchise experience, you may want to begin again in franchising. Here are some options:

- **Becoming a franchisee of the same chain:** Maybe you want to relocate to another area (warmer weather, here you come), buy multiple units, or become an area developer this time. Or how about taking the concept to Paris, *oui?*

- **Switching to another franchise system:** You could stay in the same industry or try a totally different industry. Perhaps you had a retail store before and now you want to try a service business — one that doesn't require as much overhead. Check your noncompete clause before doing anything.

New beginnings also could include the following:

- **Trading up to be a franchisor:** A handful of former franchisees have bought the very franchise companies they were a part of or have become franchisors of different systems. The insight they've gained from being on the front lines is invaluable. ***Remember:*** Dave was an early KFC franchisee.

- **Working for the franchisor:** You may want to stick with the same franchise, but work on the inside — at regional or corporate headquarters, for example. More commonly, the reverse happens — corporate employees become franchisees.

- **Becoming a consultant:** You may want to compete with coauthor Michael and become a franchise consultant. (He was a franchisee and a franchisor before he became a franchise consultant.) Depending on your years in the industry and your expertise, you may have a lot of insight to offer franchise neophytes. You've come a long way, baby!

Double-checking your old agreement before moving forward

If you've learned one thing from your franchise experience, it's to always check the rulebook. Well, the rules are no different after you've relinquished your title as franchisee. Before you plan your next move, go back to your franchise agreement to see whether you're bound by any restrictions.

Virtually all franchise agreements (other than hotel franchise agreements) have noncompete clauses in effect both during and after the contract. Post-term, the contract usually prevents you from owning or operating a competing business in a defined geographic area for a certain number of years. Two years is typical, but it can be longer. The noncompete clause may cite specific businesses, industry segments, or whole industries. It also may cite specific distances from the original franchise, another franchisee, or a company-owned location, or it may have a blanket restriction.

Whatever your long-term plans, whether you choose to stay the course and continue with your location, expand the business into different cities, or sell and go to Tahiti, the one underlying thing you need to remember is that if you do your homework on the front end, if you understand the agreement, and if you plan for your future, you'll have more options and probably a happier future.

Part V

On the Flip Side: Building Your Own Franchise

The 5th Wave   By Rich Tennant

Don't be ridiculous. This is for ordering food. Job interviews are being conducted straight ahead on the left.

NOW HIRING

In this part . . .

Understanding what it takes to become a franchisor and how franchisors operate and grow their businesses is essential if you want to become a successful franchisor yourself. In this part, we look at the elements necessary for business owners to know if they're ready to become franchisors and how great franchisors are set up to provide their franchisees with the support they promise to provide. We also discuss how franchisors support and expand their systems domestically and internationally.

Chapter 14

From Small-Business Owner to Franchisor

• •

In This Chapter

▶ Franchising your business: What are the chances?

▶ Qualifying as a potential franchisor

▶ Finding the help you need to get started

▶ Launching your new franchise: Strategic planning

• •

*B*efore a single franchisee can exist, a franchisor must be born. In the next few chapters, we give you a very brief glimpse of what it takes to make the transition from running your own independent business to becoming a successful franchisor and operating a chain under your brand.

By now, you probably realize that you need more than just legal agreements and disclosure documents to be a franchisor. You need to assess a host of business issues before you even hire a lawyer to help you prepare your legal documents. To develop a franchise correctly, you need to first decide whether you should expand your business, and then, if franchising is the right method to use, determine how you should structure your franchise program.

In just a single chapter, we can't fill you in on everything having to do with feasibility and the development of your franchise system and legal documents — but we give you a start.

The Feasibility of Turning Your Tiny Garden into a Farm

Before you do anything else, the first thing you want to know is whether you should franchise your business in the first place.

Feasibility has nothing to do with whether you can sell a franchise. Trust us, selling franchises — even for a bad concept — is not all that hard. Feasibility also has nothing to do with being the first one in the market selling your products or services. All you have to do for inspiration is take a look at Dave Thomas and John Schnatter, who certainly had a bit of established competition when they started Wendy's and Papa John's, respectively.

When Dave started Wendy's, many pundits said that the market for hamburger chains was already saturated. After all, large, established franchised hamburger chains existed back in August 1972 when Wendy's sold its first franchise to L. S. Hartzog. The same thing was said about John Schnatter's chances in the pizza industry when he founded Papa John's Pizza in 1983. Pizza Hut had begun selling franchises in 1959, Domino's in 1967, and Pizza Inn in 1963 — and those were only a few of the established franchisors against which John had to compete. Looks like the experts got it wrong. No matter what the pundits say, the market will always accept great products, services, and concepts that provide consumers with what they want in the way they want it.

Large, established companies often suffer from *incumbent inertia.* That's a term we use to describe companies that feel so secure in their market position that they don't innovate their products/services and methods of delivery, don't feel threatened by new small competitors, and ultimately wake up to find out that they're not the big boys on the block anymore. Upstart businesses thank their lucky stars for incumbent inertia — it allowed for the creation and success of Amazon.com, Starbucks, FedEx, Home Depot, CNN, Toyota, and thousands more. Smaller firms can move quickly and introduce new products and services that the larger companies can't possibly put out as fast.

In this section, we look at the feasibility of taking your small business and growing it into a nationally known franchisor. You may even want to compete with Wendy's and Papa John's. Impossible? It happens every day.

Deciding whether your business should be franchised

Believe it or not, in the United States, except for the few states that require pre-sale registration of a franchisor's disclosure document, no regulator ever has to see your franchise documents before you give them to a prospect. Becoming a franchisor is that easy. Even Uncle Sam doesn't want to see a copy of your offering circular and agreements before you begin to offer franchises. Outside the United States, having a disclosure document may not even be required.

On the CD-ROM, we include a document on international laws (CD1401), which was assembled by Andrew Loewinger, a partner in the Washington, D.C., office of Nixon Peabody, and by Dave Koch, a partner in the Reston, Virginia, office of Plave Koch.

Whatever business you're in, if you want to know whether you *can* franchise your business, the likely answer is absolutely. But the real question to ask yourself is whether you *should* franchise your business.

Not everything should be franchised. You need a concept that you can teach and that's very simple to execute. There has to be an advantage to franchising for you and your future franchisees, and the concept has to be able to make money.

Putting the legal requirements in context

When you franchise your business, you're offering a license to someone to operate under your brand name. In a handful of states (the registration states), before you begin to offer franchises you have to present your legal document, the Franchise Disclosure Document (FDD; see Chapter 6) to state regulators, whose approval is required before you begin to solicit franchisees.

You need to understand, though, that all the regulators are doing is making sure that your franchise documents meet the minimum legal standards in their states. No regulatory requirement says that you must base your franchise on a good idea. No requirement says that you have to test it or show that it's ever made a dime. And no requirements exist under the law for a franchisor to have any level of competence in the business it's planning to franchise before it does so.

Think of franchise registration as an automobile emissions test: If your car passes the test, you can legally drive it on the street. A passing grade, however, doesn't mean that the car will make it at Indy, or even that the car will make it out of first gear. Truthfully, passing the text doesn't even assure you that you have enough gas to get it off the lot and down to the corner.

All franchise registration means is that you can legally drive your franchise off the lot. But before you begin to develop your franchise system, before you invest in the creation of brochures, before you invest in the creation of legal documents and hire franchise sales and support staff, you'd better first find out whether what you have is franchisable.

Looking at the Criteria for Becoming a Franchisor

When Michael H. Seid & Associates (MSA) looks at determining whether a client is franchisable, we examine a broad spectrum of her business by conducting a systematic franchise diagnostic examination. We compare the client's performance and readiness against other franchised and non-franchised businesses (called *benchmarking*), conduct analytical examinations, and perform other tests — all designed to help the client determine whether she should become a franchisor. Most professional franchise consulting firms, in one form or other, conduct similar feasibility examinations before they begin to develop a franchise program for a client.

At MSA, we have a basic principle about working with companies that want to start a franchise system. Even before we begin a feasibility examination, we look for the following warning flags in a client's business:

- ✔ It's only a concept.
- ✔ It has only a limited operating history.
- ✔ It hasn't had a history of sustained profitability.
- ✔ It isn't currently achieving a reasonable return on investment.

If we see any of these potential danger signs, then likely the business isn't franchisable — at least not yet. Regardless of what a client may have been told by someone else or what she may hope for, chances are good that the company isn't ready to begin franchising. MSA and other professionals will usually recommend to the client that the company first put its house in order and operate the business for a while before developing a franchise system. (Don't be surprised if a franchise packager leaves this step out of the process so that it can keep its fees low. Conducting a proper feasibility review is an essential step before you jump into the deep waters of franchise system development.)

The bottom line is that *franchisability* means that the franchisee is not the guinea pig in the relationship. You've operated the business — profitably and usually more than once. When working with start-up franchisors, good consulting firms and lawyers recommend and encourage clients to conduct a feasibility examination prior to developing a franchise system.

So, what do we look for in determining whether a business can successfully franchise its concept? That all depends on the business. As in most things, one size doesn't fit all. The following are some of the general criteria that

MSA reviews in evaluating whether a client should expand his business and include franchising in his downstream mix:

- ✔ Reality of the existing business
- ✔ Consumer demand for the product or service
- ✔ Management and commitment
- ✔ Ability to expand and availability of franchisees
- ✔ Systemization
- ✔ Skill transfer
- ✔ Localization
- ✔ Differentiation
- ✔ Capital resources required for expansion
- ✔ Economics of the business

Do you have an operating business?

If you don't have an operating business, stop. Go develop one. Run your prototype for a long while; make sure it works. Make sure you understand its ebb and flow, seasonality, customers, suppliers, competition, positioning, and branding. You need to have an understanding of everything about your business. After you've developed one location, develop another one, maybe more, and if you can, do it in more than one city. Then come back.

You need to be able to define, at a minimum, the following from experience:

- ✔ Locations that work for your concept and those that don't
- ✔ Interior and exterior design, décor, and signage
- ✔ Construction costs and requirements
- ✔ Business seasonality
- ✔ Competition and competitive advantage
- ✔ Brand personality
- ✔ Marketing
- ✔ Operating expenses
- ✔ Labor and training requirements
- ✔ Pricing strategies
- ✔ Sources of products

Will consumers need or want your products and services tomorrow?

To better predict your franchise's future, you must have a measurable set of results — that is, you've been in business for a sufficient period of time. Your success will be dependent on whether sufficient consumer demand exists for your brand's products and services in your targeted markets. Ideally, you've based your business either on a well-established consumer demand or on a trend that will keep your company's products and services in demand for the foreseeable future. In addition, you want to operate in a technological environment that is beneficial to the concept's long-term success.

Ask yourself these basic questions about your own business when reviewing whether you should franchise:

- ✔ Is it based on a well-established consumer demand or trend?
- ✔ Can it distinguish itself from the competition?
- ✔ Does it have a high return-customer base?
- ✔ Does it have ownership of its trademarks and service marks?
- ✔ Does it have a recognizable brand?

Most any business lends itself to franchising, but historically, restaurants, retailers, and service providers have had the widest appeal. Here's some advice on deciding whether you can successfully franchise your company:

- ✔ Most restaurant concepts are good candidates, but those that need chefs rather than cooks or have intricate menus and recipes are more difficult.
- ✔ Companies whose products and services have broad consumer acceptance are a natural as long as the market trends support long-term viability and growth.
- ✔ Companies whose operating margins allow for franchise fees and still leave an adequate return on investment for both the franchisee and franchisor usually are suitable for franchising.
- ✔ Companies in fragmented industries (industries where most of the businesses are independent operators) that would benefit from branded consolidation are franchising candidates.
- ✔ Companies in a stable or growing industry, unburdened by significant regulation, are franchisable.
- ✔ Companies with systems that are simple to execute, that can draw from a large pool of qualified candidates, or that can train franchisees to use the technology in a reasonable period of time will work as a franchise.

Are you committed to franchising?

If you're going to be successful as a franchisor, you need to understand that you're entering into a whole new business that may require you to learn a new set of skills and to bring on new management experienced in expanding and supporting a growing franchising system.

Prospective franchisees are attracted to franchise systems whose management is experienced, ethical, and has a history of financial and personal accomplishments. You'll be more attractive to prospective franchisees if you can add sustainable value to the relationship, including product and service enhancements, management and staff training, operations manuals, field consulting, consumer marketing, multi-unit operations skills, franchise system expansion skills, and other support systems they've seen in other successful franchise systems. Therefore, the bios you include in your FDD about your management's background must show the potential franchisee that you know how to run the business you're franchising.

When you start a franchise, you need to be emotionally and financially committed and have the capability to make the necessary investments in the long-term growth and support of the franchise system. Your franchise system will need to have the necessary resources to adapt the system to local market conditions, evolve the product and service offerings, motivate franchisees to achieve successful operations, and enforce system brand standards. The organization you'll develop must be ready to implement, support, and evolve the franchise system after you launch it. Simply drumming up the necessary capital to obtain your FDD and sales material isn't sufficient. After the franchisees come onboard, they expect you to deliver on the promises you made in the franchise agreement, and you'll need additional capital to meet your commitments. Ask yourself these questions:

- ✔ Can you and your existing staff operate and grow the business?
- ✔ Can you afford to hire any additional franchise talent you may need?
- ✔ Do you have the resources necessary to meet your commitments to your new franchisees?

Having the right people in place to execute a franchise strategy is important. If all you can afford to hire is you and your spouse, and you're already running your existing business, you're in for some interesting times.

Great franchisors try to deliver all the elements that their franchisees need for success; others provide very little. However, if you want to see your system grow, you should try to deliver a sustainable competitive advantage by continually providing local support and new products, services, and marketing that enable your franchise system to operate at the head of the pack for the long term. Try to answer the following questions:

✔ What type of support programs do you need to put into place to assist your franchisees and to operate and grow the franchise system?

✔ Can you put those systems into place yourself, or do you need outside advisors to help you?

✔ How will you provide continual training, field and headquarters support, marketing support, new product introduction, and all the other services required to make yours a great franchise system?

✔ What about research and development? Can you develop additional products or improvements to those you currently offer, in order to keep your franchise fresh and your franchisees profitable? Before you say yes, be sure that you know how you'll do it.

Do you have enough potential franchisees?

We know that your mom keeps telling you that you should start a franchise. Everybody she knows says so. But has anyone besides your mom ever told you that? Eventually, people outside the family have to step up to the plate. Will they?

Before you develop your franchise, you should know something about your potential franchisees:

✔ Do you know the profile of your prospective franchisee?

✔ Who's going to be attracted to your opportunity? Are they the same people you want as franchisees?

✔ Do you have an understanding of what geographic expansion strategy is appropriate, and what you can readily support?

✔ Are your growth plans realistic? Can you support your new franchisees financially?

✔ Does an adequate pool of potential franchisees exist — candidates that are ready, willing, and able to become franchisees of your franchise system?

✔ Will your franchise system be attractive to only one class of franchisees, or will you be able to attract several types, including single-unit and multi-unit operators and investor groups?

✔ Can you operate your existing business while you're developing and operating the new franchise system?

✔ What happens when you begin to open in more than one market?

✔ What happens when two or more franchises open in the same week? Can you meet your commitments to all the franchisees at the same time?

✔ Will this be the type of franchise that people will be proud to own?

✔ Will prospects be able to afford your franchise? We're not talking about simply affording your franchise fees and royalties but everything, including site development, interior design, equipment, training costs, and working capital — all the costs to get into the business. If your targeted prospect can't afford to get into the business, you have to either rethink and adjust who your prospect is or find a way to reduce the entrance costs.

You can't wait until you're trying to sell franchises to figure out the answers to the preceding questions, because you may find

✔ The pool of potential franchisees may not be sufficient to meet your expansion goals.

✔ The pool of franchisees may be sufficient, but the pool has little interest in what you have to offer.

✔ The cost of acquiring the franchises may be too high or take too long.

The cost and timing of acquiring franchisees will affect your financial viability and, therefore, your franchisability.

Many of the stories in the pop-culture media lead you to believe that franchising is a quick-growth strategy. It can be, but for most new franchisors, it's not as fast as they expected. Depending on the industry and the investment range, a typical franchisor opens fewer than ten locations in the first year of operation; the average is probably closer to five. Five to ten new locations in a year is still a pretty impressive growth rate for a new company. Given these numbers, you need to focus your efforts on achieving critical mass and sufficient market share to support your brand and achieve victory over the competition in the markets you do enter.

Do you have a system?

Throughout this book, we keep talking about a system, but what do we mean when it gets down to the local level? You need to base your business on a set of refined and unified operating processes that you've tested and proven in actual operating locations. You must clearly define and document your processes. Operations manuals and training programs? You'll need those, too, making sure they include the necessary forms and checklists.

Use the following questions to gauge how well defined your system is:

- ✔ Can you deliver the "look" to franchisees: the design, décor, signage, site criteria, and plans for construction?

- ✔ Are you able to tell franchisees how much it costs to develop the location? This figure includes not just the fixed costs but the expenses from the day they meet you until the day they no longer have to fund working capital out of their own pockets. Remember that the franchisee is relying on you to be knowledgeable — especially in getting the business up and running.

- ✔ Do you have systems for operating your business? ***Remember:*** As a franchisor, you want your locations to run consistently so that every customer is delivered the same product, the same way, every time. Are you able to document those procedures in operating manuals, and do those procedures work all the time?

Can you teach others how to operate your system?

Your franchisee generally won't know much about running your particular business, unless you're fortunate enough to have as your potential franchisees former management and staff. Therefore, you need to train franchisees, their management, and other personnel on how to run the business. And, you need to do it quickly. If your potential franchisees will need to spend the next five years in class before they can open their doors and operate to your minimum standards, you have a serious problem. To expand your franchise system, you need franchisees who can do the job. Here are some questions you need to ask yourself:

- ✔ Are the skills that your prospects need so specialized that finding enough prospects will be difficult?

- ✔ Will your franchisees be able to hire enough help with the necessary skills?

- ✔ Are you able to train franchisees and their staffs in your procedures, policies, and systems?

- ✔ Can the training be completed satisfactorily in a reasonable period? (See Chapter 8 for a discussion of training.)

In order for your business to be franchisable, you need a pool of potential franchisees who are not only willing to buy your franchise but also can operate it to your standards. They also have to be able to recruit sufficient staff with the skill level to do the job. Is a skilled labor pool available to support your franchise system's development and growth?

Are your products and services any good?

Although having great products and services is no guarantee you'll succeed, it sure can't hurt. Check out the following questions to see if your products measure up:

- How do your customers view your products and services?

- Are they different from, or better yet, are they superior to, your competitors' products?

- Will your products and services carry to the next town, the next state, or across the country?

If you see new faces every day but wish some of the old ones would come back, you may have a problem. At some point, you'll run out of new customers. Having a product that someone wants to come back to buy — hopefully, often — is the measure you have to meet.

As a franchisor, your product and services also have to meet the test of distance and of time. Even if you have the best products and services in town, do you know whether anyone outside your neighborhood will want them? To determine whether your concept has franchisability, opening up locations out of town is often necessary. Also, bear in mind that the marketplace changes rapidly today. Products and services often have a half-life equivalent to that of a fruit fly in September. What's hot and essential today could be a faint memory tomorrow. Here are some things you need to consider:

- Are consumer-purchasing patterns changing, and will they affect the popularity of your product and services?

- Can other companies absorb your product or service? If they do, will that place you at a competitive disadvantage? Do you have any competitive advantages or points of differentiation that no other company can offer?

- Are competitors introducing, or even discussing, alternatives to your products or services?

- Do you have a strategy to adapt to changing market conditions (culture, real estate, consumer preferences, and regulations)?

You need to be alert that your business isn't simply the latest fad. Franchise systems need staying power and must be built on a consumer demand that is growing and secure.

Will the economics of the business support a franchise expansion strategy?

Likely, the most important criteria for the determination of whether a business is franchisable is its ability to meet minimum economic requirements. You're going to expect your franchisees to pay you a fee to get into the business (called a *franchise fee*), continuing fees (called *royalties*), and maybe other fees, such as for additional training, marketing, and advertising.

Maybe you'll earn income through the sale of products to your franchisees or collect income or rebates from manufacturers on system-wide purchases. Some franchisors lease equipment or property or have other sources of revenue. After those fees are deducted from the bottom line, you need to know the answers to these questions:

- Will the franchisee still be profitable?
- Will the franchisee receive an acceptable return on investment?

Even if the answer to both of those questions is yes, you still have to consider other issues:

- How many prospective franchisees can afford your franchise?
- What will be each franchisee's total upfront investment?
- How much of the initial investment will the franchisee need to pay in cash?
- Can a franchisee finance any portion of the initial investment?
- Do any regulations in your industry make it costly or difficult to franchise?

If your prospective franchisee is the operator of a single-unit, mom-and-pop business, she may be asking herself whether the franchise will give her a better income than the job she's thinking of leaving. However, if the franchisee is a multi-unit operator or a sophisticated or institutional investor, and many franchisees are, he'll ask whether the franchise can generate a sufficient return on his investment consistently and predictably. He'll want to know how the return on investment in your franchise stacks up against other investment opportunities available to him, and how long before he can break even. When looking at the total investment required by a franchisee, you also need to factor in some other realities of your business:

- Does your type of business have any serious short-term or seasonal cash-flow problems? If so, these problems could affect franchisees' total investment, depending on when they buy your franchise. These issues may also impact when you should start offering franchises.

✓ Will franchisees need to carry a significant level of inventory?

✓ How often will franchisees be able to turn over their inventory?

✓ If food is involved, what's the rate of spoilage?

✓ Will you need to set up any commissaries or central kitchens to support your expansion strategy? What is the investment required, and whose responsibility will that investment be?

You need to have a complete grasp of your assumptions and facts in order to determine what initial investment will be required by your franchisees.

And don't forget that the franchisee is not the only one in this relationship. To meet your own needs, you must know the answers to the following questions as they relate to your future franchise company:

✓ How much will it cost to develop a franchise system for your company?

✓ Can you afford to develop a quality system?

✓ Will you be able to finance any shortfall in your development costs?

✓ Will the fees you charge be enough to sustain you?

✓ Will you be able to achieve a reasonable return on your investment?

✓ If you're using a broker, will enough be left over after commissions to meet your commitments and still obtain a good level of return?

Often, when you speak to a new franchisor and ask the question "How's business?" his answer will be something like "Franchise sales are good — sold five franchises last month." However, if you ask the same question of a unit operator or the executive of a large franchise, she'll likely talk to you about same-store sales (SSS) or other key performance indicators (KPIs). If you're going to be a great franchisor, your head has to be in the bottom line of the underlying business. If your economics are solid, and your concept is well designed and supported, marketing your franchise is not really very difficult. Indeed, one of the easiest things to do in franchising is to sell franchises. The hard part is making sure that the franchise system is sustainable, that everyone is making a reasonable return on their investments (including you as the franchisor and each class of your franchisees), and that you're selecting and not just selling franchises.

So, what do you think? Are you ready to become a franchisor? Feasibility is only the first step. You still have a lot more to do.

Although we've given you some of the criteria MSA and other professional consultants use in evaluating a client's readiness to franchise, we haven't given you the experience necessary to make a realistic judgment on your own. From experience, we know that prospective franchisors often have trouble objectively determining whether their businesses are franchisable. They're emotionally tied to the business, and usually they have a ready answer for every concern or issue. For additional information on conducting a feasibility examination, visit the MSA Web site at www.msaworldwide.com.

The CD-ROM includes the International Franchise Association's Code of Ethics (CD1402) so you get an idea of the standards of conduct that members of the IFA expect.

Beginning Your Franchise Program: Who Should Take the Reins?

Developing a franchise program is a complicated procedure. In addition to all the business issues that franchisors need to address is the reality that franchising is also a highly regulated business. How you choose to proceed with the development of your franchise is important to your success as a business and as a franchisor.

Doing it yourself: Success or suicide?

Sometimes prospective franchisors try to save money on professional fees by going it alone. They order self-help kits with fill-in-the-blank forms for franchise agreements and FDDs from companies masquerading as franchise consulting firms and advertising in the back of magazines (see Chapter 6). Or they buy a copy of an established franchisor's FDD from FRANdata (www.frandata.com) or get one for free from the State of California (www.corp.ca.gov/caleasi/caleasi.htm). They figure that if it worked once for someone, it should work again for them. They scan the document into their computers and cut and paste the other franchisor's data and add their own information. Is this an option? We don't think so. In fact, we think it's a recipe for disaster almost all the time.

The design, development, and implementation of any franchise system are complex. And believe it or not, the legal issues aren't the most complex part of the franchising process. The legal documents — the FDD, the franchise agreement, and all the other forms and agreements — are fairly straightforward, but they're made up of the unique business decisions you'll need to make. Unless you've spent your professional life as a franchise executive (and not simply as a franchise salesperson), established one or two or more franchise systems before, and understand what is and isn't working in franchising today, designing and developing a franchise program is not for the novice. The risks for you and your future franchisees are too high for you to take someone else's strategy (frequently a strategy used by a mature system or a system with different resources, history, and goals) and simply copy or modify it for your use.

If your goal is to save money because you're short on capital to pay professional fees, remember that the fees are the least expensive portion of developing and operating a franchise system. If you're short on the capital needed to hire professional help, maybe you should wait until you have the money you need before you begin, or maybe you should seek other sources of funding.

Going it alone may not be an immediate suicide, but it may be a slow death for what could have been a promising system, as well as for the franchisees who relied on you to do it right.

Watching out for "franchise packagers," wolves in pros' clothing

We're going to spend a bit of time talking about franchise packagers and companies that take shortcuts. Many of these firms provide little real value for the money they charge. And, you really need to understand the difference between working with franchise professionals and those that feed on the "red meat" part of franchising — the inexperienced company looking to become a franchisor.

Most professionals providing business and legal advice to companies in franchising are highly trained and experienced. Some of these professionals may have even obtained their Certified Franchise Executive (CFE) designation from the IFA Education Foundation. Some may have other licenses and designations (CPAs, for example). (In the next section, we give you a way to locate the professionals serving franchising.) These professionals usually follow the standards of practice required by the organizations providing them their certification. Non-certified professionals legally may not have to meet those higher standards, but you may be at risk if they don't. Other firms primarily package companies into franchisors for a living. These companies are referred to as (and this is not a flattering term) *franchise packagers* by the professionals in franchising.

Lawyers and experienced consulting firms, such as MSA, who work with mature franchise systems in addition to start-up franchisors, criticize franchise packaging the loudest because we often see a franchisor client for the first time after the company has experienced difficulties with regulators, is having difficulty with their franchisees, is unable to expand, is losing money, or is experiencing any number of problems it could've avoided. In many cases, these difficulties result simply from bad business advice and structural problems in the design of the franchise system because the client was provided an inappropriate, boilerplate approach to franchise development. Or the company's problems may be the result of legal issues that it should've addressed with qualified franchise lawyers at the outset of the franchise program's development. Often, when professionals get involved in these situations, we even find that the client should never have franchised when they did, and they could've avoided all their problems had they conducted a proper feasibility review and had proper business and legal representation at the beginning.

Franchise packagers generally market their services to people who are inexperienced in franchising and who are looking for a simple way to achieve their dreams of becoming franchisors by buying complete packages of documents and services at one-stop shops. Franchise packagers masquerade as consultants, but instead of helping you evaluate, design, and develop your franchise system in a strategic and tactical manner, these firms sell you a package of boilerplate documents and services that they "customize" for you. They provide you with legal documents, marketing brochures, public relations materials, sales videos, operating manuals, training programs, and so on. Some are a bit more honest and advertise as doc-in-the-box merchants in the back of magazines and sell you generally the same fill-in-the-blank materials at a much lower cost.

What surprises many new franchisors is that working with franchising professionals not only provides them with a higher quality of services and materials, but they can get those services at about the same relative cost they would pay the packager. What you get from professionals usually will be measured in improved performance of your franchise system long term. What you'll get could mean the difference between your franchise system succeeding and failing. So, from our point of view, steer away from the franchise packagers and work with the recognized pros.

So, how do you tell if a company is a franchise packaging firm? Try the following:

- **Google its list of clients.** See how many of the companies it lists as clients are still franchising today.

- **Listen to its sales pitch.** Does it recommend that you conduct feasibility examinations before you begin to develop your franchise? If you mention feasibility, does the company brush it aside as not really being important in your case?

- **Does it make all franchise systems out as the same?** Does it claim that all you need to do is fill out its 60-page questionnaire, wait for your legal documents, manuals, brochures, and video, and then sit back as dozens of franchisees line up to buy your exciting opportunity?

✔ **Does it provide you with a set of legal documents its lawyers prepared for you and then require you to bring those documents to another lawyer for review and approval?** Guess what? Consulting firms are not allowed to practice law. The packagers need you to get a real lawyer to bless the documents before you use them. Wouldn't you be better off hiring a real lawyer in the first place to prepare the legal documents rather than paying an additional $5,000 to $10,000 for some other lawyer to review the boilerplate forms?

✔ **Does it simply sell you fill-in-the-blank legal documents?** If you're that short on cash, we already told you where you can get other franchisor's documents for free. Even if those documents aren't right for your franchise system, why would you want to pay for something you can get for nothing?

✔ **Does it offer to develop your franchise system so that it can then sell your franchises for you?** These packagers may be the scariest of all because they'll take up to 50 percent of your franchise fee when they sell a franchise for you and usually another 20 percent of your royalty stream forever. When the franchise system has problems, and the franchisees fail to open, you're left holding the bag, but they still usually get to keep their sales commissions.

✔ **Are its consultants independent contractors who may be working for them only while they're between jobs?**

Unfortunately, franchise packaging is not relegated solely to consultants and brokers. Just as attorneys are rightly critical of the franchise packagers, professional business consultants are rightly critical of those attorneys who have a similar style of developing legal documentation for new franchisors. Some attorneys who work with start-up franchisors seem to believe that the legal documentation, being necessary to sell franchises, is also sufficient to define the franchise system. In fact, you need to address far more business issues than legal issues in developing a franchise system. The business determinations must define the content of the legal documents, not the other way around.

Finding professional advisors to guide your way

Properly developing a franchise system requires a team of qualified professional advisors, including the following:

✔ Franchise consultants

✔ Franchise lawyers

- Accountants and auditors
- Marketing professionals (advertising, public relations, and so on)
- Web site and intranet designers
- Professionals to help you design your operations manuals and training programs, and so on

Usually, in the beginning, the consultant acts as the quarterback for the design and development team. After you launch the system, and you no longer need that level of coordination, you're left with a group of professional advisors who can help you grow and manage your franchise system long term. This approach is the one that successful franchisors generally follow.

You may already know of a consultant, an attorney, and others who are qualified to give you the help you need. If not, here are some tips for finding the right companies to work with:

- **Don't rely on yellow-pages listings or advertisements in the back of the trade magazines.** The firms with the best reputations are well known by franchisors and other professionals in franchising. Get referrals from people who know you and the type of business you're in, and who have gotten good results from the professionals they're referring.

- **Google *franchise consultants* or *franchise development* and then review each firm's Web site.** Get to understand its reputation in franchising and Google its client list to see whom it has worked for in the past.

- **Meet with several consulting firms before you choose one.** If a consulting firm is vague or speaks only in technical terms, search for someone else who can answer your questions clearly.

- **Make sure the consulting firm is familiar with businesses of your size and within your industry.**

- **Choose an experienced consulting firm with solid industry credentials and a reputation with large, established franchise systems and not just the small, emerging franchisors.**

- **Be prepared to speak candidly about the firm's fee structure and what services they include.** Make sure that you understand what you'll be getting.

- **Talk to some of the firm's start-up and more mature clients.** See whether they're satisfied with the level of service they've received.

- **Be comfortable that the professionals you choose are not only qualified but will communicate with you throughout the development process about the future of your business and how they can help you reach your goals.**

After you select a consulting firm, the firm can help you choose a law firm and other professionals experienced in franchising. When selecting your lawyer, check out the American Bar Association Forum on Franchising (www.abanet.org/forums/franchising). Your consultant or your other business lawyer can provide you with a list of attorneys who belong to the ABA Forum on Franchising. Make sure that your franchise lawyer is not just a member of the ABA Forum on Franchising but also regularly attends their meetings and is invited to be a speaker and present papers to their franchise peers.

 One of the best sources for consultants, lawyers, public relations firms, insurance agents, and pretty much everyone who services the franchise industry is the IFA's Supplier Forum. Most of the knowledgeable legal and consulting firms are members of the Supplier Forum (www.franchise.org/supplierforum.aspx). (Coauthor Michael and his partner Kay are past chairs of the Supplier Forum.)

See if your advisors have obtained the CFE designation from the IFA's Education Foundation (IFAEF). If they have, they're probably keeping abreast of the latest in franchise system structure and management.

If you've noticed, we never mention the need to select an advisor who is nearby. The right professional for you may be right around the corner or across the country. Franchise professionals really comprise a small community, and professionals are accustomed to working with clients wherever they're located. In the age of electronic communication, your distance from your advisor is really of little, if any, consequence.

Passing Go with Your Franchise Idea

Assume for the time being that your concept is franchisable. Congratulations! Do you hurry up and start to develop your legal documents and marketing brochures? Hold off a bit more. You have a host of business issues to focus on and decisions to make before you bring in the legal and marketing troops.

Brainstorming a strategic plan

The business blueprint, often referred to as a *business plan* or *strategic plan,* examines the issues and makes the determinations needed to design and implement your franchising strategy. Although each company looking to franchise will differ, some of the key areas to consider in developing your franchise strategic plan generally include the following:

- Accounting (control and reporting systems)
- Capital requirements for the franchisor and franchisee
- Communication with the franchisees
- Consumer and other market research
- Conversion strategy for independent operators
- Cooperatives and buying groups
- Core and tertiary market expansion strategy, including determination of the various classes of franchisees to use for expansion
- Development and implementation of the internal structural elements of the franchise system
- Franchise relationship strategies, including dispute resolution and dispute prevention
- Franchisor field services
- Financial planning and analysis
- Franchisee operations
- Franchisee recruitment, selection, and closure
- Franchisee staffing, training, and certification
- Franchisor organization and training requirements
- Insurance requirements
- International expansion and support
- Investment hurdles to determine fees and other system revenue and costs
- Legal documentation, including FDD and franchise and other agreements
- Location (selection, acquisition, development, and management)
- Management information systems and point-of-sale systems
- Marketing (advertising, publicity, and promotion)
- Merchandising standards and plan-o-grams
- Monitoring mechanisms for product and service quality and consistency
- Ongoing services provided to franchisees and a la carte fees, if any
- Packaging and labeling for products sold to consumers by franchisees
- Policy formation
- Warranty and guarantee programs

The franchise system you ultimately develop and the franchisor-franchisee relationship you establish will be shaped by the determinations you make in designing the franchise system. You decide upon planning, policies, procedures, ongoing administrative monitoring, and support services in the strategic and tactical plan.

Fleshing out your strategies

After you develop your tactical and strategic plan, you also need to begin to develop some of the components required for executing your strategy. These include the following:

- All the operating systems and procedures

- Operations manuals for each class of franchisee, their management, and staff

- Operating manuals for the franchisor's headquarters and field and other support personnel

- Training programs required for all the system participants

- Marketing programs for use by local operators to attract and retain retail and system customers

- Marketing programs to recruit franchisees, including discovery days, Web sites, brochures, trade shows, and so on

- The fee structure for the franchise system

- Required documentation (developed by specialized franchise legal counsel)

Creating a plan for action

Finally, you should create an *action plan,* which will organize and schedule the tasks you need to complete in implementing your franchise development plan. Your plan should provide for controls and feedback to ensure a clear direction for the company, an understanding of who is responsible for what, and the timeline for making everything happen. Control over the timing of your plan's implementation is critical. The action plan ensures that something is going to happen and describes when to do it.

A reason that many franchise packaging firms skip the process of developing a strategic plan and instead substitute a lengthy questionnaire is that strategic planning is time-consuming and can raise issues that you need to address if you're to properly design, implement, grow, and support your franchise system. It also allows them to artificially keep their fees low but puts you at risk.

The reason start-up franchisees for mature franchisors have a higher success rate than independent start-up companies usually has little to do with the quality of their products or services, the ambition and hard work of the owners, or even their available capital. Instead, franchisees in mature systems are better prepared to begin and to operate their businesses because the franchisor has the experience to answer all the strategic questions necessary to develop and support the relationship properly. New franchisors need to go through a strategic process to achieve similar results.

The strategic development is the first step in providing those future franchisees with the tools they'll require to succeed.

On the CD-ROM, we provide a whole document of explanations on writing a business plan for your franchise (CD1403).

Developing the legal documents

The final output of the initial strategic development is the legal documentation of the franchise system. You should base all the legal documents required to offer franchises on the determinations you made during your strategic planning process. The agreements convey the information that legally binds you and your franchisee, spelling out the relationship between you and all your franchisees and describing the system you're franchising. They provide prospective franchisees with at least the minimum information required by law and professional practices; the legal agreement incorporates these disclosures into the contract, which generally spells out each party's obligations to the other. In the United States and some other countries, you also have to prepare a disclosure document. (See Chapter 6 for a discussion of the FDD.)

Because the laws and practices governing franchising are evolving constantly, the use of specialized legal counsel with current experience is essential. Saving money on the development of your legal documents by doing it yourself or placing your trust in well-intentioned general practitioners is not a wise choice.

Properly developing the FDD and franchise agreements takes a business strategy developed by a qualified franchise consultant. Experienced franchise lawyers (who understand the rules that govern franchising and who have the experience to draft the documents properly) then craft that strategy into the FDD and agreements. To give you a better understanding of structure of the FDD, we include an analysis of the document's structure — prepared by partners at DLA Piper's Washington, D.C., and Reston, Virginia, offices — on the CD-ROM (CD1404).

In preparing the FDD and franchise agreements, many lawyers require their clients to complete a lengthy FDD questionnaire. To prepare you, we include a sample FDD questionnaire (CD1405) on the CD-ROM. This questionnaire was prepared by Arthur Pressman and Andrew Loewinger, partners, Nixon Peabody's Washington, D.C., and Boston, Massachusetts, offices.

Tactical planning documents are long and may contain information that your attorneys really don't need. Besides, they're usually so voluminous that your attorney probably doesn't want to see them anyway. But, to be effective, your attorney needs information.

We recommend that you prepare for your counsel a document similar to what MSA produces for its clients. At MSA, our proprietary document is called a *business overlay,* which is an enhanced version of your tactical plan that explains all the key issues to your attorney so that they can prepare the franchise agreements, franchise offering circular, and other required legal documents. It also provides guidance to the rest of the development team in areas concerning real estate, manuals, training, retail marketing, franchisee marketing, IT, and so on.

After you complete the tactical plan, meet with your attorneys and present them with an outline of your business plan. Seek their input and advice, because they have experience that should prove beneficial to your franchise system. Respect your lawyer's advice regarding the law. (If you were smart in the design of your franchise system, you involved them in much of the tactical and strategic planning process already.) However, remember that franchising is primarily a business strategy, not a legal strategy. Your legal agreements need to reflect the decisions you made in your plan. If the language in your agreements doesn't reflect the thinking of management and your business plan, speak to your attorneys before the documents are completed. Although customs and practices exist in franchising, and some elements are routinely found in many franchise systems, none of those matter if they don't work in the structure of the franchise you developed.

Question any changes your attorneys make to the business elements in your franchise documents.

Most attorneys practicing franchise law have forms and checklists to help their clients prepare legal documents. These are usually well-developed forms that deal with many of the business and other issues you may have addressed during your tactical planning. Review these forms and checklists and make sure that you answer all your attorney's questions in the business overlay. Doing so ensures that your attorneys can prepare the required documents for your system in an efficient and reasonably priced manner and that their end product reflects the business realities of your system. This process is not something you should do only when you start your franchise system.

Thoroughly reviewing your franchise agreements and making changes, as your tactical plans require, is an ongoing effort.

One last bit of advice: Take your time and don't get caught up in entrepreneurial fever ("I must get it done now"). Most of us who work in franchising as franchisors, franchisees, consultants, and lawyers learn something new every day about business and franchising. Professionals seize every opportunity to attend professional forums where we can exchange ideas with other professionals about best practices and worst practices in franchising. Take the advice we give you, thoroughly review all the chapters in this book, and seek out professionals who can help you through the process. When franchising is done well, there's no better method of business expansion.

Chapter 15

Growing Your Franchise Family

. . . .

In This Chapter

▶ Sifting through potential franchisees

▶ Selecting the right markets

▶ Recruiting franchisees

▶ Increasing franchisee diversity

▶ Giving franchise sales presentations

. . . .

Before you can really call yourself a franchisor, you need to recruit and sign up your first franchisee. That seems simple enough. But, to be a great franchisor, your first job will be to select carefully from candidates who have the knowledge, skills, abilities, and financial capabilities required to operate your business concept successfully. Your candidates will need to fit the distinct culture of your company. You also need people who are willing and able to follow your direction in delivering your products or services using only the unique methods of operations you've defined as your system.

This chapter will provide you with a method for recruiting, selecting, and closing the right franchisee. If you choose to simply *sell* franchises instead of *selecting* franchisees, the music your system will play may not even be a tune you recognize.

If you want to do it with your own staff, look for a consulting firm that can train your sales team and help you structure your unique selling program. At Michael H. Seid & Associates (MSA), we conduct these services for many of our clients who are brand-new to franchising and even for those who have done it for many years.

Forming the Essence of the Ideal Franchisee

Most new franchisees see themselves as entrepreneurs, which poses a problem for franchisors — true entrepreneurs have trouble following anyone's direction except their own. So, what's really wrong with an entrepreneur as a franchisee? After all, entrepreneurs have energy, drive, ambition, and a clear focus on what they want to create. But that's the essence of the problem for franchisors. A true entrepreneur wants — no, *needs* — to tinker and make changes to your brand until it fits his own image. And, if you allow that to happen, each franchisee will do his own thing, and your system will never be able to achieve the consistency the public expects when they shop at a brand.

To create a brand in franchising requires people who will follow your lead and understand that consistency throughout the network of locations is essential for their success as well as yours and the other franchisees in the system. The type of person you're looking for, therefore, is an "entrepreneur lite." He understands that his first obligation is to follow the system and execute your strategy flawlessly but still have the burn to own his own business. Those are the people you want to bring into your system.

Great franchisees often come up with great ideas that can improve your offering to the public or allow you to do things better. We all remember the story of Jim Delligatti, a McDonald's franchisee who invented the Big Mac at his franchise in Uniontown, Pennsylvania. It's one of the most popular burgers McDonald's sells today. But before the Big Mac saw the light of day, McDonald's tested the innovation and then made the decision whether Jim's great idea was even offered in his location let alone throughout the system.

Not everyone who wants to become your franchisee will make a good franchisee. And picking the wrong franchisee is not only annoying but potentially devastating over the long haul. Take your time and be disciplined in your approach to recruitment and selection. In the long run, a bad franchisee diverts you from doing productive work and hogs the attention and resources you need to support the rest of your network. The money they pay you will never be enough to make them a worthwhile franchisee.

Focusing Your Market Strategy

Saying that you want to grow in the top 100 cities is not enough. If you're going to succeed, you need to determine where and when you should open in new markets. Franchisors usually begin by determining which markets are their primary targets, which are their secondary targets, and what is the geography in which they can affordably support their franchisees.

You need to have a market penetration strategy tied to your franchise recruitment strategy in order to determine the timing for entry into new markets and the critical-mass requirements in those markets. (*Critical mass* refers to the number of units a franchisor should optimally develop in a market over time.)

Expanding without a plan is potentially dangerous for any franchisor. Servicing distant, isolated locations will take human and financial resources that will be precious and scarce in your early days. If you stretch yourself too thin, your entire system may suffer for lack of attention to quality standards. Expanding too fast and far and without critical mass is risky. MSA develops for each emerging franchisor client a comprehensive written plan for the expansion of the client's franchise network based on the following:

✔ The company's expansion goals and objectives.

✔ The company's contractual obligations to the franchisees and the franchise system's ability to provide them with support, both initially and ongoing.

✔ The franchisor's ability to recruit, train, certify, and motivate only highly qualified franchisees.

✔ The franchisor's ability to efficiently provide start-up support with limited corporate staff and sometimes limited financial resources.

✔ Critical mass and availability of the proper locations.

✔ The vendors' ability to support the franchisees.

✔ The franchisor's ability to continue to operate its own businesses.

✔ The franchisor's ability to efficiently enforce brand standards.

✔ An understanding of the franchisor's goals and exit strategy. (Knowing your long-term goals upfront is important for any business owner, including franchisors.)

An unfocused market development strategy (one in which the areas for development are selected by where the phone calls from prospective franchisees come from) causes the company to be reactive rather than proactive, at all levels. For example, without a market development plan, the company may miss sales opportunities because of failure to register its franchise in key states, or it may incur unnecessary expenses to register in states where it probably shouldn't expand yet.

An unfocused market strategy doesn't allow you to make business decisions based upon measurable criteria. For example, franchisors need to evaluate the various methods of expansion (including company-owned, individual, and various multi-unit strategies) in different markets. To be prudent, a franchisor should include critical-mass and other reviews when making its market selections. Critical-mass reviews help a franchisor reduce its field service and distribution costs per unit; they're the most effective way to capitalize on the local marketing possibilities.

The goal isn't merely to enter new markets but to enter them successfully, distinguishing your core market opportunities (in major and secondary urban areas) from tertiary market opportunities (in all other areas) so that you can profitably provide field support, advertising, and other support functions. Defining your critical-mass requirements in advance enables you to plan your growth.

If you already have company-owned locations spread out over a host of markets, evaluate whether you should franchise those stores to new franchisees and put the proceeds they pay you into growing company-owned units elsewhere. Doing so is part of a retrofranchising approach.

Reeling In Great Franchisees

Not every person who calls you or contacts you through your Web site is going to be the right candidate, even if he's been successful in someone else's system.

Franchise systems that let all candidates in simply because they have the money use a franchisee selection strategy often called *fogging the mirror*. If the prospective franchisee is alive, as indicated by his breath on a mirror, and has enough money in his checkbook, welcome aboard. Don't fall into that trap — it's an easy mistake to make in the early days of your franchise.

Defining the franchisee profile

First, you need to understand your company and who would make the perfect operator for a successful location. You need to define what will make successful franchisees, such as those who have the following traits:

- The ability and discipline to successfully operate a location to brand standard
- A willingness to follow your system
- The financial resources not only to open the location but also to get through the hard times that often follow a new business's opening
- Basic background and skills needed to run the business
- The ability to absorb the new lessons you're going to teach them about running your concept
- Enthusiasm for your concept
- A track record for success
- The ability to operate independently and have a stable employment history

- ✔ The trait of being a self-starter

- ✔ A willingness to take risks necessary for success

- ✔ No history of litigation

- ✔ Living, or being willing to live, near the location

- ✔ No burning desire to change the business strategy simply because of a belief that this market is different

- ✔ The ability to delegate responsibilities, especially if the candidate will operate more than one location

You need to know, before you close the deal, whether a franchisee will fit well with your concept, organization, and other franchisees. You want franchisees who will

- ✔ Be able to relate to their customer bases

- ✔ Create the proper environment to motivate their employees

- ✔ Fit your distinct culture

You also need to be sure that your franchise opportunity can meet the income expectations of your potential franchisees.

The franchisee profile you develop will serve as a set of guidelines that will help you select suitable candidates for operating a successful franchise. In developing the profile of your franchise candidate, you begin to understand who your potential franchisees are and what sources of marketing will be most productive for you to use in recruiting them. Make sure that your first group of franchisees is the right one — the future of your company hinges on this group.

One of the latest and potentially one of the more dangerous "innovations" in franchising is the emergence of broker/packagers (see Chapter 14 for information on packagers), who both develop your franchise system and also act as your exclusive franchise sales agent. Broker/packagers frequently sell you on working with them based on lower or even no professional fees in exchange for taking a percentage of your franchise fee, your continuing royalty, and sometimes even some equity in the franchisor. The broker/packager's income comes from the commissions he makes on selling your franchises. But remember: Your focus needs to be on developing a franchise system that is sustainable because you selected the right franchisees and have the necessary revenue to support your obligations to them. Broker/packagers tend to set initial and continuing fees so that they can sell franchises quickly, regardless of whether those fees are right for the franchisor or the franchisee. After giving up often 50 percent of your franchise fee and 20 percent or more of your continuing royalty to the broker/packager, what are you left with to sustain your franchise system long-term and earn a reasonable return on your investment? This type of broker/packager relationship has the potential for serious conflicts of interest and long-term financial problems, and it's a relationship that emerging franchisors should avoid.

Reaching out through the right medium

After you know who your potential franchisees are, you need to determine their media habits as a group, which will help you reach your profiled candidates. Pay attention to the following characteristics:

- ✔ Geographic
  - Local
  - State
  - National
  - International
  - Alternative distribution possibilities in stadiums, arenas, airports, hospitals, universities, and other mass-gathering locations
- ✔ Demographics
  - Age
  - Income
  - Gender
  - Family size
- ✔ Psychographics
  - Values
  - Interests
  - Attitude
  - Personality
  - Lifestyle

As you begin to market franchises, you'll quickly find that following up on leads takes up a lot of human and financial resources. So, you must develop a media mix that will generate the most productive lead flow that fits within your budget, instead of just trying to get as many leads as possible.

Marketing for franchisees

Shotgun advertising indiscriminately may generate a lot of franchise leads but may not generate franchisees you want and need. That's one of the basic problems many franchisors have with the abundance of leads coming from the Internet. Although getting leads over the Internet is great and paying

Google an additional fee for directing those searches to your site is often worth the investment, you need to remember that many of your leads may actually be coming from 12-year-olds with a mouse.

Your franchise marketing material should contain a filter in the message that focuses it on the person you want and helps those who aren't your candidate self-select out of the process. One common technique is a minimum net-worth requirement or a minimum cash-investment requirement.

In establishing your marketing plan, answer for yourself these four basic questions:

- ✔ What are the appropriate sources for recruiting franchisees that best fit the franchisee profile you've established?

- ✔ What methods (financial, personal, and so on) will you use for evaluating potential franchisees?

- ✔ What procedures are appropriate for approving franchisees?

- ✔ What administrative procedures and negotiating strategies will you need to have in place to close the sale — and do it legally?

To be successful in marketing your franchise, you need to address these basic issues before you start spending money on marketing — not after.

Franchisors use a wide variety of marketing and advertising vehicles. They select the ones they believe will effectively reach their targeted prospect and achieve a reasonable cost per prospect lead, and ultimately an effective cost per franchise sold. Some of these include

- ✔ Search engine optimization (SEO; making the Internet work for your brand)

- ✔ The Internet (Yahoo!, Google, and so on)

- ✔ Franchise sales brokers (outside franchise sellers)

- ✔ Lead generation sites, such as the International Franchise Association (IFA; www.franchise.org) and Franchise Bison (www.bison.com)

- ✔ Franchise trade shows

- ✔ National, regional, local, weekly, and trade newspapers and magazines

- ✔ Business journals

- ✔ The electronic media (television, radio, and even infomercials)

- ✔ Franchise directories such as those published by the IFA (www.franchise.org)

- ✔ General business publications

- ✔ Franchise-specific magazines and other publications

- ✔ Referrals from franchisees and others who know the brand
- ✔ Consumer and franchise Web sites
- ✔ Articles in publications developed through public relations
- ✔ Newsletters
- ✔ Community involvement and charity tie-ins
- ✔ Franchise literature exhibited in existing locations
- ✔ Targeted mailings to potential franchisees who meet the franchisor's criteria
- ✔ Trade missions

The marketing is supported by sales tools such as the following:

- ✔ Brochures
- ✔ Electronic brochures and videos
- ✔ Folders
- ✔ Sell sheets
- ✔ Interactive CDs
- ✔ Web sites
- ✔ *Webinars* (Web-based seminars)
- ✔ Invitations to *discovery days* at your headquarters or locally (where you present the company to the prospect)
- ✔ PR kits
- ✔ Broker newsletters
- ✔ Franchisee referrals
- ✔ In-store programs

So many different media options are available that you can pretty readily target a specific audience. Each media has its own unique characteristics in terms of the audience it reaches and how it delivers an advertising message. Any given media may be right for one type of message or one target audience and wrong for another. Having a marketing plan and an understanding of the profile of your franchisees will make for a more effective use of your budget.

Don't make the mistake of taking a "survey of one" in choosing your media or your message. Unless *you* are your profile of the right franchisee, what you like and read doesn't really matter. Get the help of franchise marketing professionals who do this for a living.

Every year, *Franchise UPDATE* magazine publishes its "Annual Franchise Development Report," which examines what franchisors spend on recruiting franchisees and what the best sources for leads were in the prior year. The report is available for $199 at www.franchise-update.com/magazine/franchisedevelopmentreport/. (Be sure to include that last / when you go to this address, or you won't get to the right page.)

Putting out ads

You can choose among endless Web-site and advertising avenues for franchise recruitment advertising. (For a list of available lead-generation Web sites, refer to CD0402 in the Chapter 4 folder on the CD-ROM.)

How do you know whether your ad dollars are being spent wisely?

When investigating any ad source, talk with other franchisors that have used the sources for a minimum of six months. Ask them about the following:

- Quantity (cost per lead)
- Quality (cost per sale)
- Responsiveness to change and working with you on tuning the lead flow

In tracking your leads from multiple sources, you *must* use and manage a contact management system. The cost of the system will pay for itself in additional sales and avoiding lost opportunities.

You don't have to wait for a sale to measure the effectiveness of your ad dollars. Gather reports weekly to track the effectiveness of each site at the critical steps of the process, highlighting the following information:

- Applications
- Franchise Disclosure Document (FDDs; see Chapter 6) given to franchise candidates
- Office visits
- Awarded franchises

Be sure to balance the talent of the sales professional and track each one separately on each lead source so you have a solid analysis.

Accounting for Diversity in Franchising

Although you won't encounter a special type of franchise arrangement for members of minorities or women looking to invest in a franchise, many franchise systems have developed opportunities designed to increase the diversity of their franchisee ownership and management.

In most franchise systems, women and members of minorities are still underrepresented. Many minority franchisees were excluded from franchising in the past, primarily, among other causes, because of limited equity in homes that most new franchisees use to finance their first franchise purchase. Women, who traditionally were also underrepresented in the general workforce, weren't considered prime targets for franchisors. But the rapidly expanding minority middle class and the increase in the numbers of Hispanics, Asians, other immigrants, and women, both entering the workforce and achieving management positions, have changed the economic climate and the potential pool of franchisees.

Franchisors also are finding that, because of the economic problems the United States has experienced during the past few years, people may be candidates for franchise ownership because jobs in their industry are scarce. Minorities and military veterans are great candidates to look at because they may be actively seeking franchise ownership as job replacements.

Franchisors recognize the social implication of this historic fact of underrepresentation of minorities. They also realize that improving diversity is important to their brands and to their bottom lines. And with the aid of local, state, and federal programs designed to level the playing field for minority investments, as well as lenders in franchising who are targeting franchise systems, the diversity of franchise ownership is increasing rapidly. The IFA Education Foundation (IFAEF; www.franchsie.org) has established its Diversity Institute to focus on bringing more minority candidates into franchising as franchisees, franchisors, and franchise system management.

Franchisors aren't talking about *redlining* (targeting minority franchisees to particular markets). However, many minority franchisees are electing to open locations in underserved inner-city and urban areas (the emerging markets) where franchise brands are underrepresented. Others, in growing numbers, are investing in opportunities in markets that are more traditional to franchising (that is, the suburbs). Because of the strong diversity movement in the United States, many minority candidates now live in the suburbs, so the distinction between traditional and nontraditional markets is thankfully fading quickly.

Some franchisors are offering special arrangements to minority franchisees and military veterans to stimulate the growth of their franchise systems. In addition to reducing some of their fees, some franchisors are adjusting their net worth and liquidity requirements for new franchisees, and some are even providing financing. Others are providing increased levels of support and are developing retail marketing programs tailored to these neighborhoods.

Why are these emerging markets so attractive to franchisors? The following are contributing factors:

✔ **Opportunity:** In the past, many franchisors avoided inner-city and urban locations — the emerging markets — simply because opportunities in their more traditional markets were readily available and the opportunities in the emerging markets didn't appear as strong. Now that many of the traditional markets have been fully developed, these franchisors are looking for new opportunities. The emerging markets provide them with a ready customer base that knows their brand and is ready and willing to buy.

✔ **Strategic location:** Many of these locations are strategically located near downtown, mainstream markets. This makes them perfect locations for establishing businesses that can service customers in those areas, because the location of the franchisee to the customer is less important than in other types of businesses. This includes franchisors in industries such as printing, janitorial services, personnel agencies, maintenance and repair, delivery, and others that don't require a local market demand.

✔ **Real-estate availability:** Often, large tracts of real estate exist within these markets that franchisees can assemble and develop at a lower cost than in suburban markets.

✔ **Labor:** Because of a higher-than-average rate of unemployment in these areas, labor is plentiful and often available at a lower cost than in areas where job opportunities are more abundant. Also, training programs run by government and nonprofit organizations train a significant portion of this labor pool in the skills that small businesses require.

✔ **Government programs:** Government programs — including tax credits, tax-free bonds, depreciation advantages, and other assistance — make operating in these markets economically advantageous.

✔ **Local demand:** Although *per-capita spending* (the amount of money each person spends) may often be lower, these markets are usually high-density areas — many people in a small area. In fact, spending in some emerging markets actually exceeds per capita spending in suburban markets for certain products and services. Therefore, the combined demand for goods and services in these markets often exceeds that of suburban markets.

✔ **Lack of existing merchants:** Although the demand for products and services is high, quality suppliers are often in short supply. The absence of quality retail, services, and restaurants in some areas forces residents to travel great distances to get what they need. Locally based and owned businesses have the opportunity to secure these customers as their own.

To give you a better understanding of the importance of minorities in franchising, we include an article (CD1501) by Ronald N. Langston, National Director of the Minority Business Development Administration, in the U.S. Department of Commerce, on the CD-ROM.

Women in franchising are beginning to become recognized as an important pool of investment capital for franchisors. To give you a better understanding of the importance of women in franchising, we include an article (CD1502) by Joyce Mazero, partner, Haynes & Boone, Dallas, Texas, on the CD-ROM.

Developing the Recruitment Organization

Although selling franchises is an art, it's an art that anyone can learn who speaks well, is disciplined, and can think on her feet. The secret is that selling franchises isn't really that hard, mostly because many potential franchisees are actively looking for an opportunity. At MSA, we know that 90 percent of the battle to get a franchisee to select your franchise will be emotional. And the best way to trigger that emotion is to get the franchisee to see you and your entire staff's passion for the business. You need to tailor your sales process to support why the prospect should also share those same emotions. When you can establish a sense of trust with your prospect and are able to get him to see himself in your business, the sale is done.

The prospect needs to see that your business is operated by individuals who understand how your brand operates. Yet, often, the first person they meet is a professional salesperson who really doesn't have a history of operating or understanding the brand and is really only interested in the sale and not always the long-term relationship. Your focus needs to be on the long term. So, before looking outside your company for a hired-gun franchise sales professional or broker, we generally recommend to our clients that they look internally for individuals who understand how your brand functions at the local level: how you schedule your staff at the unit level, order your products, market for customers, open in the morning, and close at night. Training people how to market your franchise successfully is a learnable skill that we teach to our clients' sales staffs every day. Conveying to the prospect a detailed understanding of the business he's investing in is a little harder. You need war stories from experience to close the sale. Look for an experienced person; your consultant can train that person how to market franchises well.

If you're going to recruit a salesperson, look for an executive search firm that is a member of the IFA's Supplier Forum (www.franchise.org/supplier forum.aspx), or ask your franchise lawyer or consultant to help you find the right sales professional.

Having one person in your organization who can shepherd a franchise candidate through the franchise selection process is essential. Doing so allows you to

✔ Establish trust and rapport with each prospect.

✔ Prevent viable candidates from slipping through the cracks.

✔ Give each prospect the attention he needs, allowing for a more thorough fact-finding and interview process.

✔ Customize the selling process to each candidate's buying style.

✔ Avoid a situation where a prospect plays one person in your organization against another.

REMEMBER

Use a contact management system such as GoldMine (`www.frontrange.com/goldmine.aspx`) or ACT! (`www.act.com`). Many franchisors have developed their own software to track discussions with prospective franchisees. Being disciplined about using contact management software allows you to track a candidate's progress through the process, maximize your recruitment investment, capture the important dates and commitments, monitor the sales process, and record the essence of each contact a member of your staff has had with each candidate. This system will keep the process disciplined, ensure that a prospect stays on the sales track, and record each discussion with each candidate.

For a successful franchise recruitment program, you'll need to staff four basic functions:

✔ The franchise development staff

✔ The screener or administrative assistant

✔ The compliance officer

✔ The approval committee

The franchise development staff

The franchise development staff is tasked with the following responsibilities:

✔ Fielding all inquires

✔ Prequalifying candidates

✔ Shepherding each qualified lead through the recruitment and approval process

✔ Closing the sale

The screener or administrative assistant

The screener, or perhaps an administrative assistant, is responsible for the following:

- Responding initially to all sales leads that come into the system
- Staying in touch and understanding the deal flow coming from the brokers working with the franchise system
- Conducting the initial screening with the candidate
- Receiving and verifying completeness of the basic information required by the franchise development staff (applications and so forth)
- Coordinating appointments for the franchise development team
- Completing all scheduled mailings in sequence and on time
- Coordinating all the resources necessary for discovery days
- Scheduling the candidates for meetings, including discovery days
- Ensuring that market research and other studies are scheduled and conducted and that the development team has the necessary information for their discussions with the candidate
- Maintaining the prospect file and ensuring that all information, including the receipt for the FDD, is on file
- Ensuring that the franchise agreement is complete and that a copy of the final contract is in the prospect's hands at least five business days before the scheduled contract signing
- Taking care of a zillion other little tasks so that the development team can focus on the recruitment process and not on administrative details

The compliance officer

The compliance officer is not really a member of the selling team, so he shouldn't be a direct report to anyone involved in the franchise recruitment process. Salespeople are paid to close deals and are usually on a bonus or commission structure tied to the sale. The compliance officer's role is to avoid mistakes.

Usually, the compliance officer is a member of the accounting or legal department and should be the most detailed-oriented person you can find in the organization. You can also include an outside professional, such as your franchise attorney or a member of her staff. The compliance officer needs to

> ✔ Be able to stop a contract signing if he isn't satisfied that the company has followed all the necessary procedures and fully completed all the required paperwork
>
> ✔ Be well trained in regulatory compliance and serve as your watchdog that everything is handled according to the law and your franchise selection process

The approval committee

Although the franchise development team and the compliance officer are responsible for franchise recruitment and closure, the approval committee is responsible for making sure that each franchise candidate meets your system's entrance requirements before you allow him to sign the franchise agreement.

The approval committee is generally made up of executives and department heads that will be responsible for supporting the prospect after he becomes a franchisee. They look at the prospect from the long-term view of how well he'll do as a member of the franchisee team. Generally, the approval committee is drawn from members of the following departments:

- ✔ Executive management
- ✔ Marketing
- ✔ Operations
- ✔ Real estate
- ✔ Merchandising
- ✔ Training
- ✔ Legal
- ✔ Product sourcing
- ✔ Finance
- ✔ Compliance

The approval committee meets regularly to review candidates before they become franchisees. During their meetings, the approval committee reviews each applicant's application and rejects those who don't meet the system's criteria or approves those who have been recommended by the sales staff to become franchisees. Optimally, each member of the approval committee should have met with the prospect and be ready to discuss her perception of the franchisee. Ultimately, the approval committee makes the decision whether to accept or reject a candidate; you should never leave the decision to the salesperson or the sales broker.

Don't create a process where the approval committee earns a direct bonus or commission from the franchise sales process. This safeguard ensures that their votes aren't tainted by an economic benefit they get from any one sale.

After the approval committee discusses each candidate, they'll vote on whether to accept the candidate. If a member of the committee feels that a candidate is still not a good fit — even if this is just a gut feeling — you need to discuss and deal with those concerns. Take a vote, but other than the results of the vote, don't make a record of the discussion or keep a detailed log of the vote. Also, unless the prospective franchisee can cure the reasons for his rejection (a lack of financial resources, for example), don't provide him with a reason for his rejection. Giving a reason will almost always cause bad feelings.

Recruiting Franchisees in Just Ten Steps

You need to establish a qualification process that ensures that you follow up with every person who contacts you and wants to talk about becoming a franchisee. Creating the process for your company is a bit complex and takes time. What works for one company may not work for another. For example, for some brands, you may want to have the discovery day at the beginning of the process. For others, you may want to have it in the middle or at the end. At MSA, we tailor the franchise recruitment and selection process for each of our clients — no one method of recruitment is right for everyone.

So, we can give you some recommendations, but the procedures you use really need to make sense for your company and your prospective franchisee profile. You also need to modify our recommendations based on your experience in marketing your franchise. Put your process in writing so that everyone in your company knows what you want them to do and to ensure that you don't overlook any viable opportunities. Following your system will also help prevent the wrong person from running one of your operations.

Your recruitment and selection process needs to

- Give your candidates the information they need to make their decisions.

- Ensure that the candidates understand how committed you are to maintaining a quality system.

- Let candidates know that you aren't selling franchises but selecting franchisees, and that you'll select only the best candidates.

- Gather the information you require from candidates to move them though to the next step in the process.

✔ Keep you in contact with the candidates throughout the selection process, which will enable you to do the following:

- Obtain a better picture of whether they fit into your system

- Build the relationship for the next 20 years

- Give the candidates a basis upon which to choose your system as their investment opportunity

- Allow you to highlight the strengths of your headquarters and field support

- Assess the franchisees' willingness to follow the process and enable them to validate that your franchise is the right one

> **TIP**
>
> Creating challenges and obstacles for potential franchisees actually helps the sales process. By doing so, you let them know how serious you are in selecting only the best candidates. These hurdles also set the right tone for the rest of your relationship with them after they become franchisees.

Each time you talk to a prospect, you're able to overcome a candidate's objections, answer his questions, provide him with new information, and clear up any misconceptions he may have. You're driving him to the decision point — hopefully one that will allow you to open up another location with him as the owner and operator.

In the following sections, we outline the ten steps usually included in any recruitment process. You may have more or fewer steps, or put them in a different order, but these are the key steps to consider.

Steps 1–4: The introductory phase

The introductory phase gets the ball rolling, starting with prequalifying the candidate through the initial follow-up contact:

1. **Prequalify, or screen, the prospect.**

   You need to speak to every prospect as soon as possible after the initial contact. In today's fast-paced world, even a few hours' delay can mean a lost opportunity.

2. **Provide the candidate with initial information:**

   - Send out the information package.

   - Set a date to return the application to you.

   - Set a date for your next conversation or meeting.

If the prospect doesn't meet your criteria, don't send a packet of information. It's expensive, and you don't want to encourage people whom you likely won't approve anyway.

3. **Set up the applicant's file.**

   Establishing a file allows you to maintain all the paperwork and records in one place. Also, if the candidate becomes a franchisee, you have a complete record throughout her time in your system.

4. **Do the initial follow-up contact, and set a date for the candidate to visit your headquarters for discovery day.**

   Contact the prospect and discuss the information she sent to you. Answer her questions and continue to move her through the process. If necessary, find out why the candidate hasn't returned any promised information on time. (See the "Working the Validation Process" section, later in this chapter.)

   Use this opportunity to continue to build rapport.

Step 5: Discovery day

Discovery day is a structured day of meetings at your headquarters, where you interview the franchisee and answer her questions, and the candidate meets your team and usually receives a copy of your FDD.

Your goal is to create excitement and make the prospect feel like she's already part of your brand and your franchise family.

Make sure that you review the FDD thoroughly with the prospect. Have a set presentation to start anticipating her concerns, highlighting the positive features of the agreement, and putting the negatives in a more positive light.

If the potential franchisee will have multiple owners, make sure that all of them come to discovery day.

Step 6: Follow up after discovery day

If you're rejecting the candidate, notify her — but do it tactfully. You want to maintain her good feelings about the company. Unless she can fix the reasons for rejection, going into a discussion of the reasons really won't be fruitful.

If the candidate made the cut, let her know that she's been tentatively approved. Tell her that your approval committee will evaluate her based upon the information it has now and how well she follows through with the rest of the recruitment process.

Continue the process by making sure the candidate follows up on the tasks you gave her during discovery day, such as contacting existing franchisees.

This is the time when you can also follow up on the candidate's credentials.

Step 7: Follow up again

Stay in touch with the candidate. The 14-day delay in allowing her to sign an agreement under the Federal Trade Commission (FTC) rule is not meant to be a quiet period. Let the candidate know what's going on in the process and keep her engaged in the process by answering her questions. Let her know about events in the system so that you continue to make her feel like she's part of the family. If you have a conference or event going on, consider inviting her to it. Also, try to get her to agree upon a date for making a decision.

Step 8: Make a decision

Decision time! Get a commitment from the candidate that she wants to become a franchisee, and then agree upon a date she'll sign the franchise agreement.

Step 9: Close the prospect

Now you get to seal the deal. Convey to the prospect the decision of the approval committee. Make sure you deal with any objections or jitters the prospect may have, which will smooth the transition. Ensure that all paperwork and requirements have been met and received.

Make sure that all the terms of the agreement are complete and that the prospect has the finalized contract at least seven days before she's scheduled to sign the franchise agreement if you made changes to the agreement she originally saw.

If you make unilateral changes to the franchise agreement provided in the FDD or include information in the final agreement that your prospect hasn't had a chance to review, you need to provide her with the completed franchise agreement at least seven calendar days before signing.

Step 10: Complete the process

Congratulations! You have a new franchisee.

If at all possible and convenient, have the prospect come in to sign the franchise agreement. Making it a memorable event with lunch, a gift, and some recognition and excitement is the appropriate way to begin a long and hopefully positive relationship.

Begin the start-up process with your new franchisee. Getting her started on your training program, or getting her involved in some other task, helps to alleviate any potential buyer's remorse, which is fairly common.

Have your compliance officer review the file to ensure that it's complete. He should conduct any compliance interview and make sure you've met the 14-day and 7-day rules before the contract is signed.

To help you meet the rules that govern the offering of franchises, we include a sample franchise sales and compliance manual (CD1503) on the CD-ROM.

Many franchisors today are providing electronic disclosure of their FDDs to prospective franchisees. We include an overview of e-disclosure (CD1504) on the CD-ROM. That document was written by Lee Plave, partner, Plave Koch, Reston, Virginia.

Get a check when the contract is signed, and congratulate every member of the franchisor organization who worked hard to get you to this point.

Working the Validation Process

Your franchisee needs to prove to you that he can keep his commitments after he becomes a franchisee. And you're trying to convince him that yours is the right opportunity before he makes a decision. During the recruitment process, give the franchisees dates to meet to give you information. Hold him to those dates. You can set dates for things such as the following:

- ✔ Completing the application process on time
- ✔ Meeting with his advisors
- ✔ Applying for financing from his bank
- ✔ Looking for locations
- ✔ Visiting some of your locations
- ✔ Coming to discovery day
- ✔ Talking to your current franchisees

In Item 20 of your FDD is a list of your current franchisees and those who have left the system in the last year, along with their contact information. Tell your prospect to contact your franchisees so that they can get comfortable with your franchise system and begin to understand what being a franchisee is all about. This process allows him to ask your franchisees about your capabilities as a franchisor and also to answer questions (for example, about the financial performance of individual operations) that you may not be able to answer.

Although you shouldn't steer your recruit to your most favored franchisees or those who like you the best, you should assist by matching him up with franchisees in markets similar to his or to franchisees who share his attributes. Who he calls is his choice, however, and you should let him know that. Have him give you a list of which franchisees he's likely to call. Alert those franchisees to expect a call, which will enable your franchisees to feel free to give the prospect information about the system.

Make sure you call each franchisee whom the prospect has called so you can get feedback on the prospect. You also want to hear the types of questions the prospect is asking, which will give you a good indication of how serious he is about your opportunity and what his doubts may be.

Follow up with the prospect on the calls he's making to ensure he's getting the information he needs. Address any issues or concerns that may have surfaced during his due diligence of your opportunity. The recruiting process is a two-way street, and making sure your franchisee is comfortable with your system is as important as your being comfortable with him.

When a potential franchisee checks up with your existing franchisees, you get incredibly important feedback on your performance as a franchisor. What will your current franchisees tell a prospect about you? We hope you've lived up to the promises you made to your franchisees so that you get the positive validation necessary to convince prospective franchisees that your system is right for them. If you haven't, make it a priority for your franchise system to do better.

The Franchise Sales Presentation

The major differences between a franchise sale and any other type of sale are the legal time limitations in franchise sales and the types and format of information you may present or are required to present.

Selling any franchise without first providing an FDD to the prospective franchisee is unlawful. You must provide this information at least 14 calendar days before you sign the agreement or accept any payment. The prospective franchisee must also receive a franchise agreement containing all material terms at least seven calendar days prior to the signing of the franchise agreement, if you make any unilateral changes to the form of the franchise agreement provided in the FDD or included information in the final agreement that the prospect hasn't had a chance to review.

You can use the 14-day period to your advantage. When a prospect has your FDD, let her know that for the next two weeks you want her to learn more about your franchise program, and you want to learn more about her.

Explain that a franchise agreement is a two-way street. It requires a continuing commitment by both parties. Furthermore, it isn't an automatic process. Encourage the franchisee to seek outside legal and business advice on the franchise offering.

During the 14-day period, you may discuss the agreement with her and her advisors. The 14-day period is not a "quiet period."

Some prospective franchisees will try to turn the selling process on you by stressing their strength and importance as a candidate to you. They may try to negotiate terms of the franchise relationship. Don't allow this gambit. In addition to weakening your position, it also may have long-term impact on the future relationship. Explain to the franchisee that you have a selection and approval process and that it's designed to protect the franchise system, including the other franchisees. Explain that when they become a franchisee, the selection process will benefit them as well.

Discipline in franchise sales is an important aspect of establishing a professional relationship with your prospect and with all future franchisees.

Present the franchise program to the prospect completely. Review with the franchisee the system and the terms of the agreement. Review the history of the franchisor. This process enables you to share your strengths with the prospect and build a compelling case for her seeking admission into the franchise. You want to build her excitement in joining the system. Discuss an overview of the industry and why the opportunity is unique and beneficial. Discuss with the prospect the agreement and the franchise system, such as the following:

- Operational support provided
- Field visits
- National account programs
- Technology advances of your company
- Buying groups
- Information technology
- Training
- Advertising and marketing

- ✔ Other services provided by the system
- ✔ Other factors unique to your offering

Be prepared to discuss, with knowledge, the offering of your direct competitors. If the franchisee is smart, she'll already have obtained information and even copies of the direct competitor's FDD.

You also need to discuss the system's fee structure, including the following:

- ✔ Franchise fee
- ✔ Royalty
- ✔ Local advertising requirements
- ✔ Brand fund contribution

Don't try to justify your fees and tie them to the services you provide. Your fees are being charged as an admission cost for getting into the system and using your brand, as well as to pay for the franchisee's continuing membership. In reality, unless your lawyer has tied your fees to services in the contract, which wouldn't be a good or appropriate thing to do, the services you're providing to your franchisee are simply those services you think she needs to represent and operate your brand to your standards.

You need to make sure also that the franchisee understands her obligations to the system. Take these one at a time and get her commitment to fulfill each obligation:

- ✔ Initial investment (Item 7 in the FDD)
- ✔ The requirements to meet standards of your franchise system
- ✔ Territorial rights
- ✔ Market penetration strategy
- ✔ Term and renewal of the agreement
- ✔ Termination of the agreement
- ✔ Training
- ✔ Transfer and all the other key provisions

Be prepared to let the franchisee review the operations manual and training program outline. Go over each section of the manual if she wants. Don't let her make copies of the manuals. Have her, and anyone else who will be looking at the manual and training program, sign a confidentiality agreement prior to reviewing the manual. Explain why you selected each procedure in the manual and how it benefits the operation of the franchise and the system.

You need to be prepared for the question "How much can I make if I buy your franchise?" Your answer will depend on whether you've included a disclosure in Item 19 about the financial performance of franchisee- and company-owned units. Consult with your legal advisor, but a financial performance representation is basically any statement that claims, suggests, or provides a formula for calculating a specific level or range of past or projected sales, income, or profit. Talk to your franchise consultant and franchise lawyer about unit operating cost information that you can provide to prospective franchisees outside the FDD.

If you make a financial performance representation, you must disclose it in the FDD and must also have a reasonable basis that you can substantiate if asked to do so by the prospective franchisee. The FDD must also include the basis for your claims and any assumptions on which you based them.

What types of earnings questions should you expect to hear from your prospects? The following kinds of questions are typical:

✔ What kinds of gross sales figures should I expect from my store next year?

✔ What percentage of labor costs have you experienced at your company-operated units?

✔ I understand that I can purchase my paper products through your supplier. What do you think will be the percentage of sales for my paper costs over the course of 12 months?

✔ I know that you just opened a few restaurants in Washington, D.C. Do you know what sales figures the unit on M Street is experiencing?

Consult with your lawyers about how to answer these key and important questions from the prospect. Make sure that you answer all the franchisee's questions, clearly and honestly. Tell the franchisee the truth. ***Remember:*** She'll be in the franchise system for many years.

Your legal advisors should give you some coaching on what you should tell her she can earn. Recommend to recruits that they discuss questions regarding earnings with the existing franchisees in the system, which is a good idea even if you do provide a financial performance representation in Item 19 of your FDD.

Finalizing the Selection Process

After the franchisee has indicated that she wants to become a franchisee, your approval committee should review her application. Explain to the franchisee that this is part of your best-practices approach to the franchise system.

At the final interview, explore any unanswered questions (both yours and the franchisee's) and make sure you're mutually satisfied that the decision is the right one for both of you. At the conclusion of the meeting, assuming that it has been 14 days since you gave the candidate your FDD and that you haven't made any unilateral changes to the franchise agreement (or, if you did, that the seven-day period has elapsed), you can execute the franchise agreement and related documents! Just to be safe, check with your compliance officer or your franchise lawyer. After all, they're your safeguards to proper franchise sales practices.

Chapter 16

Building the Network: Expanding Wisely

▶ Following expansion rules of the road

▶ Going abroad with your franchise

▶ Hooking up with non-U.S. franchisors

*Y*ou're ready to begin offering franchises — certainly at home as soon as you've established a solid domestic base, maybe soon internationally. If you're at this stage of the process, here's what you already should have done:

- ✔ Developed your prototype operation

- ✔ Tested your concept and operating system in more than one location or market

- ✔ Built an operating history that shows continuing profitability and success

- ✔ Hired a recognized franchise consulting firm that verified with you that your concept is franchisable

- ✔ Recruited an executive and support team for the franchise company

- ✔ Developed a tactical strategic plan for the system

- ✔ Put together all your systems and manuals

- ✔ Properly funded the system

- ✔ Prepared your Franchise Disclosure Document (FDD) and agreements

Now all you need are some candidates who want to become your franchisees and an understanding of where and how you should grow.

At this point, you're probably nervous, which is only natural. So far, the only people you've had to convince that your creation would succeed were yourself, your employees, and maybe your banker and your family. Getting people to queue up for your franchise is the real test.

In this chapter, we let you know when — and how — to start your expansion.

Heeding the Expansion Rules of the Road

When you enter the franchise arena, you have to be ready — very ready. You have to be committed to becoming a franchisor and operating the system for the benefit of both your shareholders and your future franchisees. After all, your franchisees will be counting on you to have a system that can deliver on its promises to the consumer and to them.

If you're expanding in the United States, your company's FDD (see Chapter 6), must be prepared and ready for delivery to prospective franchisees nationwide. It's the law in the United States. If you're franchising outside the United States, you need to be aware that some countries have their own presale disclosure laws, and you need to comply with these laws.

See the file CD1401, in the `Chapter 14` folder on the CD-ROM, for information on franchise laws around the world.

If you're in a state that requires registration or filing or you plan to offer your franchise in one of those states, you're required to meet that state's registration or filing requirements before you solicit franchisees. For more on the states that require registration and filing, check out Chapter 15. (Also, refer to the file CD1503 in the `Chapter 15` folder on the CD-ROM, which is a sample franchise sales and compliance manual.)

Although you're required to have the FDD to be a franchisor, having the FDD alone is not sufficient. You have to be able to back up the statements in that document — and then some. Franchisees expect three fundamental things:

- A great concept.
- Superb support service.
- Knowledge, experience, and most important, an ethical approach to running your franchise business. Trust in franchising is key to great franchise relations.

Taking care of housekeeping

Before you begin soliciting franchisees, make sure that you've completed all the ground rules — the key operational components. Use this checklist:

✔ **Operations manuals:** Many franchisors today provide their manuals only electronically. In this age of electronic information, you can put your manual online in a secure site on your intranet, and your franchisees can access or download not only the manual but also the changes as you make them. You can even verify electronically which franchisees have accessed or downloaded the update and which haven't.

See CD1601 on the CD-ROM for a sample table of contents for a unit franchise operations manual, prepared by Marla Rosner, a senior consultant at Michael H. Seid & Associates (MSA).

In addition to the unit operations manual, you need manuals on-site for development, field services, local marketing, and multi-unit operations (if you're using an area development or master franchise arrangement as your mode of expansion), and that's just for the basics. Plan on creating manuals for your franchisee and headquarters staff and writing a section of the unit manual so that all unit personnel can understand it.

✔ **Training programs:** Make sure that training for franchisees and their employees at each level of their organization is in the bag. You also need to train your field consultants, headquarters staff, area representatives, master franchisees, and everyone involved in your franchise support organization. This task includes deciding what training to provide, formulating the curriculum, hiring trainers, establishing testing procedures to verify that you've communicated the information, and setting an exit strategy for franchisees that aren't up to snuff. For example, will you return franchise fees to candidates?

✔ **Sourcing merchandise:** Franchisees expect you to guide them on where to get merchandise, supplies, equipment, signage, insurance, and financing — consistently and reasonably. Make sure that you pinpoint suppliers, negotiate deals, or set up your own distribution facilities.

✔ **Administrative requirements:** Knowing what's going on when you're running one or two locations is easy. Now, however, you have to keep tabs on a large number of people, some of them operating in different countries and in different languages: your headquarters team, your field staff, franchisees, their staffs, suppliers, customers, and so on. To do so, you need the following:

   • Forms and procedures, either electronically or in paper to monitor franchisee compliance with the franchise agreement, to determine their financial and operational performance, and to see how well they're doing with your consumers.

- Forms for franchisees to provide you with information on their operations to help you manage your system and instructions about how they should send you your royalty fees and other payments. You need to get the advice of a good tax attorney to establish a process for repatriating funds into the United States; how you charge for fees and services can impact the tax rate and withholding taxes in different countries.

- Regional support offices or support based from your headquarters in the United States. If you decide to establish a regional office (which will cut down on telephone calls at 3 a.m.), you need to decide whether to train locals in your system or to send an American into the country. Plan ahead because arranging for work permits and visas can be difficult.

- Clearly defined roles for your field consultants (the folks on your payroll who visit franchisees to check on compliance and to provide them with local support) and the forms or methods they use to communicate with headquarters and franchisees.

- Procedures to help your franchisees obtain merchandise from vendors and manage vendor rebates. You can't expect your international franchisees to have you ship everything from your normal U.S. suppliers.

Franchisors today get their information in real time. Getting information in real time allows them to better manage the franchise system. Franchisors have introduced smart cash registers (point-of-sale systems) that quickly communicate information to the franchisor's headquarters. Field consultants have e-mail access and can often go online to their computers in the office through intranet connections. Franchisees can visit chat rooms on their franchise system's intranet site, so they can talk with other franchisees. Vendors receive current information from the purchases the franchisees make through the intranet so they can make sure that products are shipped when the stores need them and the franchisor can be sure that they're ordering merchandise to system specification. Having access to information at a speed that enables the franchise system to analyze it, share it, and use it in a timely, effective manner separates the underperformers from the leaders.

- **Food safety:** If you're in the food business, make sure that your procedures for safe food handling are in place. Establish a way to enforce your safety standards and see that your franchisees and their staffs understand and follow them. You need to rely on your international master franchisee and area developers to comply with local requirements outside the United States. The National Restaurant Association's ServSafe food-safety training and certification program (www.servsafe.com) is required by many franchise systems for their franchisees to keep the food they serve safe.

✔ **Nonfood safety:** Establish procedures that give your franchisees guidance on running their operations safely so that they can limit the chance of injuries to staff and customers. Procedures on how to wash the floor, lift boxes, store merchandise, and so on ensure that your franchisees have the tools to operate safely.

Establishing safety and security policies for your franchisees as a guide to how they conduct their businesses is important. However, talk to your attorney before you establish any mandatory requirements. Doing it wrong may set you up for vicarious liability claims by third parties. (*Vicarious liability* is when you're liable for the actions of someone else even when you weren't directly involved.)

✔ **Personnel:** Franchisees aren't going to be thrilled if they call headquarters and nobody answers. They also won't be happy if someone does answer but doesn't have answers to their questions. (This is when that regional support team will seem like a really good idea.) Carefully select your management and support team according to your tactical plan. You need to train your staff in the systems procedures, and they also need to understand how to work with your franchisees.

Although you need a franchise development team to offer franchises, that's not even the beginning. Remember that a franchisor has to operate and support a franchise system. You need operations, training, financial, marketing, merchandising, research and development, administrative, and a host of other bases covered. The personnel you need should already be onboard or scheduled to be hired and trained in time to service the system as you grow. And, in international markets, you need to understand the culture of the market you're entering and be prepared to make any necessary changes in your product or operating processes to meet local demand and culture.

Is your field staff in place? What geographic territories can they reasonably support? If your field staff is in San Francisco, think twice before selling a franchise in, say, Maine or London. Regularly servicing only one location in a distant market is unrealistic and not cost-effective. In addition to the cost of lost time, the cost of travel could wipe out any royalty payments and then some.

Many start-up franchisors have their staff perform double and even triple duty as they grow the system and gain the resources required. The head of operations also may conduct training and visit the franchisee's location in the early days. The person in charge of real-estate support also may be responsible for product sourcing. You get the idea. For new franchisors, this approach is fairly normal and cost-effective. Having adequate staff (and enough money to stay fully staffed) is one of the baseline feasibility requirements to be a franchisor. (See the discussion on feasibility in Chapter 14.)

✔ **Marketing materials:** You've whipped up brochures, ad slicks, employment applications, and a Web site. If you plan to use a public relations firm (one of the best early investments you can make), make sure that the company understands both franchising and your specific concept. The PR firm needs to know what gives you that sustainable competitive edge and be ready to pitch your virtues — wherever you need to pitch them, from small-town newspapers to *Good Morning America,* to CNN to Fox News to the BBC.

You can find public relations firms experienced in franchising by looking at the membership of the International Franchise Association's Supplier Forum at www.franchise.org/supplierforum.aspx.

✔ **Fee structure:** By this point, you've set your fees: initial franchise fee, *royalty structure* (an ongoing fee most commonly based on a percentage of sales), your system advertising fund contributions, and so on. Base these fees on the value and marketability of the franchise, the costs of providing services to the franchisees, and the return-on-investment hurdles you established for the franchisor and franchisee.

If the only thing a franchisor has to offer a franchisee or the only distinction it has from other franchisors is a lower fee structure, it has little to offer and nothing to make it very distinctive. To help you work with your professional advisor in getting your fee structure right, we provide information on how the professionals establish franchise fees, royalties, and other fees on the CD-ROM (CD1602).

Some franchise packaging firms and some lawyers who prepare your FDD and legal agreement based upon your answers to their lengthy questionnaire use a little trick: They simply advise you what the average fees are with your competitors and have you make your decision. Or, they may recommend you make your decision based upon the listings found in publications such as *Entrepreneur* magazine's annual Franchise 500. Be careful — if you set your fees too high, you'll impact the profitability of your franchisees, and you may hurt your franchise sales to boot. If you set your fees too low, you may sell more franchises, but you also may lose money on each one you sell. Don't fall into the trap of cutting corners when establishing your fees — it's much too critical a decision.

✔ **Legal:** In order for franchisees to sign on the dotted line, you must decide the terms and conditions that are included in the franchise agreements. In the United States, you need to develop an FDD (see Chapter 6), and some countries also need you to provide a disclosure document to franchisees before you make a sale. Your franchise agreement needs to define all the terms of the relationship; those terms determine the legal relationship between the franchisor and franchisee. When you use it internationally, you need to customize it for the country and the relationship you use to expand in that country. Several countries today have their own franchise disclosure requirements.

Expanding nationwide and internationally during your initial period of franchise development is potentially dangerous. Therefore, completing the registration process in all the states in the U.S. that require registration on your first day as a franchisor may be a waste of legal fees and registration costs. Establish your expansion plans during the strategic process, and if national and international expansion isn't in your immediate future, register your franchise only in the states and countries where you plan to expand. Save your money for the things you're going to need immediately. It's sort of like buying a car for your son when he's only 14: It may be nice to admire in the garage, but he won't be driving it for a while. Also, it'll make you think twice about accepting that exciting opportunity to sell one franchise on the other side of the country.

Although you don't want to rush out and prepare disclosure documents for each country you want to enter, you do want to register your trademark. Talk to your lawyer about the international trademark treaties that may benefit you and reduce your costs of registering your brand in the developed countries you're most likely to enter later. Investing in securing your international trademarks is a good investment early in a franchisor's existence.

Understanding the markets

Imagine throwing darts at a map and locating franchises wherever they land. Easy, yes. Smart, no. An unfocused expansion strategy is financially dangerous — to you and your franchisees. It wastes marketing resources, makes maintaining quality standards difficult, makes supporting the system cost-prohibitive, often leaves your franchisees in a poor competitive position in their markets, and ultimately can lead to franchisee unrest — or worse.

The only right way to franchise your concept is through planned and controlled growth. You have to select markets from the get-go that strategically make sense. What we're talking about is market planning: determining which markets are your primary targets, which are your secondary or tertiary targets, and which aren't targets at all.

Criteria for choosing markets typically include the type of products or services your locations will be selling, demographics in the markets, competition, and the location of your headquarters and regional support staff. The criteria also needs to include *critical mass* (the number of locations you need to have up and running in a market for your franchisees to be competitive and for you to effectively support the market). Having one unit in a market that doesn't have the resources to market effectively or that can't obtain supplies in a cost-effective manner makes little sense for the franchisee. Spending all your annual royalty dollars on making one or two field visits to a market or on translation costs for international markets makes no sense either. Focusing your growth into markets that you can support is the proper way to go. You need to plan market development with the goal of having enough units to compete with effectively.

Say that your franchise sells pool supplies. You don't need us to tell you to begin franchising in areas flooded with swimming pools. In a simplistic model, you can likely find great markets all over the southern and western parts of the United States. The largest pool-service franchisor in the world — PoolWerx, led by John O'Brien — is actually in, of all places, Australia.

But what if choice of location isn't quite so obvious? Say that your franchise supplies practice-management services to doctors and hospitals. Sure, these medical facilities are everywhere. But for your franchise to succeed it may need a minimum number of doctors and hospitals, maybe even a certain percentage of doctors who are in group practice. That requirement may significantly reduce the number of markets available to you — and takes some market research to narrow down.

During the strategic planning process, you have to understand who your customers are. You want to know some basics, such as their ages, races, incomes, household sizes, and ages of their children. This data gathering is called *profiling*. Understanding your customers enables you not only to select which markets to expand into but also to zero in on specific neighborhoods and even street corners in those neighborhoods that have the best chance of success.

Demographics are so important that some franchisors base franchise sales on specific populations rather than on a blanket territory. For example, Oogles n Googles, an Indiana-based franchisor, offers birthday parties for children, and Kidville, a children's edutainment franchise located in New York City, offers its services to children around 2 to 11 years old. When selecting a market, both companies look for territories based on their population of children. They have no interest whatever in the number of seniors; those folks may buy golf clubs but are not the population that use kids-only centers. Both companies look at the age of the families in those markets before establishing a territory for their franchisees.

 Don't rely on intuition or general rules in making decisions about markets. Assumptions that seem right are often wrong if you don't have the facts and a baseline to measure them against. You may be absolutely certain that cold weather is death for frozen-dessert sales. Surprise: Boston is one of the top ice-cream-consuming markets in the United States — even in frozen February.

Also consider the competition. If a market is already saturated with a similar product or service, are you offering a revolutionary twist, or is your brand name so recognizable that you'll declare war on other players? Conversely, will your franchise sit idle because customers are already well served?

Establishing a network

Now that you're eyeing specific markets, you're ready to get franchisees to fill the spots. Historically, franchisors establish networks by selling units one by one. Today, many focus on the sale of multiple units — two by two, ten by ten, and so on. Other franchisors sell area development rights or master franchising rights. (You can read more about these expansion methods in Chapter 11.) Your approach depends on how fast you want to expand and how much control you want.

So, how do you lure candidates to your team? Marketing is the name of the game. The trick is to tap media that produce leads in your target market and that resonate with your profile franchisee. A national business publication may not be the best choice if you're searching for Farmer Joe in a rural community or a specific market, but it may hit the spot if you're looking for well-heeled investors to develop larger territories.

Marketing nationally may get you leads in markets you're not interested in entering or may get you leads in states in which your franchise is not registered. A franchise sales compliance program, established by your attorney or consultant, can teach you how to deal with those prospects correctly.

Refer to the document CD1503 on the CD-ROM to help you establish, alongside your lawyer, a sales compliance program for your franchise.

Most franchisors successfully use the Internet to generate leads. For example, PostNet — a major player in the franchising of postal and business service centers — has substantially reduced its cost of recruiting franchisees and has increased the quality and number of franchisee leads through its system's Web site and sales procedures.

Because every 5-year-old knows how to use the Internet, many franchisors are finding that, although the number of leads coming from the Internet is impressive, sifting out qualified leads and leads in the markets they're interested in is a big problem. Processing leads costs money — a lot of money. Working out the issues on how to effectively process Internet leads is one of the challenges that franchisors face today. Plan on developing an Internet screening process to work through this issue.

Franchise and business-opportunity trade shows have been a staple for recruiting franchisees, and for years many franchisors became lukewarm on franchise shows in general as a recruitment vehicle. The smaller shows, especially the ones that blend business opportunities with franchises, aren't as effective as they once were and actually may place your franchise in a setting that doesn't display it in the best light. However, some of the larger shows still draw considerable crowds interested in acquiring franchises both in the United States and internationally. The International Franchise Association

(IFA) sponsors several franchisor trade shows in the United States and overseas. You can check the date of the next show in your market by contacting the IFA at 202-628-8000 or via its Web site at www.franchise.org. The international department at the IFA is also a good source to tell you where shows and *trade missions* (where franchisors recruit franchisees for their overseas opportunities) are being held around the globe.

Several companies hold franchise trade shows around the world, and the largest trade shows in the United States focused exclusively on franchise sales are operated by MFV Exposition (201-226-1130; www.franchiseexpo.com; info@mfvexpo.com).

In addition, most of the franchise associations around the world regularly schedule trade shows regionally or in their home countries. (See CD1603 on the CD-ROM for contact information for franchise associations around the world.)

If you're going to succeed as a franchisor, never merely sell a franchise. Offer it to candidates you think can do a good job. Then select and approve only those candidates who meet your standards. Anybody can make a sale. Great franchisors know the difference between selling and selecting.

Taking Your Franchise Abroad: Knowing What You're Getting Into

Just because the Internet has made the world a much smaller place, and maybe people everywhere have heard of your brand and been on your Web site, doesn't mean that you're ready to expand beyond the U.S. borders just yet.

We're sorry to burst your bubble, but international franchising is not child's play. No question, international expansion can add prestige to your brand and pride to your domestic franchisees — suddenly, they're part of a worldwide organization. But to be successful, you have to go for the right reasons, at the right time, and with the right partners.

Success at home doesn't guarantee success abroad. Unfortunately, war stories abound about franchisors that have gotten wounded on the international front. Dozens of chains have pulled out entirely or ended up reselling the franchise rights to a second or even third partner in certain markets. They wasted both time and money. Worse, they ruined their image, which forced them to have to try even harder the next time around. They took their licks because they didn't dedicate resources or personnel, misjudged the market, or picked the wrong partner. Are we scaring you? Good. You need to get soaked with ice-cold water.

Kay Ainsley, coauthor Michael's partner and a managing director of MSA, warns that "Going global takes longer, costs more, and is more frustrating than you'll anticipate. Franchising internationally is not a fix for other problems in a franchise system."

You need to have a stable and profitable domestic operation and an organization that can leverage its resources to support an international presence. Selecting appropriate franchisees takes time, and supporting them requires you to internationalize your products and services to meet the demands of the new markets. Failure to prepare properly for international expansion is foolish and unnecessary. Going global simply because you received an e-mail from an exciting and intriguing overseas destination can be a serious mistake — and one that could take years and cost a fortune to correct.

When you begin to look at international operations, here are some of the elements that you should be looking at:

- ✔ **Your products and services:** What changes will you need to make so that the local population will want to buy your products and services? You must consider culture and local tastes in making your move overseas.

- ✔ **Local economic issues:** What is the availability and cost of qualified local labor? What kind of spending power do local consumers have? Will you be affected by government instability, local laws and legal systems, or corruption? Will you run into import and export issues? Will you be hindered by local supply issues? You'll need to address each of these issues before considering overseas operations.

Be prepared to cough up mucho moolah

Here's the biggest reality check: money. International streets aren't paved with gold; getting the royalties flowing your way takes some time. And revenue projections have to factor in different parameters — perhaps higher wages and social costs and benefits for employees, or real-estate availability and rental costs, including key money in many countries. Can your products or services command a higher price to make up the difference in costs?

And although jetting to Venice may sound glamorous — and a romantic ride on a gondola is very appealing — be prepared to fork over lots of euros. What often sounds like a huge upfront fee — anywhere from $50,000 to $500,000 — for the right to develop a foreign territory gets used up quickly to screen candidates, establish the franchise, and support overseas operations. Marcel R. Portmann, the former director of international development and global marketing at the IFA, issues this warning: "Don't think of the fee as money in your pocket. At least 80 percent of the master franchise or development fee goes to expenses."

Many times franchisors get the international bug and start to focus on going global in the belief that the upfront fees will provide for immediate income. The reality is that making money on your international operations, even if you do it right, will usually take several years.

Franchisors can expect to visit potential foreign markets many times. You have to conduct demographic studies — including population size, education, per capita income, standard of living, and religious and cultural issues — and determine whether the local population will buy your product or service in the way those at home do. You must eyeball the local and foreign competitors who are in the market. They'll impact your potential market share, site selection, marketing, and labor and supply issues.

Also, expect to meet with potential candidates on their turf — a lot. Wining and dining a foreign partner once won't do it; international deals usually happen after relationship building. Educate yourself to be culturally sensitive. Foreign deals are often years in the making.

Understand the necessity of hiring a good attorney

Legal fees can add up — for registering trademarks, preparing franchise agreements, and meeting other government regulations. Contrary to popular belief, the United States isn't the only country heavy with franchise laws; other countries also require government filings and/or disclosure documents for prospective franchisees and have franchise relationship requirements. Even if a disclosure document isn't required in the country you're entering, smart prospects are going to ask for one, so be prepared.

The most avoidable mistake when franchising internationally is the failure to meet that country's legal requirements — including any disclosure requirements, withholding taxes, relationship laws, currency exchange restrictions, letters of credit, and your options for dispute resolution, among other issues that will likely be different from what you're used to in the United States. Besides understanding the local requirements, attorneys experienced in international franchise law understand the nuance of how the laws are applied in each jurisdiction and the traps you can inadvertently fall into — even when you think you understand that country's law. When you're ready to cut a deal, you want to be able to move quickly. Experienced attorneys both in the United States and in the country you're planning on entering — along with business consultants knowledgeable about international commerce — can save you time and money in getting the deal done correctly. Many lawyers and consultants in the United States have a network of lawyers and consultants internationally who they respect and can recommend to you.

The IFA's Supplier Forum (www.franchise.org/supplierforum.aspx) and the American Bar Association's Forum on Franchising (www.abanet.org/forums/franchising) can provide you with information on attorneys who specialize in franchise law. In addition, the International Bar Association's International Franchising Committee has over 600 members from 78 countries who regularly work in international franchising. You can reach the IBA, located in London, at (0) 20 7691 6868 or through its Web site at www.ibanet.org. Another source for qualified international franchise counsel is *Who's Who Legal,* published by Law Business Research Ltd at www.whoswholegal.com; use it to search for lawyers specializing in franchise law around the world.

ON THE CD

If you're a franchisor in the United States or in another country that requires pre-sale disclosure, you're probably used to giving prospects a copy of your disclosure document. Ask your attorney whether this step is required as you enter a particular country. (Refer to CD1401 in the Chapter 14 folder on the CD-ROM for more information.)

If you're a U.S. franchisor, you don't need to provide your domestic FDD to an international prospect. A court decision in the United States, *Nieman v. Dry Clean U.S.A., Inc.,* concluded that the FTC rule doesn't apply to franchises that will be operated outside the United States. In addition, the Federal Trade Commission (FTC) adopted its new franchise rule, confirming that the rule doesn't apply to international transactions. In any case, most professionals in franchising feel that giving international prospects information about the franchise offering in your home market doesn't make any sense (and may be misleading); the offering may not resemble what you'd be providing them in their markets. Instead of giving a prospect your domestic FDD, consider putting together an international disclosure document (conformed for the particular country's laws, if necessary). Just as with domestic prospects, your overseas prospects need to know as much as they can about your company, the background of your team, and what the deal is so they can make an educated decision. Making the sale is relatively easy — the long-term relationship takes the hard work.

After you strike a deal, you aren't going to take the money and run. You have to translate documents, marketing materials, and signage; train partners; and schedule more on-site visits. (Maybe then you can sneak in a gondola jaunt, or if you're entering the United States, the wine country in Northern California is lovely in the spring.)

Consider the implications of language and culture

Many U.S. franchisors naturally make English-speaking countries their first stop. After all, they speak English, so it should be a cinch, right? Don't let the common tongue fool you. Even English-speaking countries have different mentalities, consumer attitudes, and ways of doing business. And pity the non-Spanish-speaking franchisor who thinks that the markets in Madrid and Mexico City are the same just because the language is similar.

Lease negotiations may vary, and labor laws or hours of operations may be more restrictive. Consider this: A chain that delivers food by car in the United States could navigate the crowded streets of Japan only by moped, raising new issues about security and handling hot food. Language, although English, still has its quirks. For Decorating Den, the word *color* is vital to its business. Years ago, when it swept into the United Kingdom, it had to change the spelling to *colour* in all its literature. The implication of a word is as important as its spelling. Church's Chicken became known as Texas Chicken in the Muslim world, where a church may not be perceived as a good thing.

So, no matter the language spoken, expect to modify your system and, most likely, your product or service. What at first glance can appear to be minor changes can be major changes for systems that thrive on consistency. For example, available real estate with your specified square-footage requirements may be somewhat limited and force you to downsize your units and redesign them to use more of the vertical space within the site. A restriction on meat in foreign countries may alter your menu. Are your domestic marketing materials suitable? Don't take things for granted. At home, your franchisees may automatically send in their sales reports and royalty checks. Abroad, some countries require invoices before franchisees can send money out of the country. And you have to adjust reporting requirements based on a Monday through Friday week for countries whose weekend is Thursday and Friday.

Keep in mind that since September 11, 2001, the United States has had new rules on international commerce called the Patriot Act. You need to comply with this complex law. For example, one of the requirements of the Patriot Act is that you need to do a background check on your foreign franchisee and make sure that he isn't on a terrorist watch list. Make sure that your lawyer works with you on an international due-diligence process that keeps you on the right side of the Patriot Act.

Also, no singular solution or plan execution exists for what we know as the "international market." Paris and Bonn are as different as Cincinnati and Carmel, which are as different as Hong Kong and Shanghai. So, despite due diligence and support in one market, you may have to start from ground zero in the next. The reality is that many franchisors either forget or don't fully realize what has been accomplished in the previous decade(s) to build the brand and their system. International expansion is as close as it comes to pioneering your brand; it compels the franchisor to prove its concept and products in every foreign market it attempts.

Remember that you're still under laws and taxes

Depending on the country, you may face tariffs, currency-exchange restrictions that prevent the *repatriation* (transfer back to your home country) of profits or limit royalties, taxes, restrictive labor laws, and prohibitive import rules. For example, what's the point of setting up a frozen-yogurt franchise if you can't import your proprietary product and revenues don't justify setting up a local dairy?

In the following sections, we cover a few of the issues you may face.

Product sourcing

Not every country has what you need, when you need it, at a price you can afford. If you do source locally, your franchisee will save import tariffs and transport costs.

A word to the wise: Thoroughly check out local distributors to ensure that your secret sauce remains a secret. The U.S. embassy can help you identify sources for raw materials and products. You can also contact the local branch of your commercial bank, accounting firm, and law firm in the country to provide you with assistance. After you find suppliers, check often that what they produce is, indeed, your secret sauce and not their local variation.

Trademarks and trade names

Watch out for countries with loose trademark protection laws. Check the cost and time involved with registration. Just because you own a name at home doesn't mean you can count on it abroad. Because many countries' trademark laws grant trademark rights to the first party to file for trademark protection, trademark pirates may have registered your very name right under your nose, hoping that you'd sniff them out and hand over big bucks to get it back. Otherwise, it's a waiting game. The bottom line again: time and money.

Deal with trademark issues at least a year or more before you begin to seek franchisees in an international market.

Other franchise-specific laws

Depending on what country you're entering, you may need to be concerned with other laws as well. Every country has laws that, although perhaps not aimed explicitly at franchising, affect franchising as well (for example, the local equivalent of our own antitrust laws). Many countries have laws that deal with the offer of franchises (or the franchise relationship) in their countries. Understand the requirements to offer franchises before you begin to solicit franchisees in a foreign land.

Deciding whether to Leave Your Turf

To go or not to go? That is the question. The answer to whether to expand internationally really boils down to timing.

Most franchisors head overseas after an unsolicited query gets their adrenaline pumping. Others pursue international markets out of ego. They figure that being the head of an international company will make interesting cocktail-party chatter or that globalization will attract more domestic franchisees. Others are lured by the idea that going international is a quick fix for domestic cash-flow problems. (As we say throughout the book, the opposite is true.) Still others simply like the appeal of international travel — hey, it's a great excuse to buy new luggage. Sorry, these are all the wrong reasons to expand internationally.

Smart franchisors head overseas only after intensively planning for international expansion. If you're crossing the border because the timing is right, give yourself a healthy pat on the back. That's strategic development. Kay Ainsley says, "The most difficult part of getting started with an international franchise program is knowing how to evaluate and price a market. The days of the enormous upfront fees are history. Today's franchisor must try to estimate the potential of the prospective market and determine a fair price. The instant gratification of a large upfront fee needs to be replaced with long-term royalties from a greater number of units. To do that, the price must be fair to both sides." Kay knows how much the market has changed after having structured and negotiated franchise agreements in over 50 international markets.

Before entertaining international proposals, you should have a strong and profitable base at home. To do otherwise is like serving dessert before the main course. We can't pinpoint an exact number of units you need at home, but your domestic operation should have a significant number of franchises in various regions and be supporting itself from royalties before going international. A saturated domestic market is a strong incentive to look outside but doesn't necessarily mean that your concept is ready for international expansion.

Other things also need to be in place. Internally, executive management must be committed to being in the game for the long haul. Too many international programs are severely damaged or killed when franchisors pull back resources because early results fall short of expectations.

Long-term commitment to international franchising includes shifting or adding staff that solely focus on foreign turf. Having field staff, marketing support, product sourcing, operations, and training staff all dedicated to international expansion and being supported by the rest of the organization is not unusual. As your international operations get even larger, you may need to establish whole divisions that mirror your domestic organization. Franchisors need to have surplus capital resources for providing support services, modifying operations, and making on-site visits.

In addition, no training is universal. You need to weave adaptations for operational variations and cultural differences into your standard training. If you offer franchises to master franchisees who will select franchisees in their markets and also provide franchisees with support, you need to be prepared to train them on how to be "franchisors" at home. After all, they'll be performing many of the same tasks you do as a franchisor: franchisee selection, training, and support. They need training in the following areas:

- ✔ Recruiting and selecting franchisees
- ✔ Administrative functions
- ✔ Site selection
- ✔ Marketing and advertising
- ✔ Training for personnel who will be trained locally
- ✔ Local product sourcing and vendor management
- ✔ Standards enforcement and discipline procedures
- ✔ All those other services they'll provide in the market

If you don't train them, who will?

Don't try to keep one eye on international operations and one eye on domestic. Appoint one person or group to be in charge of international expansion. It's a full-time job — not something that can be done in your spare time. Don't forget about the here and now in your excitement of looking to the future. So many times, franchisors let their focus stray from their domestic business — the thing that got them where they are in the first place — and get caught up in the excitement, sometimes fantasy, of going global. Make sure that you have the organization to manage both areas adequately — or wait until you do.

Externally, you must have a product or service that meets the needs of consumers in that market — or you have to be willing and able to invest in creating a need. Despite a shrinking world, not everyone needs or wants everything just the way you have it at home. Make sure that your product or service — and your operating system — can fly within the framework of local laws and cultural differences, and that you can make any necessary adaptations while maintaining the integrity of your concept. Food franchises, for example, must weigh religious and dietary issues. If, for example, a residential cleaning franchise has to retool its mops to accommodate the smaller hands in some markets, that's not nearly as big a deal as a convenience-store chain built on 24-hour service that has to greatly restrict trading hours due to local laws. A residential maid service has little market in countries with no sizable middle class; the wealthy have live-in help, and the poor *are* the help.

In addition, registering a franchisor's trademark as early as possible is a critical ingredient in border hopping. As soon as you select the countries you plan on entering, you should begin the process. No joking around here: You have to work with your local and international attorneys. And make sure that the political and economic climate is ripe for building a business. No one wants to risk employee safety or the economic viability of a start-up if unrest fills the air.

Look at the flip side for a moment. Don't leave home if

- ✔ You're looking for a quick fix to cash-flow problems.
- ✔ Executive management is not committed to long-term development.
- ✔ You're not prepared to invest time, effort, and resources.
- ✔ Your product or service doesn't meet local needs.
- ✔ You're unwilling to or can't modify your product or service to the local market.
- ✔ You can't secure trademark protection.
- ✔ Your operating procedures are so rigid that you can't or don't want to accommodate cultural or legal differences or requirements.
- ✔ Political or economic instability will create problems.
- ✔ You can't get your money out of the country.

If You Decide to Cross Borders . . .

If you decide to take the plunge, you want to tread carefully as you try to find your initial franchisees. You want to partner up with a franchisee with expertise in the foreign market and its customs, and you need to learn the tricks of overseas negotiations as you try to steer your initial efforts toward success.

Finding the right partner

So, you've got your passport in hand? Not so fast. A big chunk of international expansion hinges on teaming up with the right partner. If you're a U.S.-based franchisor, the exceptions may be Canada and Mexico; many franchisors sell directly to franchisees because proximity is not much different than, say, an East Coast company servicing franchisees on the West Coast.

Leaving North America, however, is a different story. Except in the hotel and some casual-dining restaurant concepts, partnering is pretty much the way to go to speed the learning curve because of a franchisor's distance and unfamiliarity with local customs. As much as you may think you know a foreign culture, you don't. (Your post-college trek around the globe doesn't cut it.)

Franchisors typically expand in these ways:

- **Master franchising:** A master franchisee follows a development schedule that calls for x number of units over x number of years. The master franchisee opens her own outlets or subfranchises them, or both. As a mirror image of the franchisor, it provides support on the local level in exchange for a percentage of franchise fees and royalties.

- **Area development:** A franchisee follows a development schedule to open her own outlets in an area (no subfranchising) and relies more on the franchisor for support services than in master franchising. Area development is becoming more popular.

- **Joint ventures:** The franchisor and a local partner form a company to pool their expertise and cash. This option gives the franchisor both more control and more risk. But the franchisor's equity participation may make a deal more credible to the local partner and to the government banks, among others.

Not just any warm body will do when you're looking for a franchisee. The biggest reason international franchise attempts fail is poor matchmaking — someone who is undercapitalized, is inattentive, doesn't adhere to a development schedule, or wants to do it his own way. Distance makes this a double-whammy; nipping a problem in the bud is more difficult and more costly when you're thousands of miles away and in a different country. By the time you find out about the problem, you may be too late to do anything about it. You could spend more money that you were paid straightening — or litigating — it out.

In scouting a franchisee, trust should top your list of qualities in a candidate. You're entrusting this person to build a network, protect and grow your brand name, and uphold your standards. You want some assurance that this person will put her heart and soul into the deal. What you may not want is a large company swimming in so many directions that your franchise drops to the bottom of the ocean. Your brand deserves capital and staff to support a development schedule, and your brand deserves focus. A foreign franchisee with access to real estate and local suppliers is a real plus. And he should be knowledgeable about local customs, laws, and business methods. If he's up on franchising, all the better.

Internationally, your franchise prospect may differ from the candidate you typically look for in your home market. The prospect may be bigger and better financed and have more resources and more bargaining power. This has its minuses as well as its pluses. You may consider (or even target) the type of franchisee you'd probably shun at home: the company that already owns other franchises.

The one criterion that is key in either domestic or international is that your franchisee has to be someone you like and want to work with on a long-term basis. You must have a clear meeting of the minds where each side understands what they can expect from the other and what will be expected from them. It's mutual, or it's wrong.

Entering a foreign market

Let's cut to the chase and round up some international partners. Just as at home, everyone wants to attract the best-suited franchisees — efficiently and without a lot of problems.

The first in line isn't always the best in line. Check out all prospective franchisees very, very carefully and remember to consult with your lawyer about meeting the requirements of the Patriot Act (see "Consider the implications of language and culture," earlier in this chapter). Rely on national franchise associations, local franchise attorneys, the local office of your accounting firm, knowledgeable consultants, potential suppliers, officers at foreign branches of your country's embassy, Interpol, and the international credit and reference services. If you're a U.S. franchisor, check out the International Trade Administration's Trade Information Center at 800-872-8723.

And, don't be surprised if you have a lot of foreign-based competition for good franchisees. Gone are the days when international franchising meant U.S. companies venturing forth to populate the world with U.S. products and business acumen. Alas, the gospel of franchising has spread. Foreign-based concepts are franchising with increasing frequency — in their home countries and abroad.

Begin your search with the following organizations and techniques:

- ✔ **Trade missions:** The IFA organizes trade missions. These missions last five to ten days and span two to four countries. They include meetings at U.S. embassies and one-on-one appointments with potential investors, prescreened to meet your requirements for a franchisee.

- ✔ **Trade shows:** The annual International Franchise Exposition (IFE) held in the United States typically draws thousands of foreign visitors in search of franchise opportunities. Contact the exposition's producer, MFV Expositions, at 201-226-1130 or visit `www.franchiseexpo.com`.

MFV also sponsors franchising events in other countries where U.S. franchisors can learn from local professionals how to enter the country, and foreign franchisors are able to learn from U.S. franchising professionals.

You can also check out franchise trade shows sponsored by many of the national franchise associations held all over the world.

✔ **Embassies:** These government offices in foreign countries can help you network and qualify locals. You can also try joint chambers of commerce and industry associations.

✔ **Referrals:** Contact franchise consultants and attorneys with affiliate offices in foreign countries. Franchisors of noncompeting concepts may also be willing to share leads. Give them a call.

✔ **World Franchise Council:** The World Franchise Council (`www.world franchisecouncil.org`) is made up of approximately 30 national franchise associations. Its purpose is to encourage international understanding and cooperation in the protection and promotion of franchising worldwide.

You won't find an American Franchise Association or a United States Franchise Association — so you can stop looking. Back in 1960, Bill Rosenberg, the founder of Dunkin' Donuts, together with several of the leading franchisors in the United States at the time, decided they needed an organization that would be the voice of franchising, and they formed the International Franchise Association. Many of the other national associations may feel that the IFA should change its name to the American or the United States Franchise Association, but the IFA is not likely to change its nomenclature anytime soon. Members of the IFA aren't trying to show their global ego — they simply like the name chosen by the founders, and it's pretty descriptive of the IFA's global reach, purpose, and function. The IFA is the leading association in the world representing franchisors, franchisees, and suppliers. As franchisors in the United States have expanded internationally, the IFA has led the way in working with governments around the world and with other national associations to develop franchising internationally. For information about the IFA, check out its Web site at `www.franchise.org`.

✔ **Suppliers:** A growing global economy probably has opened doors for your suppliers, and they may have contacts in the countries you're targeting. Besides, if they help you find the right franchisee, they'll end up selling more products.

✔ **Advertising:** You can advertise for foreign franchisees in print and online publications that cover franchising, international business, or industries in specific markets. In choosing a publication, keep your audience in mind.

If you're thinking about using a broker to handle your international expansion, think again. Making a mistake in selecting your franchisee overseas is likely to be more devastating to your expansion plans than making a similar mistake domestically. Always use internal personnel in your international expansion program. If you use a broker, limit the broker's role to making introductions, and be careful that you do a thorough due diligence on each of the prospective franchisees the broker has brought you.

Consider not just tying their total compensation to a percentage of the upfront market fee you may be paid by the franchisee, but prorating some of the broker's commission over the time the units are expected to be opened. Making a sale of a franchise, after all, isn't that hard. Recruiting, selecting, and introducing franchisees who can actually get the job done is what you really want to pay for.

Negotiating the deal

If you think you can saunter in and crank out a franchise agreement like you do in your home market, forget it. If you're used to saying "take it or leave it" at home, don't expect this approach to get you far on the international scene. Internationally, negotiation is definitely the name of the game. Because you're usually dealing with larger territories and big front-end fees, much more is at stake — for you and your prospective franchisee. So, get ready to negotiate.

The key to negotiating is building a trusting relationship. Make sure that your foreign prospect understands his obligations — and that you understand yours. Because of potential language barriers, review everything — and then review it again — to avoid miscommunication.

Keep cultural differences in mind when you're negotiating. People frequently want to establish friendships before getting down to business.

Your flexibility should depend on your thirst for the deal and that particular partner. If a prospect is thinly capitalized and lacks experience, you don't have much reason to bargain. When in doubt, walk. However, if your prospect is well capitalized, has sources for products, owns real estate perfect for your concept, has a great reputation as an ethical businessperson, and wants to open up a bunch of locations, this prospect is worth negotiating with.

Strike a balance, though. The key is not to give away the store. Too much flexibility doesn't bode well for your system.

Don't be surprised if fees are a bone of contention. Your asking price should reflect your size, your trademark, and your expenses. But to prospects, international price tags often sound like they're for the rich and famous. Reducing the fee, however, may be bad precedent for future relations. Rather, smart franchisors throw the following items on the table to make the front-end fee more palatable:

- ✔ Extra training
- ✔ More on-site support
- ✔ Translation of materials
- ✔ Additional advertising support
- ✔ Discounts on the initial inventory

Building in growth incentives also works as a bargaining chip. You could reduce royalties based on exceeding sales targets, or lower per-unit fees for surpassing development schedules.

Talking about development, specify a certain number of units that a master franchisee must build himself before subfranchising so that he works out any bugs in the translation and has a pilot operation available for training subfranchisees. Other contract issues include noncompetition covenants, termination rights and obligations, supplier restrictions, and local insurance requirements.

Dispute resolution is a big topic everywhere. Although many of the same methods available for resolving problems in your home country are likely available in foreign markets (arbitration and mediation), let your attorney — in conjunction with your in country lawyers — guide you down this path.

Striking a deal is just a small first step. The giant step is making the deal work. But the two go together — in order for the deal to work, you must be satisfied with a deal that makes economic sense. If your ego demands a press release announcing a huge franchise fee and aggressive development schedule, you may be headed for trouble. Remember that the franchisee will need resources to meet her obligations and your expectations and that money may no longer be available to her because she paid you such a large fee. Make sure that you're planning for the future success of your business. Just as you do in the United States, make sure you select franchisees who have the resources necessary to do their jobs. The bulk of your income should come from continuing fees from a growing network of locations and not from a one-time payment.

Bringing Foreign Franchises to the United States

Although many Americans may not believe it, the United States isn't the only mother of invention. Companies worldwide are giving birth to their own franchised concepts — with increasing frequency — and are crossing borders and offering franchises all over the world.

Because of its size, the U.S. market is extremely attractive to many foreign franchisors. Americans have a deep-rooted fascination with franchising, have high disposable income, and enthusiastically embrace new products. We're also the consummate consumers — just check out our credit card debt.

The biggest problem for foreign franchisors is fear. They have exaggerated fear of being sued because of the U.S. reputation for litigation, they know that playing the game in the United States costs a lot of money because of the regulatory environment, and they're daunted by the size and diversity of the market.

Foreign-based franchisors entering the United States are often patterning after the U.S. chains that land on their soil — typically selling master franchises or setting up joint ventures. But companies entering the United States need to understand the market and answer the same key questions we posed for U.S. franchisors going overseas. Even if you're convinced that the concept will work, you could drain your financial resources if you miss the mark.

Working far from home presents challenges that you have to be ready for:

- Will you adapt the concept to the local market? Who will control the adaptations?

- Are inventory and equipment available locally? If you must import them, what are the duties, shipping costs, and time constraints?

- Will you store inventory locally to make up for potentially longer delivery times to your franchisees of the products and supplies they'll need?

- Does your brand have enough name recognition to demand a higher price — especially compared to local competition — to cover any increased costs?

- What happens if things don't work out?

- What are your termination provisions and dispute resolution procedures?

- What's your corporate culture like? Do you have open communication? How will you communicate with franchisees who speak a different language from the language spoken by everyone else in the system?

Just because a franchisor is from overseas doesn't mean that it doesn't have to meet all the requirements of a domestic franchisor. If a franchisor is offering franchises in the United States, it must provide an FDD (see Chapter 6). If a franchisor is offering franchises in other countries, it may have to meet those countries' disclosure rules. Just as with U.S. franchisors going overseas, franchisors entering the United States should work with U.S. consultants and legal counsel. The United States is a tough and unforgiving market. Historically, few foreign franchisors, including those from nearby Canada, have prospered in the United States. The size, costs, diversity of markets, and different culture of the American franchisee and consumer often overwhelm foreign franchisors. Testing your concept first in a local market is a good idea; try out a market, such as Dallas or Chicago, with an area development agreement before offering larger master franchisees territories in the United States.

The CD-ROM includes helpful material on foreign companies entering the U.S. as franchisors (CD1604). It was written by Dave Koch, a partner in the Reston, Virginia, office of Plave Koch.

Part VI
The Part of Tens

The 5th Wave — By Rich Tennant

ORIGINAL WAITRESS UNIFORM FOR "HOOTERS" RESTAURANT

"Think of all the ornithologists we'll attract."

In this part . . .

In this part, we give you some insight into the ten keys to franchise success. We also list the ten questions to ask before you buy a franchise.

Chapter 17

Ten Keys to Franchise Success

In This Chapter

▶ Having enough money, discipline, and personal support

▶ Recruiting, retaining, and training your employees

▶ Serving your customers, community, and franchise

Making any business reach its full potential takes talent, and ensuring that your customers are always satisfied isn't that easy. If you've selected your franchise well, your franchisor will be able to help you avoid many of the mistakes that new independent start-up businesses make. However, they can't guarantee your success — that's up to you. Your contribution is critical, too.

In this chapter, we offer you our list of considerations that may help your franchise experience be a success and (we hope) help you stay in front of the pack.

Make Sure That You Have Enough Money

Before you make your decision to invest in a franchise, make a personal financial plan. Decide how much you have to invest, how much you're willing to risk, and how much you'll need to live on for at least 12 months. Remember that you and your family still have to live, and fun is something you need to budget for also. Unfortunately, so are emergencies. Carefully go over your personal finances with your accountant or some other investment advisor so you know what you can afford to do.

Follow the System

Following the system sounds like obvious advice. Who wouldn't follow the franchisor's system after going through all the effort and expenses required to join the franchise? You'd be surprised. Franchisees, on more than the rare

occasion, will get the business up and running, and then they begin to tinker —
changing or adding products, modifying the advertising, customizing the services, the hours, and even the quality and consistency of the products and
services that they're licensed to deliver. They want to be entrepreneurial.

By following the system, you preserve the brand and protect your investment
and those of your fellow franchisees, because you're giving consumers what
they expect. You hope they'll reward you by spending their money at your
location. However, if you have what you think is a good idea, don't sit on it.
Inform your franchisor so that the franchisor can consider it, possibly test it,
and maybe even approve it. Many of the most successful innovations in franchising have historically come from the franchisees already in the system.
You have a role in evolving your system, and most franchise systems have
clear procedures to help you do so.

Don't Neglect Your Loved Ones

Starting any business is hard work. When you couple starting a business
with franchisor-provided training and the requirement to follow procedures,
starting a franchise can take even *more* work. You'll feel pressure — some
self-imposed, some imposed by the franchisor — to get the job of opening the
business done on time. And you'll feel some fear — primarily of failure. Hard
work, pressure, and fear can impact your personal life. Be prepared.

You need the support and understanding of your loved ones during the launch
of your new business — especially when the pressure puts you in moods that
even your mother couldn't love. Don't forget to acknowledge their sacrifices.
Set aside time for just you and the important people in your life. If the only time
you have for your kids, for example, is when you grab a quick bite with them at
night, be sure to spend that time focused on them, not on the business.

Be an Enthusiastic Operator

The success of any business is linked to the level of enthusiasm the unit management brings to the job. In franchising, the most enthusiastic operator is
usually the one who has the most to lose if it fails: the franchisee.

Enthusiasm is contagious:

- ✔ It brings a level of excitement and energy to the operation that
  everyone — including your customers — can feel.
- ✔ It motivates your staff by making your location a better place to work.

Your mood translates immediately into the mood of your entire operation. No matter how you feel, no matter what the problem is, no matter who you're mad at, when you come to work, be enthusiastic and upbeat. You may be trying to fool only your staff and your customers, but if you keep it up long enough, you may even fool yourself!

Recruit the Best Talent and Treat Them with Respect

Good help is hard to find; great help is essential. Even when you're faced with a tight labor market, you can still find ways to attract the best people into your business. Your job is also to keep them there.

Don't overlook the senior citizen. Many seniors like working and have a wonderful work ethic that makes them terrific additions to your team and role models for younger employees.

 Another sizable pool that the marketplace is only now tapping into is the physically and mentally challenged. We're not suggesting that you set up a program that makes you feel good because you're hiring the "handicapped." We're recommending it strongly because it will show that you're a smart businessperson who doesn't allow perceived problems to get in the way of the reality of improving the performance of your business.

Before you hire your staff, make sure they understand their jobs, their pay, the hours they'll be required to work, their benefits, their days off, and their vacations. When you find the right people, train them before you put them to work. Nothing is more frustrating to employees than being thrown into a job they don't know how to do. To retain good staff, you must respect individuals, recognize where they're happiest, put them there, and keep them there as much as possible (see Chapter 8).

Teach Your Employees

Why recruit the best employees in town if you don't plan to properly teach them how to do their jobs? The happiest employees are the ones who get proper training so that they can do a good job.

In franchising, training should be continuous (see Chapter 8). Employees are your front line. They're the ones who meet and greet your customers and the ones you rely on to help grow your business. Poorly trained staff can break you because they're the ones likely to create dissatisfied customers.

Training classes are a good way to show your employees that they matter to you — and to the success of the business. A good manager praises employees — after making sure they have the knowledge they need to do their jobs.

Give Customers Great Service

One of the reasons you invested in your franchise was because it had a system to provide consistent products and services. Following your franchisor's procedures is a good place to start. In a good franchise system, the products and services should be the same from franchisee to franchisee to company-owned location. This consistency is what customers expect and why they may have come into your store or called you for your service in the first place. But consistency doesn't answer the question of why some franchisees do better than others.

Treat the brand with respect. Make sure that your staff is well groomed, your bathrooms are clean, and you treat your customers as if they were guests in your house.

Get Involved with the Community

As a local businessperson, you should be as interested in your community as any baby-kissing political candidate. You need to be seen as part of the fabric of your community. Customers like to shop in places that support them. We're not talking about advertising — we're talking about real marketing to your community.

The following activities help show your community that you care about them and want to support what is important to them:

✔ Sponsor a Little League team.

✔ Participate in civic groups.

✔ Start a nursing-home visitation program.

✔ Conduct tours of your business for school groups.

✔ Set up a kiosk at community events (if your franchisor allows).

✔ Get together with other franchisees in the market and sponsor an event together.

✔ Set aside a day to give a portion of your proceeds to charity.

✔ Provide students with good grades a discount or free products when they bring in their report cards.

✔ Celebrate good citizenship by supporting a youth group.

✔ Join and support your Better Business Bureau, Chamber of Commerce, Rotary Club, or other local community-based organization.

Stay in Touch with Your Franchisor and Fellow Franchisees

Most franchisors invest heavily in communications about new product development, troubleshooting tips, employee relations, upcoming meetings and conventions, franchisee achievements, and other important news. Some of the methods may be old-fashioned: letters, newsletters, phone calls, and faxes. Some may be high-tech: e-mails, forums on intranet sites (an *intranet* is a closed-system version of the Internet, accessible only to the company's employees), and Internet sites. Many will be face-to-face: training programs, field visits, conferences, and conventions. You should take advantage of every method of receiving information from your franchisor and take advantage of every chance to provide the franchisor with information.

Contact the International Franchise Association at 202-628-8000 or go to www. franchise.org, and find out if it has a grass-roots meeting in your community. These meetings are attended by franchisors and franchisees from many franchise systems, as well as suppliers to the industry. The gatherings are great networking opportunities where you can learn from other people in different franchise programs.

Watch the Details

Success is in the pennies. To run a successful business, you must minimize costs and maximize sales. Minimizing costs goes beyond cutting the best deal for your raw materials or inventory. Minimizing costs means you have to be diligent and observe how your business operates day-to-day:

✔ Watch out for your *shrinkage,* the merchandise that is missing and unaccounted for due to employee theft, customer theft, vendor theft, or maybe simple bad management, inventory, and ordering procedures.

✔ Establish a friends-and-family policy — and that includes the friends and family of your employees. *Remember:* You're in business at your business. Most people have family and friends they invite to their houses for dinner. Often, though, those guests think that coming to your business is the same as coming to your home — it's free.

✔ Although store operation costs take into account some shortages (your franchisor probably has the percentages), you also need to keep a sharp eye on shipment deliveries, storage, product handling, and store theft. Every time products disappear, are damaged, or are prepared but not sold, that's money out of your pocket.

✔ When you see a vendor improperly handling your delivery, bring it up immediately. The same thing goes for employees who aren't handling products correctly.

✔ Plan your labor. Look at any business: Some days are busier than others, and some hours during the day are busier than others. Learn how to schedule to meet your needs.

✔ Work hard every day. Some days you may want to kick back just a little and coast, putting the business out of your mind for a while. We're not recommending that you deprive yourself of breaks from the business, just that you choose your time away from the franchise wisely.

Chapter 18

Ten Questions to Ask Yourself before Buying a Franchise

This time of your life is an exciting one. You're looking at your future and weighing your options. Maybe you're a recent escapee from the corporate ranks, or perhaps you've owned your own business before and want a little more support, training, and backup than when you were going it alone. Whatever your reason, we're glad you're considering franchise ownership. This chapter offers ten questions that, together, we think are a good jumping-off point when you consider buying a franchise. Take a look at Chapter 1 for more questions on becoming a franchisee.

Do You Know the Franchisor?

You need to know a potential franchisor on a deeper level than just as a nice person with a winning smile and a great golf swing. In addition, you need to know if the opportunity is as solid as the glossy brochure represents.

We want you to know the person behind the handshake — to know the beliefs, convictions, and ethics of your franchisor. To get that information, you need to conduct an investigation of the opportunity, including talking to as many existing and former franchisees as possible. Don't be shy about asking questions. Your future could depend on the information you're able to gather. When in doubt, walk away from the opportunity. You'll find plenty more to choose from.

Personal Inventory: Are You Ready to Be on Your Own?

If your calling card is self-reliance, congratulations. Having that quality means you're used to taking care of yourself and doing what needs to be done. Some of the most successful franchisees we know have an enthusiasm and a commitment to making their businesses the best in the system.

Maybe, however, you're independent and accustomed to doing things your own way, which can become a problem when you have to play by the franchisor's rules. You have to consider many issues before you decide whether you're ready to join the ranks of franchisees. So, ask yourself a few questions:

- Can you follow somebody else's road map, or do you have to be in control all the time?

- Are you the type who will resent the franchisor two or three years from now when you don't need as much active support?

- How much do you need to live on? Can you live on the anticipated money you'll earn from the business?

- Do you like to work with people? Do you like to make decisions and have people report to you? Do you trust that you have what it takes to be a success?

Can You Afford a Franchise?

Buying a franchise is an investment, often the largest investment you'll ever make.

Although you can finance some opportunities on your credit card for a few thousand dollars, others will require you to come up with ready cash or loans of over $1 million. So don't cut corners when you do your financial homework. Take your time and run the numbers:

- How much do you have to invest? How much can you risk losing? How much do you need to live on?

- What is the total investment required for getting into the franchise? What portion of the investment can you finance? Can you find anyone who is willing to invest in you and your future?

✔ How much can you earn as a franchisee? How long before you'll break even? What return can you get on your investment? Can you get a better return from another investment? Are the risks equal?

✔ Make sure your research is thorough, and do the research yourself instead of using franchise brokers. Research the industry and the company on the Web, review the company's disclosure document, talk to current franchisees, and talk to former franchisees.

✔ Get the assistance of professional advisors — your banker, accountant, attorney, or someone whose business judgment you trust.

Reviewing your financial situation isn't the most exciting part of investing in a franchise — but it must be the cornerstone of the process.

Do You Have the Support of Your Loved Ones?

Keep the lines of communication open with the important people in your life; talk with them freely about the pressures of running your own business and the demands it will likely have on your time. Let them in on the pressure you may be feeling by discussing the risk with them — after all, investing in a franchise is not a 100 percent guarantee of success.

Make sure they're comfortable with your decision before you move forward. You're going to need their support along the way. You'll also need to keep your focus trained on your business, not deflected by pressures from home.

In a very real sense, not only are *you* investing in a franchise, but so is everyone who is close to you.

Do You Understand the Terms of the Contract?

Franchising is a relationship between a franchisor and franchisee that is governed by a written agreement — the contract. In the process of investigating a franchisor, you meet franchise executives and franchise salespeople who will make you promises. Remember, though, that the franchisor's obligations and promises to you, and your obligations and promises to the franchisor — the obligations that are legally binding — will be found in the written agreement you sign. Keep a written log of promises the franchisor makes that you're relying on. You want to make sure that those promises are in the franchise agreement.

Even if you're experienced, having a qualified franchise attorney work with you is always a smart idea. Franchising is a complex business and legal relationship. The attorney you hire needs to be qualified and experienced in franchise law. The business advisors you consult need to understand the franchise relationship and, ideally, the industry your franchisor operates in.

If you're satisfied that all your concerns have been answered, work with your attorney in finalizing the agreement.

Are the Other Franchisees Happy with Their Investments?

The franchisor will provide you with a Franchise Disclosure Document (FDD). In that document, you'll find a list of franchisees in the system and a list of those who recently left the system. Get on the phone and start calling. Sound like a lot of work? Maybe, but if you take a second mortgage on your house to buy this franchise, shouldn't you try extra-hard to make sure you choose wisely and that your family won't end up sleeping in a pup tent?

If the franchise system has an association of franchisees — a franchise advisory council or franchisee association — get the president's number and give her a call. The president can be a great help in educating you about the franchise system.

Does the Franchisor Have a History of Litigation?

How would you feel about buying into a company that has a history of lawsuits with its franchisees? Although having lawsuits is not always an indication of a bad franchisor, it's something that should concern you and something you need to investigate.

As a rule, you should be very concerned if you find a franchisor whose franchisees seem to be constantly bringing lawsuits against it. These frequent lawsuits are a warning bell of the loudest kind. Although lawsuits certainly are an indication of problems with some franchisees, they could also be an indication of a poorly managed franchise system or a franchise system that is not meeting its commitments. Instead of seeking solutions through active discussions, some franchisors and franchisees manage problems through the courts.

However, an isolated lawsuit may not be an indication of any serious problems. Check out the specifics of the lawsuit. What were the circumstances and the outcome? Did the lawsuit have to do with a breach of the agreement by the franchisee, such as nonpayment of fees or quality concerns?

Can You Make Money with This Franchise?

Your goal is to make a return on your investment. Even if the franchisor provides projected earnings for a location, the best indicator of how well you can actually do comes from franchisees already in the system.

When you speak with established franchisees, get as much information as they're willing to give. Here are some suggested questions for you to ask:

- ✔ Are you making money with this franchise investment?
- ✔ How long did it take you to break even? How long before you started to make money?
- ✔ Was the investment estimate that the franchisor gave you accurate? If not, how much more money did you need?
- ✔ Was the estimated working capital accurate? How much did you need to have? How long before you could take money out of the business to live on?
- ✔ Did you make any mistakes in starting up the franchise that cost you money? How can I avoid the same problem?

Although the franchisees probably won't share their profit-and-loss statements with you, go ahead and ask them about their profitability. If they're willing, they can give you information that'll help you develop your own projected financial information for your location.

The type of information to look for is

- ✔ Size of location.
- ✔ Number of staff hours required per week.
- ✔ Type of labor required. You want to determine how much it'll cost you to get the same quality labor in your market.
- ✔ Amount and types of local advertising required.

You get the idea.

Is the Franchisor Making Money, and Where Is the Money Coming From?

You'll be relying on the franchisor to provide the promised services and to keep the concept fresh. You want a franchisor that is financially solid — not just today, but for the long term. A franchisor that has financial problems is not a franchise system you want to get involved in — unless you like added risk.

New franchisors may receive the majority of their income from the initial fees they charge the franchisees. That's normal. Franchisors that have been around a while, however, should be supporting their systems from continuing revenue — such as the royalties paid by the franchisees. (*Royalties* are the continuing fees paid by the franchisee to the franchisor for the use of the trademarks and the system.) If royalty income is not able to pay for the support services, what will happen to the franchise network if expansion slows down or stops?

Be sure that your franchisor is on firm financial ground and able to provide support over the long term. Have your accountant review the franchisor's financial statements.

Does the Franchisor Understand Franchising?

For a franchisor to be able to work the grill or change a muffler is not enough. That's your job, the job of the other franchisees, and the job of the managers of the company-owned operations.

Operating and expanding a franchise system, as well as providing support to franchisees, requires different skills than simply running a single location or multiple locations. To make sure your franchisor has the necessary skills, you need to answer the following questions:

✔ Does your franchisor have adequate staff, resources, and trained personnel to meet its commitments to you?

✔ From your meetings with the franchisor, review of its disclosure document, and conversations with the existing franchisees, do you feel that the franchisor has the appropriate temperament to operate a franchise system?

- ✔ Does the franchisor staff attend seminars on franchising and management? Do they know about the latest changes in their industry? Are they active in the trade associations for their specific industry, and are they active in the International Franchise Association, the industry trade association for franchising?

- ✔ Are members of the franchisor's staff and management Certified Franchise Executives (CFEs), or are they candidates for the CFE?

- ✔ Is the chain growing? Is the franchisor adding new locations on a regular basis? How many locations closed in the past few years? (If any stores have closed, you need to find out why.)

- ✔ Are the same-store sales on the increase? This statistic is different from whether sales for the entire chain have increased. The franchisor could've added new stores to the system, and even if unit sales went down, the system sales may still go up. You want to determine if individual store sales are increasing and you want to know about other key performance indicators.

- ✔ Does the company have an active research and development department that introduces new products and services?

- ✔ Do the field staff act as consultants and advisors, or do they act as police personnel (inspecting franchises and writing up violations, but not offering help and guidance)?

Part VII
Appendixes

"I have 8 children from my first marriage and 6 children from my second, and you're asking me if franchising myself is something I'm comfortable with?"

In this part . . .

This book references many terms that you may not recognize. Although we explain them along the way, Appendix A is here to give you some further input on the definitions as well as to serve as a handy reference tool so you don't have to put sticky notes all over your book. Don't look in any dictionary for these definitions exactly as we wrote them — we wrote them in a way that we hope makes them more meaningful for you.

Possibly the most exciting change in this revised edition of *Franchising For Dummies* is the addition of the bonus CD-ROM. On the CD, you find a plethora of workbooks, forms, checklists, guidelines, and so on to give you a great start in your franchising pursuit and to guide you along the way. Be sure to check out the CD, because it contains things that, up until now, only lawyers and other professional advisors could bring you.

Appendix A

Glossary of Common Franchise Terms

• •

Don't look for the following definitions in any legal journal. We want to give you a sense of what people in the industry mean when they say something — not turn you into a franchise attorney. In this glossary, you find some of the more common terms used in franchising.

acknowledgment of receipt: Item 23 of the Franchise Disclosure Document (FDD) that is signed by the prospective franchisee and provided to the franchisor (in hard copy or electronically signed) as proof of the date the FDD was received by the prospect.

advertising fee: Franchise systems advertise to consumers — a lot — and most of the cost of developing the consumer marketing material is paid for out of a fund. Depending on the system, the fund also may pay for the cost of placing the ads you see on TV and hear on radio or elsewhere. The money to produce and place the ads gets there when the franchisee makes a contribution to the fund. That's what we call the advertising fee.

advertising fund: See *system brand fund.*

agent: A party that has implied or expressed (oral or written) authority to act on behalf of another.

approved advertising materials: Materials provided by a franchisor for the franchisee's use in his local market. These may also be materials created by the franchisee that the franchisor has approved for use.

approved site: A location that the franchisor determines meets its criteria for a location. Site approval does not usually indicate any level of sales or guarantee of the success of the location.

arbitration: A method of resolving disputes.

area franchisee (multi-unit): If you want to open and operate many locations and are willing to make the commitment to a franchisor that you'll develop an agreed-upon number of locations during a defined period — and in a defined territory — you're an area franchisee. You usually pay an area fee for the rights granted by the franchisor.

authorized or designated supplier: A supplier of products and/or services who has been approved by the franchisor to sell to franchisees. An approved supplier may be the franchisor or an affiliate company.

broker: An outside salesperson or firm. For a fee — usually a commission — brokers sell franchises for a franchisor. Some brokers like to call themselves franchise consultants but that's a misnomer (see *franchise consultant,* later in this glossary).

business-format franchising (BFF): Wendy's, Meineke, and PostNet are business-format franchisors. In a business-format franchise, the most important thing you get from the franchisor is the method to conduct the business. See also *product and trade name franchising* to understand how BFF differs.

business plan: A planning document that details the objectives for the business and established processes and the measures for meeting those objectives.

capital required: The initial investment or required amount of investment necessary to conduct the business.

certification: Program by which a franchisor or franchisee tests and attests to the ability of an employee to perform certain job functions within the franchisor's standards. The franchisor or franchisee can usually revoke certification if the employee fails to maintain standards in performing the job function.

churning: Sometimes franchises fail, and the franchisor becomes the owner of the failed location. In the hands of a non-franchisor, who does not have the ability to franchise the location to another person, the location may be a candidate for closure, if the non-franchisor didn't think that the location could be turned around. In the hands of some franchisors, though, that location, even with the prospect of continuing failure, is resold, sometimes again and again to new franchisees, who also eventually fail. Churning is not a common practice in franchising, but it does happen. Beware of franchisors that churn.

company-owned location: The locations owned and operated by a franchisor. They should be identical in appearance and operations to those locations operated by the franchisees.

continuous training: In most franchise systems, you, your managers, and your staff receive initial training when you join the system. In a good franchise system, the training is continuous, meaning that the franchisor offers you training throughout the term of the franchise relationship.

conversion franchisee: An independent businessperson who agrees to convert her business to the franchisor's brand and operating procedures. She changes the business name, adopts the franchise system's methods of operation, and agrees to pay fees.

copyright: The franchisor's ownership rights over the manuals and other published materials you use in the system.

culture of compliance: The franchisor's culture whereby franchisees and staff do what is right for the system based on a feeling or knowledge that it's the right thing to do within the company philosophy rather than because it's in the agreement or someone is watching.

customer information: Any information gathered by or for the franchisor or its franchisees about an actual or potential customer, including, without limitation, names, addresses, e-mail addresses, telephone numbers, and all other personally identifying information, regardless of whether such information was gathered prior to the commencement of the agreement; customer credit information; billing information; and records. Customer information is usually considered confidential information of the franchisor.

days: Generally refers to calendar days.

day-to-day management: As an independent owner, the franchisee is obligated to manage the day-to-day affairs of his business to meet the franchisor's brand standards.

default: Generally refers to the failure of either the franchisor or the franchisee to meet their obligations under the franchise agreement.

design: Includes everything that makes a location look like all the other franchise locations — the layout, colors, signage, logo, and so on.

disclosure document: Also known in the United States as the Franchise Disclosure Document (FDD). In the United States, all franchisees must receive an FDD at least 14 days before they sign an agreement with the franchisor or write the franchisor a check. Disclosure documents are not required everywhere around the world. In the disclosure document, you find information about the franchisor, including the obligations of the franchisor and the franchise, fees, start-up costs, and other required information about the franchise system.

distributorships: The right granted by manufacturers or wholesalers to individuals or businesses to sell their products.

financial performance representation: Generally refers to the Item 19 disclosure made by franchisors in their FDD and unit performance.

exclusive (protected) territory: If a franchisor agrees to give you an area around your location where it will not put another franchise or company-owned location, you have an exclusive or protected territory. The area can be quite small (the four walls of your store) or it can be quite large (cities, counties, states, or countries). Most often, the size is somewhere in the middle.

FDD: Franchise Disclosure Document. See *disclosure document.*

feasibility study: A study of a company that is thinking about becoming a franchisor. The company usually hires a franchise-consulting firm that looks at the company and gives management its opinion on whether the company can become a successful franchisor.

Federal Trade Commission (FTC): The agency of the U.S. government that regulates franchising.

field consultant: Field consultants usually work for a franchisor. Their job is to make sure that the franchisees are following the franchisor's rules. In good systems, field consultants are also responsible for giving the franchisees advice and assistance in running their businesses.

footprint: The layout of a location, including placement of all furniture, fixtures, and equipment.

franchise: Every franchise is a license, but not every license is a franchise. Confused? Many people are. A franchise is a special type of license that usually has three elements: (1) The franchisor lets the franchisee use the franchisor's name and marks, (2) the franchisor provides the franchisee with assistance or has some control over how the franchisee operates the business, and (3) the franchisee pays the franchisor some money. In the United States, the fee is $500 or more during a six-month period.

franchise agreement: The written contract between the franchisor and franchisee. The franchise agreement tells each party what it's supposed to do and what it isn't supposed to do.

franchise attorney: An attorney who specializes in franchise law.

franchise consultant: A business advisor with significant knowledge of the design, development, and operation of franchising and the underlying franchise relationship. Some brokers like to call themselves franchise consultants, but that's a misnomer (see *broker,* earlier in this glossary).

franchise fee: When a franchisee signs a franchise agreement, he usually writes a check to the franchisor — that's the franchise fee. The fee is the cost of joining the system. The fee is typically a flat fee, as opposed to a percentage of sales like the royalty.

franchisee: The person or company that gets the right from the franchisor to do business under the franchisor's trademark and trade name.

franchisee in good standing: A franchisee who is operating her business in full compliance with the franchisor's operating and other standards per the franchise agreement and is current with all payments due to the franchisor.

franchising: A method of distribution; in other words, a method of growing a business.

franchisor: The person or company that grants the franchisee the right to do business under their trademarks or service marks.

gray marketing: When a franchisee sells or uses products or services obtained through his franchise relationship in another business or sells products or merchandise to another company without the authorization of the franchisor.

gross sales: Generally the total sales of the business, before the collection of any sales taxes and after specified deductions. Generally used as the basis for percentage royalty calculations.

initial investment: The initial costs of getting into business, which usually include the franchise fee, the cost of the fixed assets, leasehold improvements, inventory, deposits, other fees and costs, and the working capital required during the start-up period.

inquiry: Anyone requesting information about a franchise opportunity, whether via the Web site, by telephone, by fax, and so on.

International Franchise Association (IFA): The industry trade association that represents franchising.

Internet sales: Any sale initiated and completed on the World Wide Web.

key supplier or vendor: A supplier with whom the franchisor has negotiated pricing or product availability and whose products or services are an integral part of the franchise system.

lead: An inquiry who is pre-qualified after the initial interview with a member of the development staff as meeting the minimum criteria to become a franchisee and is invited to submit a franchise application.

location: The site of the franchised or company-owned operation.

manual: The bible of a franchise system. The manual is the place to look for instructions on how the franchisor wants the locations to operate and for other policies concerning the system.

market introduction program: Marketing, advertising, and public relations activities used to launch a franchisee's business. Also known as *grand-opening marketing*.

master franchisee: Take a look at the definition of *area franchisee*. Now, in addition to operating its own locations, the master franchisee also gets the right to sell franchises to subfranchisees within the master franchisee's specified territory. The master franchisee may provide to the subfranchisee some of the services provided by the franchisor and will typically split with the franchisor the franchise fee and royalties paid by the subfranchisee.

multi-unit franchisee: A franchisee who owns more than one franchise but may not have an area development agreement.

operating principal: Franchises owned by more than one person that appoint a single individual authorized to make decisions on behalf of the franchisee. This person is the operating principal and is usually the person with whom the franchisor consults regarding the operation and conduct of the franchise.

product and trade name franchising: Pepsi and Ford are product and trade name franchisors. In a business franchise, the franchisee sells or distributes a specific product using the franchisor's trademark, trade name, and logo (for example, automobile dealerships, truck dealerships, farm equipment, mobile homes, gasoline service stations, automobile accessories, soda, beer, and bottling). The most important thing you get from the franchisor is the product that the franchisor manufactures, not the system of running the business, as in business-format franchising.

prospect: A person who has expressed interest in continuing the approval process by completing and submitting the franchise application and whose application has been preliminarily approved by the approval committee or the development director.

protected or exclusive territory: Prohibition of the franchisor from opening company-owned locations or granting a franchise within the territory assigned to a franchisee.

quality standards: Some systems have high quality standards; others don't. If franchisors want to control quality, however, they tell the franchisees what those standards are in their training programs, manuals, and other communications. Quality franchise systems tightly control these standards for the benefit of the franchise system and its franchisees.

registration: Some states in the U.S. require the franchisor to send the state its disclosure document for approval prior to offering franchises. No registration is required at the federal level.

registration states: The various states that require franchisors to submit their FDD for approval prior to offering franchises.

retrofranchising or refranchising: Retrofranchising and refranchising are not the same as churning. These are existing locations that may or may not have ever been franchised before but are currently operated by the franchisor. The franchisor that is retrofranchising or refranchising locations is selling the operating business to a franchisee. In these situations, the franchisor has an expectation that the business will be successful. See also *churning*.

royalty fee: The franchisee sends the franchisor a check on a regular basis to stay part of the franchise system. Usually, the payment is based on a percentage of the franchisee's gross sales, but it can be a fixed fee or calculated on some other basis. That continuing fee is the royalty fee.

service mark: A mark used to identify the services of one company as distinguished from the services of another. Service marks are afforded similar protection under the law.

single-unit franchise: A franchisee who owns and operates a single franchise.

start-up costs: The initial investment that the franchisee will make in becoming a franchisee. It's also known as an Item 7 disclosure. It generally includes the franchise fee, the cost of fixed assets, leasehold improvements, inventory, deposits, other fees and costs, and working capital required during the start-up period.

success: How do you define success: profit, growth, or return on investment? In some franchise systems, success often simply describes the absence of failure or the closing of a location. It may have nothing at all to do with unit sales or profitability.

successor agreement: The franchisee's ability to continue in the business for additional terms following a successful completion of their initial term. Also known as *renewal.*

system brand fund: A fund established and usually managed by the franchisor to which all franchised and company-owned units contribute monies to be spent on promoting and protecting the franchisor's brand. Often called an *advertising fund.*

trademark: The marks, brand name, and logo that identify a franchisor. It's the name that the franchisor licenses to the franchisee.

turnkey: A location that a franchisor builds and then sells to a franchisee fully equipped and ready to operate.

Appendix B

About the CD

The CD-ROM that comes with this book is a fantastic resource. In this appendix, we tell you what you need to know to use it.

System Requirements

Make sure that your computer meets the minimum system requirements shown in the following list. If your computer doesn't match up to most of these requirements, you may have problems using the software and files on the CD. For the latest and greatest information, please refer to the ReadMe file located at the root of the CD-ROM.

- A PC with a Pentium or faster processor, or a Mac OS computer with a 68040 or faster processor.

- Microsoft Windows 98 or later, or Mac OS X system software 10.3 or later.

- At least 32 MB of total RAM installed on your computer; for best performance, we recommend at least 64 MB.

- A CD-ROM drive.

- A sound card for PCs; Mac OS computers have built-in sound support.

✔ A monitor capable of displaying at least 256 colors or grayscale.

✔ A modem with a speed of at least 14,400 bps.

If you need more information on the basics, check out these books published by Wiley: *PCs For Dummies,* 11th Edition, by Dan Gookin; *Macs For Dummies,* 10th Edition, by Edward C. Baig; *Mac OS X Tiger For Dummies, Mac OS X Leopard For Dummies,* or *Mac OS X Snow Leopard For Dummies,* all by Bob LeVitus; or *Windows XP For Dummies,* 2nd Edition, *Windows Vista For Dummies,* or *Windows 7 For Dummies,* all by Andy Rathbone.

Using the CD

To install the items from the CD to your hard drive, follow these steps:

1. **Insert the CD into your computer's CD-ROM drive. The license agreement appears.**

   Note for Windows users: The interface won't launch if you have autorun disabled. In that case, choose Start⇨Run. In the dialog box that appears, type **D:\start.exe**. (Replace D with the proper letter if your CD-ROM drive uses a different letter. If you don't know the letter, see how your CD-ROM drive is listed under My Computer.) Click OK.

   Note for Mac users: The CD icon will appear on your desktop; double-click the icon to open the CD, and then double-click the Start icon.

2. **Read through the license agreement, and then click the Accept button if you want to use the CD.**

   The CD interface appears. The interface allows you to install the programs and run the demos with just a click of a button (or two).

What You'll Find on the CD

The following sections are arranged by category and provide a summary of the software and other goodies you'll find on the CD. If you need help with installing the items provided on the CD, refer to the installation instructions in the preceding section.

Software

You'll find the following software on your CD:

- **Adobe Reader:** Adobe Reader is a freeware program that allows you to view (but not edit) PDFs.

- **OpenOffice.org (PC) and NeoOffice (Mac):** These programs are free multi-platform office productivity suites. They're similar to Microsoft Office or Lotus SmartSuite, but OpenOffice.org and NeoOffice are absolutely free. They include word processing, spreadsheet, presentation, and drawing applications that enable you to create professional documents, newsletters, reports, and presentations. They support most file formats of other office software, so you should be able to edit and view any files created with other office solutions.

Shareware programs are fully functional, free, trial versions of copyrighted programs; if you like particular programs, register with their authors for a nominal fee, and receive licenses, enhanced versions, and technical support. *Freeware programs* are free, copyrighted games, applications, and utilities; you can copy them to as many PCs as you like — for free — but they offer no technical support. *GNU software* is governed by its own license, which is included inside the folder of the GNU software; there are no restrictions on distribution of GNU software. (See the GNU license at the root of the CD for more details.) *Trial, demo,* or *evaluation* versions of software are usually limited either by time or functionality (such as not letting you save a project after you create it).

Chapter files

The chapter files on the CD all fall into one of the following categories:

- **PDFs:** Most of the files on the CD are PDFs, so you can't change them, but you can print them out and record the answers to the questions as you go through the process of becoming a franchisee or franchisor, and we highly recommend that you do so. Many of the documents work well for bringing along on your research ventures and various interviews and meetings so you can make sure you've covered all your bases.

- **Word documents:** One file is a Word document, created to provide helpful links to various franchising Web sites. Feel free to add to the list as you discover other sites you find useful.

- **Excel spreadsheets:** One file is an Excel spreadsheet, which you can use to help you do calculations at the touch of a key. Simply plug in the numbers and you're on your way.

The following list summarizes all the chapter files on the CD:

CD0101	Article about the Economic Impact of Franchising
CD0401	Evaluating a Franchisor's Services: Financial and Local Operational Issues
CD0402	Internet Franchise Opportunity Web Sites
CD0403	Evaluating Franchise Brokers: Questions to Ask Before You Agree to Work with Them
CD0404	Evaluating a Franchisor's Services: Consumer Research and Marketing
CD0405	Evaluating an Existing Franchise
CD0406	Evaluating a Franchisor's Services: Franchise Ownership
CD0407	Evaluating a Franchisor's Operations and Success
CD0408	Evaluating a Franchisor's Services: Continual Services
CD0409	Evaluating a Franchisor's Financial Requirements
CD0410	Evaluating a Franchisor's Services: Site Development
CD0411	Evaluating a Franchisor's Services: Your Market or Area
CD0412	Evaluating a Franchisor's Services: Training
CD0413	Evaluating a Franchisor's Services: Products and Services
CD0414	Evaluating a Franchisor's Services: Marketing and Advertising
CD0415	Evaluating a Franchisor's Services: Field Support
CD0416	Evaluating a Franchisor's Services: Operations Manuals
CD0417	Evaluating a Franchisor's Services: Territory
CD0418	Evaluating a Franchisor's Services: Other Questions to Ask
CD0419	Federal Trade Commission's Consumer Guide to Buying a Franchise
CD0420	Making the Franchise Decision Comprehensive Workbook
CD0501	Looking Closely at Your Finances Worksheet
CD0502	Estimating Business Start-Up Costs Spreadsheet
CD0503	Franchise Start-Up Costs: The Details
CD0601	Letter about NASAA and State Franchise Authorities
CD0701	Evaluating a Site for Your Franchise Worksheet
CD0702	Tips for Doing Your Own Market Research

CD0703	Eight Steps to Development Success (how to secure real estate)
CD0704	Sample Franchisee Site Submittal Package (for franchisor's reference)
CD0705	A Breakdown of Leasing Costs
CD0706	Checklist for Selecting a Contractor
CD0707	Tips for Finding and Evaluating a Supplier
CD0801	Sample Employee Handbook
CD1001	Checklist of Advertising Questions
CD1201	Discussion of Dual Branding and Its Legal Issues
CD1401	List of Franchise Laws around the World (by country)
CD1402	International Franchise Association's Code of Ethics
CD1403	Planning for Growth: Creating and Using the Business Plan (how to start one from scratch)
CD1404	UFOC Guidelines: A Practical Guide
CD1405	Sample UFOC Questionnaire
CD1501	Article about the Minority Business Enterprise: The National Priority
CD1502	Article about Women and Franchising
CD1503	Franchise Sales and Compliance Manual
CD1504	Article about eDisclosure: Best Practices
CD1601	Sample Basic Franchisee Unit Operations Manual Table of Contents
CD1602	Discussion of Pricing of Franchises
CD1603	Contact Information for Franchise Associations Worldwide
CD1604	Q&A on Foreign Companies Entering the U.S. as Franchisors

Troubleshooting

I tried my best to compile programs that work on most computers with the minimum system requirements. Alas, your computer may differ, and some programs may not work properly for some reason.

The two likeliest problems are that you don't have enough memory (RAM) for the programs you want to use, or you have other programs running that are affecting installation or running of a program. If you get an error message such as Not enough memory or Setup cannot continue, try one or more of the following suggestions and then try using the software again:

- ✔ **Turn off any antivirus software running on your computer.** Installation programs sometimes mimic virus activity and may make your computer incorrectly believe that it's being infected by a virus.

- ✔ **Close all running programs.** The more programs you have running, the less memory is available to other programs. Installation programs typically update files and programs; so, if you keep other programs running, installation may not work properly.

- ✔ **Have your local computer store add more RAM to your computer.** This is, admittedly, a drastic and somewhat expensive step. However, adding more memory can really help the speed of your computer and allow more programs to run at the same time.

If you have trouble with the CD-ROM, please call the Wiley Product Technical Support phone number at 800-762-2974. Outside the United States, call 317-572-3994. You can also contact Wiley Product Technical Support at http://support.wiley.com. John Wiley & Sons will provide technical support only for installation and other general quality-control items. For technical support on the applications themselves, consult the program's vendor or author.

To place additional orders or to request information about other Wiley products, please call 877-762-2974.

Index

• Y •

• Z •

Wiley Publishing, Inc.
End-User License Agreement

READ THIS. You should carefully read these terms and conditions before opening the software packet(s) included with this book "Book". This is a license agreement "Agreement" between you and Wiley Publishing, Inc. "WPI". By opening the accompanying software packet(s), you acknowledge that you have read and accept the following terms and conditions. If you do not agree and do not want to be bound by such terms and conditions, promptly return the Book and the unopened software packet(s) to the place you obtained them for a full refund.

1. **License Grant.** WPI grants to you (either an individual or entity) a nonexclusive license to use one copy of the enclosed software program(s) (collectively, the "Software") solely for your own personal or business purposes on a single computer (whether a standard computer or a workstation component of a multi-user network). The Software is in use on a computer when it is loaded into temporary memory (RAM) or installed into permanent memory (hard disk, CD-ROM, or other storage device). WPI reserves all rights not expressly granted herein.

2. **Ownership.** WPI is the owner of all right, title, and interest, including copyright, in and to the compilation of the Software recorded on the physical packet included with this Book "Software Media". Copyright to the individual programs recorded on the Software Media is owned by the author or other authorized copyright owner of each program. Ownership of the Software and all proprietary rights relating thereto remain with WPI and its licensers.

3. **Restrictions on Use and Transfer.**

   (a) You may only (i) make one copy of the Software for backup or archival purposes, or (ii) transfer the Software to a single hard disk, provided that you keep the original for backup or archival purposes. You may not (i) rent or lease the Software, (ii) copy or reproduce the Software through a LAN or other network system or through any computer subscriber system or bulletin-board system, or (iii) modify, adapt, or create derivative works based on the Software.

   (b) You may not reverse engineer, decompile, or disassemble the Software. You may transfer the Software and user documentation on a permanent basis, provided that the transferee agrees to accept the terms and conditions of this Agreement and you retain no copies. If the Software is an update or has been updated, any transfer must include the most recent update and all prior versions.

4. **Restrictions on Use of Individual Programs.** You must follow the individual requirements and restrictions detailed for each individual program in the "About the CD" appendix of this Book or on the Software Media. These limitations are also contained in the individual license agreements recorded on the Software Media. These limitations may include a requirement that after using the program for a specified period of time, the user must pay a registration fee or discontinue use. By opening the Software packet(s), you agree to abide by the licenses and restrictions for these individual programs that are detailed in the "About the CD" appendix and/or on the Software Media. None of the material on this Software Media or listed in this Book may ever be redistributed, in original or modified form, for commercial purposes.

5. **Limited Warranty.**

    (a) WPI warrants that the Software and Software Media are free from defects in materials and workmanship under normal use for a period of sixty (60) days from the date of purchase of this Book. If WPI receives notification within the warranty period of defects in materials or workmanship, WPI will replace the defective Software Media.

    (b) WPI AND THE AUTHOR(S) OF THE BOOK DISCLAIM ALL OTHER WARRANTIES, EXPRESS OR IMPLIED, INCLUDING WITHOUT LIMITATION IMPLIED WARRANTIES OF MERCHANTABILITY AND FITNESS FOR A PARTICULAR PURPOSE, WITH RESPECT TO THE SOFTWARE, THE PROGRAMS, THE SOURCE CODE CONTAINED THEREIN, AND/OR THE TECHNIQUES DESCRIBED IN THIS BOOK. WPI DOES NOT WARRANT THAT THE FUNCTIONS CONTAINED IN THE SOFTWARE WILL MEET YOUR REQUIREMENTS OR THAT THE OPERATION OF THE SOFTWARE WILL BE ERROR FREE.

    (c) This limited warranty gives you specific legal rights, and you may have other rights that vary from jurisdiction to jurisdiction.

6. **Remedies.**

    (a) WPI's entire liability and your exclusive remedy for defects in materials and workmanship shall be limited to replacement of the Software Media, which may be returned to WPI with a copy of your receipt at the following address: Software Media Fulfillment Department, Attn.: *Franchising For Dummies,* 2nd Edition, Wiley Publishing, Inc., 10475 Crosspoint Blvd., Indianapolis, IN 46256, or call 1-877-762-2974. Please allow four to six weeks for delivery. This Limited Warranty is void if failure of the Software Media has resulted from accident, abuse, or misapplication. Any replacement Software Media will be warranted for the remainder of the original warranty period or thirty (30) days, whichever is longer.

    (b) In no event shall WPI or the author be liable for any damages whatsoever (including without limitation damages for loss of business profits, business interruption, loss of business information, or any other pecuniary loss) arising from the use of or inability to use the Book or the Software, even if WPI has been advised of the possibility of such damages.

    (c) Because some jurisdictions do not allow the exclusion or limitation of liability for consequential or incidental damages, the above limitation or exclusion may not apply to you.

7. **U.S. Government Restricted Rights.** Use, duplication, or disclosure of the Software for or on behalf of the United States of America, its agencies and/or instrumentalities "U.S. Government" is subject to restrictions as stated in paragraph (c)(1)(ii) of the Rights in Technical Data and Computer Software clause of DFARS 252.227-7013, or subparagraphs (c) (1) and (2) of the Commercial Computer Software - Restricted Rights clause at FAR 52.227-19, and in similar clauses in the NASA FAR supplement, as applicable.

8. **General.** This Agreement constitutes the entire understanding of the parties and revokes and supersedes all prior agreements, oral or written, between them and may not be modified or amended except in a writing signed by both parties hereto that specifically refers to this Agreement. This Agreement shall take precedence over any other documents that may be in conflict herewith. If any one or more provisions contained in this Agreement are held by any court or tribunal to be invalid, illegal, or otherwise unenforceable, each and every other provision shall remain in full force and effect.

Internet

Blogging For Dummies,
3rd Edition
978-0-470-61996-4

eBay For Dummies,
6th Edition
978-0-470-49741-8

Facebook For Dummies,
3rd Edition
978-0-470-87804-0

Web Marketing
For Dummies,
2nd Edition
978-0-470-37181-7

WordPress
For Dummies,
3rd Edition
978-0-470-59274-8

Language & Foreign Language

French For Dummies
978-0-7645-5193-2

Italian Phrases
For Dummies
978-0-7645-7203-6

Spanish For Dummies,
2nd Edition
978-0-470-87855-2

Spanish
For Dummies,
Audio Set
978-0-470-09585-0

Math & Science

Algebra I
For Dummies,
2nd Edition
978-0-470-55964-2

Biology For Dummies,
2nd Edition
978-0-470-59875-7

Calculus For Dummies
978-0-7645-2498-1

Chemistry For Dummies
978-0-7645-5430-8

Microsoft Office

Excel 2010 For Dummies
978-0-470-48953-6

Office 2010 All-in-One
For Dummies
978-0-470-49748-7

Office 2010 For Dummies,
Book + DVD Bundle
978-0-470-62698-6

Word 2010 For Dummies
978-0-470-48772-3

Music

Guitar For Dummies,
2nd Edition
978-0-7645-9904-0

iPod & iTunes For
Dummies, 8th Edition
978-0-470-87871-2

Piano Exercises
For Dummies
978-0-470-38765-8

Parenting & Education

Parenting For Dummies,
2nd Edition
978-0-7645-5418-6

Type 1 Diabetes
For Dummies
978-0-470-17811-9

Pets

Cats For Dummies,
2nd Edition
978-0-7645-5275-5

Dog Training For Dummies,
3rd Edition
978-0-470-60029-0

Puppies For Dummies,
2nd Edition
978-0-470-03717-1

Religion & Inspiration

The Bible For Dummies
978-0-7645-5296-0

Catholicism For Dummies
978-0-7645-5391-2

Women in the Bible
For Dummies
978-0-7645-8475-6

Self-Help & Relationship

Anger Management
For Dummies
978-0-470-03715-7

Overcoming Anxiety
For Dummies,
2nd Edition
978-0-470-57441-6

Sports

Baseball
For Dummies,
3rd Edition
978-0-7645-7537-2

Basketball
For Dummies,
2nd Edition
978-0-7645-5248-9

Golf For Dummies,
3rd Edition
978-0-471-76871-5

Web Development

Web Design
All-in-One
For Dummies
978-0-470-41796-6

Web Sites
Do-It-Yourself
For Dummies,
2nd Edition
978-0-470-56520-9

Windows 7

Windows 7
For Dummies
978-0-470-49743-2

Windows 7
For Dummies,
Book + DVD Bundle
978-0-470-52398-8

Windows 7 All-in-One
For Dummies
978-0-470-48763-1

Available wherever books are sold. For more information or to order direct: U.S. customers visit www.dummies.com or call 1-877-762-29*
U.K. customers visit www.wileyeurope.com or call (0) 1243 843291. Canadian customers visit www.wiley.ca or call 1-800-567-4797.